SWIFTBOATING AMERICA

SWIFTBOATING AMERICA

Exposing the Russiagate Fraud, from the Steele Dossier to the FBI's Crossfire Hurricane Investigation

HANS MAHNCKE

Skyhorse Publishing

Copyright © 2024 by Hans Mahncke
Foreword copyright © 2024 by Aram Fuchs

All rights reserved. No part of this book may be reproduced in any manner without the express written consent of the publisher, except in the case of brief excerpts in critical reviews or articles. All inquiries should be addressed to Skyhorse Publishing, 307 West 36th Street, 11th Floor, New York, NY 10018.

Skyhorse Publishing books may be purchased in bulk at special discounts for sales promotion, corporate gifts, fund-raising, or educational purposes. Special editions can also be created to specifications. For details, contact the Special Sales Department, Skyhorse Publishing, 307 West 36th Street, 11th Floor, New York, NY 10018 or info@skyhorsepublishing.com.

Skyhorse® and Skyhorse Publishing® are registered trademarks of Skyhorse Publishing, Inc.®, a Delaware corporation.

Visit our website at www.skyhorsepublishing.com.

Please follow our publisher Tony Lyons on Instagram @tonylyonsisuncertain

10 9 8 7 6 5 4 3 2 1

Library of Congress Cataloging-in-Publication Data is available on file.

Cover design by David Ter-Avanesyan
Cover image from Getty Images

Print ISBN: 978-1-5107-8287-7
Ebook ISBN: 978-1-5107-8289-1

Printed in the United States of America

Contents

Foreword		vii
Introduction:	Finding Danchenko	xiii
Chapter 1:	The Origin of the Swiftboat Project	1
Chapter 2:	Swiftboating America—The Clinton Campaign	9
Chapter 3:	Swiftboating America—The Government	17
Chapter 4:	Russian Disinformation or Dirty Trick?	27
Chapter 5:	Christopher Steele	41
Chapter 6:	Framing Millian	51
Chapter 7:	Report 80—Made-to-Order Fairytale	71
Chapter 8:	Reports 86 and 95—Pinning WikiLeaks on Russia	83
Chapter 9:	How Did Crossfire Hurricane Begin?	91
Chapter 10:	Spying on the Trump Campaign	115
Chapter 11:	The Alfa Bank Hoax	129
Chapter 12:	The Media Strategy	147
Chapter 13:	The Intelligence Community Assessment	163
Epilogue:	The Butterfly Effect	179
Notes		191
Index		235

Foreword

Never did I think that I would have to worry about being branded as a Russian spy, especially considering my family's and country's history. It was 2017. We had just finished two terms of the Obama administration. I had voted for him based on what I had thought was his brave leadership in rejecting the Iraq war and his optimistic and unifying message that there is "no white America, no black America; only the United States of America." He won the vote of millions of people who had rejected a dossier produced by former British intelligence agents, which then-President Bush had presented, asserting that Iraq had Weapons of Mass Destruction. Bush went to war based on these assertions, but he found no weapons.

Despite this, hundreds of thousands of Iraqis and over four thousand American and allied soldiers were killed. The damage caused by the first fake dossier made many in our country realize what a previous generation had learned during the Vietnam War. Trusting anonymous sources from what President Eisenhower had called the "military-industrial complex" could lead to horrific outcomes.

When BuzzFeed published the now infamous Steele dossier on January 10, 2017, purportedly written by ex-British intelligence agent Christopher Steele, I was suspicious. The Steele dossier asserted that there was a conspiracy between the Russian government and American citizens, led by Donald Trump, to steal the 2016 election. Three thoughts immediately came to mind:

1. It was not true.
2. It was produced by Trump's enemies.
3. Few Americans would believe it is true.

I ended up being correct about the first two elements but not the third; millions of people believed it. Surprisingly, when I started talking to friends in New York, I was amazed to find that most people who had protested against the Iraq dossier believed the Trump one to be truthful.

Given that many people I knew, who believed the first dossier was fake, thought the second one was real, I decided to become an internet sleuth, along with many other citizen journalists that had become citizen journalists looking into the provenance of the dossier.

I scrolled through the dossier and on page five, paragraph three, my jaw immediately dropped, and my face warmed with fear. It was so frightening that I hit the exit button and walked away. *This cannot be*, I thought to myself. Eventually, I gathered my strength and returned to reading the paragraph that scared me so much:

> In terms of "foreign" agents, the FSB was approaching US citizens of Russian (Jewish) origin on business trips to Russia. In one case a US citizen of Russian ethnicity had been visiting Moscow to attract investors in his new information technology program. The FSB clearly knew this and had offered to provide seed capital to this person in return for them being able to access and modify his IP, with a view to targeting priority foreign targets by planting a Trojan virus in the software. The US visitor was told this was common practice. The FSB also had implied significant operational success as a result of installing cheap Russian IT games containing their own malware unwittingly by targets on their PCs and other platforms.

Steele, who was then still anonymous with unknown backers, asserted without evidence that Jewish Americans with Russian ancestry in the Information Technology sector served as "foreign agents" in service to Russia. The specific claim was that these Jewish-Americans used their power to drive "downloads" and "games" to install "malware" on users' computers. They did this to assist the Russian government in some unexplained manner.

I am a third-generation Russian-Ukrainian-Jewish-American, and I am the CEO of a company called eGames.com. We sell our games through downloads on Google Play and the iTunes App Store. It is fair to speculate that if Hillary Clinton had been elected, and Obama, Biden, and Clinton's support of the Steele dossier had never been exposed, eGames.com's business would have been negatively impacted. No one would have trusted our code if they thought its CEO might be in service to a malevolent foreign power.

But it wouldn't be just my small company. Google was founded by Sergey Brin, a first-generation Russian-American Jew. Given the size of Google, if it were not trusted, the US tech sector, and maybe even the US economy itself, might have suffered. Do you really think the awful dunces who perpetuated the Steele dossier hoax could have resisted summoning a prominent Russian-American Jewish CEO to testify before Congress? There is a long history of governments accusing Jewish people of being a fifth column for foreign governments. France suffered from the Dreyfus Affair, while Russia endured the Protocols of the Elders of Zion.

And indeed, this is not the first time someone named Fuchs has been caught up in this sort of thing. "Fuchs" is actually a German family name meaning "Fox." It is quite common among both Jews and Christians in Eastern Europe. My father endured some pain during the McCarthy era because Klaus Fuchs was actually a Soviet spy while working on the Manhattan Project during World War II and the early parts of the Cold War.

My father was teased in the schoolyard because he had the same name as a spy. However, he used that mild pain as a way to teach his children to judge people by their character and not by their family name, ethnicity, religion, skin color, title, vocation, or political party.

I believe the authors of the Steele dossier included this "Jews as a Fifth Column" canard because they truly believed that the United States is full of a "basket of deplorables," and they had seen such a hoax work in France and Russia. They probably imagined that these so-called "deplorables" would vote for Clinton, their candidate, if they could convince the deplorables that Jews formed a Fifth Column in America.

In truth, the Steele dossier is as bogus as the Protocols of the Elders of Zion. There was no Trump malware found on any American's computer put there by Russian-Jewish-Americans like me or Brin. No game published by Russian-American-led companies was found to assist the Russian government.

Even worse, the Horowitz report, published by Inspector General Michael Horowitz on December 9, 2019, was the first to mention an FBI interview with the Steele dossier's purported source. Hans Mahncke and a group of internet researchers later identified that purported source as Igor Danchenko. Danchenko admitted to investigators that he "never expected Steele to . . . present [the Steele dossier] reports as facts"[1] and that the things he told Steele were said in "jest" derived from a "conversation that [he] had with friends over beers."[2]

Not only was there no evidence supporting the conspiracy theory, but there was also witness testimony admitting that the accusations were fabricated.

One could only imagine what someone might have overheard during Danchenko's brainstorming session over beers. "OK, guys, my boss, Steele, has Hillary Clinton as a client. Let's come up with the most absurd ideas and see if we can make some money here. How about we claim that Trump was engaged in sexually perverted acts in the same Moscow hotel room as the Obamas?" one might have said. The other might have replied, "I can one-up that—let's create an internet-era Protocols of the Elders of Zion. Let's say the Jews helped Putin assist Trump with spyware."

Even after being caught as the source of these absurdly evil apocryphal tales, Danchenko managed to convince the FBI to hire him as a confidential human source, even though he had previously admitted that his stories were made in "jest" and that the "corroboration was zero."

I believe that the individuals in our government who initially received and later distributed the dossier knew from the beginning that it was fake. But even if we were to stipulate that those in the highest echelons of the government, the military-industrial complex, and our institutions more broadly fell for the dossier hoax, any such stipulation would have automatically collapsed after Horowitz published his report in December 2019. However, unlike the rest of us, the FBI did not have to wait until December 2019 to find out the truth. They knew in January 2017 that there was "zero corroboration," but they concealed this fact, as well as the fact that the dossier was entirely fake. The FBI's deception has come at a significant cost to American society.

Did they not know the history of what such bigoted smears, false accusations of treason, and manufactured hysterias have done to societies in the past?

Or did they just not care?

At the time when I first read the Steele dossier, I thought that this was going to be my painful time, similar to what my father and many others had experienced during the Cold War hysteria. We would endure it, and then we could teach our children to judge people, including the heads of our corrupt institutions and everyone unfairly maligned in the dossier, by the same moral code. Judge each individual by their character.

But the dossier's lies proved more durable. While Joseph McCarthy's reputation lies in tatters, none of the key figures involved in the Russia collusion hoax have faced consequences. Indeed, many of the principals secured multimillion-dollar book and TV deals. Worst of all, Joe Biden,

Foreword

who himself played a role in perpetuating dossier lies, was rewarded with the presidency.

People with malicious intentions have realized that falsely accusing individuals of crimes is a tactic in the arsenal of ambitious Americans in the internet era to gain power. There have been a slew of false Russian agent conspiracy theories attacking everyone from Glenn Greenwald to Bernie Sanders to Tulsi Gabbard. It's not just false accusations of treason; it has also spread to fake sex and hate crimes. Our country is drowning in fake hoax hysterias not seen here since Abigail Williams brought Salem, Massachusetts asunder in 1691.

Importantly, when placed on a historical chronology, the Steele dossier, witch hunts, and anti-Semitism are manifestations of the same strategy that people have used to gain power since the beginning of recorded history. Philip of Macedonia coined the term "divide et impera," which translates as "divide and conquer."

In France and Russia, the elite believed that inciting anti-Semitism would lead the powerless to direct their anger toward Jews rather than toward the ruling class. Today's bigoted smears and fake crime accusations create divisions similar to those seen during the Dreyfus affair in France, the Protocols of the Elders of Zion in Russia, or the divisions Philip of Macedonia created among the people in the Balkans.

Powerful individuals have exploited these modern American divisions to acquire official control over the resources of the American government. Once they obtain power over the state tools, it is fair to speculate that they will continue using the strategies that helped them achieve that position.

My father, like most of his generation, had a canon of quotes, aphorisms, and poems about the fragility of liberty. One of my favorite quotes on this theme was from an erudite German Lutheran minister named Martin Niemöller who initially supported Hitler but later resisted him. As a result of his resistance, the Nazis put him in a concentration camp for seven long years.

After he was released, he gave a speech and said:

> First they came for the socialists, and I did not speak out—because I was not a socialist.
>
> Then they came for the trade unionists, and I did not speak out—because I was not a trade unionist.
>
> Then they came for the Jews, and I did not speak out—because I was not a Jew.
>
> Then they came for me—and there was no one left to speak for me.

We have just witnessed two blatantly false smears: the Iraq dossier and the Steele dossier. These have incited significant violence and division, enabling the perpetrators to seize control of the levers of power. But they do not have total power yet. I often wonder what Father Niemöller would write if he were alive today. Perhaps in his sequel, he would say something like this:

> Did you not learn the lesson that I learned too late?
>
> First, they came for Iraq and the Muslims. But you were neither, and you were riled up by what the TV told you after 9/11, so you did not speak up about the first false dossier.
>
> Then they came for Trump and the MAGAs, but you were neither, and you were riled up by what the TV and social media told you, so you did not speak up about the second false dossier.
>
> But do you really think they are going to stop at the Muslims and the MAGAs?
>
> What will happen when they launch a third dossier, and it comes for you? Brave men like Chief Comperatore have already been sacrificed. Will there be anyone left to rescue you?

Swiftboating America lays bare the full catalog of lies and deceptions employed by a group of divisive, power-mad fraudsters. If I had been told in 2015 that the FBI was corrupt to its core and that many of its agents participated in a massive campaign of law fare against Trump, I would not have believed it. If I had been told in 2016 that, based on a transparently fraudulent dossier, Obama and Biden had created a giant booby trap for Trump, I would probably not have believed it. But these things happened. Understanding the lessons of *Swiftboating America* will better prepare you to identify Goebbelsian "Big Lies" when they attempt to deceive us again. Let's learn the lessons of Father Niemöller, President Eisenhower, and my dad, and all stick together.

—Aram Fuchs, July 2024

INTRODUCTION

Finding Danchenko

It had become a tradition for me to take the kids camping each summer for my birthday. In the past, we had rented an RV or a cabin, but this time the kids wanted the barebones experience. Our journey took us to a lush forest near the shores of Lake Huron. We arrived on Thursday, July 16, 2020. Little did I know that the next three days would turn out to be anything but the tranquil camping trip for which we'd come.

After pitching our tent, we started our campfire. It was a perfect summer evening, with the sky slowly turning dark and a gentle breeze rustling through the leaves. Soon, the kids disappeared into the tent. They wanted to lie in their sleeping bags and watch the night sky. The weather forecast was good, so I decided not to use the rain tarp. The kids were gazing at the stars above. It reminded me of when I was a kid, doing the exact same thing. I was still outside watching the embers glow. It was beautiful.

We woke up early the next day to the sound of birds singing. It was my birthday. Everything was perfect. We had picked up some canned coffee on the way, which became my breakfast. We also brought cake, although without any candles. After tidying up, we started making our way to the beach. Having spent their early childhood in the Caribbean, the kids were not very familiar with Great Lakes beaches, but they quickly adapted to them. They liked that the water wasn't salty. And so they set off to splash about and build sand castles. I happily lay down and started reading *The Case Against Reality*, Donald Hoffman's book on simulation theory. I spend most of my time reading legal texts, so I was happy to take my mind somewhere completely different.

Lunchtime arrived early, as it tends to do when kids are out playing. They were starving. By this time, the sun was at its peak, so we moved to a shaded area. That's when my phone lit up. Most of the area did not have cell coverage, but we must have passed through an area that did. The messages were from my friends and fellow internet sleuths: Fool Nelson, Walkafyre, and Stephen McIntyre. A year earlier, Fool Nelson had identified Eric Ciaramella, the so-called whistleblower who had triggered the first impeachment of President Trump. Ciaramella was upset that Trump had asked the president of Ukraine to coordinate with Attorney General Bill Barr to investigate the Biden family's financial and other involvements in Ukraine. Ciaramella himself was involved in those entanglements, at least to the extent that he had organized the White House meeting where the idea of firing the Ukrainian prosecutor—what Trump wanted investigated—was first raised. Fool Nelson uncovered that as well. Although I knew their real names by that point, I often thought that it might be better for Fool Nelson and Walkafyre to remain anonymous.

I knew Stephen the best out of the group. We first met two years earlier. At the time, I was working in the Caribbean and was not involved in any online research projects. In contrast, Stephen had been doing it for a while, having made crucial discoveries along the way, including exposing the hockey stick deception as part of the Climategate controversy.

My interest began in 2018 when I read about the peculiar case of George Papadopoulos. Papadopoulos was a foreign policy advisor to the Trump campaign. He is supposed to have kicked off the FBI's Trump-Russia investigation in July 2016 by bragging about his Russian connections to Alexander Downer, the Australian ambassador in London. To this day, that entire story remains shrouded in mystery. What is known is that the ambassador's alleged account of his meeting with Papadopoulos was used by the FBI as a pretext to initiate the Crossfire Hurricane investigation into the Trump campaign for collusion with Russia. What is also known is that what Downer later told Special Counsel John Durham, the man appointed to investigate the origins of the Russiagate hoax, does not match the FBI's official story for how the Crossfire Hurricane investigation was opened.[1]

Another aspect of the Papadopoulos case that piqued my interest was how Robert Mueller's special counsel team dishonestly used the Papadopoulos story to promote the false Russia collusion narrative. Their court filings, in which they alleged that Papadopoulos had lied to the FBI, were filled with anti-Russian and anti-Trump insinuations. That was par for the course. What wasn't normal, at least not at the time, was that the

Finding Danchenko

legal documents did not match the facts. *Why would Papadopoulos admit to things that did not happen*, I wondered, *especially when Mueller's team knew the truth?* Something wasn't right.

In August 2018, I reached out to Papadopoulos's wife, Simona. This was after Papadopoulos had pleaded guilty but before his sentencing hearing. Despite how she has been portrayed by some in the media, Simona is a very kind and thoughtful person. It became clear to me that she and Papadopoulos were stuck in a terrible quagmire. Mueller's team of lawyers convinced Papadopoulos to plead guilty to incidents that did not transpire. Papadopoulos's legal counsel, rather than resisting, appeared to have supported Mueller's tactics. It is possible that he agreed with Mueller's narrative on Russia collusion, or he might have considered it beneficial for Papadopoulos to admit guilt to a minor offense and move forward with his life. While I would have disagreed with that legal strategy, if indeed that is what it was, I have some sympathy for it. Papadopoulos, as I would soon find out, has a tendency to change his story. People like that are not exactly ideal clients.

Over time, I discovered that the story of George Papadopoulos is a microcosm of Russiagate, the conspiracy theory alleging that Donald Trump colluded with Vladimir Putin to steal the 2016 election from Hillary Clinton. From the FBI's spying on the Trump team to Mueller pressuring Trump associates to fabricate stories, Papadopoulos went through it all, at times completely unaware of what was going on. But Papadopoulos's story is not one of pure victimhood. He made plenty of mistakes along the way. But 2018 wasn't a time for reflection. What mattered to Simona and George Papadopoulos was that he was a few weeks away from facing a federal judge, having already pleaded guilty to things he did not do. Simona, a fellow lawyer, must have shared my concerns. She recognized that her husband had been railroaded and was looking for ways for Papadopoulos to undo his plea. In reality, it is incredibly difficult to retract a guilty plea—as we all learned later in the case of Lieutenant General Michael Flynn. Ultimately, Papadopoulos and Simona decided to follow their lawyer's advice, face the situation head-on, and move forward.

Papadopoulos's plight, whether deserved or not, is what prompted me to connect with Stephen. I knew of Stephen from his Climategate wars. Stephen was the first person to uncover the hockey stick deception,[2] which suggested that global temperatures were expected to rise sharply, resembling the blade of a hockey stick on a graph. Stephen originally comes from a mining background, but he is truly a polymath. He studied for a Philosophy,

Politics, and Economics (PPE) degree at Corpus Christi College, Oxford. Back in the day, graduating with a PPE at Oxford was considered one of the highest forms of academic achievement. It might still be. I doubt it, though. Higher education has undergone significant deterioration. But I digress. Stephen is undoubtedly the smartest person I have ever met. He also happened to be the only person that I could find on the internet who understood George Papadopoulos's predicament. Without any hesitation, he agreed to meet. He, too, was perplexed that Papadopoulos was pleading guilty to things that he did not do and that, in any case, could easily be explained. Why would he do that? What was Mueller's team up to? We both agreed that Papadopoulos had been pressured to fabricate stories, or perhaps to repeat stories that Mueller's team had fabricated. Perhaps, in return, Mueller had agreed not to charge Papadopoulos with other offenses, such as the potential foreign agent charge that Mueller's team was considering. That potential charge stemmed from Papadopoulos bragging about his Israeli connections to an undercover FBI informant. In truth, Papadopoulos wasn't an Israeli agent, and everyone who knew him was aware of that fact. He wasn't an agent of any country. He was just a young man who stumbled into the Trump campaign, where he tried to impress beyond his abilities. When asked about Papadopoulos boasting about his Russian connections, his former teacher at DePaul University, Professor Richard Farkas, told the media that his former student was simply pretending to be in touch with top Russian officials as a means of enhancing his status on the campaign.[3] Papadopoulos was a braggart, a grandstander who portrayed himself as a big shot. It was his business model, and it had been very successful. How else would a completely unknown twenty-eight-year-old with next to no real-life experience become an advisor to a presidential campaign?

Engaging in conversation with Stephen can make you easily lose track of time. Our first meeting in a small coffee shop in Toronto's East End lasted five hours but felt like only twenty minutes. We bounced ideas off each other and ended up making real progress in understanding Mueller's special counsel operation, something that we would both end up referring to as an attempted coup against Trump. It was also the beginning of a close friendship that would develop over the months and years to come.

Not much was known about Russiagate when I first met Stephen in August 2018. Other than a few court filings that were trickling out of Mueller's operation, our main focal point was what had become known as the Steele dossier.[4] The dossier is a collection of sixteen reports on Trump's alleged Russian ties that former British intelligence officer Christopher

Steele compiled for Glenn Simpson, the owner of Fusion GPS. Fusion GPS had been hired by the law firm Perkins Coie, which, in turn, had been hired by Hillary Clinton's campaign. You can say what you want about the Clintons, but they run their operations tightly. Utilizing numerous middlemen provided them with ample plausible deniability.

Steele's task was to write reports about Trump's connections to Russia, but it would be more accurate to say that his task was to fabricate stories about Trump's alleged connections to Russia. The corporate media has often portrayed Steele's work as if it had been initiated by Trump's fellow Republicans seeking dirt on him,[5] but that is not true. Steele was hired by Clinton campaign contractors Fusion GPS in May 2016, after Trump had secured the Republican nomination.[6] Steele worked for Clinton.

The dossier was an incontrovertible bunch of garbage. I remember reading it the day it was first published by BuzzFeed,[7] the now-defunct online news platform. That was on January 10, 2017, before Trump had even been inaugurated. I did not take long to figure out that the whole thing was frivolous drivel. The first sentence reads: "Russian regime has been cultivating Trump for at least 5 years."

According to Steele, this operation was the brainchild of Vladimir Putin, who somehow had the foresight in 2011 that Trump would one day become president. There are quite a few issues with this claim. While it is true that Trump briefly sought the Reform Party's nomination for president in 2000, his efforts notably coincided with the release of a new book, *The America We Deserve*, in January 2000. A few weeks after his book was released, Trump left the race. By the time the 2004 presidential election came around, Trump was the host of the hugely successful reality TV show, *The Apprentice*. Then there's the Clinton problem. Having contributed to Hillary Clinton's campaigns over the years, Trump donated an additional $110,000 to the Clinton Foundation in 2010.[8] Why would Putin cultivate a man he had never met who was openly supporting the likely future Democratic candidate for president? He didn't. In fact, before Hillary Clinton became Trump's opponent, they were friends. The Clintons attended Trump's wedding. He played golf with Bill Clinton. Trump encouraged Hillary to run in 2008. He sang her praises again in 2012, claiming, "Hillary Clinton, I think, is a terrific woman"; "I think she really works hard and does a good job"; and "I like her."[9]

It is also often overlooked that when Trump announced his candidacy for president on June 16, 2015, he was dismissed as a joke candidate.[10] No one but Trump himself and his core supporters thought he had a chance.

But somehow, Putin had secretly determined five or more years earlier that Trump was going to win the presidency. It was laughable.

As I read on, the list of transparent lies grew page by page. The dossier mentioned Russian operatives operating from the Miami consulate. There is no Russian consulate in Miami. It was reported that Russia had offered Trump advisor Carter Page "the brokerage of up to a 19% (privatized) stake in Rosneft." To anyone with even a hint of business acumen, this was completely fantastical. Rosneft is a Russian oil giant. It has a market capitalization of $50 billion. The claim was preposterous on its face.

There were many more claims like that. The one that stuck with me the most—because it was so incredibly crude and immature—was Steele's exclamation that Trump hated Michelle Obama. Steele wrote: "[Trump] knew President and Mrs OBAMA (whom he hated)." Who would write such a childish thing, let alone in a purported intelligence report? The entire dossier read as if it had been written by a twelve-year-old with a vivid imagination.

Stephen and I had both come to that conclusion long before we ever met. Anyone with a modicum of sanity would have come to the same conclusion. But why did the FBI rely on what was an obvious fraud? Why was the media echoing the false claim that the dossier had been corroborated? We wanted to find out. Incidentally, to this day, nothing in the dossier has been corroborated.[11] The only verified information consists of names and places that are easily accessible online. And yet, this apocryphal document was used by the Clinton campaign, the media, the FBI, and the CIA as the centerpiece of an all-out effort to bring down a presidential candidate and later, the president himself.

Stephen and I suspected that the entire dossier had been fabricated in Steele's office. But how do you disprove a fantasy? For that, we needed to know who Steele's alleged sources were. We suspected there weren't any credible sources, at least not individuals with genuine insight into Vladimir Putin's thinking. We suspected that the sources were cutouts that were used, wittingly or unwittingly, to masquerade as real sources.

At the time, we were unaware of the existence of a "primary sub-source" that was responsible for conveying most of the accusations in Steele's dossier. The existence of this individual only became known when the inspector general of the Department of Justice (DOJ), Michael Horowitz, published his report on the FBI's failures in applying for warrants to surveil Trump campaign aide Carter Page.[12] The identification of that source would later become the core task of our small group of four, which included Stephen and the two Russiagate researchers we had met online: Fool Nelson and Walkafyre. Had we known about the existence of the primary sub-source earlier, it might have provided a new perspective for our research. It is inherently more difficult for two people to keep a secret than it is for one. The primary sub-source posed a potential liability for Steele and later for the FBI when they began using Steele's information to target Trump. This is why the existence of Steele's secret source was concealed from the public for many years, both by Steele and the FBI. The efforts were so extensive that, upon discovering Steele's primary sub-source in December 2016, the FBI promptly enlisted him as a confidential human source.[13] This meant they could deny the existence of the source and prevent any inquiries into the entire matter, whether by Congress, through Freedom of Information requests, or otherwise. The FBI kept the primary sub-source on their payroll until 2020. Our group effectively forced the FBI's hand when we were finally able to identify him.

After I first met Stephen in 2018, which was more than a year before we knew about the primary sub-source's existence, we focused on specific issues for which we had information. For instance, we had Mueller's court documents in the Papadopoulos case. Indeed, Papadopoulos, being Mueller's initial target, naturally became the primary focus of our investigation. There were also bits and pieces of information that we gleaned from Congressman Devin Nunes's March 2018 memo, which later served as the foundation for Lee Smith's superb book, *The Plot Against the President*.[14] So we plodded along with the little information we had.

On September 7, 2018, Papadopoulos was sentenced to two weeks in jail for lying to the FBI.[15] The sentencing did not aid our efforts, both due to the absence of new revelations and the perception that a Trump campaign advisor being imprisoned was evidence of collusion with Russia.

The first significant batch of new materials for us to utilize arrived in April 2019 with the release of Special Counsel Mueller's report on Trump-Russia collusion.[16] After carefully parsing the 448 pages of the report, we discovered that it confirmed much of what we had already suspected from analyzing Papadopoulos's case. The entire report was a significant exercise in narrative creation, far removed from the facts. Some of Mueller's information was clearly false.

To give an example, Mueller claimed that: "With respect to the sanctions, Flynn requested that Russia not escalate the situation, not get into a 'tit for tat.'" Mueller was referring to Trump's first national security advisor, Michael Flynn, whom he had charged with lying to the FBI, similar to

Papadopoulos. The problem was that Flynn never mentioned sanctions. We suspected this at the time, but confirmation only came a year later when Flynn's lawyer, Sidney Powell, finally managed to obtain the transcripts of Flynn's call.[17] In truth, Flynn's "tit for tat" statement had nothing to do with sanctions.[18] Flynn never once mentioned sanctions. Just as Steele had done before him, Mueller fabricated information to construct a false narrative of Trump-Russia collusion.

There were other blatant lies. But Mueller's main tools are more appropriately described as subterfuge, half-truths, and smoke and mirrors. In that way, the Mueller operation was far more sophisticated than Steele's operation. One example emerged fairly soon after the Mueller Report was released. Mueller's team had altered the transcript of a voicemail message from President Trump's then-attorney, John Dowd. Dowd's message was for Flynn's lawyers and requested a heads-up on Flynn's potential cooperation with Mueller. The message was standard communication between lawyers who were essentially on the same side. There was nothing unusual or unethical about it, especially since Dowd added, "without you having to give up any...confidential information."[19] However, Mueller's team deliberately omitted the last part of the message and instead made it appear as if Dowd was illegally requesting confidential information from Flynn's lawyers to assist Trump. Why would Mueller need to fabricate evidence if there was any genuine wrongdoing on Trump's part?

Another example of Mueller's deceptions concerns Papadopoulos. Mueller stated that "on May 6, 2016, Papadopoulos suggested to a representative of a foreign government that the Trump Campaign had received indications from the Russian government that it could assist the Campaign through the anonymous release of information that would be damaging to candidate Clinton."[20]

If true, this may well have provided the FBI with a semblance of justification to investigate contacts between the Russian government and the Trump campaign. The problem is that it was not true, as confirmed by the foreign government representative, former Australian Foreign Minister Alexander Downer himself.[21] Special Counsel John Durham's report later confirmed that Mueller's claims regarding Downer did not align with what Downer told Durham.[22]

Mueller's entire narrative about Papadopoulos aimed to portray him as a Russian spy or stooge. Papadopoulos's communications were recounted by Mueller in a manner that would serve this purpose. One central message Mueller relied on to create the impression that Papadopoulos had nefarious Russian ties was when, early on in the campaign, Papadopoulos emailed Sam Clovis, Trump's foreign policy coordinator. The email, which was later reproduced in its entirety in the Senate Intelligence Committee's Russia Report, is completely innocuous.[23] In typical fashion, Papadopoulos bragged about his high-level contacts and meeting the Russian ambassador in London. In fact, Papadopoulos never met the man. It was just another example of Papadopoulos's frequent embellishments. In the same email, Papadopoulos also mentioned his connections to leadership in Vietnam. But Mueller needed to make it look as if Papadopoulos was all about Russia, so he simply omitted the part about Vietnam. Mueller did the same again when it came to his depiction of Trump's foreign policy meeting on March 31, 2016, during which Papadopoulos was in attendance. Mueller's report suggests that Papadopoulos was encouraged by other people in attendance, including Trump himself, to pursue Russian ties. In fact, a series of Mueller interview transcripts that have since been released under the Freedom of Information Act have revealed that every person at the meeting remembered that the idea of pursuing Russian ties had been firmly rejected by everyone except Papadopoulos himself.[24]

Another interesting aspect of the Mueller Report that caught Stephen's and my attention is the dog that did not bark. Incredibly, the Steele dossier is hardly mentioned at all, and when it is, it is only in passing. In 448 densely packed pages, Steele is mentioned only fourteen times, and there is no attempt to verify or even discuss his dossier. To put that in perspective, Papadopoulos is mentioned 343 times. Trump's first attorney general, Jeff Sessions, who was never charged or even accused of anything, is mentioned 491 times.

Overlooking Steele seemed odd, considering that Steele is the only person who has ever explicitly alleged collusion between Trump and Russia, the very issue that Mueller was supposedly investigating. This is one of the most central facts about the entire Russiagate affair, a fact that the corporate media has tried to suppress. It was Steele and Steele alone who alleged collusion, yet Mueller had no interest in him. This was not an oversight. Mueller's team knew from day one that the dossier was a pile of garbage that they needed to steer clear of.

Not even the Intelligence Community Assessment of January 2017,[25] which Barack Obama had ordered as a parting gift to incoming President Trump, claimed that there was collusion. However, it did include a summary of Steele's dossier as a roundabout way of introducing the claim without anyone in the US intelligence community having to actually make the claim themselves. Everyone who was deposed by Congress, including a multitude of FBI agents, stated under oath that there was no evidence of collusion.[26] Mueller's own report had to grudgingly accept that fact, leaving Steele as the only person to actually claim collusion.

Just as Stephen and I had concluded on January 10, 2017, that the Steele dossier was garbage, Mueller's team must have reached the same conclusion. But instead of admitting this fact, they did everything they could to avoid talking about Steele.

As more information started filtering out in the months after the Mueller Report was published, it became clear that Steele was hiding behind someone. At the time, we did not know who it was and weren't even sure that such a person existed. We inferred this assumption from a description of Steele's source in a book by journalists Michael Isikoff and David Corn, who were themselves deeply involved in the Clinton campaign's attempt to associate Trump with Russian collusion.[27] Isikoff, who had written a critical article about Trump advisor Carter Page in September 2016,[28] and Corn, who had provided copies of the Steele dossier to the FBI in October 2016,[29] reported that Steele had a "collector" who was his "primary source."[30] Unfortunately, there was no further information available. Given Isikoff's and Corn's less than stellar reputations for factual reporting, we had to take it with a grain of salt. In 2019, validation was obtained when Fusion GPS's proprietors, Glenn Simpson and Peter Fritsch, published a book in which they referred to Steele's source as a "collector."

Simpson and Fritsch noted that this collector was "among the finest [Steele] had ever worked with, an individual known to U.S. intelligence and law enforcement."[31] This detail, among others, led us to believe that the primary sub-source must be a credible individual with a background in the KGB or FSB. Ironically, we would later find out that the primary sub-source was known to US intelligence and law enforcement, but for reasons that made him even less credible. Specifically, the primary sub-source had run-ins with the law and was the subject of an FBI counterintelligence probe while working at the Brookings Institution in 2009 and 2010.[32]

So, we had some hints that Steele had a main source, but we were unsure of who it was and what their role was. Was Steele's source a patsy? Or was it Steele who was the patsy? Had Steele been fed false information by a foreign government? It was highly unlikely, but we wouldn't know for sure until we identified the mysterious source.

There weren't a lot of clues, so we were essentially making educated guesses. Our basic premise was that the alleged source had to have a measure of credibility; otherwise, the FBI would never have given Steele the time of day. We completely misunderstood that part. As we would later find out, the primary sub-source was an unknown individual residing in Washington, DC with no ties to the Kremlin. That's a measure of how naive we were, or perhaps, of how much the Overton window has shifted in recent years regarding the public's perception of the FBI. Corruption of the kind we once thought was unthinkable just a few years ago is now perceived as commonplace within the FBI.

We thought Steele's source would probably turn out to be a former member of the KGB or its successor organization, the FSB. Perhaps Steele had met someone during his assignment in Moscow in the 1990s, where he had worked for British intelligence. But our initial assumptions were incorrect. As subsequent events revealed, Steele had the ability to provide the FBI with any information he desired, and they would have proceeded with the investigation regardless—which is exactly what happened. Steele's source was as credible as any individual selected randomly from a phone directory. But the FBI did not care. Like Steele, they only had one goal. To get Trump.

Our luck changed with the release of the Horowitz report in December 2019.[33] Under the American system of government, federal agencies have inspectors general who are tasked with overseeing operations to prevent inefficiency or unlawful practices. Michael Horowitz holds the position of inspector general at the Department of Justice, where he supervises various agencies, including the FBI. Horowitz was tasked with the investigation of the Foreign Intelligence Surveillance Act (FISA) warrants issued against Carter Page, an advisor to the Trump campaign.

Similar to Papadopoulos, Carter Page was recruited to join the Trump campaign as a foreign policy advisor in March 2016.[34] In contrast to Papadopoulos, Page possessed the necessary credentials. However, he did not originate from the typical Beltway circle that Republican candidates usually rely on to select advisors. Establishment Republicans continued to distance themselves from Trump, prompting him to seek advisors elsewhere. As recounted by Page himself, in early 2016, he walked from his office in Manhattan to Trump Tower and approached the campaign manager at the time, Corey Lewandowski, expressing his interest in joining the team.[35] On March 21, 2016, Page was appointed as a campaign advisor, joining other notable figures such as future Attorney General Jeff Sessions, counter-terrorism expert Walid Phares, former Defense Department Inspector General Joe Schmitz, and retired Lieutenant General Keith Kellogg. At that time, Page held the position of managing partner at Global Energy Capital. He possessed expertise in global energy and had held the position of vice president at Merrill Lynch in Moscow. All this information was publicly known, making Page vulnerable to be used by individuals seeking to incriminate him and, consequently, implicating Trump. This is precisely what transpired. Steele implicated Page through his dossier, and the FBI used Steele's information to obtain a FISA warrant for the direct surveillance of Page, which indirectly extended to monitoring Trump.[36] Eventually, the Carter Page affair was brought to the attention of the inspector general's office. This action can be interpreted as the bureaucracy's way of superficially rectifying its own errors. Horowitz's limited responsibility involved evaluating the FBI's compliance with proper procedures in their decision to surveil Page.

Horowitz's investigation found that the FBI had failed to adhere to appropriate procedures. Indeed, Horowitz ended up producing a 476-page report, almost all of which is extremely damning of the FBI.[37] That is unusual for an inspector general report. Things must have been really bad. And they were. Horowitz found massive procedural abuses in how the FBI had obtained the warrants against Page. Despite the damning nature of the report, it was limited to Page alone. Other abuses, such as why the Trump-Russia investigation was initiated in the first place or why the FBI had relied on a fraudulent dossier, were not within Horowitz's purview. That was by design.

However, the report did serve another purpose, at least for those of us who wanted to uncover the entire Russiagate affair. It was the first time that it was officially confirmed that Steele had a primary sub-source. Even more significantly, Horowitz's report contained real, tangible clues about the identity of the primary sub-source.

Straight off the bat, the most shocking revelation in Horowitz's report, one that was largely ignored by the corporate media, was that the person whom Steele cast as his primary sub-source had disavowed him. Almost everything that the Steele dossier had attributed to this source was denied by the source. Horowitz lamented that when the FBI obtained the Carter Page warrant from the Foreign Intelligence Surveillance Court (FISC), the court was never informed about these denials. Instead, the FBI told the court that the primary sub-source was "truthful and cooperative."[38] That may have been technically correct, but what the FBI didn't tell the court was that by "truthful and cooperative," the FBI meant that the source had truthfully and cooperatively disavowed Steele.

Another falsehood propagated by the FBI, both in congressional briefings and in its Carter Page warrant application, as revealed by the conviction of FBI lawyer Kevin Clinesmith, was the claim that Steele's primary sub-source was located in Russia.[39] He was not. He resided in a suburb of Washington, DC. The fact that he was not based in Russia would have raised concerns for the court regarding his potential lack of access to the information that Steele attributed to him. According to Horowitz, Clinesmith received a warning from a colleague about the inaccuracy but failed to revise Carter Page's FISA application to indicate that the source was not located in Russia.[40]

The fact that the primary sub-source was not based in Russia was inexplicably redacted from Horowitz's report, perhaps because DOJ censors, who reviewed the report before its public release, were aware of its implications. Notably, the 122-word footnote describing Clinesmith's actions is largely un-redacted, except for the term "Russian-based."[41] This strongly indicates that DOJ censors were concealing information both to protect Clinesmith, who was not charged with spawning this falsehood, and to shield the FBI, which provided false information to the FISC.

After the publication of the Horowitz Report, Stephen invited Fool Nelson and Walkafyre to participate in our search for the primary sub-source. With their assistance, we were able to work out what was behind the DOJ's redaction. Horowitz's reference to the Carter Page FISA warrant, which indicated that the primary sub-source was "Russian-based," was helpful in this regard. Subsequently, it was possible to deduce that Horowitz had discovered that the source was, in fact, not "Russian-based." Based on additional clues provided by Horowitz, we inferred that the source was likely located in the United States. Our findings were subsequently validated when Attorney General Bill Barr ultimately disclosed the FBI's interview transcript with the primary sub-source.[42]

Curiously, Clinesmith was never charged for lying about the primary sub-source's location. Instead, he was later charged with doctoring evidence regarding Page's status as a CIA source. Clinesmith made it appear that Page was not a source, when in reality, he was a source.[43] If the FISC had known that Carter Page had been a CIA source, that would have provided a credible explanation for why he traveled to Russia and why he had contact with Russian individuals. Not that traveling to Russia or knowing Russians is a bad thing, but the FBI portrayed it that way, so they should have at least told the court why Page was doing it. They didn't. Instead, they lied about it.

Armed with small clues from the Horowitz Report, our group of four also deduced that the primary sub-source lived in Northern Virginia, based on the indication that the source had been interviewed in Washington, DC over an extended period. This, too, turned out to be true. Thus, we started looking for former KGB or FSB personnel who lived in Northern Virginia and had a history with Steele. We identified a few candidates. What we didn't know at the time was that our initial assumption about the source's professed credibility was incorrect. While we were looking for someone with a semblance of credibility, the actual primary sub-source did not have such credibility. We could have never imagined that the source whom the FBI ostensibly believed had obtained Putin's innermost secrets—something that no professional intelligence service has achieved so far—would turn out to be an amateur with no significant experience. We could never have imagined that the FBI would proceed with their investigation based on an entirely unbelievable source. But they did, which takes us back to the shores of Lake Huron.

It was July 17, 2020. Stephen, Fool Nelson, and Walkafyre were exchanging messages about a significant breakthrough in our project. They asked me, "Have you seen it?" I didn't know what they were talking about. "Lindsey released the primary sub-source interview!" read the next message. Lindsey was Lindsey Graham, the senior senator from South Carolina and the then-chairman of the Senate Judiciary Committee. Attorney General Bill Barr had provided him with a rough transcript of one of the primary sub-source's FBI interviews, and fortunately, Graham released it to the public, although in a heavily redacted form.[44]

This was huge news. The Horowitz Report revealed that the primary sub-source was interviewed by the FBI in January 2017 and again later in the same year. We also knew that the primary sub-source had disavowed Steele. But we did not know who this person was. Was it some bigwig defector with insider knowledge of Kremlin politics, or rather a retired intelligence official, as we had been suspecting? Graham only released the notes of one of the interviews that took place in late January 2017. But that one interview would turn out to be enough for us to identify Steele's mysterious source.

I asked Fool Nelson for a link, informing him that I was camping with limited internet access and no computer. Before I could type anything else, I had lost my connection. I spent the next half hour desperately pacing around the beach, trying to find a spot with cell coverage.

My kids were wondering what was going on. I tried to explain, but they just assumed Daddy couldn't get away from the internet, which is something they like to joke about. There is some truth to that, of course, but this was an all-hands-on-deck situation, and I was out of commission. Eventually, I found a spot where my phone worked. By this time, I had received a dozen or so additional messages. My three friends were way ahead, discussing what they had found. I hadn't even downloaded the file. Fool Nelson had sent a link, so I started downloading it. It was only thirty-three megabytes, but with barely one bar of cell reception, it was taking ages. And then I lost reception again. This was not good. I had to come up with another plan. I gathered the children and told them that we needed to return to our campsite. There had been limited cell coverage there the night before. But it was gone, so we ended up driving to the nearest town. The nearest town required a forty-mile round trip. The kids weren't thrilled, but as luck would have it, we found a Burger King three-quarters of the way along, which made up for the inconvenience. Not exactly how camping is supposed to work, but the kids were happy.

With the help of Burger King's Wi-Fi, I got my first look at the source's interview notes. They were astounding. Although the source's name and many other details were redacted, it became clear that this individual was not a former KGB official. Despite the redactions, we were able to glean from the biographical part of the interview that the source was still a child when the KGB was dissolved in 1991. We also noted that the source claimed to have never met a Russian intelligence or security officer in his life. The claim was later disputed when it became known that the source may have had such contacts while working for the Brookings Institution in Washington, DC.[45] But the overall picture remained: this guy was an amateur. At least that part of the puzzle was resolved. Steele was not a patsy. Instead, he had hired a Russian speaker to serve as an intermediary to assist him in fabricating a story. If later asked why things hadn't panned out, Steele could blame his source.

As I read on, things only got worse. Steele had paid his source to fly to Russia to go drinking with his childhood friends. As the primary sub-source described it to the FBI, he clearly enjoyed these trips. The problem was that Steele wanted some gossip in return, so the source told Steele whatever he wanted to hear. An un-redacted portion of the notes stated that the source "felt like he had to report something back to Steele."[46]

Another un-redacted section revealed that Steele had initially asked the primary sub-source to provide him with information about Paul Manafort.[47] The source told the FBI that, at the time, he had no idea who Manafort was. This didn't sound right. When Steele asked the source for stories about

Manafort, Trump was the presumptive Republican nominee for president, and Manafort was Trump's campaign manager. You would have had to completely shut yourself off from the world not to know who Manafort was.

If that wasn't enough, the corporate media constantly portrayed Manafort as a pro-Russian puppet because he had once worked for the allegedly pro-Russian then-president of Ukraine, Viktor Yanukovych. How could the primary sub-source, who was an alleged expert on all things Russia, not have heard of Manafort? To us, it was almost inconceivable that the primary sub-source had never heard the name Manafort. The source had either lied to the FBI or was even less knowledgeable than we feared.

As we continued dissecting the fifty-seven pages of interview notes, we were able to deduce that the primary sub-source and his childhood drinking buddies had grown up in what appeared to be a large four-letter city in Russia. We narrowed the search down further and concluded that the city had to be Perm, a city located near the Ural Mountains, about a thousand miles east of Moscow.

We continued what had by then become a game of deducing the redactions. Walkafyre was particularly skilled at it. Up to that point, the FBI's reports had always used a monospaced font, which means a font where each letter and character occupies the same amount of horizontal space. Courier is probably the most well-known monospaced font. This was extremely helpful to us because it allowed us to determine the exact number of characters hidden under any redaction. A few weeks after we identified Steele's primary sub-source, the FBI changed their font. Because of us, they no longer use monospaced fonts in their reports.

Luckily, the interview report we had was monospaced, which helped us determine that the primary sub-source's name was fourteen characters long, including the space between the first and last name. That narrowed it down considerably. But none of our usual suspects fit. That was not surprising, as we had looked at ostensibly credible sources, not a complete nobody whom no one had ever heard of.

We used the same redaction trick to piece together additional information. We deduced that, after finishing school, the primary sub-source had studied at a twenty-one-character college. Perm State University. The one after that was trickier but turned out to be a very helpful clue. As a student, Steele's source had participated in a global leadership initiative. We knew the initiative had an eighteen-character name. We eventually figured out that this was the Open World Program, which brings students from Eurasia to the United States for a ten-day trip. It is somewhat ironic that this program was developed in the 1990s to cultivate cultural and political connections between the United States and Russia. In this particular instance, the individual brought to the United States played a crucial role in the attempted takedown of the Republican presidential candidate and subsequent president.

By this point, I had persuaded the kids that we were going to move to a campground that had Wi-Fi. I promised we would go back to barebones camping as soon as possible, and I kept that promise. But this was very important. Plus, it was still my birthday, so I had some leeway. We got a cabin with a bunk bed, which the kids loved. Now that I had proper internet access, I was able to delve into it more deeply, albeit on an iPhone.

Our next task was to figure out where the primary sub-source had studied after leaving Russia. All we knew was that it was a university with a ten-character name, "University of 1234567890." There were also some clues that he had moved to the United States after attending the Open World Program. There was mention of another ten-character university, this time spelled as "1234567890 University." Was this intentional, or were these the same universities? Both Georgetown and Louisville comprise ten letters. We found out that Perm is twinned with Louisville, which drew our attention there. By employing the same modus operandi, we deduced that Steele's source probably had a connection to the Brookings Institution and was acquainted with Fiona Hill, one of the key witnesses who testified against President Trump in the Ukraine impeachment proceedings. Washington, DC seems to be an extremely incestuous city.

We had also begun sharing clues in real-time with other internet researchers. Some of our old friends, @CasualSemi, @BlackJackBoGreı, @SamSimeonSays, and Dutchman Jaap Titulaer were helping with the heavy lifting. CasualSemi had managed to extrapolate from the way the source's name was redacted at the end of a line that the primary sub-source's name comprised a four-letter first name and a nine-letter last name. We were looking for someone originally from Perm, who had participated in the Open World Program, studied at Louisville or Georgetown, or both, and had a four-letter first name and a nine-letter last name. The next step was to analyze any social media contacts of individuals known to be associated with Steele. Maybe we could find a four-plus-nine name among them. We suspected that this would eventually reveal the name of the primary sub-source, but it was a challenging task. There were many social media accounts to check. Stephen decided to share what he knew on Twitter. Through his Climategate adventures, Stephen had gained a large following, and our efforts evolved into a crowd-sourced endeavor. While helpful in expediting our search, it would potentially alert the primary sub-source to what we were doing. We knew this but thought it was worth the risk.

By Sunday morning, barely forty hours after Lindsey Graham had released the redacted document, we received a message from someone on Twitter whom we had not met before. He went by the online handle @Hmmm57474203. He told us that he thought the source's name was Igor Danchenko. To memorialize how he had come up with that name, @Hmmm57474203 wrote a blog post describing how he utilized the different data points Stephen had publicly shared the night before to identify Danchenko. He had combed through the social media accounts of people working for Steele's company, Orbis, looking for four-plus-nine names. Eventually, he came across someone named Kieran Porter. Porter worked for Steele and had a social media friend named Igor Danchenko, which was a four-plus-nine name. The reason we knew that Porter worked for Steele was due to a previous, separate effort by Yaacov Apelbaum, another amazing internet sleuth. But Danchenko, as far as we could tell, did not work for Steele, at least not publicly. And so it was. As we later found out, Danchenko used a Washington, DC-based cutout as his place of employment. Steele paid the cutout, and the cutout paid Danchenko. We eventually concluded that this probably had more to do with Danchenko's immigration status than with trying to hide Danchenko's connection to Steele. In fact, it is almost certain that the FBI identified Danchenko in December 2016 by tracing payments that Steele sent to the cutout firm.

Danchenko seemed like a solid identification, but we needed to be sure. We embarked on the task of confirming that Danchenko was indeed Steele's source. He was from Perm. He studied at Perm State University. He participated in the Open World Program. He studied at Louisville. He also studied at Georgetown. He was friends with Fiona Hill. He had worked at the Brookings Institution. Everything fit, and it looked like we had found our suspect.

But before we were going to announce it, there was one final thing we had to check. According to the Horowitz Report, the primary sub-source had contacted Sergei Millian twice. Millian was a realtor who had once sold apartments in a Trump condominium complex in Florida. Millian had been framed by Steele and the primary sub-source as the source for almost every salacious and damning accusation in the dossier. During the lead-up to the 2016 election, Clinton operatives also maliciously spread Millian's name in the media.[48]

Later, when Millian was hounded by the press during the Russiagate hysteria that led to the appointment of Mueller as a special counsel, he was forced to give up his business and leave the country. Stephen had contacted Millian before we began our quest to identify Steele's primary sub-source, allowing us to establish a good rapport.

Millian was an affable character who was always willing to help. He wanted to know who had framed him as much as anyone else did. Millian told us that he had once met Trump at a marketing event in 2007, and there were photos online. It was that connection, as well as the fact that he was from Belarus and spoke Russian, that likely put him in the crosshairs of the Clinton campaign's plan to accuse Trump of colluding with Russia. Millian was also the former president of the Russian-American Chamber of Commerce and had appeared in the media in that role. None of those things are in any way nefarious. But they were enough for Steele and his operatives: a Russian speaker who had a connection to Trump.

What distinguished Millian from others in the Russiagate story was that he never had any contact with anyone in Steele's circle. Steele's typical modus operandi is to position his targets in the same room as his operatives. Once that is achieved, words can be attributed to anyone. But because he was never in the same room with Danchenko, Steele, or any other Clinton operatives, words could not be put in Millian's mouth. However, Steele did put words in Millian's mouth regardless. This was and remains the biggest problem in Steele's entire tale. It is the one thing he cannot wiggle out of. It is where his fantasy falls apart. You can only create a "he said, she said" situation if he and she were at some point in the same location.

The myth of Millian as a source was particularly important for Steele. Millian was allegedly the source of large amounts of Steele's intelligence. Every major Steele dossier allegation had supposedly come from Millian: The Moscow pee tape, the "well-developed conspiracy of co-operation" between Trump and Putin, the WikiLeaks email dump, and the story about secret communications between the Russian Alfa Bank and Trump. All of that and more were supposed to have come from a person whom neither Steele nor Danchenko had ever met. How was it possible for Millian to provide all this information? Steele claims that Millian told Danchenko these stories over the course of three separate meetings. But the Danchenko interview notes that we were analyzing revealed that Danchenko had never met Millian. Crucially, the notes also stated that Danchenko had sent Millian two emails that remained unanswered.

As soon as we found the character count for sub-source's name on July 18, 2020, Stephen messaged Millian and asked him to check his email archive from around July 2016 for a four-plus-nine name. The next morning, before Millian could get back to us, @Hmmm57474203 suggested the name Igor Danchenko. So Stephen asked Millian to search for that name instead. Within a few minutes, Millian replied. He found the two emails that Danchenko had sent in 2016 and shared them with us.

Millian told us that he had no idea who Danchenko was and therefore ignored the messages. In retrospect, that was very wise. Steele would have used any contact, no matter how brief, to support the false narrative of Millian as a source.

With Millian's confirmation, we had our proof. Steele's primary sub-source was Igor Danchenko. Not a Kremlin insider with important information, but a Beltway insider with no information. Danchenko knew as much about Putin's innermost thoughts as you or I.

We had achieved our goal; we finally knew who Steele's source was. But it was just the beginning. Danchenko had told the FBI that there were five other people he had used as ostensible dossier sources. These people were not insiders either. Instead, they were his drinking buddies and friends. In the document released by Lindsey Graham, names and any identifying information had been redacted. Once we had identified Danchenko, we set out to identify these other so-called sources. We also needed to try to match them with whatever they were supposed to have contributed to the dossier. In June 2021, after a Russian newspaper reported on our endeavor to find Danchenko,[49] all five alleged dossier sources came forward and swore under penalty of perjury that they had nothing whatsoever to do with the dossier and had not provided Danchenko with any information for the dossier.[50]

Despite this, many Americans still believe the Steele dossier to be at least partially true.[51] Attorney General Merrick Garland seems to be undecided. He claimed during his Senate confirmation hearing in 2021 that the information he had seen in the dossier was conflicting.[52] There is nothing conflicting about the information. The dossier was fabricated by Steele and Danchenko. It was a document tailored for the Hillary Clinton campaign to serve as both a shield and a sword. It acted as a shield to divert attention from Clinton's email scandal and as a sword to portray Trump as a Russian puppet.

The following book is the story of how the Clinton campaign's initial smear tactics targeting Trump evolved into a broader assault on the nation itself. This is a story of how a small group of online researchers connected scattered pieces of information to uncover crucial aspects of the plot against Trump. Together, we uncovered a complex scam involving various elements, including a presidential candidate, senior campaign officials, an international law firm, a public relations firm managed by two political strategists, a former British intelligence officer, an alleged Russian operative, the FBI, the director of the CIA, the president and vice president of the United States, and, perhaps most importantly, the media. Above all, this is a story about the collusion between the Clinton campaign, the media, and government agents. Initially, their aim was to elect Hillary Clinton. When that failed, their attention turned toward undermining a president who had been duly elected. In the process, these forces so badly damaged the United States and its ability to engage Russia peacefully that it resulted in the rebifurcation of the world order. Hillary Clinton's attack against Trump was the greatest act of domestic political sabotage of all time.

CHAPTER 1

The Origin of the Swiftboat Project

On May 20, 2022, Hillary Clinton's campaign manager, Robby Mook, finally admitted that it was Hillary Clinton herself who approved her presidential campaign's strategy to tarnish Donald Trump with Russia collusion allegations.[1] Mook's admission, made during his testimony in Clinton campaign lawyer Michael Sussmann's trial for lying to the FBI about Clinton's scheme, marked the final chapter in a six-year saga that ruined a presidency and turned the world order on its head.

It all began in early 2016 when Jennifer Palmieri, the director of Communications for the Hillary Clinton presidential campaign, received an email from Joel Johnson, a senior advisor to Bill Clinton. Johnson wrote, "Who is in charge of the Trump swift boat project? Needs to be ready, funded and unleashed when we decide—but not a half assed scramble." Palmieri sarcastically replied, "Gee. Thanks, Joel. We thought we could half-ass it. Let's discuss."[2]

The exchange was buried in a vast collection of emails from Clinton campaign chairman John Podesta that were released by the whistleblower group WikiLeaks in October 2016. The significance of the two emails was largely overlooked at the time. It was only with hindsight and the progressive unraveling of Hillary Clinton's scheme to vilify Donald Trump that the importance of their exchange has become apparent.

We now know that the two emails marked the inception of the dirtiest political trick of all time: Hillary Clinton's Russiagate scam, a multi-pronged and multi-layered campaign to portray Donald Trump as an asset of the Kremlin. Such a scheme was completely unheard of and beyond the bounds of anything that had happened in the murky world of American politics. On June 17, 1972, individuals associated with President Richard Nixon conducted a break-in at the Democratic National Committee (DNC) headquarters located in the Watergate office building in Washington, DC. The ostensible purpose of the break-in was to eavesdrop. But even that act pales in comparison to what Clinton did.

Clinton intended to execute an elaborate scheme that portrayed her opponent as an agent of a foreign power. It was a devious plan, and it came at a heavy price for all Americans. The Russiagate scandal not only engulfed Trump's presidency but also reshaped the geopolitical balance of power for generations to come. In her failed attempt to become president, Hillary Clinton sabotaged America herself.

Trump's slogan throughout the 2016 campaign was "Make America Great Again." One of the central tenets of Trump's platform was to extricate the United States from its numerous foreign entanglements, wars, and proxy wars. As part of that broader ambition, Trump was determined to improve relations with Russia. American-Russian relations had been deteriorating since the days of the George W. Bush administration, perhaps best exemplified by Bush's ill-considered 2008 Bucharest Declaration, in which it was announced that Ukraine and Georgia would become members of NATO.[3] Admitting these two countries into NATO was a well-known red line for Russia. Crossing that red line was not only reckless, but it also contradicted a promise made in 1990 by the administration of Bush's father, George H. W. Bush, not to expand NATO.[4]

In 2009, President Barack Obama attempted to reset relations with Russia. However, whether intentional or not, those efforts proved fruitless. By early 2014, Obama's Russian reset was dead in the water. Instead, the Obama administration decided to take a diametrically opposed direction by supporting a coup d'état in Ukraine, which is strategically crucial to Russia. The country's elected president was removed and replaced by a handpicked puppet. A leaked recording of a phone conversation between then-Assistant Secretary of State Victoria Nuland and then-ambassador to Ukraine, Geoffrey Pyatt, revealed that the selection process was orchestrated by the State Department with the approval of then-Vice President Joe Biden.[5] It was as if Russia had organized the overthrow of the Mexican or Canadian government and handpicked the new leader for that country. The United States would not have tolerated such a move, and neither did Russia. The reaction was swift. Crimea, formerly a part of Russia until Soviet leader Nikita Khrushchev transferred it to the Ukrainian Soviet

Socialist Republic in 1954, was annexed shortly after the American-led coup.

The drive by the Western establishment to antagonize Russia since the end of the Cold War has never been fully explored or understood. While the United States was pushing for the westernization of Eastern Europe, Russia was being mocked, shamed, and sanctioned. There was no obvious reason why Russia needed to be vilified. Russia and large parts of Eastern Europe share related cultures, religions, histories, and languages. They have far more in common with each other than Russia does, for instance, with China or India.

Why was one country antagonized while the others were courted? There is no clear answer to this question. Perhaps the main reason for this irrational policy was and remains the prevailing Cold War mentality and animosity toward all things Russian among Western elites and the Western foreign policy establishment.

Other reasons may include greed, as well as the predispositions of the people involved. For instance, Joe Biden's son Hunter was profiting directly from the situation that his father had created in Ukraine. When Ukrainian energy oligarch Mykola Zlochevsky lost his government position in the American-backed 2014 coup, he turned to Hunter Biden for protection. Hunter was hired at a base rate of $1 million per year. Victoria Nuland, the assistant secretary of state who was in Kiev supporting anti-government forces and directly overseeing regime change in Kiev, has family ties to this region. Alexander Vindman, the man behind Trump's 2019 impeachment, was born in Kiev.

More recently, Russia has served as a convenient scapegoat for a variety of domestic problems, with energy dependency being at the top of that list. The incessant vilification of Russia has, intentionally or otherwise, also diverted attention from China, a far more formidable threat to freedom and global order. Perhaps worst of all, the denigration of all things Russian extends to the entire Russian population, even including sports stars like Daniil Medvedev, the former world No. 1 tennis player.[6]

The vilification of Russia has come at a steep price. As Russia became increasingly isolated, it began to forge new friendships, most notably with Beijing. It was the worst possible outcome for the so-called Western alliance. And it was completely unnecessary. China and Russia are not natural partners. In 1969, the Soviet Union and China fought a six-month-long war, which was only finally resolved in 2008 when Moscow and Beijing signed a border agreement.[7]

Although it appears almost unthinkable from today's perspective, Russia and Taiwan—Beijing's archenemy—once maintained favorable relations. In the 1990s, Taiwan was on the verge of purchasing Russian SU-27 fighter jets, but was pressured by the United States to cancel the deal. In the early 2000s, Taiwan's then-new president, Chen Shui-bian, and Russia's then-new president, Vladimir Putin, maintained a friendship that dated back to 1995 when Chen was the mayor of Taipei and Putin was the deputy mayor of St. Petersburg. It was this friendship that led to the development of a joint Taiwanese and Russian spacecraft, which was launched in 2009. As recently as 2014, Russia and Taiwan initiated non-stop commercial flights between their respective capitals.

The notion that the Kremlin is inherently allied with Beijing was always as false as the idea that Russia could not be part of the Western alliance. In reality, it was reckless, thoughtless, and corrupt Western elites that pushed the Kremlin ever closer to Beijing.

Trump recognized this problem long before he became president. One of Trump's campaign promises since 2015 was to enhance relations with Russia. He would often ask at his rallies, "If we could get along with Russia, wouldn't that be a good thing, instead of a bad thing?"[8]

Trump's vision was correct. The only serious adversary the United States faces in the world today is China. The Western foreign policy establishment's actions of pushing Russia, with its abundant supply of raw materials and energy, toward China would only serve to strengthen China. Trump intended to put the brakes on this dangerous trend and realign the relationship between Washington and the Kremlin.

Directly tied to Trump's desire to normalize relations with Russia was his view that NATO was obsolete. NATO was created in 1949 by the United States to provide ten Western European nations with a security guarantee against an attack by the Soviet Union. Once the Soviet Union was dissolved, NATO no longer had a reason to exist.

But international institutions have a persistent tendency to perpetuate their own existence. One way to perpetuate NATO was to equate Russia with the old Soviet Union. Instead of disbanding, or at least maintaining the status quo as George H. W. Bush had promised the Kremlin in 1990, NATO expanded eastward fourteen times, incorporating several former Soviet republics in the process. NATO also began transitioning its mission from a commitment by the United States to defend a select group of countries in case of a Soviet attack to a broader concept of promoting human rights.[9] The first application of this new justification for its existence came in 1999 when NATO attacked a historic Russian ally, Yugoslavia. Similar justifications were used in 2011 when NATO intervened in Libya.

Such military adventurism for ill-defined purposes did not align with Trump's America First vision. Nor did it help with containing China, which is by far the West's greatest foreign policy challenge of the twenty-first century. On top of all that, open-ended NATO expansion antagonized Russia. Unsurprisingly, the Washington establishment was alarmed by what Trump was proposing. They could not allow Trump to realign the geopolitical landscape.

Disengaging from other countries' problems would have been detrimental to the perception of American preeminence and its role as the world's so-called policeman. It would have been detrimental to globalization, which aims to promote increasing interconnectedness and interdependence among the world's economies. That, in turn, would have been detrimental to China, something the Chinese Communist Party's numerous allies in Washington, DC and corporate America could not allow to happen. Lastly, American disentanglement from overseas military adventures would also have been detrimental to the military-industrial complex. For all these reasons, the combined forces of the pushback from the American establishment were strong.

Trump's views were well-known. In his first foray into public policy writing in 2000, Trump articulated in *The America We Deserve* that the expenses associated with stationing troops in Europe are substantial, suggesting that these resources could be more effectively allocated elsewhere.[10] Trump reiterated these views during his presidential campaign. In August 2015, he stated that he "would not care that much" about Ukraine's entry into NATO.[11] This was anathema to the DC foreign policy establishment. The media ran breathless headlines proclaiming that Trump had abandoned Ukraine and ditched Europe.[12] Most notably, all of this was happening long before Hillary Clinton kicked off her Russia-focused smear campaign against Trump.

The apprehension among Washington, DC elites that Trump might disrupt their favored world order laid the groundwork for Hillary Clinton's choice to prioritize the Trump-Russia collusion narrative in her swiftboat project. Like all political campaigns, the Clinton campaign was looking for an issue to use against her opponent. There was a lot to choose from, including Trump's checkered past in the real estate industry and his philandering. But those issues had strings attached. Reminding voters of Trump's business background might have enhanced his image as an outsider who could accomplish tasks effectively. Highlighting his extramarital affairs would not have had the same impact as it would have had in the past. Ironically, it was Hillary Clinton's husband, Bill, who broke that particular glass ceiling.

What was needed was something that would catalyze traditional political smears involving suspect business deals and extramarital affairs into something more explosive. Russia was the catalyst. Best of all, it was an issue that the entire Washington, DC establishment could coalesce around.

By painting Trump as a Russian stooge, the Clinton campaign aimed to gather a broad coalition of support, including globalists and war-mongering neoconservatives. The Russian stooge story could be interspersed with more familiar stories about shady business dealings and illicit affairs. Placing Trump and the Kremlin in the same corner also served as an insurance policy for Hillary Clinton in case any of the thirty thousand deleted emails from the covert server she used during her tenure as secretary of state were leaked. Any disclosure could be attributed to the Russian government and, consequently, to Trump, thereby diverting attention from the content of those emails. In the end, Clinton's thirty thousand missing emails never surfaced. But that did not affect the implementation of Hillary Clinton's devious plan. When unrelated emails from the DNC were released in July 2016, Clinton initiated her carefully planned swiftboat project.

It was Clinton's communications director, Jennifer Palmieri, who initially got the swiftboat plan rolling, as we would later find out from WikiLeaks's release of Clinton campaign chairman John Podesta's emails.

The term "swiftboating" originated from the 2004 presidential campaign when a group of veterans, known as Swift Boat Veterans for Truth, attacked the war record of presidential candidate John Kerry, who had served as a swift boat commander in the Vietnam War.[13] Just like the Clinton campaign's ruthless tactics against Trump, the swift boat attack on Kerry was similarly aggressive. The Swift Boat Veterans for Truth challenged aspects of Kerry's military service record and the circumstances surrounding the conferral of his combat decorations. And just like the Clinton campaign attack against Trump, the swift boat attack on Kerry was multi-pronged. It cast doubt on various events involving Kerry during the Vietnam War and publicized its claims through different television ads, media appearances, and a book titled *Unfit For Command*. Moreover, Kerry's opponent, George W. Bush, disavowed any connection with the Swift Boat Veterans for Truth campaign. The Clinton campaign too was very careful to distance itself from their own swiftboat project. In fact, it wasn't until a year into Trump's

The Origin of the Swiftboat Project

presidency that Clinton's involvement in, and funding of, the infamous Steele dossier first became known.

But this is where the comparisons end. No matter how viciously Kerry was swiftboated, the 2004 attacks are dwarfed in planning, scope, and effect by Clinton's 2016 swiftboat project.

CHAPTER 2

Swiftboating America— The Clinton Campaign

Three days after the February 2016 exchange between Palmieri and Johnson regarding "the Trump swift boat project," Peter Fritsch emailed a "senior figure in the Democratic Party," exclaiming that Trump "has to be stopped." The response was affirmative, "Yes. Let's talk."[1]

Peter Fritsch is the co-founder of Fusion GPS, a firm of political operatives that he established with Glenn Simpson, who, like Fritsch, is a former *Wall Street Journal* reporter. Soon after Fritsch's email, Fusion GPS was hired by the Clinton campaign to develop and promote the Swiftboat project. Ten months later, after Trump miraculously won the election against all odds, the Fusion GPS founders' *Wall Street Journal* connection would become crucial in efforts to conceal the existence of Clinton's Swiftboat project. But more on that later.

The unidentified "senior figure in the Democratic Party" whom Fritsch had contacted soon arranged for Fritsch and Simpson to meet Marc Elias. Elias is a Democratic Party elections lawyer who was known at the time for leading the political law unit at Perkins Coie, an international law firm aligned with the Democratic Party. He was also known for his efforts in overturning the contested Minnesota Senate election in 2008 in favor of Al Franken. Elias spearheaded the Democratic Party's highly successful "fortification" efforts in the 2020 presidential election.[2] The term "fortification" originated from a *Time Magazine* article in 2021, in which a left-wing activist boasted about engineering Biden's win: "They were not rigging the election; they were fortifying it."[3]

In 2016, Elias was the attorney of record for the Clinton campaign. He was not only in charge of every aspect of campaign lawyering but also led the Swiftboat project, which included shielding the campaign from any fallout associated with the project. In practice, this meant establishing multiple layers of deniability for Hillary Clinton herself. The Swiftboat project would be run out of Perkins Coie, the law firm where Elias was a partner until his sudden departure in 2021.[4]

In March 2022, the Clinton campaign was fined by the Federal Election Commission for violating election laws. Specifically, they were penalized for concealing that they had funded the phony Steele dossier.[5] The campaign had claimed in its filings that the Steele dossier payments were legal expenses incurred by Elias on behalf of the campaign.

Elias's associate in representing the Clinton campaign was his fellow Perkins partner Michael Sussmann, who was indicted in September 2021 for lying to the FBI on Clinton's behalf.[6] The general modus operandi was that Elias and Sussmann would hire external operatives, creating a first layer of deniability. In addition, they would claim attorney-client privilege over all communications between themselves and these operatives. That would create the second layer of deniability. In reality, outside the world of Clinton campaign machinations, attorney-client privilege does not apply when the communication is not intended for requesting or receiving legal advice. But they claimed that it did.

Most, if not all, aspects of the Swiftboat project, such as planting fake stories about Trump with sympathetic media outlets, cannot be categorized as providing or receiving legal advice. There simply was no basis for invoking the privilege. But it is very difficult to persuade a judge to pierce supposed attorney-client privilege. Elias and Sussmann were counting on this, and they were proven right. The falsely claimed privilege was not pierced, so we never found out exactly what Elias and Sussmann were telling their contractors.

As a next step, those contractors, such as Fusion GPS, would outsource tasks to their own subcontractors. This added another layer of distance to the campaign. Ideally, the subcontractor would then use their own subcontractor, which would result in the Clinton campaign being five steps removed from any potential malfeasance.

One of Fusion GPS's subcontractors was Steele. In turn, Steele had his own subcontractor, Igor Danchenko, whose main purpose was to provide

Steele with a layer of deniability. In case the entire scheme blew up, Steele could claim that he was just reporting what Danchenko told him. In fact, this is exactly what Steele later claimed in various interviews and legal disputes that arose from his authorship of the dossier.[7] There were other subcontractors, particularly in the media. The extent of their contractual relationship with Fusion remains shrouded in mystery. What can be said with certainty is that members of the media, including those from ABC and the *Wall Street Journal*, were involved in performing tasks for Fusion related to the Swiftboat project.[8]

After Elias hired Fusion GPS on April 20, 2016, Fusion immediately began writing a dossier on Trump.[9] This wasn't the Steele dossier but rather a proto-dossier consisting of a fifteen-page report written by Jake Berkowitz, an in-house operative at Fusion GPS. The Fusion dossier's claims followed familiar patterns, asserting that "Donald Trump's connections to Vladimir Putin's Russia are deeper than generally appreciated and raise significant national security concerns."[10] Fusion's preliminary dossier highlighted Trump advisors Paul Manafort and Carter Page, Trump's alleged visits to Moscow, and Trump's purported financial connections to Russia. These themes were later adopted and repackaged by Steele.

But it wasn't just Fusion's in-house dossier that was making the media rounds in the spring of 2016. A Clinton operative named Cody Shearer had authored his own memos on Trump. We know of the existence of two Shearer memos, titled "Donald Trump—Background Notes—The Compromised Candidate" and "FSB Interview."[11] FSB stands for the Russian Federal Security Service, which is roughly equivalent to the FBI.

Shearer is the brother-in-law of Bill Clinton's Oxford study mate, Strobe Talbott. Talbott later served as a deputy secretary in Bill Clinton's State Department, while Shearer is said to have worked as a behind-the-scenes fixer under the direction of another Clinton operative, Sidney Blumenthal.[12]

Shearer shared his memos with favored members of the media, as well as with Jonathan Winer, who was the State Department's special envoy to Libya.[13] In September 2016, at the height of the Clinton campaign's efforts to promote the Russia hoax, Blumenthal provided Jonathan Winer at the State Department with a copy of at least one of Shearer's two memos. In turn, Winer gave the memo to Steele, who then passed it on to the FBI.[14]

It was the same modus operandi the Swiftboat operatives used throughout: creating the impression of separate information streams and establishing distance by employing various layers of messengers to disseminate the false information to the media and the FBI.

Shearer's initial memo echoed Steele's broader narrative on Russian collusion. However, it stood out by explicitly identifying journalist Brian Ross, who was working at ABC at the time, as the source for the story alleging that Trump had been compromised sexually during a trip to Moscow. The reason why Ross was named as the source is unknown. What is known is that Ross would later play an important role in helping Fusion GPS frame an innocent man, Sergei Millian, as the source for most of the Steele dossier's allegations.

In Shearer's account, Trump was "invited to a private hotel located in a shopping mall called Crocus about an hour's drive from Red Square. It is at this hotel that Trump is filmed with a young woman. The film shows a woman urinating on Trump."[15] In Steele's account, these events occurred at the Ritz Carlton hotel, which is situated less than a thousand feet from Red Square.[16]

Shearer's memos are also notable because they appear to contain the early seeds of what would later become known as the Alfa Bank hoax. This fabricated story, promoted by both Steele and Clinton campaign lawyer Sussmann, alleged that Trump was communicating with Putin through Russia's Alfa Bank. Like the rest of Steele's dossier, the Alfa Bank story was made up. However, unlike Steele, Shearer attributed the story to a known individual, Robert Baer, a self-proclaimed intelligence and security analyst for CNN. Baer is quoted as claiming that the "Russians had established an encrypted communication system with a cutout between the Trump campaign and Putin."[17] Steele was more circumspect, stating that his source was "a trusted compatriot" of "a top level Russian government official."[18] Much later, we would find out that the trusted compatriot was Steele's in-house operative Igor Danchenko and that no "top level Russian government official" ever spoke to Danchenko, let alone about the stories featured in Steele's dossier.[19]

Baer's mindset is illustratively captured in his recent claims that Elon Musk's efforts to restore free speech to Twitter were something the Russian government had been waiting for: "Putin is going to be all over Twitter if there's no regulations on this, fake accounts, spoofed accounts, the rest of it, this is a great opportunity for him. And so when he's talking about the popular voice, Musk, he's really talking about Russian intelligence. The Russians are waiting for something like this."[20]

Stories from both Fusion's proto-dossier and Shearer's memos were shared with members of Clinton-friendly media, including ABC's Matthew Mosk, Reuters's Mark Hosenball, and Slate's Franklin Foer.[21] As email exchanges between Fusion and these media allies would later reveal, this wasn't just a symbiotic relationship but rather a full-fledged collaboration.[22] As early as April 2016, Foer, who would become one of Fusion's most important media figures, was actively shaping the narrative of Trump-Russia collusion.[23] By July 4, 2016, Foer was publishing articles portraying Trump as "Putin's puppet."[24] Mosk received a copy of Fusion's proto-dossier in May 2016, before Steele had even arrived on the scene. In early July 2016, Fusion assigned Mosk to pursue an innocent man, Sergei Millian, whom Steele falsely accused of being a major source of the Steele dossier.[25] It is not known whether Mosk knew that his task was directly related to fabricating a narrative for the Steele dossier.

Notably, all of this occurred long before the tip the FBI received from Australian diplomat Alexander Downer on July 26, 2016. That tip would later be characterized by both the media and the FBI as the official starting point of the FBI's investigation into Trump-Russia collusion.

Foer's initial critique also preceded the launch of the public rollout of the Swiftboat project on July 24, 2016. On that day, Clinton's campaign manager, Robby Mook, announced to the world that Russia was assisting Trump in his election campaign: "Experts are telling us Russian state actors broke into the DNC [Democratic National Committee], stole these emails, and other experts are now saying that the Russians are releasing these emails for the purpose of actually of [*sic*] helping Donald Trump."[26]

Just before Mook's announcement on July 24, WikiLeaks had released a trove of DNC emails. The emails were not particularly damaging to Clinton or Trump. The emails were mainly about how the Democratic Party had sidelined Hillary's primary opponent, Bernie Sanders. There was speculation at the time that the emails had been leaked by a disgruntled Sanders supporter.[27]

It is not known why the Clinton campaign chose July 24 to implement its Swiftboat plan. It is likely they did so in anticipation of more damaging email leaks, perhaps also fearing that Clinton's 30,000 deleted emails from her homebrew server might be released. Whatever the reason, Mook had fired the starting shot, and the Swiftboat project was in full swing. Within hours of Mook's statement, media coverage of alleged Russian interference in the 2016 election was widespread, exemplified by Politico's headline the next day: "Why Putin hates Hillary."[28] In fact, as per an intercepted communication from July 26, 2016, which was disclosed in 2020 by Director of National Intelligence John Ratcliffe, Hillary Clinton had personally sanctioned the strategy to discredit Trump by linking him to Russia "as a means of distracting the public from her private email server."²⁹ Mook later confirmed that Clinton had personally approved a plan to spread the Trump-Russia collusion narrative among the media.³⁰

A lot of preparation had gone into the project, starting long before Mook pulled the trigger. While Fusion's proto-dossiers were sufficient for dissemination by a select group of Fusion's familial media collaborators, something bigger was needed to make the story go viral with other media outlets. Clinton needed a 007, and she found him in London. It was Christopher Steele who was hired in May 2016.³¹

Hiring Steele had several advantages. First and foremost, as a former British intelligence officer, he brought a significant amount of persuasive power. A British agent who had uncovered a conspiracy involving the Kremlin and a billionaire real estate magnate sounded like a scene straight out of a James Bond movie. Steele had another significant advantage. He had extensive contacts in both the FBI and the State Department, and his background lent credibility to the Trump-Russia allegations within those agencies. This was something that Fusion GPS, Fusion's proto-dossier author Jake Berkowitz, and Cody Shearer did not possess. Lastly, Steele created distance and deniability. Anything that Steele did or said could be disavowed by Fusion, Perkins Coie, and the Clinton campaign itself. Berkowitz and Shearer did not provide such distance.

But there was also a problem. Fortunately for Steele, it was uniformly glossed over by the media, the FBI, and the State Department. The problem was that Steele had as much access to the Kremlin as anyone else, which is to say, none whatsoever. Steele worked at the British embassy in Moscow in the early 1990s but had not traveled to Russia in at least a decade. His contacts, if he had any, were outdated. But even if he had any real sources, penetrating the Kremlin's inner circle is next to impossible, a fact that Western intelligence agencies had been complaining about for decades.³² The idea that Steele could magically accomplish what the combined efforts of Western governments could not was preposterous from the start. But no one seems to have cared.

The allegations of collusion by Steele were entirely fabricated. Igor Danchenko, Steele's primary sub-source, later informed the FBI that there was no corroboration for any of Steele's stories.³³ In fact, any factual statements in Steele's reports pertained to information that was already in the public domain. For instance, it was reported at the time that Trump campaign advisor Carter Page had traveled to Moscow in July 2016.³⁴ In contrast, Steele's allegations about Page's activities in Moscow, particularly his meeting with Igor Sechin, the head of one of the world's largest energy companies and former Russian deputy prime minister, were not reported anywhere. Those allegations were fabricated. Not coincidentally, at the same time that Steele was writing his fictitious Carter Page dossier stories, Fusion GPS was promoting the same narratives to their media partners. When the *Washington Post*, whose reporter Tom Hamburger had links to Fusion, took the effort to investigate the Sechin claims through their established network of sources in Moscow, those sources promptly refuted the allegations as "bullshit" and "impossible."[35] But again, no one cared. The Sechin story not only made it into the media but was also later used by the FBI to obtain a warrant to surveil Carter Page and, consequently, the Trump campaign.[36]

Similarly, public reporting has also revealed that the Russian government was looking to sell 19 percent of its stake in Rosneft.[37] That percentage value was adopted by Steele but not in the way it was publicly reported. In Steele's account, that 19 percent, amounting to billions of dollars, was designated for Carter Page. The allegation was completely ludicrous. But again, it was repeated throughout the media.[38]

Steele used the same modus operandi repeatedly: he would start with a known fact as the foundation and then embellish it with numerous fabricated stories. To this day, not a single statement in the dossier that had not been previously reported has proven to be true.[39]

Just as Clinton, Elias, and Fusion had done, Steele also made sure to insulate himself by creating his own layer of deniability. For Clinton's Swiftboat project, Steele used Danchenko, a Russian analyst based in Washington, DC as his conduit. Steele would pay Danchenko to fly to Moscow and meet old school friends and acquaintances. Danchenko would then attribute stories in the dossier—stories that had been written by Steele and Danchenko themselves—to these old friends. That way, if anyone asked uncomfortable questions, Steele could say that he had heard the allegations from Danchenko, who in turn could say that he had heard them from people in Moscow. Those individuals in Moscow who were unaware of their role as sources for the fake dossier were at least five steps removed from the Clinton campaign, making it extremely challenging to trace the scheme back to Clinton. Eventually, our group, centered on Stephen McIntyre, Walkafyre, and Fool Nelson, did identify these fake sources, but it was far too late.[40] By the time we unraveled the entire plot, Trump's presidency had been hindered by Steele's false allegations for three and a half long years. The Trump-Russia collusion narrative was, and continues to be, firmly entrenched.

As an added insurance policy, Steele insisted, first to Fusion GPS and later to the FBI, that he could not disclose Danchenko's name as that would have allegedly put Danchenko's life in jeopardy. Of course, Danchenko's urbane life in the Washington, DC suburbs was never under any threat. In fact, in 2018, long after the events that allegedly put Danchenko in grave danger, he happily attended an event inside the Russian Embassy in Washington, DC.[41] There was never any fear of being fed a plutonium cappuccino by one of Putin's henchmen. That story, too, was made up. But it bought both Steele and Danchenko plenty of time.

There was, however, also another reason for Steele to guard Danchenko's name so closely. Five years before the dossier, Danchenko had been the subject of an FBI counterintelligence investigation that assessed his documented contacts with Russian intelligence officers.[42] To this day, Danchenko's status as a suspected Russian spy has never been resolved.[43]

We can only speculate about what might have happened if the FBI had known at the time it received Steele's first dossier report in July 2016 that the source of the information was a Washington, DC-based think tank staffer suspected of being a Russian spy. Clinton's FBI gambit might have been over before it even began. However, considering that the FBI's lead investigator, Peter Strzok, and many of his colleagues were anti-Trump fanatics, it is also possible that, like many other red flags, Danchenko's status would have been concealed by FBI leadership to undermine Trump.

CHAPTER 3

Swiftboating America— The Government

A question that has never been answered, and which Special Counsel John Durham, despite his mandate to get to the bottom of the hoax, punted on, is how much of the Swiftboat project was the work of the Clinton campaign and how much was orchestrated by factions within the federal government? We know that there is no doubt that after Trump won the November 2016 election, FBI leadership repurposed the Swiftboat project for its own efforts to smear and ultimately oust Trump. And they were joined in this endeavor by then-CIA Chief John Brennan and then-Vice President Joe Biden, as well as President Obama himself. The efforts of these three men, along with many of their associates, resulted in the creation of the notorious Intelligence Community Assessment. This document, although lacking in detail, accused Russia of influencing the election in favor of Trump. The document was released by the Intelligence Community in the days before Trump's inauguration, ensuring that his presidency was tainted from day one.

By the time Trump won the presidency, the FBI needed Steele's reports to be credible. For one thing, they had used the Steele dossier to obtain a Foreign Intelligence Surveillance Act (FISA) warrant for Trump campaign advisor Carter Page. It was unthinkable for FBI leaders to go to the Foreign Intelligence Surveillance Court (FISC) and admit they had obtained a warrant to spy on the campaign of the Republican nominee for president based on a bunch of lies.

It is therefore not surprising that the FBI doubled down. In fact, the FBI was instrumental in creating the Intelligence Community Assessment and in ensuring that Steele's catalog of lies was included in the assessment. There was no turning back for the FBI, regardless of Danchenko's unresolved status as a suspected Russian spy, and despite the fact that, four days into Trump's presidency, Danchenko had disavowed the dossier.[1]

In the years that followed, the FBI took great pains to bury Danchenko's name, his past, and even his existence. We would likely still not know that Danchenko was not in a position to know Putin's secrets if then-Attorney General Bill Barr had not released Danchenko's FBI interview notes in July 2020.[2] These notes provided our group with the necessary puzzle pieces to identify Danchenko. We would probably also not know about Danchenko's brush with counterespionage authorities had Barr not revealed this fact in September 2020.[3]

We now know that by December 2016, the FBI had identified Danchenko and was aware of both his broader problems and the issues with the stories he told Steele. Yet, instead of coming clean, the FBI doubled down. In other words, by December 2016, the FBI was a full-fledged participant in the Swiftboat project. But how did the FBI get there? Were the FBI's efforts to target Trump a result of his election victory, or did the FBI hijack Clinton's Swiftboat project from the beginning?

While feeding Trump-Russia collusion tales to the media might be considered by some as nothing more than an ambitious political smear, the Clinton campaign did not plan to stop there. The Swiftboat project was built on two main axes. Once a sufficient amount of allegations against Trump had been compiled, a new phase of Clinton's Swiftboat project kicked in. That phase involved triggering an FBI investigation of Trump. That aspect of the plan surpassed traditional smear campaigns.

Once an investigation into Trump's alleged ties to the Kremlin was initiated, the information about the investigation would be leaked to the media. In theory, that should have effectively ended Trump's hopes of winning the presidency. By design, this part of Clinton's Swiftboat project did not concern itself with whether the allegations would stand up to scrutiny; it just had to work long enough to ensure a Clinton victory. If Clinton had won on November 8, everything would have been quickly forgotten. The FBI would have ended its investigation. The dossier, which had not been published and had only been superficially mentioned in the media, would have disappeared. And the fact that the dossier had been commissioned by the Clinton campaign would likely have never been discovered.

Swiftboating America—The Government

To put it another way, if Clinton had won, we would never have discovered the Swiftboat project. The term "Trump swift boat project" would have remained an obscure reference in one of thousands of leaked emails. The fact that it did not turn out this way is, at least in part, due to the fact that Clinton's attempts to push the Swiftboat smears into the FBI remained largely unsuccessful during the pre-election period. To be more precise, the push was successful in itself; however, it did not lead to the expected leaks and media uproar. Consequently, unlike his entire presidency, Trump effectively did not have to deal with false Russia collusion allegations during the 2016 campaign.

There is no simple explanation for why the Clinton plan to trigger an FBI investigation worked, but the accompanying plan to get the fact that there was an investigation into the media did not succeed. The most plausible explanation is that the FBI was so confident in a Clinton victory that they did not see the need for an elaborate media leak strategy on their part.

The element of the plan that worked perfectly was getting the FBI to investigate Trump. The architects of the Swiftboat project had devised two parallel paths to accomplish this goal. The Steele path and the Sussmann path. Steele provided an early dossier report to an FBI agent with whom he had prior interactions. That was on July 5, 2016,[4] before the Clinton campaign initiated the Swiftboat project in earnest on July 24, and before the FBI officially opened its Trump-Russia investigation, codenamed "Crossfire Hurricane," on July 31.[5] After Steele submitted his initial dossier report to his FBI handler, Michael Gaeta, Gaeta forwarded the report to an assistant special agent in charge at the FBI's New York office.[6] From there, the report quickly made its way up to the top levels of the FBI in Washington, DC.[7]

It is unknown who within Clinton's Swiftboat group instructed Steele to provide the FBI with the dossier. Given that Steele had just been hired a few weeks earlier, it is unlikely that he would have voluntarily approached the FBI so soon without being prompted to do so. This inference is supported by the fact that Steele must have known that, by taking this route, he would ultimately destroy whatever credibility he had. For instance, if Steele had not provided his dossier to the FBI, it would not have been used to secure the Carter Page FISA warrant. In turn, there would not have been an investigation by Inspector General Michael Horowitz into the dossier's provenance.

What is also not known is the extent to which the existence of the dossier influenced the FBI's decision to open an investigation into Trump-Russia collusion. The FBI's official stance is that the dossier did not influence that decision. Yet the timing of the delivery of the dossier to the FBI and the subsequent opening of the investigation suggest that the dossier played some role.

There was also a second prong to push false information about Trump to the FBI. The plan involved setting up a false Russia collusion trail, a cyber trail.[8] However, while the Steele dossier prong was executed perfectly, the cyber prong, orchestrated by Clinton campaign lawyer Michael Sussmann, did not go as planned. Sussmann had been put in charge of a cyber links offensive against Trump. The plan was to create the appearance of internet connections between Trump and the Kremlin, which would substantiate Steele's dossier allegations with tangible, real-world evidence.[9]

With the assistance of a tech executive named Rodney Joffe and a team of cyber operatives, Sussmann began compiling data that allegedly indicated secret communication between the Trump Organization and Russia's Alfa Bank.[10] In parallel, Steele wrote reports alleging the existence of a secret communications channel between Trump and Alfa Bank. The mysterious communications would then be used as a basis for claiming that Alfa Bank was acting as a conduit between Trump and the Kremlin. The problem was that the purported cyber links were either entirely insignificant artifacts or blatantly fabricated.

When Sussmann took his cyber data to the FBI on September 19, 2016,[11] it did not take the FBI long to figure out that the data was "51–50ish," which is a reference to a section of the Welfare and Institutions Code that allows someone experiencing a mental health crisis to be involuntarily detained.[12] In other words, the FBI knew that the Alfa Bank data was borderline crazy. Coincidentally, or not, six additional Steele dossier reports arrived at FBI headquarters on the same day, September 19, 2016.[13]

Sussmann also provided the FBI with a fourteen-page dossier on Alfa Bank, referring to it as a white paper. He billed the Clinton campaign for his work on the phony cyber data and the Alfa Bank dossier, as well as for delivering it to the FBI. The billing is important because Sussmann, who was later charged with providing false information to the FBI, claimed that he was merely acting as a Good Samaritan.[14]

As we discovered when Sussmann was indicted in September 2021, the tech operatives who provided the phony cyber data privately discussed its lack of credibility, with one individual emailing the others: "We cannot technically make any claims that would fly public scrutiny."[15] The same operative went on to add, "the only thing that drives us at this point is that we just do not like Trump."[16] The Clinton operatives behind the cyber data knew it did not say what they claimed it said.

Even more incriminating is the fact that the white paper that Sussmann delivered to the FBI bore a striking resemblance in formatting and style to the proto-dossier prepared by Fusion GPS in April 2016, before Steele or Sussmann had even entered the picture.[17] The similarities suggest that Fusion may have been involved in drafting, editing, or formatting the white paper that Sussmann took to the FBI, once again highlighting Fusion's central role in all matters related to the Swiftboat campaign.

Just as Sussmann's cyber data and white paper were, the Steele dossier was also submitted to the FBI in an apparent attempt to prompt an investigation of Trump. But unlike the cyber prong, the Steele prong was far more successful. Steele's first dossier report was completed on June 20, 2016.[18] It was the infamous "pee tape" report—Report 80—that laid the groundwork for the Clinton Trump-Russia collusion narrative. It alleged that the Kremlin was assisting Trump in his election campaign and possessed compromising material in the form of lewd sex tapes from Trump's 2013 visit to the Miss Universe competition in Moscow. The dossier contains many paradoxes, such as why Trump, a well-known germaphobe who would reprimand individuals for simply coughing in his vicinity,[19] would participate in "golden showers."

The "pee tape" story, along with the other stories in Report 80 and subsequent Steele reports, was transparently false. But accuracy was not the point. The point was to get these stories into the media and to the FBI.

By July 5, 2016, Steele had personally shared Report 80 with FBI agent Michael Gaeta.[20] Coincidentally, July 5 was the same day on which FBI Director James Comey held his press conference, absolving Hillary Clinton of wrongdoing regarding her use of a clandestine email server. Comey infamously stated that "no reasonable prosecutor would bring such a case."[21]

One of the reasons Steele was such an appealing choice for the Swiftboat conspirators was his previous connection with the FBI. This was due to his involvement in providing information about suspected vote rigging within the international soccer governing body, FIFA.[22] As our group would discover, Steele's FIFA reports bore a remarkable resemblance to his Trump reports, even using the same Russian villains for his stories, such as Igor Sechin, the CEO of Russian energy company Rosneft, whom Steele falsely accused of colluding with Carter Page.[23] According to "one of Steele's best sources," Sechin traveled to Qatar at the same time as Russia's World Cup bid team in order to "swap World Cup votes."[24]

By late July, Steele's Report 80 was circulating in the upper echelons of the FBI.[25] The first sentence of that report read: "Russian regime has been cultivating, supporting, and assisting Trump for at least 5 years."[26] A few weeks later, in Report 97, Steele exposed the dossier's lack of credibility by altering "five years" to "eight years."[27] That's what happens when things are made up on the fly; inconsistencies arise. A later report would also detail additional stories of Trump's alleged sexual escapades in St. Petersburg and a bribery scheme.[28] To top it off, according to Steele, the entire collusion operation was orchestrated by Vladimir Putin himself.[29] Steele's stories were transparently fake, as anyone with a modicum of sanity would have realized within a few minutes of reading his dossier. Indeed, that was the reaction of many people who read the dossier on January 10, 2017, when it was first publicly released by Buzzfeed.[30] By January 13, *Forbes* magazine ran a story headlined: "The Trump Dossier Is Fake—And Here Are The Reasons Why."[31] But the FBI did not care. Now that Trump had been elected, Steele's dossier became the focal point of concerted efforts by Washington elites to bring him down.

Only days before the dossier was publicly released on January 10, 2017, the euphemistically named Intelligence Community, under the guidance of CIA Director John Brennan, issued an Intelligence Community Assessment (ICA).[32] The assessment alleged, with extraordinary certainty, that the Kremlin had interfered in the 2016 election with the express goal of helping Trump. In 2020, Brennan made headlines once again, this time for influencing the 2020 presidential election by signing a statement that falsely asserted Hunter Biden's laptop exhibited all the "earmarks of a Russian information operation," implying it was part of a Russian plot.[33]

Perhaps Brennan was trying to make amends for not intervening earlier in the 2016 election on behalf of Hillary Clinton. But his actions after the 2016 election proved equally destructive. The January 6, 2017 ICA, written under Brennan's direction, was a laughable assortment of talking points. It included the claim that the Russian state TV channel RT had made negative remarks about Hillary Clinton, as if an obscure TV channel that most people have never heard of could influence the outcome of an election. The assessment's real purpose was to legitimize the Steele dossier, a summary of which was attached in the annex. While the media had been reluctant to promote an unverified—and unverifiable—dossier, the ICA changed that. Overnight, the entire focus of the media's breathless reporting on Trump shifted to the Steele dossier. This is what Clinton had hoped would happen during the election. It did not. Instead, Clinton's failed dirty trick was repurposed by government actors to undermine Trump's presidency. If they could not stop Trump one way, they would do it another way.

The Trump-Russia collusion hysteria, fueled by linking the Steele dossier to an official government report, quickly bore fruit for those aiming to bring down Trump. Within weeks of the dossier being released, the media frenzy forced Trump to fire his national security advisor, General Michael Flynn.[34] Flynn had been dragged into the Russia collusion scandal shortly after the FBI opened its Crossfire Hurricane investigation. A Steele dossier report dated August 10, 2016, alleged that Flynn had ties to the Kremlin.[35] The ostensible basis for these claims was a well-publicized trip that Flynn had made to Moscow in 2015 at the invitation of RT, the Russian TV channel. During a gala dinner, Flynn was seated at the same table as Vladimir Putin. There was nothing unusual about this trip. Jill Stein, the Green Party candidate for president in 2016, sat at the same table as Flynn. Willi Wimmer, a German politician, and Cyril Svoboda, former deputy prime minister of the Czech Republic, also sat at that table. Mikhail Prokhorov, the former owner of the Brooklyn Nets, was also present.[36] A few years earlier, at the same time when then-Secretary of State Hillary Clinton was opposing sanctions against Russia, Bill Clinton delivered a speech in Moscow. For his troubles, Bill Clinton was paid half a million dollars.[37] No one seemed to care, but somehow, when it was Flynn's turn to go to Moscow, the visit became a five-alarm fire.

On February 14, a day after Flynn was fired, the *New York Times* ran a front-page story titled "Trump Campaign Aides Had Repeated Contacts With Russian Intelligence."[38] In truth, there were no such contacts. The story was entirely made up. By the end of February 2017, former President George W. Bush was increasing the pressure, stating to the media that "we all need answers" regarding the Trump campaign's ties to the Russian government.[39] In March 2017, FBI Director James Comey informed Congress that there was an ongoing investigation into those ties—ties that, in light of the Crossfire Hurricane predicate having blown up, he must have known did not exist.[40] Within months, the combined pressure from the media, political figures, and government officials resulted in the appointment of a special counsel, Robert Mueller.[41]

Although Clinton's Swiftboat scheme failed to get her elected, its post-election repurposing by the outgoing Obama administration, the FBI, and the intelligence services ensured that Trump's entire presidency was marred by Russia collusion claims. Crucially, Trump's hands were effectively tied regarding his ambition to improve relations with Russia. Whenever he spoke to a Russian official, even if it was just the Russian ambassador in Washington, DC, the media immediately depicted such meetings as proof of collusion.[42] When Trump met Putin in Helsinki in July 2018, the media went into full meltdown mode, portraying Trump as a traitor.[43] All that Trump had done was express his doubts about the ICA's conclusion that Putin had interfered in the 2016 election to help Trump. Hysterical headlines proclaimed that Trump was Putin's "poodle" and that he had committed treachery by casting doubt on US intelligence during the post-meeting press conference.[44] By the time of the Helsinki summit, the FBI had known for over a year and a half that the dossier was phony, and the CIA had known for the same amount of time that the allegations about a secret communications channel between Trump and the Kremlin were false. In fact, when Clinton's lawyer, Sussmann, presented the alleged evidence of this secret communications channel to the CIA, CIA analysts immediately recognized that the data was not "technically plausible" and was "user-created."[45] The fact that the FBI and CIA withheld that information while Trump was under scrutiny by the press and a special counsel proves that Trump had every reason to question not only the conclusions but also the motives of US intelligence services. But the media did not care. It was probably the biggest media pile-on against Trump since the *Access Hollywood* tape was released in October 2016.

And it got even worse. During the Helsinki meeting, which took place shortly after the conclusion of the soccer World Cup in Russia, Putin presented Trump with one of the official balls used in the tournament. The ball was intended for Trump's son, Barron, who is a big soccer fan. CNN promptly reported that the ball was considered a national security threat because it may have contained a transmitter chip. The hysteria knew no bounds.[46]

Hillary Clinton and her media allies had thoroughly poisoned the well. The repercussions were devastating. Instead of détente with Russia, relations grew worse. Trump's hands were similarly tied concerning Ukraine, the strategically crucial neighbor of Russia, where the United States government—led by Joe Biden and Victoria Nuland—had supported a coup d'etat in 2014. It is not a coincidence that when the Russia collusion hoax nominally ended after Special Counsel Mueller found no collusion, Trump was confronted with a new hoax. Trump's infamous July 25, 2019 phone call with Ukrainian President Volodymyr Zelenskyy,[47] which was used as a pretense for Trump's first impeachment, happened the day after Mueller testified to Congress that there was no evidence of collusion.[48] What had started as a Clinton campaign dirty trick had turned into an all-out effort by factions within the federal government to drive out a sitting president.

CHAPTER 4

Russian Disinformation or Dirty Trick?

One of the enduring narratives about Russiagate is that it is fundamentally rooted in Russian disinformation. No one is at fault because everyone was duped. Senator Lindsey Graham, who asserts that Steele dossier source Igor Danchenko was played "like a fiddle" by Russian intelligence services, strongly advocates for this perspective.[1] In truth, this is a false narrative designed to blame a foreign scapegoat and deflect attention from the actual culprits, Hillary Clinton, and, more insidiously, factions within the federal government.

As reported by Danchenko, his first assignment related to Trump took place in March 2016 when Steele requested him to investigate Paul Manafort, focusing on corruption issues and Manafort's ties to the deposed Ukrainian president Viktor Yanukovych.[2] The alleged timing of this request is odd because Steele was not formally tasked to write the Trump-Russia dossier until May 2016. However, the March 2016 time frame perfectly aligns with Manafort's appointment as Trump's convention manager.[3] The reason why Steele assigned Danchenko with anti-Trump efforts before he was hired by the Clinton campaign is not known. Perhaps the Manafort work had a different origin. If that was the case, then it was most fortuitous for Steele that just as he was hired to write the Trump dossier, Manafort was elevated to the role of Trump's campaign manager.[4]

Manafort had a colorful past, including serving as an advisor to Yanukovych at one point. Maybe Steele thought he could offer his services to Democrats by compiling disparaging stories about Manafort. Danchenko claims that he did not know anything about Manafort before Steele mentioned his name.[5] This stretches credulity as Manafort was in the media on a daily basis. Either Danchenko lied to downplay his own role in the dossier, or he wasn't familiar with the elementary knowledge required to perform his work. Danchenko later told the FBI that his task was subsequently expanded from looking for dirt on Manafort to looking for information on Trump. Tellingly, Danchenko admitted that even though he did not feel comfortable traveling to Russia to inquire about these topics, "he felt like he had to report something back to Steele."[6] Once this modus operandi is understood, everything else falls into place. Danchenko had the task of providing Steele with stories, and that is exactly what he did. Steele did not seem to care much about the provenance of those stories. He just needed someone to pin the blame on if the stories did not check out—which is exactly what Steele ended up doing.[7]

Steele had originally met Danchenko years earlier. The introduction was given by Fiona Hill, senior director for Europe and Russia at the National Security Council during the Trump administration. Hill became widely known due to her testimony against Trump in the Ukraine impeachment inquiry. Hill had been a colleague of Danchenko's at the Brookings Institution, where Danchenko worked in an intern type role from 2006 to 2010. We know that Hill wrote a generous appraisal of Danchenko on his LinkedIn page: "Igor has built an extensive network of professional research connections that complements his network in Russia and Europe."[8] In 2015, Hill expressed gratitude to Danchenko in her book: "Igor Danchenko, as research assistant and later senior analyst at Brookings, provided us with a wealth of insights into and information about Vladimir Putin's life, career, and connections in St. Petersburg."[9] In another strange coincidence, Hill had worked with Steele from 2006 to 2009 while she was an intelligence analyst at the National Intelligence Council and Steele was still at MI6.[10]

When Danchenko's time at the Brookings Institution ended in 2010, Hill assisted him in finding new employment, notwithstanding that his departure coincided with an allegation that he had attempted to recruit Obama administration officials, reportedly on behalf of Russian intelligence. An FBI report on Danchenko, which was only released in September 2020, revealed that Danchenko was at a work-related event in late 2008 when he suggested to two individuals that they could "make a little extra money" if they got "a job in the government and had access to classified information."[11] Danchenko allegedly told these two individuals that he knew some people they could speak to if they were interested. The person who reported the conversation to authorities, whose identity is not known, said that there was no pretext for the conversation with Danchenko. The person could not recall a specific pitch for classified information.

According to the FBI report released in September 2020, Danchenko had already attracted the attention of the intelligence services in 2006 when he was in contact with a known Russian intelligence officer. This was while he was at Brookings. According to the FBI report, Danchenko informed the Russian intelligence officer that he aspired to join the Russian diplomatic service in the future. The two discussed a time when Danchenko could visit the officer. Four days later, the Russian intelligence officer contacted Danchenko and suggested meeting on that day to collaborate "on the documents and then think about future plans." Subsequently, Danchenko contacted the Russian intelligence officer to request a response "so the documents can be placed in tomorrow's diplomatic mail pouch."[12]

These are undoubtedly odd occurrences, and they form the basis of the false narrative that the Swiftboat project is, at its core, a Russian disinformation operation. Unfortunately, other than the little tidbits contained in the FBI report, not much is known about these events. Danchenko appears not to have been asked about them in his January 2017 interview with the FBI. In that interview, he stated that he had never knowingly met a Russian intelligence officer, a claim that now seems to have been false.[13] It is not known why Danchenko was not charged with lying about his previous contacts with Russian intelligence officials.

What is noteworthy about Danchenko's apparently false claim is that at the exact point in the interview when Danchenko made that statement, his attorney, Mark Schamel, interjected to emphasize that Danchenko had not met a Russian intelligence officer "to his knowledge." What's remarkable about this is that, according to the FBI's interview notes, Danchenko himself had already qualified his answer by saying the same thing. Why did Schamel feel the need to repeat what his client had already said?

I have been in this type of situation many times where a client is briefed ahead of an interview or deposition, and to me, this only means one thing. I would be willing to make a small wager that, prior to Danchenko's FBI interview, Danchenko and Schamel discussed his interactions with Russian intelligence officials in 2006. Any discussions between Danchenko and Schamel are fully protected by attorney-client privilege, and Danchenko likely confessed to Schamel about exactly what had happened in 2006 and again in 2008. They would have both known that this was a serious problem that they had to address before Danchenko was questioned by the FBI. In my view, they settled on the "not to my knowledge" qualifier. They might have rationalized that the Russian intelligence officer never identified himself as such, or at a minimum, no one could prove that he had. It's a risky strategy because the officer's conversations may have been recorded, but Danchenko probably thought it was his only option. As to why Danchenko wanted to create distance between himself and Russian intelligence, it is likely that he wanted to continue his life in the United States without having to deal with his past, especially if the interaction with the intelligence officer was benign. If it wasn't benign, he probably wouldn't have hung around for the FBI interview in the first place.

It is common practice for persons of interest to be confronted directly rather than being given several weeks to prepare for questioning in order to elicit truthful answers. Unusually, Danchenko was inexplicably given the luxury of several weeks to prepare for his FBI interview.[14] The person who gave Danchenko time to get his story straight was the chief of counterintelligence at the Department of Justice, David Laufman. Laufman, who became known for his anti-Trump views, claimed that he had given Danchenko time in order to "build a cooperative relationship that could . . . result in the Bureau's being in a position to assess the validity of information in the [Steele election reporting] resulting from [the Primary Sub-source's] activities or the collection of [his/her] sub-subsources."[15] Laufman abruptly resigned from his post in 2018, allegedly for personal reasons.[16] He later reappeared as Joe Biden's personal lawyer when Biden was found to have unlawfully retained classified documents after he left the vice presidency in 2017.[17]

Not surprisingly, the revelations about Danchenko's past have been used to portray him as a Russian spy who provided Steele with a lot of disinformation.[18] It is a convenient excuse for everyone involved. If they were ever held accountable, the FBI could justify their actions by arguing that Steele's information originated from Russia, and they could not be blamed for it being disinformation. If pushed, Steele could also shift the blame to an elaborate Russian hoax. The media, which endlessly parroted dossier lies, could do likewise. It's a perfect alibi. But it is fatally flawed. First and foremost, if Danchenko had been an actual Russian spy, he would have shared much more interesting information with Steele, originating from far more significant individuals. But he didn't. He told Steele gossip from his childhood friends. Steele knew who these friends were. Steele knew that these people did not have any more insight into Putin's secrets than anyone else.

Importantly, Danchenko was also in need of money. Danchenko's social media accounts, which he scrubbed as soon as we identified him, reveal the life of someone who struggled financially and was constantly seeking ways to make ends meet. He may have dabbled in spying for a few bucks here and there, but it is inconceivable that he was a Russian agent, let alone by the time the Steele dossier was written. Danchenko was a Russian individual who had encountered the American way of life during a study trip and, like many others with similar experiences, desired to stay in the United States. Everything else can be derived from these simple facts.

Danchenko leveraged his knowledge of Russia and his ability to speak Russian, which is possibly why he was of interest to the Brookings Institution. Little is known about his departure from Brookings, other than the fact that it coincided with Danchenko being investigated by the FBI for spying. What is known is that shortly after concerns were raised about his alleged attempted recruitment of US citizens, he left the country—or so we thought. The FBI's report on Danchenko states, "Because the Primary Sub-source had apparently left the United States, the FBI withdrew the FISA application request and closed the investigation."[19] This report was written in September 2020 in response to a congressional inquiry. Thus, it was assumed that Danchenko left the country in 2010 rather than facing scrutiny over his alleged spying and recruitment activities. But the report was wrong. Danchenko never left the country. As Special Counsel John Durham disclosed in 2023, "the FBI incorrectly concluded that Danchenko had left the country and returned to Russia."[20] Whether this was just incompetence or if there is more to it remains unknown. But the fact that Danchenko did not leave the country suggests that there is at least the possibility that he was completely oblivious to the fact that he was under FBI investigation.

All this means that we still do not know why Danchenko left Brookings. However, we do know that Special Counsel John Durham, as part of his investigation into the origins of the Trump-Russia collusion hoax, subpoenaed Brookings's records. Judging by Danchenko's FBI interview and his social media posts, both of which depict him as someone constantly seeking financial gain, it is plausible that the alleged intelligence recruitment attempts were motivated by promises of monetary rewards. The person who reported Danchenko to the FBI was skeptical that Danchenko was earnestly trying to recruit anyone. The earlier 2006 incident involving the Russian intelligence officer is also open to various interpretations. Maybe Danchenko was just trying to make some money. Maybe he genuinely wanted to join the diplomatic service. This was Danchenko the hustler and not Danchenko the Russian spy.

What is also overlooked by adherents of the spy theory, such as Lindsey Graham, is that Danchenko never left the United States. Surely a real spy would have been happy to escape without being caught. And even if we stick to the original story that Danchenko left the United States in 2010, it did not take Danchenko long to return. Why would he come back if the FBI was looking for him? Why would his Russian handlers allow him to go back if he was a real spy? Why would he go back, having just dodged the bullet? How did he get past airport security? How did he manage to live under his own name in Virginia for six years before the FBI came to talk to him about the Steele dossier? All of this suggests that Danchenko's involvement with Russian intelligence was not quite as significant as it was later portrayed.

It was around the time when Danchenko left the Brookings Institution that he was first introduced to Steele. The introduction was apparently made via email by Cenk Sidar, an acquaintance of Danchenko's who ran Sidar Global Ventures, a company specializing in commercial intelligence.[21] The reason this information is not confirmed is that most of the parts related to Danchenko's life during this time are redacted from his FBI interview transcript. However, using their ingenious methods for filling the gaps, Stephen McIntyre, Fool Nelson, and Walkafyre were able to deduce that it was Sidar who put Steele in touch with Danchenko.

One interesting note about Sidar is that, although he seems to have had no involvement in the Swiftboat project, either knowingly or unknowingly, his name surfaced during Danchenko's 2022 trial for lying to the FBI. According to Durham, Danchenko wrote Sidar an email in 2016 in which he "advised Sidar, when necessary, to fabricate sources of information."[22] It is not known in which context Danchenko gave this advice to Sidar, but it aligns perfectly with the excuse he gave the FBI regarding the dossier, stating that he felt he had to tell Steele something.[23] Of course, it also fits perfectly with the fact that so many dossier stories were, in fact, made up.

According to Danchenko's January 2017 interview with the FBI, Steele was not interested in his background but rather in his contacts in Russia. Initially, Steele did not assign any tasks to Danchenko, but later he hired him to conduct open-source analysis on investment risks. Danchenko says he was paid a few hundred dollars for this, which was very welcome as he had no income. At some point, Danchenko claims to have been given a more formal role by Steele, which involved signing a confidentiality agreement with Steele's company, Orbis.

Although Danchenko claims to have had no insight into Steele's clients, he told the FBI that he was always "trying to understand the tangible results of his work."[24] Notably, Danchenko's attorney, Schamel, interjected to stress that Danchenko was never informed nor questioned about Steele's clients. Danchenko elaborated that his tasks were kept vague, saying, "Can you do some checking on this?"[25] Sometime later—the exact date is redacted—Steele asked Danchenko to travel to Russia for what Danchenko described as a due diligence assignment that preceded the Trump-Russia collusion tasking. He was paid $3000, which included the airfare and expenses. This would not have left much money as remuneration, a fact that stands in stark contrast with the notion that Danchenko was being portrayed as a super source with access to Kremlin secrets. It appears that Steele was aware of Danchenko's financial circumstances and was keeping him on a tight leash. Another trip followed, and Danchenko made a stopover in London on his way back to Washington, DC to share the latest gossip with Steele.

Danchenko told the FBI that when the parent company of his primary sponsor in the United States—whose name is redacted but seems to be Cenk Sidar's company Sidar Global Ventures—went bankrupt, he turned to Steele for help. There is no record of Sidar Global Ventures itself going bankrupt, and as of this writing, the company seems to be up and running. Thus, it is far from clear why Danchenko would have had to leave the company, let alone why he told the FBI that the company was bankrupt. In any case, the FBI does not seem to have cared. We also know that he wanted to remain in the United States, which meant that, whatever the reason things did not work out with Sidar, he needed a new sponsor. Steele was initially unable to help because his British firm could not sponsor US employment visas. Based on Danchenko's FBI interview notes, it seems that Steele, Danchenko, and a US-based firm named Target Labs devised a plan for Danchenko to stay in the United States. Danchenko would be employed by Target Labs in name, and they would sponsor his visa. However, in reality, he would be working for Steele full-time. Danchenko described the arrangement to the FBI as a "contract vehicle," whereby Steele would pay Target Labs, and Target Labs would pay Danchenko.[26] Thus, from around 2014 onward, Danchenko worked solely for Steele. None of this aligns with the idea that Danchenko was covertly working for the Russian government to disseminate disinformation.

The most striking aspect of the story Danchenko told the FBI about his relationship with Steele is dependency. Steele had groomed Danchenko for a number of years, providing him with small amounts of money and fostering an increasing dependency. Danchenko transitioned from working on various projects to becoming a full-time employee, although he did so through a cutout firm. The bottom line is that without Steele, Danchenko would have had no income and no visa.

The FBI does not appear to have questioned Danchenko about his potential involvement in other Steele projects, such as the FIFA dossier, which shows a notable similarity to the Trump dossier. Instead, the FBI jumped straight to Danchenko's role in the Trump-Russia report. According to Danchenko, after completing the first task of the Manafort assignment, Steele sent him to Russia to gather information on Trump. This trip took place in June 2016. As we will see later, the trip provided Steele with the fake sources, or cutouts, needed for Report 80, the first of the Steele dossier reports. The next phase, according to Danchenko, was to inquire about Kremlin spokesman Dmitry Peskov. The last phase was to inquire about Trump Organization attorney Michael Cohen. All phases match the Steele reports at that time. The modus operandi was always the same. Steele asked Danchenko to share stories about X. Subsequently, Steele would write whatever Clinton required about X, attributing those stories to Danchenko and his alleged sources. The success of the scheme depended on Danchenko and his associates not being identified—or so Steele thought. Little did Steele know at the time that the FBI did not care about having credible sources.

And so Steele proceeded, concealing himself behind multiple layers of deniability. It was an impressive array of safeguards that Steele and the Clinton campaign had set up. The first step was for the Clinton campaign to hire a law firm, Perkins Coie. That was doubly advantageous. As a contractor, Perkins Coie provided a layer of deniability, but they were also a law firm, thus shielding their clients behind attorney-client privilege. Of course, the privilege does not ordinarily extend to dirty tricks campaigns, but they had thought of that. Perkins Coie was formally hired to prepare for any potential election challenges after the 2016 presidential election. It was a line that Steele would often repeat. If the work was related to legal services, such as an election challenge, they could all claim attorney-client privilege. They all knew how the game worked. In turn, Perkins Coie hired Glenn Simpson's firm, Fusion GPS. At this point, the Clinton campaign was two steps removed from the dirty tricks campaign they were about to carry out.

Russian Disinformation or Dirty Trick?

But it didn't end there. When Simpson hired Steele, the Clinton campaign was three steps removed. Four steps after Steele tasked Danchenko. When Danchenko spoke to his high school friends and drinking buddies, they were five steps removed. Steele was the source. Danchenko was the sub-source. Danchenko's drinking buddies were sub-sub sources. And the people the buddies were talking about were sub-sub-sub sources. In total, the Clinton campaign was at least six steps removed from the false stories that they themselves had conceived. Steele himself had pretty good cover as well. He was three steps removed.

The reason we finally discovered the names of Steele's fake sources is largely due to Congressman Devin Nunes's persistence. It was through his dogged determination in the face of a media and Democratic Party onslaught, including a phony ethics investigation, that we first found out the connection between Perkins Coie and Steele.[27] Without that, Steele's dossier might have never been publicly linked to Hillary Clinton. But Steele still had many layers of deniability in reserve. Danchenko and the various sub-sources were his insurance policy. As long as their identities remained unknown, Steele was safe.

Once our small group of researchers broke through that barrier, the full extent of Steele's deception was revealed. He had literally made it all up. It wasn't Russian disinformation; it was British disinformation tailored to the needs and wants of the Clinton campaign.

And this brings us back to the Crossfire Hurricane investigation. This topic is discussed in detail in chapters 9 and 10, but it is worth reflecting briefly on it here to illustrate how ridiculous the Russia disinformation narrative is. The entire history of the Crossfire Hurricane investigation is littered with red flags. Steele approached FBI agent Michael Gaeta with his Trump-Russia collusion story on July 5, 2016. This was before anyone had even heard of Trump campaign aide George Papadopoulos. There is also the fact that State Department official Victoria Nuland later admitted that she had received reports from Steele in July 2016 and immediately passed on those reports to the FBI.[28] Then there is the fact that Stefan Halper, an FBI informant whose connections with Steele remain largely unknown, invited Trump campaign aide Carter Page to Cambridge University. That was also in July 2016.[29] This turned out to be extremely fortuitous for Halper, as only a few weeks later he was assigned by the FBI to spy on Page. Steven Schrage, a PhD student who worked with Halper, later claimed that the timing of Page's invitation, just before Halper was assigned to spy on him, was merely a coincidence.[30]

In addition to Page, Halper was also assigned by the FBI to entrap Papadopoulos. The plan was to bring Papadopoulos to London in September 2016 under the false pretense of commissioning him to write a paper on energy policy. While in London, an FBI honeypot using the alias Azra Turk would engage Papadopoulos in friendly conversation and offer him alcohol, before Halper would intervene to gather information on Trump-Russia collusion.[31] Like many of the FBI's schemes, it was a madcap plan that was never going to work. There was no indication that Papadopoulos was particularly susceptible to getting drunk. The FBI would have already known that when Papadopoulos met Australian diplomat Alexander Downer a few months earlier he did not stay for more than one drink. But the main problem for the FBI was that there was nothing useful Papadopoulos could tell them.

Despite Halper's growing belligerence in trying to get Papadopoulos to say something incriminating, Papadopoulos stood firm. When Halper asked Papadopoulos whether the Trump campaign knew anything about the DNC "hack," Papadopoulos not only denied any knowledge but also correctly added that "No one has proven that the Russians actually did the hacking." When Halper provoked Papadopoulos by suggesting that assistance from WikiLeaks or the Russians "could be incredibly helpful," Papadopoulos responded that the Trump campaign did not "endorse this type of activity because ultimately, it's illegal." Papadopoulos also made it clear to Halper that collusion was "illegal" and that espionage was treasonous. Papadopoulos even addressed the media's ridiculous efforts to portray Trump's "Russia, if you're listening" remark about Clinton's email scandal as something nefarious. In July 2016, Trump jokingly said, "Russia, if you're listening, I hope you're able to find the 30,000 emails that are missing."[32] Papadopoulos told Halper that, "Of course, he didn't mean for them to actively engage in espionage." None of this had anything to do with Russian disinformation. This was the FBI trying to entrap Trump campaign associates.

Despite Halper's extensive efforts to elicit incriminating statements from Page or Papadopoulos, all the FBI was able to uncover was a plethora of exculpatory evidence. Yet, none of the exculpatory information, including Papadopoulos's vehement denials of any connections to either WikiLeaks or Russia, was included in the FISA warrant against Carter Page. The FISA warrant not only permitted surveillance but also provided access to his email archive. Additionally, it enabled monitoring individuals who had been in contact with Page. The FBI even secretly searched Page's home.[33] It all turned up nothing. There was nothing. It had all been made up by Steele, a contractor for the Clinton campaign.

By November 2016, as is discussed in greater detail in chapter 13, the needs of the Clinton campaign had shifted, as well as those of certain elements within the federal government. Clinton had lost the election and needed a scapegoat. The initial plan to pin Russia collusion on Trump, both as an end in itself and as a means to deflect from her own email scandal, failed to get her elected. Perhaps the main cause of this failure was the fact that the media did not embrace the Steele dossier until after Trump's victory. Had the media treated the Trump-Russia collusion allegations as a DEFCON 1 situation—as it did throughout Trump's presidency—it is possible that Clinton would have eked out a win. Be that as it may, Trump was going to become president in a few weeks. Consequently, the plan shifted from a dirty tricks campaign aimed at preventing his election to a dirty tricks campaign focused on making his life as difficult as possible and ultimately removing him from the presidency. The Trump-Russia collusion story was recycled for this purpose. This wasn't Russian disinformation. This was part of the federal government targeting a sitting president with a massive campaign of smears and lawfare.

For his part in this scheme, President Obama ordered an Intelligence Community Assessment (ICA), supposedly to investigate Russia's alleged involvement in the 2016 election.[34] An essential goal was to construct a narrative suggesting that Trump's victory was owed to Vladimir Putin. That aspect of the ICA scheme was almost guaranteed to ruin Trump's presidency. But the ultimate goal was to have him removed or to force him to resign. For this reason, the collusion narrative would also need to be resurrected. But intelligence officials did not have anything concrete to offer. After all, there had been no collusion, so the main part of the ICA ended up being a bland regurgitation of baseless talking points. The essence of the ICA's accusations is encapsulated by the following quote: "RT's coverage of Secretary Clinton throughout the US presidential campaign was consistently negative."[35] The ICA was a transparent hoax. It was embarrassing. But it didn't matter because the outgoing Obama administration had a trick up its sleeve: the Steele dossier. By including the dossier in the ICA, it would gain the credibility it never had and never deserved. It was that move that transformed the dossier from laughable flimflam, which even the media was not comfortable talking about, into a potent weapon against Trump.

It is rarely acknowledged, if ever, that the Steele dossier is the only document to date that alleges collusion. Sure, there have been plenty of people, such as FBI Director James Comey, who have insinuated collusion. However, when asked under oath, not a single person has ever stated that they have evidence of collusion. The House Intelligence Committee's Russia probe included over fifty witness interviews, which involved all senior FBI personnel participating in the investigation.[36] House Intelligence Chairman Adam Schiff implied otherwise during an appearance on ABC, where he claimed, "I've been very clear over the past year, year and a half, that there is ample evidence of collusion in plain sight."[37] However, when the interview transcripts were finally declassified in 2020 by then-acting Director of National Intelligence Richard Grenell,[38] not a single witness was able to provide any evidence of collusion.

In the end, the FBI only had Steele. And they knew it. Without it, the ICA was the sort of platitudinous gibberish that often characterizes these reports. Even fervent anti-Trump individuals would have struggled to maintain the collusion narrative, which was based on a fringe news channel with minimal viewership somehow influencing the outcome of the 2016 election. With Steele's information, the media would have the hook it needed to perpetuate the collusion narrative for years. The collusion angle was also necessary to prompt the appointment of a special counsel. The accusation that Putin had favored Trump wasn't enough; there had to be a specific allegation involving Trump. As FBI Deputy Director Andrew McCabe stated, "the Steele election reporting qualified [for inclusion in the ICA] at a minimum due to concerns over possible Russian attempts to blackmail Trump."[39] The purpose was obvious. To pursue Trump, a personal angle was necessary. Crossfire Hurricane was a broader effort aimed at Trump's campaign. It thus comes as no surprise that McCabe initiated the investigation into Trump personally in May 2017.[40] By doing so, McCabe guaranteed that a special counsel would have to be appointed because, as a matter of perception, an FBI under the Trump administration could not investigate Trump.

The ICA, which ultimately included a summary of Steele's dossier, marked the beginning of the next phase of the campaign to oust the newly elected president. It was a concerted effort, carried out at the highest levels of government in conjunction with the media, to whom a litany of false stories was leaked. The result of these efforts was the appointment of Robert Mueller as special counsel. The hope was to entangle Trump in something that could be used to force his resignation or impeachment. It didn't have to do with the Russia collusion, which everyone had realized did not exist by that point. But just as the investigation by a special counsel—who at the time was still called independent counsel—into Bill Clinton's involvement in the Whitewater real estate scandal ended up with Clinton's impeachment for lying about an extramarital affair, anything was possible. Indeed, when the Mueller investigation concluded, no nefarious connections to Russia were uncovered, despite a significant effort by Mueller's team to pressure Trump associates such as George Papadopoulos, Roger Stone, or Paul Manafort. Instead, the entire focus of the investigation had turned to something extraneous, namely Trump's alleged obstruction of the investigation.

As mentioned earlier, in 2020, the Biden campaign used the same Russia collusion playbook to discredit something they knew to be true. Hunter Biden's abandoned laptop was found in a Delaware computer repair shop. The laptop had nothing to do with Russia. It was a simple matter of Hunter having dropped it off for repairs and forgetting about it. But the absence of a Russian angle did not prevent the Biden campaign and the media from portraying it in that manner. Biden even explicitly blamed Russia during the second presidential debate. Trump pushed back against the ridiculous claim, but he was cut off by the debate's moderator, Kristen Welker.[41]

Just as Clinton had been supported by the intelligence services for her plan to tarnish Trump, Biden also received similar assistance. In Biden's case, it did not come in the form of a phony FBI investigation but rather in the form of a letter signed by more than fifty former US intelligence officials. The letter claimed that Russia had fabricated Hunter Biden's laptop.[42] In truth, Russian disinformation had nothing to do with Hunter's laptop,[43] just as it had nothing to do with the Swiftboat project or the subsequent efforts by some factions of the government to oust Trump.

CHAPTER 5

Christopher Steele

Christopher David Steele was born in 1964 in Aden, Yemen. At that time, Yemen was part of the Federation of South Arabia, which was a British protectorate. His father and mother had met while working at the Meteorological Office, the United Kingdom's national weather service. Eventually, the family moved back to England, where Steele grew up with his older sister Alison and younger sister Claire. In 1982, after finishing secondary school, Steele entered Cambridge University, where some of the Russiagate stories would unfold three-and-a-half decades later.[1] Steele became president of the Cambridge Union Society, a debating society, before graduating in 1986. He then joined the Foreign and Commonwealth Office, which is the United Kingdom's equivalent of the State Department. Steele was recruited by the Secret Intelligence Service, commonly known as MI6. MI6 is also known as Her Majesty's Secret Service, which might explain the media's James Bond references in relation to Steele. At the tender age of twenty-six, Steele was sent to Moscow, where he spent the early 1990s at the British Embassy, working for MI6 under diplomatic cover. He returned to London in 1993. Assignments in France and Afghanistan were to follow before he finally ended up heading the Russia Desk at MI6 in London in 2006. During this time, Steele became the case officer for Alexander Litvinenko. Litvinenko was a former officer of the Federal Security Service (FSB) of the Russian Federation. In 2000, Litvinenko fled Russia and was granted asylum in the United Kingdom. In 2006, Litvinenko was poisoned in London with polonium-210, a highly radioactive metal. Steele investigated Litvinenko's death and concluded that it was a Russian state-sanctioned assassination.

Tragedy struck in 2009 when Steele's wife, Laura, passed away at the young age of forty-three due to cirrhosis of the liver. It was a terrible blow, and Steele was left to care for their three children. In 2009, Steele, along with British ex-diplomat Christopher Burrows, founded Orbis Business Intelligence.

Orbis describes itself as a "leading corporate intelligence consultancy," providing "senior decision-makers with strategic insight, intelligence and investigative services." Whatever Orbis was actually doing, it was lucrative, certainly far more profitable than a desk job at MI6. According to a profile of Steele in the *New Yorker*, Orbis grossed $20 million between 2009 and 2017.[2]

One of Orbis's clients was Oleg Deripaska, a Russian oligarch. Deripaska claims that he hired Steele in 2012 to work on a research project related to a legal dispute he had in England.[3] Curiously, Steele also arranged a meeting between Deripaska and Department of Justice official Bruce Ohr.[4] In 2016, Deripaska conducted his own investigation into Trump's campaign manager, Paul Manafort. According to Bruce Ohr's later testimony to Congress, Steele informed Ohr on July 30, 2016, that Deripaska's attorney, Paul Hauser, was investigating whether Manafort had embezzled money from a joint venture in Ukraine in which Deripaska was also involved.[5] Deripaska had previously hired Manafort as a consultant.

In September 2016, Deripaska was one of the first individuals interviewed by the FBI's Crossfire Hurricane team. It is not known what the interview was about as the FBI's notes are almost entirely redacted.[6] Another attorney for Deripaska, Adam Waldman, claimed that Deripaska was in New York as part of Russia's United Nations delegation when three FBI agents visited him and "posited a theory that Trump's campaign was secretly colluding with Russia to hijack the U.S. election. Deripaska laughed but realized, despite the joviality, that they were serious."[7] Deripaska supposedly told the FBI that they were trying to create something out of nothing.

The Deripaska story is particularly odd because Deripaska is said to be close to Vladimir Putin. Why would such a person hire Steele, a known Putin critic? It is not known what role, if any, Deripaska played in any of Steele's schemes, other than hiring Steele for a legal case in 2012.

What is equally odd, and has gone largely unnoticed, is that between May 2014 and some point in 2015, Steele wrote over a hundred reports on Ukraine that were funneled to Victoria Nuland, then-assistant secretary of state for European and Eurasian Affairs.[8] It remains unknown who paid Steele to provide his Ukraine dossier to the State Department, presumably to influence policy. While only portions of that dossier have been published, one thing that jumps out immediately is its uncanny similarity to Steele's Trump dossier.

The background to Steele's Ukraine reports is the February 2014 Ukraine coup. Ukrainian nationalists, with the support of the Obama administration, overthrew the administration that was led by Ukrainian President Viktor Yanukovych. The Maidan Revolution led to a civil war in Ukraine's Donbass region, Crimea separating from Ukraine, and an increasing vilification of Russia. This, in turn, pushed Russia toward China. It was a foreign policy disaster on all fronts. It also elevated Ukrainian oligarchs. After the democratically elected government of Yanukovych was deposed, an unelected interim government took over the reins. The government had been chosen by State Department official Victoria Nuland, with the approval of Joe Biden.[9]

Eventually, in May 2014, billionaire oligarch Petro Poroshenko was elected president, once again with generous support from the Obama administration. Around this time, Hunter Biden, whose father, Vice President Joe Biden, had effectively become the de facto viceroy of Ukraine, was paid millions of dollars to join the board of the Ukrainian gas company Burisma. Notably, by his own admission, Hunter knew nothing about gas and even less about Ukraine.[10] It is a little-known fact that Hunter has never traveled to Ukraine, neither before he was appointed nor since.[11]

In 2015, a few weeks after the head of Burisma's board demanded that Hunter end criminal investigations into Burisma, Joe Biden allegedly blackmailed Poroshenko. He threatened that either Poroshenko would fire the prosecutor who was leading the investigations into Burisma, or Joe Biden would withhold a billion dollars in US loan guarantees.[12] It was this fact, which Biden admitted in a talk before the Council on Foreign Relations, that Trump asked then-new president of Ukraine, Volodymyr Zelenskyy, to investigate in their now-infamous July 25, 2019 phone call. It was this phone call that led to Trump's first impeachment.

With that background, it is probably not surprising that Steele was involved in the Ukraine situation. Steele's Ukraine reports bear a striking resemblance to his Trump-Russia reports. The same language and phrases are used throughout both reports, such as cryptic references to "speaking in confidence to a trusted compatriot" or "speaking in confidence to a trusted Western interlocutor," in order to conceal the fact that there are no real sources, at least not credible ones. Even the same people are used. Igor Sechin, the CEO of Rosneft, whom Steele falsely accused of meeting Carter Page, is mentioned sixteen times in the Trump-Russia dossier and nineteen times in the Ukraine dossier.[13]

Sechin also appears in a previous report written by Steele regarding corruption at FIFA, the international governing body of association football, commonly known as soccer in the United States. England had hoped to host the 2018 Football World Cup, which was eventually awarded to Russia. The English Football Association, the organization responsible for the bid, hired Steele to investigate whether the bidding process was corrupted. Steele alleged that Igor Sechin, while he was still in government and before he joined the Russian energy group Rosneft, had bribed officials to secure the World Cup for Russia. The FBI interviewed Steele about his findings in 2015 as part of its own investigation into FIFA corruption.[14]

Immediately after the publication of the Steele dossier by Buzzfeed, Reuters's Mark Hosenball, a reporter associated with Fusion GPS,[15] released an article asserting that Steele's alleged involvement in the FIFA investigation lent credibility to his Trump-Russia claims in the eyes of the FBI.[16] However, there is no evidence that Steele contributed to the FIFA investigation in any meaningful way. The only documented information is that Steele met with the FBI's Eurasian Organized Crime Unit in 2010. That doesn't mean anything. The fact that Steele kept casting the same character, Sechin, as a villain in his reports further undermines any claims that his FIFA report offered any useful information. The media's narrative that Steele's alleged contributions to the FIFA investigation made him reliable in the eyes of the FBI is further undercut by the fact that Sally Moyer, an FBI attorney who worked on the Carter Page FISA warrants, informed Congressional investigators that, by autumn 2016, the FBI was still seeking "further clarity about Christopher Steele and his reliability."[17]

Although Sechin is a central figure in at least three Steele dossiers—Ukraine, FIFA, and Trump—he is not Steele's only go-to bogeyman. There is also Sergei Ivanov, the head of Russia's presidential administration. Ivanov is mentioned twenty-one times in the Ukraine dossier and twenty-six times in the Trump-Russia dossier. These figures pertain to known reports. There are other unpublished reports on Ukraine, Trump-Russia, and possibly FIFA, so the actual number of mentions might be even higher. As a State Department employee, Jonathan Winer later admitted that Steele provided the State Department with over a hundred reports on Ukraine, only a fraction of which have been released.[18] There are also at least three Trump-Russia dossier reports—reports 132, 137, and 139—that have not been released, and their contents remain unknown.

Just as with Steele's Trump dossier, Steele's Ukraine dossier purports to be sourced from individuals with insights into Putin's innermost thoughts and secret deliberations. In a September 2014 report, Steele describes the Kremlin's evolving views on the Ukraine conflict. Steele claimed that Putin was most afraid of European Union sanctions and that he was unhappy about Poroshenko's rise. In another report, Steele claims to know about a company that is secretly owned by Putin and Putin's mistress. None of these things are knowable. Also, similar to the Trump-Russia reports, the Ukraine reports consist mostly of boilerplate information. For instance, Steele claims that the Kremlin was discussing its options regarding Eastern Ukraine. A five-year-old could have figured that out. Such trivialities are interspersed with nuggets of supposed intelligence, such as Putin's secret company. It's all a game, a very transparent one: Copy and paste 90 percent of the reports from common internet searches and inject 10 percent fabricated intelligence. In fact, it is far too transparent to believe that anyone with a semblance of sophistication fell for it. What is worse is that Steele wasn't even good at copying and pasting. The call sign of the Malaysian Boeing 777 that was shot down over Ukraine on July 17, 2014, was MH17. Steele copied and pasted it as ML17. Incidentally, that tragedy was a direct result of the Donbass war, which had been triggered by the February 2014 revolution. Similarly, there are many elementary errors in the Trump-Russia reports, such as misspelling Alfa Bank as Alpha Bank or incorrectly locating a Russian consulate in Miami where no such consulate exists.

While the Ukraine dossier does not have the targeted, made-to-order feel that the Trump-Russia dossier has, there are instances of the same kind of blatant influence operation that characterizes several of the Trump-Russia reports. Ukraine reports 162a and 194a provide a good example. As an aside, the gaps between the numbers assigned to Steele's reports are also observed in the Trump-Russia reports. Steele claims he does this to throw off potential infiltrators. Appended between reports 162a and 194a is an email that Steele wrote to State Department official Jonathan Winer:

> From: Chris Steele <chrissteele@orbisbi.com>
> Date: August 13, 2014 at 4:21:47 PM EDT
> To: Jonathan Winer
> Subject: Russian 'Aid' Convoy- Latest Orbis Intelligence
> Dear Jon,
>
> We have just received some new intelligence on the Russian 'aid' convoy approaching Ukraine which, although from a source whose reliability is not yet fully established, we thought we should share with you.

> *According to this source, bilateral talks between POROSHENKO and the Kremlin over the conditions for the convoy entering Ukraine have broken down and the Russians are rerouting it through a pro-Russian rebel held border checkpoint near Lugansk.*
>
> *Clearly there is now the potential for a confrontation, which we believe may have been the Kremlin's intention all along.*
>
> *Best, Chris*[19]

Notably, Steele put the word "aid" in scare quotes, as if to suggest that the convoy was about something other than aid. It is unfathomable that Steele would know more about Russian military movements than US military intelligence with their network of satellites and other sources. Steele also claimed to know that Russia wanted a confrontation. Again, this is, on its face, ludicrous. It is unfathomable that anyone would have believed what these reports were claiming.

As State Department Freedom of Information Act releases have shown, Steele sent his Ukraine reports to Jonathan Winer.[20] Winer then shared them with Victoria Nuland. The Freedom of Information Act emails also indicate that Steele's approach was unsolicited. As mentioned, it is not known who was paying Steele to try to influence US government policy with these reports. What is known is that despite their laughably absurd claims, Winer and Nuland seem to have found Steele's information useful and were eager for him to continue providing reports. Nuland wasn't entirely sold, though. When Steele sent a report about "Yulia's return to power," referring to Yulia Tymoshenko, Nuland's response was, "Some of this rings true, some not." Tymoshenko is the former Ukrainian prime minister who, in 2011, was imprisoned for embezzlement, a charge that was later overturned. In another instance, Nuland noted that Steele's information "rings a bit extreme." It appears that Nuland, despite being a fervent critic of Putin and one of the architects of the Maidan Revolution, had misgivings about Steele's anti-Russia reporting. It is not known whether she relayed these concerns to the FBI or whether the FBI even asked.

It is also unknown whether Steele sent his Ukraine reports elsewhere or what other purposes they may have served, apart from attempting to influence US government foreign policy regarding Ukraine and Russia. The real question—and one that has yet to be answered—is who paid Steele to write these reports and give them to the State Department?

A related issue concerns the Foreign Agents Registration Act (FARA). Every individual or organization that engages in lobbying on behalf of a foreign principal is required to register under FARA. The foreign principal does not necessarily need to be a foreign government. FARA was used against Trump associates Papadopoulos, Manafort, and most notably, Michael Flynn. However, it was not used against Tony Podesta, the brother of Clinton campaign chairman John Podesta, who was engaged in a similar kind of lobbying as Manafort.[21] Steele's modus operandi was to bypass any FARA problems by providing his information to the State Department under the guise of reporting national security matters. Similarly, he later provided information to the FBI disguised as reporting significant national security issues.

Between the Ukraine dossier and the Trump-Russia dossier, Steele worked on another operation called Project Charlemagne. It was a sort of dry run for the Trump-Russia dossier. Steele reported on alleged Russian interference campaigns in Europe aimed at supporting right-wing forces in France, Germany, Italy, Turkey, and the United Kingdom. According to Glenn Simpson of Fusion GPS, Steele reportedly discovered that the Kremlin had a "secret black budget of tens of millions of dollars" that was being funneled to European politicians who opposed the European Union.[22] Incredibly, in 2019, despite all the information available at the time about Steele's falsehoods in the Trump-Russia report, the Intelligence and Security Committee of Parliament, a statutory committee of the Parliament of the United Kingdom, which was investigating potential Kremlin interference in British politics, invited Steele as one of only five expert witnesses.[23] To be fair to Steele, he wasn't the odd one out. Among the other four individuals were Anne Applebaum, known for her strong anti-Russia stance and affiliation with the *Washington Post*,[24] and William Browder, a controversial businessman who amassed wealth in Russia before his dispute with the Kremlin. Subsequently, he began advocating for sanctions against Russia.[25] Unsurprisingly, given the composition of its panel of supposed experts, the British Committee's report found widespread Russian interference in Western democracies. As with the Ukraine dossier, it is not known who funded Project Charlemagne.

Shortly after Project Charlemagne, Steele started working for Fusion GPS. Being assigned to a project investigating alleged Russian interference in US elections right after completing a project on alleged Russian interference in European elections must have felt like a very serendipitous circumstance. Or perhaps that is why Fusion went straight to Steele. Steele did not require any coaching. He knew what to do.

At the time the dossier was conceived, Clinton was dogged by an email scandal. As secretary of state, she used a private email server to conduct her official business. She claimed to have done this out of convenience. A more plausible explanation is that she did it to avoid freedom of information requests for her communications. Not surprisingly, when those freedom of information requests were made, Clinton deleted thirty thousand emails from her private server, claiming they were personal emails related to her yoga classes and her daughter Chelsea's wedding. Of course, all 30,000 of them weren't about that. The secret server was, in many ways, the initial driving force behind the Swiftboat project. Clinton needed to insulate herself in the event that someone had obtained her thirty thousand emails before they were deleted.

There was much speculation at the time that foreign governments had access to those emails, possibly from China, Iran, or Russia. That wouldn't have been surprising, since the emails were stored on an unsecured, mom-and-pop server that was apparently located in the Clintons' spare bathroom. Long before anyone fixated on Trump-Russia collusion, there were articles detailing that foreign governments had access to Clinton's emails. Professor Paul Gregory, a foreign policy advisor for Ben Carson's 2016 presidential campaign, published an article in *Forbes* on February 12, 2016, outlining the possibility that Russia could have access to Clinton's emails.[26] In February 2016, former National Security Agency and CIA director General Michael Hayden went on CNN claiming that it was a "near certainty" that the Russian government had Hillary Clinton's emails.[27] On May 5, 2016, former New Jersey superior court judge and TV analyst Andrew Napolitano informed Maria Bartiromo of Fox News that China, Russia, and even Israel had access to Clinton's emails from the private server.[28] Four days later, on May 9, Napolitano informed Megyn Kelly, who was still at Fox News at the time, that the Russian government did indeed possess Clinton's emails and was planning its next move.[29]

Incidentally or not, Napolitano's May 5 statement came a day before Papadopoulos's meeting with Erika Thompson, an assistant to Australian ambassador Alexander Downer. The meeting set in motion what would later become the FBI's official narrative for why they opened the Crossfire Hurricane investigation into Trump-Russia collusion. Allegedly, Papadopoulos told the Australian diplomats that Russia had damaging information on Clinton.

Napolitano's statement on May 9 came a day before Papadopoulos's infamous wine bar encounter with Downer himself. It remains unclear which of the two meetings with Australian diplomats allegedly triggered the FBI to open their investigation into Trump. The widely accepted story is that it was the May 10 meeting, but tellingly, the Mueller Report cites the May 6 meeting.[30] Could Papadopoulos's mention of Russia having damaging information on Clinton have been influenced by watching Napolitano on Fox News? Could it have been inspired by Professor Paul Gregory's article about Putin having Clinton's emails? After all, both Gregory and Papadopoulos were on the Carson campaign. Either one of these is certainly far more credible than the notion that Papadopoulos had some secret source. Be that as it may, the point that is not nearly made enough is that there was nothing at all unusual about people having conversations about Clinton's missing emails. Many people were having those same conversations at the time when Papadopoulos met with the Australian diplomats.

The scene was set for an October surprise. If the Russian government, or perhaps another government, were to release the thirty thousand deleted emails, it could have potentially dealt a fatal blow to the Clinton campaign. This would be especially true if the emails revealed information about the Clinton Foundation or other questionable activities, rather than just being about yoga and Chelsea's wedding. Clinton had to insulate herself against that possibility, and the plan was to blame Trump. By also blaming the Russians, she got two for the price of one. If and when the emails were released, the plan was to blame Russian disinformation. Steele was the perfect person to execute this plan. His task was simple: to attribute email hacking to Russia and blame Trump for colluding with them.

CHAPTER 6

Framing Millian

Why have Steele's lies been so successful? Why have they persisted? To understand this, we need to go beyond the media and intelligence community that covered for both Steele and, more recently, for Biden. They can only achieve so much without a compelling narrative. And a good narrative is what the Clinton campaign provided. The Clinton campaign did not just release a story for the media to echo. They planned it meticulously, and they had the backing of the intelligence community. They also incorporated layers of complexity and deniability into their plan. They used a former British intelligence officer to give the story a veneer of credibility. They used compromised journalists to advance not only the overall narrative but also specific aspects of it. One of the most egregious episodes in the entire Swiftboat plan was the framing of Sergei Millian. It is an episode that combines all the various layers of the plan: the initial smear, collaboration from the media, and help from the intelligence services.

On November 4, 2021, Igor Danchenko was arrested in the early morning for lying to the FBI. Later that day, Special Counsel John Durham unveiled a five-count indictment. Four of those indictments related directly to Danchenko's lies about Millian. Stephen, Fool Nelson, Walkafyre, and I had made the exact points that Durham put forward many years earlier. While Danchenko would later be acquitted by an Alexandria, Virginia jury, the facts were never contested. Millian was never a source for anything. He never even met Steele or Danchenko. And yet, he was put through hell for the simple reason of being a Trump supporter with a Russian-sounding name.

As his long-time friend from New York described him to me, Millian was a gregarious character who enjoyed life. But that changed after what the Swiftboat project's operatives did to him. He became wary. The wary Millian is the one I have gotten to know. Millian first heard of me online when I was posting my research on Russiagate. He could see that I knew his story in great detail and that I knew that he had been framed. But it still took a long time to gain his trust. Every now and then, I catch glimpses of the vibrant man his old friend described to me, but they are fleeting. When you have been framed as the fall guy in an elaborate scheme to take down the president of the United States, you don't trust anyone.

Originally from Belarus, a former Soviet Union satellite state, Millian first came to the United States in his early twenties after being offered a scholarship. He speaks seven languages, so it is not surprising that he ended up taking a job as a translator in Atlanta. He also started a real estate business, which briefly brought him into the Trump Organization's orbit in 2007. Like any real estate agent, Millian made sure to let people know he had sold Trump apartments. There was nothing nefarious about it, but it would end up being used against him. Millian later moved to New York, where he was based when he was framed during the 2016 presidential race.

While Millian was likely identified as a potential scapegoat early in the Swiftboat project, it was an interview he gave to Russian media in April 2016 that ensured he would be the primary target.[1] Having represented the Russian-American Chamber of Commerce and been interviewed many times before, including a Fox News interview with Maria Bartiromo in 2014,[2] the interview was nothing unusual for him. During the interview titled "Sergei Millian: Donald Trump Will Improve Relations with Russia," Millian expressed his support for Trump.[3] As Millian later recounted to me, it was that interview that solidified the interest of the Clinton operatives in him. "Imagine," he tells me, "you have been instructed to tie Trump to Russia. The first thing you would do is conduct an internet search on Trump Russia, and one of the initial results might have been the Russian-language interview in which I voiced support for Trump."[4] Undoubtedly, the name Millian would have come up pretty quickly in any search for Trump and Russia. There was his real estate business, his role with the Chamber of Commerce, and the fact that he had expressed support for Trump. Millian's business also required him to be highly visible.

All they needed was a Russian speaker with connections to Trump. The fact that he was already in the media made it easier to find him. The fact that he publicly supported Trump was the cherry on top. Everything else could be fabricated and later attributed to Millian.

Curiously, Glenn Simpson, the Clinton campaign contractor who hired Steele to produce the Trump-Russia collusion dossier, employed his own researcher, Nellie Ohr, who also identified Sergei Millian. Simpson claims that although Ohr had encountered the name Millian in 2015, she only began investigating him after Steele informed Simpson about Millian.[5] If it truly was a coincidence, it is one that reinforces how perfectly Millian was suited to the Swiftboat conspirators.

Steele told a London court that he was first tasked by Simpson during a meeting they had at Heathrow Airport in May 2016, which was followed up by a phone call from Simpson formally engaging Steele.[6] This matches the account in Simpson's book.[7] Ohr's first report on Millian is dated June 25, 2016. Ohr eventually handed her research on Millian to her husband, Bruce, who then passed it to the FBI. There was nothing nefarious about what she had found. It was all open-source information, but handing it to the FBI still served a purpose. It created the false impression of a second source stream, suggesting that Millian was truly worth looking into. Such was the sophistication of the operation. As luck would have it, Bruce Ohr was also a close friend of Steele's. After the FBI was forced to formally cut ties with Steele for leaking stories to the media, Bruce Ohr became the informal intermediary through which Steele and the FBI maintained communication. Steele's ties to Ohr had another benefit. When the FBI finally figured out that Steele's super source was Danchenko, Steele panicked that his web of lies would unravel. He bombarded Ohr with incessant messages, claiming that Danchenko was in serious jeopardy and imploring Ohr to take action.[8] This fabricated narrative suggested that if Danchenko distanced himself from Steele, he was only doing so to safeguard himself. Put another way, Steele was creating a cover story for the likely eventuality that Danchenko would disavow the dossier when interviewed by the FBI. Unbeknownst to Steele, his panicking was completely unnecessary. FBI leadership had his back. They had an even bigger interest in covering up Steele's lies than Steele himself did. After all, based on Steele's lies, they had already spent six months investigating the campaign of the person who had become the president of the United States, including his national security advisor. The FBI had also lied to the Foreign Intelligence Surveillance Court (FISC), a fact that the FBI wasn't going to concede so easily. But far more importantly, FBI leadership, including individuals like Comey, McCabe, and Strzok, wanted to bring down Trump. They needed Steele's lies to be true.

By July 2016, Millian was unwittingly being utilized by Ohr, Steele, and Simpson, as well as Matthew Mosk and Brian Ross of ABC, as the central figure of the fabricated collusion narrative. When Mosk called on July 5, 2016, asking for an interview, Millian agreed. Millian was traveling on business in Asia at the time but agreed to do the interview in New York upon his return. The interview was scheduled for July 29. Steele had intended to place Millian in a room with his operative Danchenko in the days leading up to the interview. This was crucial to the plan because you cannot plausibly frame someone as having said something unless you are able to place that person in the same room as your purported source. So Steele needed Danchenko to be in the same room as Millian. By doing so, he could assert that Millian had informed Danchenko about the Trump-Russia collusion. Danchenko emailed Millian on July 21, pretending to pose a question on behalf of a construction company in Switzerland. Danchenko also mentioned China and Trump. Open-source materials online would have shown that Millian had business connections with all three. The issue lies in the absence of a connection between Trump, Switzerland, and China. The sole purpose of mentioning them was to lure Millian. Thus, the email, which was written in Russian, reads like a potpourri of bait. Danchenko had clearly not worked out a plan to approach Millian; thus, he just threw out whatever he could find that might interest Millian. That is not particularly good spy craft. Danchenko wasn't as skilled at this game as Steele would have us believe. The entire email, as translated into English by Stephen McIntyre, reads as follows:[9]

Hello Sergei,

Colleagues from RIA NOVOSTI gave me your contact. You spoke with Dmitry Zlodorev about Donald Trump and his travels to Russia. I wanted to ask you: what projects did he consider, or were they purely fashion trips or beauty contests? There has been a lot of speculation on this topic for a month. It would be interesting to talk about this topic.

Question from a construction company in Switzerland. I think there is a political component, but it can't be leveled. I am also very interested in Russian-Chinese cooperation, the sanctions aspect including. There are projects in Russia that are looking for investors and equipment suppliers. Like many in Russia, they look back at Asia——China, Hong Kong, but they don't know how to approach.

> *Confidentially, of course——I have thing to do with the media, although there are certainly acquaintances there. In any case, it would be interesting if possible to talk to you by phone or meet for coffee/beer in Washington or New York where I will be next week. I myself am in Washington. You can also by email. Mail in Russian or in English.*
>
> *I sent you a request on LinkedIn——my work is clearer there.*
>
> *Igor Danchenko*
> *Business Analyst*

Danchenko dispatched a subsequent email on August 18. Once again, it was written in Russian and is provided here in English, courtesy of Stephen McIntyre:[10]

> *Hello Sergei,*
>
> *I wrote to you a few weeks ago. We are in touch on LinkedIn.*
>
> *There is a proposal for a site in the Kaluga region, not far from New Moscow. I am attaching the information in a separate letter. My friends are lawyers. They repeatedly asked me to suggest someone. I thought that you or your contacts might be interested.*
>
> *The cadastral value is about 300 million rubles, respectively, the market value is slightly higher. When selling, you can immediately take into account the share of the intermediary. Attached are 8 jpegs. If there is an opportunity and interest, let us meet and talk about this and other projects. Other projects also involve investments in existing sites, but production is there. And, in some cases, technology is needed, in others—investment.*
>
> *The stakes in Russia are high—you know it yourself, so I would like to consider some simple and profitable schemes.*
>
> *Write, call. Contacts below.*
>
> *Respectfully,*
> *Igor Danchenko*
> *Business Analyst*
> *Target Labs Inc.*

The second email was slightly more focused. Danchenko's ruse was a project in Russia. But again, the delivery was extremely sloppy. Why would

Danchenko, out of the blue, think of Millian and Millian's friends, neither of whom he had ever met, as business partners? It made no sense, and Millian wisely ignored the messages. Millian tells me that it was Danchenko mentioning beer that made him realize something was amiss. Why would a serious business inquiry mention meeting for beers? Millian smelled a rat. And he was right.

Despite this, in late July 2016, Danchenko traveled from his home in Northern Virginia to New York to locate Millian at his office. We know this because of geolocated photos that Danchenko posted on his social media. He took down the photos, as well as his entire social media presence, when we discovered Danchenko's name on July 19, 2020. The fact that Danchenko had traveled to New York to try and meet Millian was later confirmed by Special Counsel John Durham.[11]

It is almost certain that Danchenko chose the late July 2016 timeframe for his visit because of Steele, who needed Millian as an imaginary source for an upcoming dossier report. Perhaps Steele had informed Danchenko about the ABC interview scheduled for July 29 and directed him to contact Millian before the interview. In any case, Steele urgently needed the two men in the same room. Unbeknownst to both Steele and Danchenko, Millian was in Asia and only returned to New York right before his ABC interview. Steele's and Danchenko's ploy failed. There would be no face-to-face encounter with Millian, and therefore, no opportunity to put words into Millian's mouth.

Despite Danchenko's failure to get Millian in the same room, Steele proceeded to use Millian as a source anyway. Steele's infamous Report 95, in which Steele cites Millian as having confessed that there was a "well-developed conspiracy of cooperation" between Trump and the Russian government, was produced by July 28. It is perhaps the most obviously made-to-order report of all his reports. Steele had been instructed on what needed to be included in light of the July 22, 2016 DNC email leak: blame the Russians and link Trump to them. We may never know why Steele proceeded without a plausible explanation for how he obtained information from Millian. He must have known that his story about an imaginary New York meeting would fall apart under the slightest scrutiny. Maybe Steele had no choice in the matter because Simpson or another Swiftboat operative had set a deadline for Report 95. Maybe it had something to do with the FBI opening its own investigation into Trump-Russia collusion on July 31. There is at least one other possibility, and that is that Danchenko lied to Steele. Perhaps Danchenko told Steele that the meeting with Millian had taken place after all. Whatever the reason, history will prove it to be Steele's undoing. The fact that it is left to history at all, and that Steele was not immediately discredited, is owed to the FBI, which incredibly never bothered to investigate Steele's implausible story about Millian.

It would have been extremely easy for the FBI to verify that Millian could not have told Steele or Danchenko anything. That is because he never met them. But the FBI never looked into it, not even after Danchenko admitted during his January 2017 interview that he had, in fact, never met Millian. To be fair, by that time, the FBI was one of the main drivers of the Swiftboat project, so there would have been no incentive to investigate. What is perhaps even more incredible than the case of the imaginary New York meeting is that Steele also cited Millian as a source for an earlier report, Report 80, dated June 20, 2016. This was more than a month before Danchenko ever reached out to Millian. Time and again, the shoddiness of Steele's dossier workmanship becomes apparent. The fact that he got away with it for all these years is a testament to the corruption of the FBI and US intelligence agencies more generally.

For some reason, perhaps out of embarrassment for failing in his mission to be in the same room as Millian, Danchenko tried to manipulate the situation. He knew he couldn't say that he had met Millian. That would have been an outright lie, which might have landed him in jail. So, he told the FBI a story about a mysterious, anonymous phone call that he had allegedly received. He said the call might have come from Millian because the voice sounded similar to a YouTube video of Millian. It was an absurd claim, made even more absurd by the fact that Danchenko was adamant that the mysterious Russian on the other end of the line didn't say anything negative about Trump. There were more red flags. Danchenko claimed that he received the call after sending his second email. That would put the call after August 18, 2016. Yet, he also claimed that it was the call that prompted him to travel to New York in late July to try to find Millian. But the biggest giveaway is the fact that Danchenko, by his own admission, spent a few days hanging around in New York trying to find Millian. Not once during this period did Danchenko email Millian or call back the strange person who had allegedly contacted him. Why would someone spend a few days in New York looking for someone without bothering to contact them? It was an obvious case of Danchenko not getting his story straight. He fibbed and fudged because he had failed to meet Millian as instructed by Steele. Despite Danchenko's obvious lies, the FBI kept forging on with its "get Trump" agenda.

In fact, the FBI continued to spy on Michael Flynn using warrantless National Security Letters, persisted in leaking information to the media about Trump-Russia collusion, pursued Papadopoulos, and obtained additional FISA warrants against Carter Page. The pursuit of Papadopoulos is particularly instructive. The FBI's Danchenko interview, which stretched over the course of three days, ended on January 26, 2017. The following morning, the FBI's Crossfire Hurricane team arrived at Papadopoulos's residence in Chicago to conduct an ambush interview. Instead of ending the investigation, the FBI intensified it. Their efforts culminated in the appointment of Special Counsel Robert Mueller in May 2017. Five years later, in May 2021, during Michael Sussmann's trial, FBI's Bill Priestap testified that Comey was "fired up" when false leads about Trump reached the FBI.[12] It was Steele's luck that the FBI wanted to get Trump even more than Steele did.

Millian returned to New York late on July 27, 2016, just in time for his interview with ABC. The interviewer was ABC's chief investigative correspondent, Brian Ross, who was later fired from ABC for filing a false report on Michael Flynn.[13] Ross claimed that candidate Trump had ordered Flynn to contact Russian government representatives. That was not true. But Ross's exposure as a dishonest journalist came too late for Millian.

Millian thought he was being interviewed because of his role at the Russian-American Chamber of Commerce. But Ross had set up the interview under false pretenses. According to Michael Isikoff and David Corn, two journalists who were used by Steele to disseminate his stories, Steele informed Simpson about Millian, after which Simpson "tipped off ABC News, which conducted an on-air interview with Millian."[14] However, this does not fully explain why Ross arranged the interview. Simpson's main goal, as he admits in his own 2019 book *Crime in Progress*, was for Ross "to get Millian on camera."[15] Simpson needed footage that the Clinton campaign could use. And he got it. Despite spending an hour answering Ross's questions, Millian's interview was never broadcast. That was Millian's first clue as to what was really going on.

Two months later, on September 22, ABC's *Good Morning America* finally aired a short clip of Ross's interview.[16] The interview had become stale by that point, but ABC's George Stephanopoulos, who had previously been Bill Clinton's White House communications director, pretended it was serious breaking news. In fact, it was a huge nothing-burger. Donald Trump sold apartments to Russian nationals. So what? But ABC wanted to escalate the innuendo. Stephanopoulos even managed to get George W. Bush's White House ethics lawyer, Richard Painter, to chime in. Painter eagerly declared, "The appearance is that a foreign government or other foreign organizations have influence over the president of the United States." It was a planned hit job that facilitated the release of the Millian footage for the Clinton campaign to use.

On that very same day, the Clinton campaign began airing advertisements featuring Ross's Millian clip. This was a coordinated effort. For all the talk about foreign election interference, the real interference has always been on the part of the domestic media. The ad ran under the heading "The man who could be your next president may be deeply indebted to another country. Do you trust him to run ours?"[17] In the ad, Millian can be seen stating that Trump had made millions from selling property to Russian businessmen. Of course, this is entirely normal for a billionaire who made his money selling apartments to affluent clients worldwide. But that is not the way the Clinton campaign portrayed it. The damage was done. Steele's operation not only framed Millian as their main source for the collusion claims against Trump but also collaborated with a major American network to lure Millian into a trap. This enabled them to provide clips to the Clinton campaign. To this day, there has never been an accounting for what ABC News did to Millian.

The operation was as sophisticated as it was despicable. The Clinton campaign had paid a British operative to portray an American man as the main source for their fabricated collusion claim. They destroyed Sergei Millian's life. Tellingly, when Simpson was asked by the House Intelligence Committee whether Millian was a source, he claimed that he couldn't disclose this information, allegedly for security reasons.[18] He had no such concerns when he sent Ross to hunt down Millian.

Things only got worse from there. In September 2016, the *Daily Beast* published an article about Millian titled "Meet The Man Who Is Spinning For Donald Trump In Russia."[19] In October 2016, a friend of Steele's, journalist Catherine Belton, published a hit piece about Millian in the *Financial Times*. The article portrayed him as a "shadowy Russian émigré" and suggested that Millian could be Moscow's link to Trump.[20] Millian was neither Russian nor was he Moscow's link to Trump.

In an unrelated case, Belton was sued for defamation by a Russian oligarch and the former owner of Chelsea Football Club, Roman Abramovich. While that case was not about the Steele dossier, it revealed Belton's anti-Putin zealotry. She claimed that Abramovich allegedly bought Chelsea at Putin's direction. Allegedly, this was part of Putin's wider plan to raise Russia's profile in the West. Belton's apparent source, Sergei Pugachev, an ex-Russian investor, had previously been deemed "self-serving" and "impossible to believe" by London's High Court. Abramovich allowed the case to be settled after Belton agreed to change the offending sections of her book.[21]

At another High Court hearing in London, Steele admitted that he and Belton were friends.[22] But he denied telling her about the dossier. That seems implausible. How would Belton, a personal friend of Steele's, have known to write a hit piece on Millian? Millian tells me that by October 2016, he was receiving multiple calls from the media every day. His responses became understandably agitated. When Belton sent Millian a pre-publication request for comment on her critical article, Millian replied, "Hi Catherine, I can recommend a good psychologist in NYC or London to anyone who came to these conclusions."[23] Millian was fed up with the media circus being orchestrated to smear him. He was wondering what was behind it all. Like most people, he had no clue about the existence of a dossier, let alone that he was its main protagonist.

Even though Millian did not know at the time that Steele had fed Belton the fake story, he immediately understood that the Clinton campaign was directly behind the attack. After Belton's smear article was published, Millian reached out to Hope Hicks, who was the Trump Campaign's press secretary. The reason Millian contacted Hicks was that she was mentioned in Belton's hit piece. Hicks had told Belton that there was no connection between Trump and Millian other than Millian meeting Trump for a photo op in 2007. Millian confirmed that he had indeed met Trump only once in 2007 at a marketing event for the Trump Hollywood project in Hollywood Beach, Florida. He told Hicks that Belton's accusations were completely baseless and that the article was entirely fabricated. Presciently, he added that the "Hillary camp is out of playing cards against Mr. Trump and the Russian card is her biggest card right now (that she still actively uses)."[24] Around the same time, Millian started receiving death threats, which continued for many years.

But things got even worse. In January 2017, Mark Maremont of the *Wall Street Journal*, hiding behind a "person familiar with the matter"—likely either Steele himself or a Steele associate—published an extraordinarily slanderous piece alleging that Millian was the key source for Steele's dossier.[25] It was through this hit piece that Millian figured out what was going on. The cat was out of the bag. Millian had been framed as the main source of the dossier. It was all a lie, and as Millian recounts, he told Maremont that it was all a lie. As we went through the article together, Millian showed me a request for comment he received from Maremont, as well as his own reply. Maremont claimed in his piece that Millian did not respond to a long list of other questions, including whether he was a source for the dossier. That is typical tradecraft for dishonest journalists. I have seen Millian's response. Millian outright rejected all claims against him unequivocally. Why should he have bothered with providing a detailed answer to each and every question, of which there were many, if he had already dismissed the entire premise of the article?

But it was not just Maremont. The same ABC reporters who, at the behest of Fusion GPS, had lured Millian into the July 2016 interview under false pretenses, published a similar smear piece on January 24, the same date that the Maremont article appeared. Ross and Mosk identified Millian as "[t]he source of the most salacious allegations in the uncorroborated dossier," stating that their source was "a person familiar with the raw intelligence provided to the FBI."[26] Referring to someone matching the description of Danchenko, whose name and even existence would not become known for several more years, Ross and Mosk suggested that Millian may "have unwittingly described Trump's alleged tryst, during a conversation with someone who was secretly reporting to Christopher Steele." Ross and Moss even alluded to the existence of Report 139, which had not been published at the time and remains unpublished: "While the published dossier never names Millian, a version provided to the FBI included Millian's name as a source, according to someone who has seen the version given to the FBI." Whoever fed Steele's lies about Millian to Maremont—the only viable candidates appear to be Fusion's owners or Steele himself—also fed them to Ross and Mosk. The reason why it is not likely that the FBI seeded these false stories is not because the FBI is somehow less devious, but because Maremont, Ross, and Mosk were all closely associated with Fusion's owners. In Maremont's case, he was a friend and colleague of Simpson and Fritsch when they all worked at the *Wall Street Journal*. They even published under the same byline in the *Wall Street Journal*.[27] Similarly, Mosk, who collaborated closely with Ross, was also a longtime acquaintance of Simpson.[28] In contrast, when FBI Deputy Director Andrew McCabe was investigated by Inspector General Horowitz for lying about his leaks to the media—as deputy director, he was apparently entitled to leak but not to later lie about it—the names of Fusion GPS-friendly reporters did not show up in Horowitz's thirty-nine-page report.[29] It wasn't that the FBI didn't leak; they just leaked to their own coterie of reporters.

The *Wall Street Journal* and ABC articles made Millian realize that he had no chance of clearing his name. The entire media and political establishment were out to get him. What Millian did not know at the time is why the article was published when it was. It was obviously intended to damage Trump, who had just been inaugurated, but why January 24? As we would later find out, this was the day of Danchenko's FBI interview. It appears that the two hit pieces were intended to provide Danchenko with a pretext to fabricate a false story about Millian being the primary source, to persuade the FBI that Millian was the main source, or both. January 24 also happened to be the day when FBI Director Comey sent Peter Strzok to ambush Michael Flynn at the White House. Once again, it is notable that just as the Trump-Russia investigation should have been winding down, it was being ramped up. ABC later took Ross's and Mosk's names off the byline and changed the article's date from January 24 to January 30.[30]

Millian told me that he was in Washington, DC at the time of the ABC and *Wall Street Journal* smears, having attended Trump's inauguration, and that he was also poisoned at his hotel. He said that he had never felt so sick in his life. Millian blamed a spiked bottle of water. While we may never know exactly what happened, it is easy to appreciate the situation from Millian's perspective. Here was a completely innocent man who had never heard of, let alone met, Steele or Danchenko, and yet the media was claiming he was behind the Steele dossier. It is a testament to Millian's courage and tenacity that he kept his mind. Most people would have crumpled under such pressure.

Millian knew he had to remove himself from the firing line before anything worse happened to him. He left the country. It has been suggested that this was somehow a sign of guilt. It is doubtful that those who make such claims have experienced what Sergei Millian went through. It is a particularly tragic story when you consider that Millian came from the former Soviet Union seeking a better life. Instead, he ended up being hounded out of the country. Even if he had decided to stay, he had already lost his livelihood. Everyone except his closest friends had abandoned him. No one would talk to him. The media had ceaselessly pestered his business partners and customers. There was no way he could still be a realtor or work for the Russian American Chamber of Commerce. His business lay in ruins. Millian spent fifteen years building a life and career in the United States. His home. His company. His friends, partners, and colleagues. It had all been taken away from him in an instant, and there was nothing he could do about it. As Millian told me, if the powers that be can bring down the national security advisor with a bunch of lies, they can bring down anyone.

Danchenko, for his part, omitted the plan to frame Millian from his report to the FBI. Instead, he told the FBI that he heard the name Millian from two RIA Novosti reporters. RIA Novosti is the Russian news agency that conducted the Millian interview in April 2016, during which Millian expressed his support for Trump. Danchenko claims that the RIA Novosti reporters informed him about Millian around July 20, 2016. That would have been a month after Nellie Ohr, Fusion GPS's in-house research operative, started looking into Millian, allegedly at Steele's suggestion.[31] While it might be possible to imagine a situation where Fusion and Steele came up with the name Millian initially, it is inconceivable that Danchenko just happened to stumble upon the same name a month later and then immediately proceeded to try to ambush Millian in New York. There is also the fact that, in early July, Fusion's Simpson instructed ABC to track down Millian. Steele used Millian as a source for Report 80, dated June 20, 2016. The report was shared with Michael Gaeta of the FBI on July 5, 2016, which was more than two weeks before Danchenko allegedly first heard of the name Millian. It does not take a genius to figure out that Danchenko's story about being informed about Millian by the RIA Novosti reporters does not pass the smell test. Danchenko did not randomly learn about Millian through acquaintances while Steele and Simpson were already actively framing Millian. It appears certain that Steele had instructed Danchenko to locate Millian and set up a meeting with him. It did not matter what Millian told Danchenko. As long as they spent time together, Steele could easily invent stories.

Why would Danchenko try to conceal that Steele informed him about Millian? Why did he tell the FBI his story about the RIA Novosti reporters? Why would he hide Steele's involvement, especially after he had already disavowed Steele? My guess is that Danchenko was embarrassed for failing in his task. Similar to what Danchenko disclosed to the FBI about his assignment regarding Paul Manafort, he felt obligated to inform Steele about something, even if it never happened. It's more likely than not that Danchenko informed Steele that he had met Millian, when in reality, he had not.

Would this absolve Steele? Not at all. The earliest possible time Danchenko could have met Millian was at the end of July when he traveled to New York. By this point, Steele had already written reports citing Millian as his supposed source. So, even if Danchenko lied to Steele about meeting Millian, those lies would have occurred after Steele had already begun using information falsely attributed to Millian. In other words, whether Danchenko lied to Steele made no difference in terms of the substance of the dossier. The intention was not to elicit any incriminating statements from Millian, but rather to orchestrate a meeting between him and Danchenko with the aim of establishing a "he said, he said" situation. The dossier's stories are fabricated in any case, as Millian could not have been a source for reports that were already written, even if he had met Danchenko.

If Danchenko lied and told Steele that he had met Millian, this might explain why Steele proceeded with Report 95, the late July 2016 report that cites Millian as the source for the claim that there was a "well-developed conspiracy of co-operation" between Trump and the Kremlin. It is also possible that Danchenko did not tell Steele that he met Millian. Perhaps Steele proceeded because the Clinton campaign required Report 95, and he could no longer delay its production. In the end, it doesn't really matter. Ultimately, whether Millian met Danchenko has only one implication, and that is whether Steele had plausible deniability. If they did meet, anything could have happened. If they didn't meet, Steele's lies would eventually be exposed for everyone to see.

But why did Danchenko lie to the FBI about the RIA Novosti reporters? Danchenko might have hoped that by claiming that the Millian pursuit was just a random by-product of a conversation he had with some journalists, the FBI would not ask any questions about it. It appears that he was right, if indeed that is what he thought. If Danchenko had truthfully admitted that Steele had instructed him to find Millian instead of falsely invoking the RIA Novosti reporters, the FBI would almost certainly have asked what he told Steele after he failed to locate Millian. But that question was never asked. It would have been a crucial question. In fact, based on the FBI's notes of their interview with Danchenko, it does not appear that the FBI asked any follow-up questions.[32]

It is also possible that Danchenko constructed a parallel path to Millian through the RIA Novosti reporters. After having been instructed by Steele to set up Millian, Danchenko may have contacted the reporters, pretended to be unaware, and deceived them into mentioning Millian's name. The case of the Russian intelligence officers, whom Danchenko claimed not to have knowingly met, and his recommendation to Cenk Sidar to fabricate sources suggest that Danchenko is not averse to engaging in deceptive practices. By misleading the RIA Novosti reporters, Danchenko could later assert that the information about Millian had not originated from Steele. However, given the timing issues and the improbability of Steele, Ohr, and Danchenko independently discovering Millian, it would have been relatively simple to expose such a scheme, assuming that is what Danchenko orchestrated.

It is also important to consider that, similar to Steele, Danchenko could not have anticipated the high level of cooperation that he received from the FBI. Both Steele and Danchenko likely harbored the expectation that the FBI was influenced by anti-Trump sentiments. However, expecting the FBI to deliberately ignore a series of falsehoods may have been overly optimistic. Yet, that is precisely what happened. Steele and Danchenko probably could not believe their good fortune.

Danchenko's attorney, Mark Schamel, who had managed to obtain a number of significant concessions for Danchenko's FBI interview, such as conducting it in Schamel's office, does not seem to be a stranger to pushing boundaries either. After our group finally managed to identify Danchenko in July 2020, Alfa Bank immediately proceeded to try to depose Danchenko. The deposition was supposed to be part of a defamation lawsuit that Alfa Bank had filed in October 2017 against Fusion GPS. Specifically, Alfa Bank's owners alleged that they had been smeared in the Steele dossier's Report 112, which portrayed them as Putin's bag men. The fact that we identified Danchenko was a significant breakthrough for Alfa Bank's lawyers because they finally had a chance to uncover the source of the smears against their clients. They would certainly not have given Danchenko the same easy ride that he received from the FBI. He would likely have been forced to admit that the claims about Alfa Bank's owners had been fabricated, which would have forced Fusion into a settlement. But despite immense efforts from Alfa Bank, the deposition never materialized.

As the court docket in the Alfa Bank case reveals, Schamel obstructed and thwarted the efforts to depose Danchenko at every turn.[33] Danchenko was initially served with a subpoena in August 2020. This was a direct consequence of our group identifying him. It was at that point that Schamel stepped forward once again, as he had in January 2017, claiming to represent Danchenko. As is customary when both sides are represented by legal counsel, communications between the parties are conducted through their respective attorneys. But Schamel had other plans. After a few months of back and forth, he claimed that Alfa Bank's lawyers had failed to provide Danchenko with various documents. The problem is that Alfa Bank had given those documents to Schamel, who acknowledged receipt. But Schamel objected anyway, thereby gaining valuable time for his client. When Schamel later failed to file a response on time, he came up with yet another novel excuse. He claimed that he had recently moved to a new law firm and did not know if Danchenko was still his client. There is nothing inherently forbidden about these kinds of tactics, but they are testing the boundaries of what can and cannot be done, much like Danchenko's FBI interview. While one can abhor his tactics, Schamel is the kind of lawyer you would want in your corner when your strategy is to stonewall at all costs. Now you might ask: What good did the stonewalling do? After all, Schamel was only buying Danchenko time. There was no way he could prevent the deposition from taking place eventually. That is technically correct, but as the Alfa Bank case shows, persevering to fight another day is not a hopeless strategy. Life is full of twists and turns, and you never know what the next day might bring. In Danchenko's and Schamel's case, it was the Ukraine War. Danchenko had almost run out of time when hostilities broke out in February 2022. That changed everything. As part of Western efforts to punish Russia, the owners of Alfa Bank were sanctioned and forced to drop their lawsuit against Fusion GPS. And thus, in one fell swoop, Danchenko's problems had disappeared.

As I was writing this, the phone rang. It was Millian. We're using an encrypted service that I had never heard of. Millian suggested that we use it. He learned about these things the hard way. One day, it will be his turn to tell his story. It is not my place to preempt him, but suffice it to say that, having heard him tell it, it would easily pass muster for a new Jason Bourne-type franchise. What Steele, Danchenko, Comey, the media, and the government did to this American citizen is beyond despicable. Millian is wary of lawyers, but he knows me as a Russiagate researcher, not as a lawyer. We bounce ideas off each other. We discuss the Danchenko and Sussmann cases. Millian wants a full and complete public exoneration, and he wants Steele and his cohorts to be held accountable. The way to do it, he told me, is to expose Steele's fraud once and for all. Anything that does not involve exposing Steele for the total fraud that he is won't do. Millian knows that Danchenko is the weakest link. Just as Steele exploited Danchenko's vulnerabilities, those weaknesses will eventually come back to haunt Steele. But will Danchenko come clean? We know he has already disavowed Steele. But the FBI let him off the hook. They never asked what exactly he told Steele. They didn't want to know because they knew it would be detrimental to their case. Even if Danchenko met Millian, as Steele claims he did, it would have been after Report 80, in which Steele heavily relies on Millian. The report is discussed later on, but the logical impossibility of Steele's account is evident. Steele won't admit it, of course, but Danchenko might.

Millian and I have started discussing the cases brought by Steele's victims. He knows he has perhaps the best case of anyone because the evidence is airtight. Millian never spoke to either Steele or Danchenko, a fact that Danchenko confided to the FBI. But to win a case, there are many hurdles to overcome. At least five victims of Steele, who were falsely framed or accused in the dossier, sued Steele, Fusion GPS, BuzzFeed, or a combination of them. The results have been poor for the victims. In one case, Steele dossier victims prevailed. In that case, the owners of Alfa Bank—Mikhail Fridman, Peter Aven, and German Khan—secured a hard-fought victory over Steele's firm, Orbis, in a London court in 2020.[34] The judge ruled that Steele had not exercised proper care in vetting the information in the dossier. As discussed earlier, Fridman, Aven, and Khan also sued Fusion but had to abandon their case due to sanctions related to the Ukraine War. Another litigant, Alexei Gubarev, the owner of Webzilla, lost his defamation case against Orbis and Steele. Steele's Report 166 alleged "that over the period March-September 2016 a company called XBT/Webzilla and its affiliates had been using botnets and porn traffic to transmit viruses, plant bugs, steal data and conduct 'altering operations' against the Democratic Party leadership."[35] A London judge agreed that the statement was defamatory but ruled in favor of Orbis and Steele, stating that although Steele's information was false, Steele was not at fault because he technically did not publish the dossier.[36] Gubarev had anticipated the English courts making excuses for Steele and had therefore also filed a case in the United States, this time against Buzzfeed, the publication that initially published the dossier. But that case too failed. The court found that Buzzfeed had a valid defense under the fair report privilege and dismissed the case.[37] Lastly, Donald Trump also filed a lawsuit in London against Orbis. The case was dismissed in February 2024 because, according to the judge, Trump waited too long to bring it, and the judge was not willing to invoke a rule that would have extended the statute of limitations.[38]

The fundamental problem with every case brought thus far is that it has been based on the premise that Steele was given false information. Once that is the basis, it becomes easy for Steele to wiggle out of his legal problems. The focus should have been on the fact that Steele fabricated the entire dossier. The Millian situation, where we know that Steele used him as a source even before Danchenko had been dispatched to talk to Millian, would have been powerful evidence supporting this fact. Sadly, the London cases make it abundantly clear that it never crossed the judges' minds that Steele made it all up. We are not just talking about random judges. Talking about Steele, Barbara Fontaine, the senior master of the Queen's Bench Division—an extremely prestigious judgeship in England dating back 1000 years—stated, "This is an unusual, and probably unique, case, where the witness is in many respects in the same position as a whistle-blower." Instead of viewing Steele's actions as the political smear they were, Fontaine regarded him as a whistleblower. But it got even worse. Fontaine added that "Mr Steele's evidence is that he was 'horrified and remains horrified that the US Defendants published the dossier at all, let alone without substantial redactions.' He considers that this may have compromised the sources of his intelligence, putting their lives, their families and their livelihoods at risk."[39] In truth, Steele had demonstrably shared his fabrications with various media outlets. Yet, as soon as BuzzFeed published the dossier, he portrayed himself as the victim. Fontaine and the other judges believed him, notwithstanding that no sources of intelligence were ever compromised because there were no sources and no intelligence to begin with.

It appears that no one told Fontaine about Steele's modus operandi, or perhaps someone did, and she, like her fellow London judges, could not fathom that a former MI6 operative could have possibly been so dishonest. In the July 2020 judgment, where Steele was found responsible for mishandling the personal data of Alfa Bank's owners, Justice Warby of the High Court in London was adamant that Steele was indeed collecting intelligence. He even made excuses for Steele's lack of any documentary notes: "This was, on any view, an intelligence-gathering exercise, inherently unlikely to be heavily documented."[40]

Despite the circumstances, none of the legal cases brought against Steele appear to have been sufficiently aggressive in exposing his deceptions. It is unfortunate that the attorneys pursuing the cases against Steele did not manage to convey that Steele was not in the business of gathering intelligence. He was in the business of fabricating intelligence. To understand this one simply has to look at the Alfa Bank dossier report. Steele alleges in Report 112 that Alfa Bank was the conduit through which Trump and the Kremlin exchanged messages. During his first London trial, Steele testified with a completely different story. Suddenly, he claimed that it was Millian's organization, the Russian-American Chamber of Commerce, that was the conduit between Trump and the Kremlin.[41] There are plenty of other examples that could have been brought to the courts' attention, but this would have required plaintiffs to dispense with niceties and be more forceful. None of them did so.

The same false narrative that several judges seem to have been stuck with also characterizes Sergei Millian's portrayal in the media. Just as Steele was supposedly gathering real intelligence, Millian must have been a source. Even among those who acknowledge that Steele's information does not check out, the assumption was that, at worst, Steele must have been fed inaccurate information. There is something very persuasive about the label "former British intelligence officer" that seems to make it impossible for people to imagine that Steele would just make things up. On Millian, even ostensibly fair news reports kept falling into the same trap, consistently portraying Millian as a source. Chuck Ross, a journalist from the *Daily Caller* who has been highly critical of both the dossier and Steele, wrote an article in March 2018 about Millian titled "Book Provides New Details About Major Steele Dossier Source."[42] A Fox News article from the same month is titled "Anti-Trump Harvard Law pro Laurence Tribe falsely claims dossier source killed in Russia plane crash."[43] There are many more examples. The narrative framed Millian as a knowing or unknowing source. But there was little doubt in the media that he was a source in any case. The notion that he wasn't a source at all completely bypassed even otherwise fair-minded journalists.

The entrenched narrative that Steele's sources are supposedly credible allowed Steele to persist for many years. It helped that the FBI supported Steele, but the scheme would not have been possible without the widely accepted belief that Steele had genuine sources.

CHAPTER 7

Report 80 — Made-to-Order Fairytale

Steele's initial dossier report was Report 80. It was issued on June 20, 2016, shortly after Glenn Simpson of Fusion GPS met and recruited Steele at London's Heathrow Airport. Report 80 was intended to serve as a foundational report that introduced the idea that Trump was an agent of the Kremlin. Unsurprisingly, the very first sentence of Report 80 claims that "Russian authorities had been cultivating and supporting US Republican presidential candidate Donald Trump for at least five years."[1] In another dossier report, written a few weeks later, Steele randomly extended the period of cultivation to eight years.[2] Steele gave no reason for the change. He had probably just forgotten about his previous lie; such was the shoddiness of his tradecraft. The cultivation claim was supported by the infamous "pee tape" story, which alleged that Trump had been secretly recorded by the Russian Federal Security Service (FSB) while participating in a "golden showers" party with prostitutes at Moscow's Ritz-Carlton Hotel.

Like everything else in the dossier, the "pee tape" story was entirely made up by Steele and Danchenko, who had been tasked by Steele in June 2016 to fly to Moscow and collect gossip. Danchenko later told the FBI that he didn't really know what to do with his instructions. However, since Steele had paid for Danchenko to travel to Russia, he felt obligated to inform Steele about something. At least that's how he described it to the FBI.[3]

But while Danchenko feigned naivety, he was well accustomed to Steele's modus operandi. Steele and Danchenko had been working together for years, and Danchenko knew how the game worked. Danchenko received some money and free trips to Russia in exchange for providing Steele with gossip that could be used as the foundation for Steele's fabricated intelligence reports. Steele knew that the gossip meant nothing. He knew the identity of Danchenko's so-called sources. He knew they were complete nobodies—in fact, most of them were friends from Danchenko's school days in Perm. But that didn't matter. The arrangement provided Steele with cutouts that he needed to falsely attribute stories to.

The procedure was always the same: get Danchenko in the same room with somebody and then make up stories about what that somebody had said. The most important aspect of Steele's modus operandi was that no one would ever find out. In case anyone ever asked questions, Steele could say he had a secret sub-source whose identity he could not reveal for security reasons. If anyone dug deeper, Steele could explain that his secret sub-source had his own network of sources, but he himself did not know their identities. That way, Steele could pretend that all of these people were highly connected and influential. And that is exactly what he did. In March 2020, Steele testified before a London judge that one of his sub-sources held a high position of authority within the Kremlin.[4] But no such person has ever been identified. That is because no such person exists. When our group, led by Fool Nelson, identified Danchenko's alleged sub-sources in July 2020,[5] the most senior person among them was Sergey Abyshev, a former deputy director of the Department of Legislative Affairs within the Ministry of Energy, far removed from the Kremlin, let alone the highest echelons of power.[6]

As it turned out, Abyshev was an important part of Steele's scheme. Armed with his initial assignment, Danchenko traveled to Russia in June 2016 and met two of his old friends. In Danchenko's January 2017 FBI interview, they are identified as Source 1 and Source 2. But the FBI had left some clues about their real identities. We knew from the FBI's redactions that Source 1 had a six-plus-seven name. We also knew that he had held some positions in city and local government, but he was unable to advance further in his career. Source 1's ties with Danchenko stretched back to the Open World program, the exchange program that had brought Danchenko to the United States in the early 2000s. Danchenko told the FBI that he met Source 1 whenever he visited Russia. Danchenko also explained that some years ago, Source 1 needed help with a language course in the United Kingdom. At the time, Danchenko asked Steele's firm to assist. This was a strong hint that whoever Source 1 was, he wasn't a big shot but rather someone dependent on financial assistance. It was also a strong hint that

Steele knew exactly who Danchenko's supposed sources were. According to Danchenko, Source 1 frequently pestered him with requests for projects he could work on, suggesting that he was not a high achiever by any means. According to Danchenko, he once assisted Source 1 with research for an academic book, which required him to visit the Library of Congress. Armed with these clues, chief among them being the six-plus-seven name, we scoured Danchenko's social media accounts to find the correct person. Chuck Ross, the *Daily Caller* journalist, eventually found a person with a six-plus-seven name among Danchenko's Facebook friends. It was Sergey Abyshev.

Steele's particular interest in Abyshev seems to have been his potential to establish a false link to former Russian intelligence officer Vyacheslav Trubnikov. Trubnikov, who died in 2022, was a Russian diplomat and intelligence officer who served as Russia's ambassador in India in the 2000s and as the director of the Russian Foreign Intelligence Service between 1996 and 2000.[7] Steele wrote in Report 80 that a "former top Russian intelligence officer claims FSB compromised Trump through his activities in Moscow sufficiently to be able to blackmail him." It is likely that the alleged source Steele had in mind when he wrote this was Trubnikov, whose name fits perfectly with the redaction in the FBI's interview notes. To be fair to Steele, Trubnikov would have been a credible source, unlike Danchenko's friends. But the problem was that Danchenko had no access to Trubnikov or anyone like Trubnikov. So the next best option was to place Abyshev in the same room as Danchenko and later assert that Abyshev was the source of the statement about Trubnikov. It made sense. If you want to attribute words to Trubnikov, you should find someone who might know him, take them to a bar, and then fabricate a conversation. However, when Abyshev was deposed by lawyers representing Alfa Bank as part of their defamation case against Steele's employers, Fusion GPS, he testified that he did not discuss anything related to the dossier with Danchenko.[8] Abyshev also stated that he believed the Steele-Danchenko part of the operation involved Danchenko fishing for gossip from unsuspecting victims that might fit the narrative put forward by Steele. When no gossip was forthcoming, they simply fabricated stories, using the same unsuspecting victims as their pawns. For his part, Abyshev claims that he never even met Trubnikov until May 2017, which was a year after his June 2016 meeting with Danchenko, which was used for Report 80.

Trubnikov emerges in another aspect of the Russiagate saga, specifically in relation to Stefan Halper, the dubious FBI informant who surveilled Trump advisors Carter Page, George Papadopoulos and Sam Clovis. Halper was also the originator of the false smears alleging that Michael Flynn had an affair with Svetlana Lokhova, a Russian-born British academic at Cambridge University. Halper hosted Trubnikov at two Cambridge University intelligence seminars in 2012 and 2015.

We know from transcripts of their conversation that Halper mentioned Trubnikov during the FBI's unsuccessful sting operation against Papadopoulos in September 2016.[9] According to the December 2019 report by Inspector General Michael Horowitz, Halper was assigned by the FBI to "ask Papadopoulos direct questions about whether the Trump campaign benefitted from, or anyone in the Trump campaign had knowledge of, Russian assistance or the WikiLeaks release of information that was damaging to the Clinton campaign."[10] While it is not unusual for Halper to have known Trubnikov, it is noteworthy that Halper brought him up as part of a sting operation against Papadopoulos while, at the same time, Steele was falsely claiming that Trubnikov was a dossier source. As previously mentioned, the connection between Steele and Halper remains poorly understood. We know that they were both Swiftboat operatives, but on opposite ends. Steele was working on the project from the Clinton campaign side, while Halper worked on it from the FBI side. Did they secretly coordinate their actions? We don't know the answer to this intriguing question.

Even when adopting a generous interpretation of Steele's narrative as merely relaying information he received, it still presents a situation where Steele obtained information from an intermediary, who in turn acquired it from another source, who in turn heard it from yet another individual. What this third person was supposed to have said was that Russian intelligence possessed "embarrassing stuff—sexual/pornographic material" on several individuals, including Trump.[11] The triple hearsay reportedly originated at a bar in St. Petersburg. The individual at the bar refutes having informed Danchenko about anything, particularly regarding Trubnikov or Trump. Recall that this is the most generous interpretation, assuming that Steele merely acted as an intermediary for information. In what manner did Steele present this information? The information was presented as follows in Report 80: "Former top Russian intelligence officer claims FSB has compromised Trump through his activities in Moscow sufficiently to be able to blackmail him. According to several knowledgeable sources, his conduct in Moscow has included perverted sexual acts which have been arranged/monitored by FSB."

Danchenko admitted to the deception—Steele's deception—during his January 2017 FBI interview. He stated that Abyshev never mentioned

Report 80—Made-to-Order Fairytale

anything about blackmail and that the dossier's depiction of events was not true. To make matters worse, Steele claimed in Report 80 that Danchenko had obtained all this information directly from Trubnikov, designated as Source B, as well as directly from Source A, described as "a senior Russian Foreign Ministry figure." As Danchenko admitted to the FBI, he had neither talked to Trubnikov nor to anyone fitting that description. The entire story had been fabricated by Steele, Danchenko, or a combination of the two, and pinned on Abyshev. But the FBI just let it go. They had a duty not only to end their phony investigation but also to inform the Foreign Intelligence Surveillance Court (FISC) that the information used to obtain the Carter Page warrant was false. The FBI, however, remained silent and concealed Danchenko's confession, as well as his very existence. Incredibly, the FBI then proceeded to secure at least two more FISA warrants using the same false Steele dossier information. Finally, in 2020, the Department of Justice conceded that those two additional warrants had been unlawfully obtained.[12] But the reason provided was not Danchenko's confession but rather alleged technical errors in the warrant applications that had been identified by Inspector General Horowitz. To this day, the FBI has not admitted that the Steele dossier was based on false information, and that the FBI knew this since at least January 2017.

But it wasn't just Source A and B that Report 80 lied about. The other alleged source for Report 80 appeared equally important to Steele's account, as they claimed to have provided information about Trump's sexual activities at the Ritz-Carlton Hotel. That story would later become the media's main talking point about the dossier. Danchenko said the information came from Source 2, Ivan Vorontsov, whose name was redacted in the Danchenko interview notes.[13]

Even though we did not know the identity of Source 2 when the interview notes were released in July 2020, we were aware that it was not Sergei Millian. That was a significant red flag—one that the FBI should have immediately noticed—because Steele had previously identified Millian as the source for the "pee tape" story. But Millian was Danchenko's alleged Source 6, not Source 2. In other words, Steele and Danchenko had conflicting accounts regarding the sources, which is quite problematic considering that all of Steele's information supposedly came from Danchenko. It was another instance of Steele and Danchenko being tripped up by their own lies, a fact that the FBI would have realized by January 2017 at the latest. Yet, they just let the lies fester.

The fact that our group immediately recognized the deceit when Danchenko's redacted interview notes were released on July 17, 2020, made identifying Source 2 a priority. From the redactions, it was clear that Source 2 had a four-letter first name and a nine-letter last name. We also deduced that Source 2 was a childhood friend of Danchenko's who had developed an interest in collecting banknotes. Although large parts of Danchenko's interview notes were redacted, we were able to piece together that when Danchenko traveled to a country whose name had been redacted but which we later worked out as being Scotland, Source 2 asked him to look for a specific Scottish banknote that was still missing from Source 2's collection. Thankfully, Danchenko shared abundant information about his international travels on his social media. That allowed us to match dates and places. From there, it wasn't too difficult to get to Scotland. Scotland uses the same currency as the rest of the United Kingdom but prints its own notes, which look different from Bank of England pound notes that most international travelers are familiar with. This sometimes causes problems, as I experienced when I lived in England. Theoretically, Scottish notes are legal tender anywhere in the United Kingdom, but not every shop accepts them. For that reason, they are rare in England but ubiquitous in Scotland. We could understand why Source 2 wanted Scottish notes, but the fact that he did was also an important clue to his identity. Not only did this information indicate that Source 2 had likely not traveled to the United Kingdom—especially not to Scotland—but it also suggested that he was not affluent. A wealthier individual would have probably sought something more unique than an unremarkable Scottish banknote. That narrowed the field, but we were not quite there yet. We knew from the interview notes that Source 2 was somehow connected to finance and had a Facebook page dedicated to his collection of banknotes.

By the time we had figured out these things, Danchenko had started deleting his entire social media presence, which complicated cross-referencing his Facebook interactions. We had always wondered how Danchenko knew to delete his entire substantial social media presence early on July 19, which was a Sunday morning. If he was concerned about the July 17 release of his heavily redacted interview notes, he should have deleted his social media accounts at that time. But he didn't. For some reason, he waited until thirty-six hours later, which happened to coincide with us finding out who he was. But how did he know that we knew who he was? On that Sunday morning, we only communicated through private direct messages on Twitter. None of us publicly posted Danchenko's name until a few hours later when Sergei Millian confirmed that he had received two strange emails from someone named Danchenko in 2016.

After Elon Musk acquired Twitter and started releasing the Twitter Files, it was revealed that Twitter staff and government agencies had access to users' direct messages.[14] We also discovered through Twitter Files that Twitter's deputy general counsel, former FBI counsel James Baker, was actively working to obstruct Musk's transparency initiative.[15] He was summarily fired for his efforts. But the revelations made us think. Was it possible that someone inside Twitter—like Baker—had been keeping an eye on our direct messages? Or perhaps the FBI had access? Stephen, Fool Nelson, Walkafyre, and I all had decent-sized Twitter accounts and were known as the go-to place for Russiagate research. Was it possible that Baker or the FBI warned Danchenko that he had been identified? In the end, we don't know, and probably never will know for sure. It might not have been that. Perhaps Danchenko had simply been procrastinating in deleting his social media accounts.

Fortunately, Stephen had managed to capture some of Danchenko's social media data just as it was being deleted. But there was no four-plus-nine name for Source 2. At the same time, I had saved a list of Danchenko's Twitter contacts, but that also did not help us find the person we were looking for. But then we got our breakthrough. On a hunch, Fool Nelson had taken a screenshot of all the people who liked a photo of a spiky-haired Danchenko on Facebook. In total, thirty of his friends liked the photo. Fool Nelson joked that we would probably find all of Danchenko's alleged sources on this list. Amazingly, he was right. All but one of Danchenko's sources had liked a Facebook photo of him. Stephen would later name the screenshot "our Rosetta Stone."

Among those who liked the spiky-haired Danchenko photo, there was a very jovial-looking fellow named Ivan Vorontsov, who had a four-plus-nine name. His social media presence suggested that he was quite the character, a partygoer with a penchant for dress-up parties. He was about forty, the same age as Danchenko. That meant they could have been childhood friends, which had been one of our clues. By this point, a few days had passed since we identified Danchenko. Even though Danchenko was aware of our identification, Vorontsov's Facebook page remained accessible. Not only was the page open to the general public, but nothing appeared to have been deleted. That suggested that if Source 2 was indeed Vorontsov, he was an unwitting source. If he had not been, Danchenko would likely have given him the heads-up, and we might never have found out that he was

Source 2, or more precisely, that he had been falsely utilized as Source 2. On Vorontsov's Facebook page, we soon found photos of Vorontsov and Danchenko spending time together in Italy. We also found numerous other photos of Vorontsov with his collection of banknotes. That is when we knew we had found the right person.

Vorontsov, it turned out, is a financial reporter and editor-in-chief of Banks-Finance.ru, a niche site that provides financial information. It is a very small website, ranking around seven millionth on the Alexa website traffic rankings. As of this writing, the website is still operational. Given the extent of the damage caused by Steele, not only to Trump but also to Russia's image and international relations, that might seem surprising, but only if we assume that Vorontsov was in on Steele's scheme. However, the Russian government knows that, like many others, Vorontsov was not a source but a victim.

While we know that neither Vorontsov nor Millian were a source, let alone the source for the "pee tape" story, it remains unknown whether Steele or Danchenko fabricated the "pee tape" story. Given the similarities between the "pee tape" story and Cody Shearer's claim that Russia had a blackmail tape of a "woman urinating on Trump," and considering that only Steele, not Danchenko, was in touch with other Clinton operatives, it is more likely that Steele was the driving force behind the "pee tape" story.[16] According to Danchenko's November 2021 indictment, the narrative was at least indirectly shaped by Charles Dolan, an associate of Clinton, who stayed at the Ritz Carlton Hotel in June 2016 during a conference planning trip to Moscow.[17] The hotel manager gave Dolan a tour of the hotel, including the presidential suite. Danchenko was in Moscow with Dolan, supposedly to compile stories for Steele's Report 80.[18] Although Danchenko stayed at another hotel, presumably to save money, he later appears to have used Dolan's accounts of his stay at the Ritz-Carlton to shape his own narrative. Despite the fact that Danchenko had never stayed there, the Ritz-Carlton, its manager, and the presidential suite would all become central themes in Steele's reporting. Thus, the most probable explanation is that Steele had set certain parameters, such as the "pee tape" story, and that Danchenko contributed made-up details, such as the location.

Danchenko later informed the FBI that he tried to authenticate the "pee tape" story with Ritz-Carlton hotel staff but was unsuccessful. Leaving aside the fact that it is extremely unlikely for Ritz-Carlton staff to discuss their guests, we know that Danchenko did not stay at the Ritz-Carlton, and there is no evidence that Danchenko even spoke to anyone at the hotel. But none of this mattered to Steele. He made the imaginary "pee tape" story the centerpiece of his first report.

After we identified Vorontsov, the Russian media followed up on the story by tracking down Danchenko's supposed sources. When asked whether he told any dossier stories to Danchenko, Vorontsov told the Meduza outlet, "No, it wasn't me. You'd need to have been there to tell such stories. I'm hearing about the mattress and Trump for the first time in my life. And this is the first time I'm hearing that Igor could somehow be connected to something like that. In conversations, he's never let anything like that slip."[19]

Vorontsov also informed Meduza that he had initially met Danchenko eight years earlier at an energy forum in Moscow. Danchenko had purported to be an expert in Washington, DC, "preparing analytical reports about various industries, which is why he was at the oil forum." They stayed in contact, but Vorontsov was very firm that they did not discuss the topics Steele alleges they did. Talking to Meduza, Vorontsov emphasized that he was naturally cautious of Russian expatriates working in the business intelligence sector. Interestingly, Vorontsov also said that Danchenko was only interested in alcohol: "I told him, 'Let's drink and be friends. No business and no politics.' 'It's a deal,' he said." Vorontsov's account appears to align with other accounts of Danchenko, especially that of Abyshev, who later testified that Danchenko had a "severe drinking problem."[20] Incidentally, the Meduza story was published on November 3, 2020, which was the day of the US presidential election. I have often contemplated the potential impact of the information regarding Danchenko—that he and Steele had fabricated everything—on that election, if the public had been truthfully informed.

In 2021, Vorontsov, along with all of Danchenko's other alleged sources, signed affidavits attesting that he did not provide any information for the dossier and that Danchenko had fabricated it all.[21]

There was also an oddity in Report 80 where Steele used the designation "Source E" for different individuals. While Steele might argue that this was meant to mislead people like us—just as his irregular report numbering was supposed to do—the truth is that Steele had inserted placeholder designations so he could later change who would be implicated as the alleged source for any specific claim. A name could be assigned later, depending on the circumstances. In Report 80, Source E was a placeholder for a staff member at Moscow's Ritz-Carlton Hotel.

However, Steele made a mistake in his scheming when he later used the same placeholder designation, Source E, to describe a Trump insider in Report 95. The supposed Trump insider was identified as Millian. Of course, in no universe could Millian have been a Ritz-Carlton staffer, not even in Steele's fantasy universe. It had long been clear that Steele was playing a smoke-and-mirrors game regarding his source for the "pee tape." But it was his sloppiness with placeholder names that gave the game away. To make matters worse, Steele told the FBI during an October 2016 interview in Rome that Source E was Millian in both cases.[22] In fact, it was not just that Steele could not get his story about Source E straight. According to Steele, Millian was described as Source D in Report 80, as Source E in Report 95, as "a Russian emigre figure close to the Republican US presidential candidate Donald Trump's campaign team" in Report 97, and as "an ethnic Russian associate of Republican US presidential candidate Donald Trump" in Report 102.

Incidentally, as we would later find out during Danchenko's trial, it was at the October 3, 2016, meeting between Steele and his FBI handler that the Crossfire Hurricane team offered Steele $1 million if he could corroborate his dossier claims.[23] He could not.

At this point, meaning on October 3, 2016, even before the Carter Page FISA warrant had been obtained, the FBI would have known, or should have known, that Steele's reporting was fabricated. The FBI had been watching Millian and knew perfectly well that he did not work at the Ritz-Carlton in Moscow. They also knew that he was not Russian and that he could not have taken on all the roles Steele attributed to him. And they knew that despite the million-dollar offer, Steele was unable to provide any corroborating evidence. But the FBI did not care and simply forged ahead. Even worse, the Page FISA warrant was obtained a few weeks after the Rome meeting based solely on Steele's say-so.

But it wasn't just the fake Ritz-Carlton story that revealed Steele's lies. Source D was similarly fabricated, and the FBI was aware of it. According to Steele, Source D was Millian. But according to Report 80, Source D was "a close associate of Trump who had organized and managed his recent trips to Moscow." There was no recent trip, only one trip, and Millian had demonstrably not organized it. During that trip, Trump traveled to Moscow for the November 9, 2013 Miss Universe pageant, an event that he owned at the time.[24] Trump's trip was organized by Aras Agalarov, an Azerbaijani property mogul who had helped finance the 2013 pageant. Aras's pop star son, Emin, performed at the pageant. Steele's description of Source D was meant to point the finger at Agalarov. When the FBI interviewed Danchenko in January 2017, he stated that Source D was actually a different individual, Danchenko's long time friend, Ivan Vorontsov. Once again, Steele was caught red-handed, and once again, the FBI ignored the obvious contradiction.

Special Counsel Robert Mueller and his deputy, Andrew Weissmann, later spent an inordinate amount of time and money investigating possible connections between Trump and the Agalarovs, even though his team knew perfectly well that Steele and Danchenko had fabricated the information. Incredibly, the name Agalarov appears seventy-nine times in Mueller's report. Steele's name appears only fourteen times.

Report 80 was Steele's attempt to anchor the Russia collusion narrative by suggesting that the Kremlin had compromising information on Trump. Once we obtained Danchenko's interview notes from January 2017, it took only a few hours to identify significant inconsistencies among Steele's statements, Danchenko's statements, and the information presented in the report. The FBI had all the relevant information to completely discredit Steele even before Trump was inaugurated. But they ignored the lies and discrepancies in their attempt to bring down a sitting president. Handwritten notes from Bill Priestap, the FBI's head of counterintelligence, that were released during the trial of Clinton campaign lawyer Sussmann, revealed that they claimed the dossier was "well-sourced" even though they knew it was entirely fabricated.[25] The FBI's talking points for a March 8, 2017 congressional briefing, which were also released during the Sussmann trial, reveal that even at that late stage, the FBI was lying about its case against the Trump campaign and about Steele.[26] The FBI falsely claimed that "some of [Steele's] reporting has been corroborated," that Steele "maintained a network of sub-sources," and that Danchenko was "a Russian-based source." The FBI knew all those things were untrue. Yet, unlike Trump associates such as Roger Stone, no one was charged with lying to Congress.

CHAPTER 8

Reports 86 and 95—Pinning WikiLeaks on Russia

With the handover of Report 80 to Steele's FBI handler on July 5, 2016, the notion that Trump was compromised by the Kremlin was planted. Steele's next task was to promote another idea: that Russia was responsible for hacking attacks aimed at interfering in the 2016 presidential election. He came up with Report 86 about one month after Report 80 was written. To underline Steele's lack of thoroughness once more, Report 86 was dated July 26, 2015, a mistake which Steele later attributed to a typo. According to Steele, he did not number his reports sequentially because he wanted to confuse potential infiltrators and spies. In truth, he just wanted to appear sophisticated and impress his audience with supposed spycraft.

But Report 86 turned out to be a total dud. Steele had asked Danchenko to compile stories about the cyber activities of the Russian Federal Security Service (FSB), an agency that is technically equivalent to the FBI. Danchenko only managed to cobble together some boilerplate stories about how the FSB had failed to penetrate first-tier targets such as the G7 and NATO. The failures had apparently been masked by successful cyber-attacks on "secondary targets," such as banks in Latvia. Report 86 contains no information about Trump. His name is not mentioned once.

While the report was completely useless to Steele's paymasters, it does offer insight into Danchenko's or Steele's prejudices. One of the stories reported claims that the FSB was actively approaching "US citizens of Russian (Jewish) origin on business trips to Russia." Allegedly, the FSB was bribing Jewish American IT executives to implant Trojan viruses in their software. According to Steele's report, this scheme was deemed a "significant operational success" as it allowed the FSB to implant Russian malware in computer games to conduct espionage on targets in the United States.

If this story sounds vaguely familiar, it might be because it loosely resembles the plot of the 1994 movie *Police Academy: Mission to Moscow*. It is not known whether Danchenko, who was sixteen when the movie came out, riffed off its script. However, as the first major Hollywood production to be filmed in Russia after the collapse of the Soviet Union—even preceding the James Bond movie *GoldenEye*—it likely captured Danchenko's attention at the time, particularly as someone who had harbored a lifelong desire to visit America.

The FBI seemingly overlooked Steele's open defamation of Jewish Americans in the IT sector. Setting aside the issue of anti-Semitism, the narrative should have been deemed implausible enough to trigger scrutiny from the FBI and potentially from the Clinton campaign.

But it didn't. Instead, the Clinton campaign was upset about the vague nature of the report. It was not what they had asked for. On July 22, 2016, three days before Steele submitted Report 86, WikiLeaks had started publishing a trove of emails from the Democratic National Committee (DNC). The email dump wasn't particularly juicy. For the most part, the emails involved only seven DNC staffers. The biggest takeaway was that the DNC had influenced the media narrative in favor of Hillary Clinton and against her primary opponent, Bernie Sanders. For instance, on May 21, 2016, National Secretary Mark Paustenbach and National Communications Director Luis Miranda discussed seeding a story that Sanders "never ever had his act together, that his campaign was a mess."[1]

In another email, DNC Chairwoman Debbie Wasserman Schultz called Sanders's Campaign Manager Jeff Weaver an "ass" and a "damn liar."[2] Wasserman Schultz later resigned as a result of the email leak. Early suspicions for the leak were focused on Sanders supporters. Perhaps a disgruntled Sanders supporter from within the DNC had sent WikiLeaks the emails. Julian Assange, the founder of WikiLeaks, has always insisted that the emails did not come from a state actor.[3] Another theory involved DNC staffer Seth Rich. Rich was murdered in Washington, DC on July 10, 2016. Although the police classified the murder as an attempted robbery, nothing was taken from Rich. What speaks against an assassination is that Rich was shot several times in the body but not in the head. To this day, the perpetrators remain at large.

While the source of the DNC email dump was—and remains—unknown, the Clinton campaign had other ideas. Their predetermined narrative was that Russia had hacked the DNC to help elect Donald Trump. On July 24, 2016, barely two days after the DNC emails started trickling out, Clinton campaign manager Robbie Mook boldly declared that experts had informed the Clinton campaign that "this was done by the Russians for the purpose of helping Donald Trump."[4]

Steele's Report 86, with all its generalities and lack of focus on Trump, was not helpful in advancing this narrative. Steele was undoubtedly informed of this in very clear terms. We can safely draw that conclusion because just a few days after producing Report 86, Steele came up with another report, Report 95. This time he delivered. If Report 80 planted the bomb, Report 95 set it off. Or, as Stephen McIntyre would say, Report 95 was the Clinton campaign's wet dream; it fulfilled all their desires and more.

Although Report 95 is undated—presumably to obscure the fact that it was a last-minute replacement for Report 86—its dissemination to Fusion GPS can be pinpointed to around July 28. This indicates that Steele only took forty-eight hours from releasing his unsuccessful Report 86 to releasing what the Clinton campaign was truly seeking. The hastily compiled Report 95 alleged that there was an extensive conspiracy between Trump's campaign team and the Kremlin, directed by campaign chairman Paul Manafort and campaign advisor Carter Page. The arrangement was described as a "well-developed conspiracy of co-operation" between Trump and Russia.

Report 95 also claimed that Russia was responsible for hacking email accounts belonging to staff of the DNC. Some might ask why, if there was extensive collusion between the campaign and Russia, the emails weren't simply given to Manafort or Page. Steele preemptively claimed that WikiLeaks was used as a conduit to establish "plausible deniability," but that senior members of his campaign, as well as Trump himself, were fully involved in the arrangement. It is noteworthy that Steele's highly detailed allegations regarding WikiLeaks were penned subsequent to the release of the WikiLeaks email dump. Once again, Steele did not provide any foreshadowing. He was merely rephrasing established facts by integrating the Clinton campaign's favored false narrative.

According to Report 95, the mechanism for transmitting intelligence from Russia to Trump was said to be Russian consulates in New York, Washington, and Miami. The problem is that there is no Russian consulate in Miami. Steele's typical approach of blending readily accessible information with made-up fantasies had once again faltered, possibly because of the haste in putting together Report 95.

But the job was done. Steele had tied Trump directly to the WikiLeaks email dump, echoing the claim made by Clinton campaign manager Robbie Mook a few days earlier. Mook's claim, made on the evening of July 24 on CNN, was that "experts" had informed the Clinton campaign that Russia had hacked and released the DNC emails to assist Trump in winning the presidency.[5] With that statement, Mook had seeded Clinton's Swiftboat offensive in the public's mind. It would hamstring Trump for years to come. In many ways, it still does.

The alleged source of all this juicy information was Source E, Sergei Millian, who had been set up by a combination of Steele, Danchenko, and Fusion GPS. Danchenko was later charged by Special Counsel John Durham with lying about his alleged communications with Millian.

As we saw earlier, Fusion GPS and Steele had identified Millian as an ideal target to be set up as a fake source. He was originally from Belarus, had a Russian-sounding name and accent, was the president of the Russian-American Chamber of Commerce, and most importantly, he had met Trump years before, with a photo taken on the occasion. Steele then instructed Danchenko to arrange a meeting with Millian under false pretenses to bring them together in the same room. Once that was done, they could put whatever words they wanted in Millian's mouth—which is exactly what they did. But because Danchenko had failed to meet Millian, Danchenko and Steele were left with no option but to pretend that Danchenko had, in fact, met Millian.

Another major allegation in Report 95, which disintegrates under even the slightest scrutiny, is that Trump's team—specifically Carter Page and Paul Manafort, as implied by Steele—supposedly "had agreed to sideline Russian intervention in Ukraine as a campaign issue" in exchange for the hacked DNC emails. Again, WikiLeaks was supposedly used to create "plausible deniability." But, according to Steele, "the operation had been conducted with the full knowledge and support of Trump and senior members of his campaign team." However, as anyone who had been following events in July 2016 knew, this was total nonsense. It seems that Steele, following his typical modus operandi, seized upon a news item and crafted an elaborate story from it. In this case, the news report he was utilizing was a *Washington Post* opinion piece that claimed that the Trump campaign had "gutted" the pro-Ukraine sections of the Republican election platform.[6] As it turned out, this was fake news. As acknowledged in an internal report by the FBI, the Trump campaign did not alter the Republican platform; quite the opposite.[7] Instead, a platform committee member, Diana Denman, who was driven by an agenda of arming Ukraine, attempted to insert language into the platform calling for the United States to "provide lethal defensive weapons to the Ukrainian government." Two members of the Trump campaign, one of whom was Jeffrey D. "J. D." Gordon, who ran the campaign's National Security Advisory Committee, argued against the change. In the end, Denman's efforts to include the term "lethal defensive weapons" were not adopted. Instead, the platform called for Ukraine to receive "appropriate assistance." Steele, relying on the *Washington Post* opinion piece, had misunderstood the situation. It wasn't Trump who wanted to change the platform, but rather an unknown Ukraine supporter. Steele's added narrative about exchanging DNC hack data for altering the GOP's platform was entirely fictional.

A day after Report 95 was issued, Steele arrived in Washington from London for an important meeting. That day, July 29, would turn out to be perhaps the most significant day since the Swiftboat project had been initiated earlier that year. Clinton campaign lawyers Marc Elias and Michael Sussmann had arranged for the key figures in the Swiftboat plot to convene at the offices of their law firm, Perkins Coie. Fusion, Steele, and Perkins Coie were all in the same room. The campaign's lawyers, media smear merchants, and a fake intelligence operative were all present. The two strands of the Swiftboat project, Steele's dossier strand and Sussmann's cyber strand, had finally converged.

Up until that point, Steele was unaware of the cyber side of the plot. Sussmann and tech executive Rodney Joffe had spent the past few months putting together the Alfa Bank smear, which was based on fake cyber connections between Russia's Alfa Bank and the Trump Organization. It remains uncertain whether Joffe was present at the meeting held on July 29 at Perkins Coie's office; however, Steele subsequently acknowledged that it was during this meeting that he was informed about the Alfa Bank narrative. He was then assigned to promote this part of the wider Swiftboat campaign through one of his fabricated reports, Report 112, which was released on September 14, 2016, just five days before Sussmann presented the fictitious Alfa Bank story to the FBI.

Sussmann was later charged by Durham with lying about whom he was representing when he took the fake Alfa Bank story to the FBI. Sussmann claimed that he was not representing anyone and was merely acting as a good Samaritan. However, the facts, including billing records from Sussmann, showed that he was acting on behalf of the Clinton campaign. Sussmann was acquitted by a partisan Washington, DC jury, with one juror later stating that it did not matter whether Sussmann had lied to the FBI.[8] The juror claimed that there are bigger issues than lying to the FBI. The jury's verdict was not surprising. Three jurors were donors to Hillary Clinton, one was a donor to Alexandria Ocasio-Cortez, and one was the mother of a close friend of Sussmann's daughter.[9] Washington, DC is an awfully incestuous place, and convicting one of their own was always a huge uphill battle for Durham.

It remains unclear why Steele was roped into the Alfa Bank side of the Swiftboat plan. Strictly speaking, he did not have a need to know. He could have simply been directed to write something specific about Trump, as was the case with previous assignments, such as Report 95. Steele did not need to know the details of the Alfa Bank plot in order to write something damaging about Trump and Alfa Bank. He had already shown that he was perfectly capable of writing fictional accounts about Trump.

When Sussmann was called to testify before Congress in late 2017, he claimed that Steele had been invited to the Perkins Coie meeting so that Sussmann could vet him.[10] That explanation never made much sense, considering that Steele was handling the dossier and operating on a different path than Sussmann. More importantly, by that point, Steele had already issued his two most consequential reports, 80 and 95. Frankly, it was too late for vetting, at least in terms of the dossier. What does make sense, however, is that Steele was being vetted for a more direct role in the Alfa Bank scam. This assertion appears even more plausible when one considers the anomaly of Sussmann, a prominent campaign lawyer, personally engaging in the dissemination of fraudulent information to the FBI. Was the original plan for Steele to take the Alfa Bank information to the FBI? It would make sense, both in terms of maintaining Perkins Coie's reputation and in terms of Sussmann's later claim that his task on July 29 was to vet Steele. If that is correct, the vetting process did not work out well for Steele. Again, that would make sense. Steele's name might have brought some superficial gravitas to the endeavor, especially by associating the "ex-MI6" label with him, but he is far less impressive in real life. Perhaps Sussmann came to that conclusion as well. In his various public interviews, he comes across as feeble and lacking substance. During his court testimony in London in 2020, he was evasive and ended up entangling himself in his own stories. Perhaps most notably, when he was interviewed by Special Counsel Robert Mueller's team in September 2017, Steele was not even able to keep his story straight.

For instance, he mangled his dossier sources. In short, he was not the kind of person you could rely on in critical situations. Sussmann and Elias, who presumably took part in the vetting process, could not have known about Steele's later missteps. However, as seasoned lawyers who had examined and cross-examined thousands of witnesses, they might have realized that Steele could not be relied upon to handle the Alfa Bank plot effectively. And so, that task may have fallen back to a reluctant Sussmann.

CHAPTER 9

How Did Crossfire Hurricane Begin?

One question that has never been fully resolved is exactly how and when the FBI's investigation into the Trump campaign really began. The official starting date given by the FBI for opening the Crossfire Hurricane investigation is July 31, 2016, which happened to coincide with a high-level meeting of all the principal Swiftboat operatives at the law offices of Perkins Coie that same week. However, both the timing of the actual opening of the investigation and the purported justification remain shrouded in mystery.

While FBI leadership later asserted that the initiation of the investigation was unrelated to Steele, it is firmly established that starting on July 5, 2016, Steele began transmitting his reports to his FBI contact, Michael Gaeta. In February 2018, Victoria Nuland, an official from the State Department, acknowledged during an appearance on CBS's *Face the Nation* that she had shared reports from Steele with the FBI in July 2016. She stated, "This needs to go to the FBI, if there is any concern here that one candidate or the election as a whole might be influenced by the Russian Federation. That's something for the FBI to investigate."[1] In December 2017, during a transcribed interview with the House Permanent Select Committee on Intelligence, Gaeta confirmed that he had passed Steele's reports to his superiors.[2] Special Counsel John Durham's report later corroborated that the FBI had indeed been receiving reports from Steele starting in July 2016.[3]

Both Durham and Attorney General Barr released statements in December 2019 contending that the FBI's stated rationale for commencing its investigation was, at a minimum, insufficient. Barr stated that "the FBI launched an intrusive investigation of a U.S. presidential campaign on the thinnest of suspicions that, in my view, were insufficient to justify the steps taken."⁴ Durham went one step further and openly challenged the official narrative for opening the Crossfire Hurricane investigation: "Based on the evidence collected to date, and while our investigation is ongoing, last month we advised the Inspector General that we do not agree with some of the report's conclusions as to predication and how the FBI case was opened."⁵ In other words, Durham objected to the official narrative both in terms of why and how Crossfire Hurricane was opened.

Barr's and Durham's statements were prompted by the publication of Inspector General Michael Horowitz's report on FISA abuse. The report, which was published on December 9, 2019, cataloged a sequence of FBI shortcomings regarding the approval of four FISA warrants targeting Trump campaign aide Carter Page. The report marked not only the first formal confirmation that Steele had a primary sub-source but also that the primary sub-source had disavowed the dossier during a January 2017 interview with the FBI.⁶ The sub-source, Danchenko, told the FBI that he "had no proof to support the statements from his sub-sources" and that it "was just talk." Danchenko added that the information in the dossier was "word of mouth and hearsay" that he had exchanged "with friends over beers." The allegations about Trump's sexual activities had been made in "jest." Danchenko claimed that he never expected Steele to include the bar talk "in reports or present them as facts." It is important to note that Danchenko made these admissions within the first few days of Trump becoming president. Upon hearing his statements, anyone with even a minimal degree of integrity would have immediately ended the Trump-Russia investigation and spared the country and the world a huge ordeal. But the FBI had other plans.

It is not known whether Horowitz was aware that the source was Danchenko. The name was a tightly held secret within FBI leadership until we discovered it in July 2020. Despite uncovering various instances of misconduct, such as the FBI obtaining further warrants for Carter Page after Danchenko had renounced the Steele dossier, Horowitz seemed to have accepted other narratives presented by the FBI. Crucially, Horowitz assumed that the FBI's official narrative explaining why they initiated their Crossfire Hurricane investigation of Trump was correct. This is what Barr and Durham objected to.

The official narrative states that Trump campaign aide George Papadopoulos met the former Australian foreign secretary and then-Australian ambassador, Alexander Downer, in London at the Kensington

Wine Rooms on May 10, 2016. During that meeting, Papadopoulos allegedly informed Downer that the Russian government could potentially release damaging information about Hillary Clinton. It was a commonly accepted fact at the time that foreign government actors had obtained Clinton's emails from her unsecured, clandestine homebrew server.[7] On the day before Papadopoulos met Downer, Fox News reported that Russia had Clinton's emails.[8] That Papadopoulos might have shared the same story with Downer should not have been noteworthy. Indeed, the information was initially deemed unremarkable by Downer. He chose not to disclose it to anyone other than documenting it in a standard meeting report submitted to his office in Australia's capital, Canberra.

The pertinent section of Downer's meeting report was subsequently disclosed in the Horowitz report: "Papadopoulos suggested the Trump team had received some kind of suggestion from Russia that it could assist this process with the anonymous release of information during the campaign that would be damaging to Mrs Clinton [and President Obama]. It was unclear whether he or the Russians were referring to material acquired publicly of (sic) through other means. It was also unclear how Mr Trump's team reacted to the offer. We note the Trump team's reaction could, in the end, have little bearing of what Russia decides to do, with or without Mr Trump's cooperation."[9]

When Downer was interviewed by the FBI about the meeting report on August 2, 2016, he stated that it was written in a "purposely vague" manner because "Papadopoulos left a number of things unexplained" and "did not say he had direct contact with the Russians."[10] Downer also stated that he "did not get the sense Papadopoulos was the middle-man to coordinate with the Russians." All of these statements should have made it crystal clear that Papadopoulos may well have been referencing the Fox News report from the night before.[11] Downer's meeting report also mentioned that Papadopoulos's story could have been derived from "publicly" available information, which aligned perfectly with the Fox News angle. Furthermore, Downer noted that Papadopoulos's musings may have been entirely speculative, which was another indication that Papadopoulos was simply rehashing what he had heard on the news. Eleven weeks passed without Downer taking any action. But then, upon learning in July that Clinton campaign manager Robbie Mook had asserted that Russia allegedly hacked the Democratic National Committee's (DNC) emails to help Trump get elected, Downer reacted. Abruptly, he recalled Papadopoulos's words and naively misunderstood the situation. What Downer did not understand is that when he met

Papadopoulos on May 10, a significant portion of the DNC emails that were later leaked had not yet been written. Papadopoulos could not have been aware of hacked emails that did not exist at the time of his conversation with Downer. Downer also did not appreciate that the exfiltration of the DNC's emails, the manner of which is still shrouded in mystery, did not begin until May 23.

Downer may be excused for hastily drawing conclusions. It was late July in an election year. The media was frantically discussing Mook's accusations, and Downer might have simply wanted to share what he had heard, just in case it was useful to American authorities. But the FBI and future CIA chief Gina Haspel do not warrant such leniency. On July 26, Downer went to the US embassy in London to pass the information about Papadopoulos to his counterpart. As fate would have it, the ambassador was on leave, so Downer instead met Elizabeth Dibble. It was fateful because Dibble, whose term as deputy chief of mission at the US embassy was going to end in five days, was not going to get herself entangled in the matter. So, she asked the embassy's legal attaché as well as the CIA's station chief to attend the meeting with Downer. The CIA station was led by Haspel, who, in another strange twist of fate, would later become the CIA director under Trump. Haspel escalated Downer's tip by deciding that it should be passed on to the FBI.[12] As a high-ranking intelligence official, she should have recognized that Downer's information was hardly noteworthy. The fact that Downer waited nearly three months to report his meeting with Papadopoulos should have served as an additional clue that this was a false alarm. In fact, both Downer and Papadopoulos later acknowledged that their encounter was completely unremarkable. It also did not involve heavy drinking, as someone in the intelligence community falsely leaked to the *New York Times*.[13] According to both men's accounts, they each had one drink and parted ways before dinnertime.

What might have been more interesting, but was probably not known to the FBI at the time, is that a few days before his meeting with Downer, Papadopoulos had met with Downer's assistant, Erika Thompson. It was that meeting that led Thompson to invite Papadopoulos to meet her boss. It may have simply been a generous offer from Thompson, who knew that Papadopoulos was eager to meet politically connected people. Downer was, after all, the former foreign secretary of Australia who, at one point, was considered a potential prime minister. An alternative theory suggests that Papadopoulos had bragged to Thompson about his attempts to organize a meeting between Trump and Putin. This might have led Thompson to believe that Papadopoulos would be an intriguing person for Downer to meet. Papadopoulos would later describe his obsession with setting up a Trump-Putin meeting as something that would set him apart.[14] He knew that he was a nobody among Trump's foreign policy advisors and felt the need to do something big to distinguish himself. Undeniably, Papadopoulos was a braggart who used his position on the Trump campaign to socialize in elite political circles, particularly in his parents' native Greece, where he portrayed himself as one of Donald Trump's closest aides and falsely claimed to be making foreign policy statements for the United States.[15]

The fact that Papadopoulos had this additional meeting with Thompson created an interesting anomaly in the Mueller Report. Mueller claims that Papadopoulos made the statements about Russia on May 6. However, an email from Thompson confirms that the meeting between Papadopoulos and Downer at Kensington Wine Rooms actually took place on May 10.[16] When Mueller's report was released in April 2019, this apparent error on the part of Mueller's team led to speculation that Papadopoulos had incriminated himself in a meeting with Thompson on May 6 and not in his meeting with Downer on May 10. However, this theory is not supported by the subsequent Durham report, which confirms that Downer's tip, given to the US Embassy in July 2016, was based on his own encounter with Papadopoulos on May 10.

Irrespective of the precise circumstances of his meetings with the Australians, the fundamental fact remains unchanged. At the time Papadopoulos met Downer and Thompson, he could not have been aware of what the FBI alleged he knew: that the Russian government had hacked the DNC's emails in collaboration with the Trump campaign. It is an incontrovertible fact that most of the DNC's emails, which later appeared on WikiLeaks, had not been written when Papadopoulos met with the Australians. Even if we were to give Haspel the benefit of the doubt for passing the information on to the FBI, or give FBI leadership the benefit of the doubt for wanting to investigate what Haspel had shared, that information would have fallen apart under minimal scrutiny. The timing simply did not work. Furthermore, Papadopoulos was a total nobody who had never traveled to Russia. Richard Farkas, who had taught Papadopoulos at DePaul University in Chicago, described his reaction upon learning that Papadopoulos had been appointed as an advisor to the Trump campaign: "We knew his expertise was virtually nonexistent. It was thin and embellished. Lots of young people, when they aspire to get close to a campaign, exaggerate their experience. George did that in spades and it was the talk of the department here."[17]

Later, after Mueller's office claimed that Papadopoulos had received information about hacked emails,[18] which were falsely assumed to be the DNC's emails from a Russian intermediary, Farkas astutely observed that Papadopoulos was likely pretending to have contact with high-ranking Russian officials to boost his status within the campaign. Without knowing it, Farkas had hit the nail on the head. Papadopoulos had indeed pretended to be in touch with top Russian officials. For instance, Papadopoulos emailed the Trump campaign to inform them that he had met the Russian ambassador in London and claimed to have also met Putin's niece.[19] Neither of these claims was true. In truth, Papadopoulos had only been in contact with two Russian nationals. The first was Ivan Timofeev, a Moscow academic who knew as much about Kremlin secrets as you or I. The second person was Olga Polonskaya, a Russian student in London whom Papadopoulos apparently wanted to date. She too knew nothing about Putin's secrets.

Papadopoulos had been introduced to Timofeev and Polonskaya by Joseph Mifsud, a professor of international relations from Malta. Papadopoulos met Mifsud through the London Centre of International Law Practice, where they both worked. The reason Papadopoulos asked Mifsud for help was simple: Papadopoulos knew no one in Russia and wanted Mifsud to make introductions.

Polonskaya was a student of Mifsud's with no apparent connections for Papadopoulos to exploit. Papadopoulos's interest appears to have been limited to the romantic sphere. However, in 2017, he attempted to distance himself from her after Mueller's team arrested him at Dulles airport. In a misguided attempt to shift Mueller's focus onto other individuals, Papadopoulos falsely claimed that Polonskaya had connections to Vladimir Putin.[20] To be fair, Papadopoulos also told the agents who arrested him that he had "a tendency to over-exaggerate a lot of things."[21] This admission might easily have explained his musings to Downer in that he had simply repackaged what he had heard on Fox News the night before. But Mueller's team paid no attention to this admission. It was not interested in exculpatory statements, only incriminating ones. And Papadopoulos could not help but make them, not out of a sense of guilt, but due to his foolhardy nature. For instance, regarding Timofeev, Papadopoulos told Mueller's office that during his second phone call with Timofeev, there were strange noises. This led him to conclude that Timofeev was acting under someone's direction and that their call was being monitored.[22] The fact that this story was entirely made up can be evidenced from Papadopoulos's many subsequent emails with Timofeev, none of which contain even the slightest hint of any suspicion on Papadopoulos's part. During his arrest, Papadopoulos also attempted to distance himself from the situation he was in by implicating Michael Flynn and Paul Manafort, suggesting that he was merely a "small fish" and questioning why Flynn and Manafort had not been arrested.[23] Similarly, in a subsequent interview with Mueller's office, Papadopoulos claimed that the Trump campaign's foreign policy coordinator, Sam Clovis, had told him that Russia was a "very important aspect of the Trump campaign."[24] Papadopoulos's behavior, which seems to have been driven by his ability to fantasize rather than a guilty mind, was not beneficial to his cause or that of Trump. Suffice it to say that it was grist to Mueller's mill.

Papadopoulos's interactions with Timofeev perfectly capture the giant chasm between the truth and Mueller's false narratives. Timofeev was a professional contact of Mifsud's. He convened the Valdai Discussion Club in Moscow, a think tank where Mifsud occasionally spoke. While Timofeev was not particularly helpful to Papadopoulos's grand scheme to organize a meeting between Putin and Trump, he did, at least, know someone at the Russian Ministry of Foreign Affairs. When Papadopoulos pushed Timofeev for an introduction, Timofeev wisely insisted that Papadopoulos needed to first provide an official letter from the Trump campaign confirming that Papadopoulos was acting on behalf of the campaign in seeking to contact the Ministry of Foreign Affairs.[25] That was a big problem for Papadopoulos. There was no way he could obtain such a letter from the campaign. The campaign was fledgling, but senior officials like Clovis were nevertheless aware that a Trump-Putin meeting was not what they wanted or needed. And if, for some reason, they changed their mind, they didn't need Papadopoulos to set it up.

Papadopoulos knew he had to find another way. Consequently, he devised a whimsical scheme that was notably juvenile yet possessed a reckless, almost sinister undertone, ultimately leading to significant negative repercussions for Trump. Papadopoulos knew there would be no letter from the campaign for the Russian Ministry of Foreign Affairs. But he also knew that Trump had given a foreign policy speech at the Mayflower Hotel in Washington on April 27.[26] So Papadopoulos came up with a madcap plan to substitute the letter he could not obtain with Trump's speech. He told Timofeev that Trump's speech itself was tantamount to a letter: "The draft letter I send cannot be better than Mr. Trump's precise speech on his intentions to repair U.S.-Russia ties."[27] When Timofeev insisted on a letter,

Papadopoulos complained to Mifsud that he had informed Timofeev that Trump's speech was "the signal to meet." It was those four words that later landed Trump in a lot of hot water. In isolation, they can appear extremely suspicious, which is precisely how the media portrayed them.[28] The media reports on those four words originated from a leak to the *New York Times*, which was the first to report on them, albeit dishonestly.[29] We know there was a leak because the four words were actually used by Papadopoulos. So, someone with access to Papadopoulos's emails, which meant either Papadopoulos himself or Mueller's office, gave them to the *New York Times*. Evidently, Papadopoulos, who was then on bail and awaiting sentencing for providing false information to the FBI regarding trivial details (specifically the timing of his initial encounter with Mifsud) did not have an incentive to leak damaging information about himself to the *New York Times*.

When the *New York Times* published their story on December 30, 2017, those four words were portrayed as tantamount to proof of Trump-Russia collusion. The *New York Times* deceptively reported that Papadopoulos told Timofeev that Trump's speech was "the signal to meet." In reality, it was hearsay. We do not know whether Papadopoulos told Timofeev about "the signal to meet." Rather, we know that he informed Mifsud that this is what he had told Timofeev. It is not known what, if anything, Papadopoulos told Timofeev. Furthermore, Papadopoulos only mentioned "the signal to meet" to Mifsud after Timofeev had made it clear that a letter from the Trump campaign was required.[30] The exchange with Mifsud took place on April 30, three days after Trump's speech, casting further doubt on the claim that Papadopoulos had informed Timofeev about "the signal to meet."

But even if Papadopoulos did use those words with Timofeev, Papadopoulos's emails—which Mueller's team had—incontrovertibly show that "the signal to meet" wasn't a signal at all but rather a harebrained Papadopoulos scheme to sidestep the fact that the Trump campaign was not interested in meeting Putin and was thus not going to issue the letter that Papadopoulos needed. In other words, the truth was the exact opposite of what the *New York Times* and the rest of the media claimed. Papadopoulos used those words because he was unable to obtain a letter. Not only did the words not suggest anything about alleged Trump-Russia collusion, but they demonstrably proved that the Trump campaign wanted nothing to do with Russia.

While Trump's Mayflower speech was falsely used by Papadopoulos as a substitute for the letter he could not obtain, it is also significant for another reason. The date of the speech is crucial evidence that Mueller's team attempted to retroactively legitimize the opening of the Crossfire Hurricane investigation by fabricating a story about Papadopoulos and Mifsud. The Mueller report alleges that, "In late April 2016, Papadopoulos was told by London-based professor Joseph Mifsud, immediately after Mifsud's return from a trip to Moscow, that the Russian government had obtained 'dirt' on candidate Clinton in the form of thousands of emails."[31] Notably, despite the fact that Mueller's 187 page report features 1283 citations, there is no citation for the claim that Mifsud told Papadopoulos about Russian "dirt" on Clinton. There is a reason for that. Mueller's team knew that Mifsud did not and could not have told Papadopoulos about any "dirt."

It took me a long time to put this particular puzzle together. Ultimately, the explanation is fairly simple yet devious on Mueller's part. The overarching context for what Mueller's team was trying to do was that they needed to substantiate the official story behind why Crossfire Hurricane was initiated. That story, as we have seen, does not hold up on its own, as it merely had Papadopoulos repeating something to Downer that had been said on Fox News the night before; specifically that Russia had Hillary Clinton's missing emails. What Mueller needed was a direct link between Papadopoulos and Russia, rather than just a connection between Papadopoulos and a story on Fox News. The narrative that Mueller's team chose was that Mifsud was the middleman who was passing the information about Clinton's emails from the Russian government to Papadopoulos. For that to have happened, Mueller needed to place the two men together at some point after Mifsud's Moscow trip but before Papadopoulos met Downer.

My first task was to determine when Papadopoulos met Mifsud after Mifsud returned from Moscow. Deceitfully, Mueller omitted the exact date in the main section of his report, stating only that the Russian "dirt" meeting occurred "in late April 2016." However, in a summary section at the back of the Mueller Report, it states that the date of this alleged meeting was April 26.[32] Why was April 26 chosen by Mueller, and how do we know that there was no meeting on that date?

We know that Mifsud gave a talk at the Valdai Discussion Club in Moscow on April 19.[33] We also know from an email to Papadopoulos that Mifsud returned to London via Italy on April 25.[34] This would have also been evident from flight records to which Mueller had access. And we know that Mifsud spoke before the Italian Parliament in Rome on April 28.[35] This left very little room for Mueller's team to construct a narrative about an alleged meeting in London between Mifsud and Papadopoulos. But there was just about enough time to fit it in somewhere between April 25 and April 28.

Mueller's team chose April 26, and Papadopoulos went along with this story, even though his own emails paint a different picture.[36] It is likely he simply told Mueller's team what they wanted to hear in order to get a better plea deal and avoid being charged under the Foreign Agents Registration Act, with which he had been threatened. His previous complaints that Flynn and Manafort had not been arrested, and his fabrications about Timofeev and Polonskaya, only amplify the inference that Papadopoulos was willing to tell Mueller's team what they wanted to hear.

But then Mueller's team must have encountered the same issue that I eventually discovered, which may be why they replaced "April 26" with "late April." If that is the case, they failed to make the change in another section of their report, which is how we know that they had initially chosen April 26. What made it impossible for Papadopoulos to have met Mifsud on April 26? It was a lie by Papadopoulos that made it impossible, a falsehood that Mueller's team may not have initially detected.

And this takes us back to Trump's Mayflower speech. Papadopoulos had told Mifsud that he was attending the Mayflower speech in Washington, DC, presumably to impress him.[37] In truth, Papadopoulos was not attending the speech. This means that although Papadopoulos was in London on April 26, Mifsud thought that Papadopoulos was either already in Washington or on his way there. This is because Trump's speech took place at 12 p.m. Eastern Time on April 27, which meant that Papadopoulos needed to leave London on April 26 to arrive on time. Some might argue that Papadopoulos could have met Mifsud on April 26 and still had enough time to fly to Washington and attend the Mayflower speech, but this does not align with an email that Papadopoulos sent to Mifsud after the speech.[38] In that email, Papadopoulos states that he will be flying back to London the next day, April 28, and asks if Mifsud has time to meet. There is no mention of having met twenty-four hours earlier. In fact, Mifsud replied that he couldn't meet because he was in Rome, a fact that Papadopoulos would undoubtedly have known had the two men met the previous day. The story of an April 26 meeting had been fabricated by Mueller and his team to shore up the FBI's phony predicate for opening the Crossfire Hurricane investigation.

While much has been made of Mifsud's alleged role as a conduit between the Trump and Russian sides of the purported Trump-Russia collusion scheme, there is no evidence that Mifsud played any such role. Indeed, the timing and content of the emails exchanged between Papadopoulos and Mifsud show that Mifsud had simply tried to help Papadopoulos by connecting him with someone in Russia. This is what Papadopoulos wanted.

Mifsud did not have any high-level contacts, so he put Papadopoulos in touch with Timofeev via email:

> Dear George, Ivan,
>
> As promised I had a long conversation in Moscow with my dear friend Ivan from RIAC about a possible meeting between the two of you. Ivan is ready to meet with you in London (or USA or Moscow). I am putting the two of you in touch to discuss when and where this potential meeting can actually take place.
> Best wishes for your endeavours. . . .
>
> Kind regards,
> Joseph [39]

There was no mention in the email of anything even remotely improper. Mifsud simply helped out a colleague by connecting him with someone in Russia. In typical fashion, Papadopoulos replied to Mifsud and Timofeev, claiming that he could come to Moscow "as part of a wider policy trip to engage with you and officials."[40] It was completely made up. Papadopoulos had no authority to go on such a trip. In fact, on March 21, immediately after Trump's foreign policy team had been named, Trump foreign policy coordinator Sam Clovis emailed everyone on the team to say that it was "OK to say that, yes, you are advising the campaign, but beyond that, we have nothing upon which we wish to comment."[41] In a separate email dated March 24, Clovis made it clear to Papadopoulos that the campaign was "not going to advance anything with Russia until we have everyone on the same page."[42] There is no evidence that that ever happened. Instead, Papadopoulos's continued freelancing and unsolicited outreach to foreign officials became an increasing irritation for the Trump campaign. When Papadopoulos did an unauthorized interview with the *Times of London*,[43] he was immediately admonished by Clovis: "No more discussion with any press until you hear otherwise."[44] On May 19, Papadopoulos was in Athens and asked Clovis if he could convey any messages from the campaign to Greek officials. Clovis replied, "No, just keep your counsel and report back."[45]

Realizing that Clovis was not going to approve his schemes to arrange unsolicited meetings with foreign officials, especially Russian officials, Papadopoulos tried a different approach. On May 21, he contacted Trump's then-convention manager, Paul Manafort, claiming that Russian officials had reached out to Papadopoulos, asking for a meeting with Trump.⁴⁶ There was no such invitation, but Papadopoulos thought he might use the ruse to get Manafort's attention. He was right, but not in the way he had planned. Unbeknownst to Papadopoulos, Manafort forwarded Papadopoulos's email to his aide, Trump campaign official Rick Gates, instructing Gates that "We need someone to communicate that DT is not doing these trips. It should be someone low level in the campaign so as not to send any signal."⁴⁷

After having failed to receive a reply from Manafort, Papadopoulos contacted another individual, campaign manager Corey Lewandowski.⁴⁸ Again, he falsely claimed that Russia had invited Trump to visit Moscow. Lewandowski, who seemed completely unaware of Papadopoulos's activities, responded, "Can you connect with Sam Clovis? He is running point."⁴⁹ Evidently, Lewandowski did not know that Clovis had been Papadopoulos's campaign contact all along. But Papadopoulos did not care. Within a few minutes of receiving Lewandowski's reply, he contacted Clovis, using the same excuse about an invitation from Moscow.⁵⁰ It is not known whether Clovis replied.

Despite these setbacks, Papadopoulos persisted in his efforts to connect the Trump campaign to foreign officials. Next, he contacted Trump campaign official Rick Dearborn, stating that he was going to meet with an Israeli official. This plan also did not work. Dearborn admonished Papadopoulos, "You are not authorized to meet with him by the campaign, nor can you reflect the views of the campaign."⁵¹ On July 14, Clovis reminded Papadopoulos that he needed to use his civilian title when meeting foreign officials: "You can express that you are a Trump supporter and have been named as an advisor on foreign policy, but that you do not speak for the campaign. Keep your nose clean on this stuff."⁵²

As for Mifsud, he and Papadopoulos remained in touch via email throughout the campaign. However, it does not appear that they met again in person. In fact, the documentary record reveals that Papadopoulos and Mifsud had only three in-person meetings: March 14, March 24, and April 12. The first meeting took place in Rome, a week before Papadopoulos was announced as a Trump campaign advisor.⁵³ Papadopoulos was in Rome as part of a delegation from the London Centre of International Law Practice. While Mifsud had long-standing ties to this group, which purports to promote peace through international law and dispute resolution, Papadopoulos had only recently joined the Centre. It has been claimed that this group framed Papadopoulos by falsely tying him, and through him, the Trump Campaign, to Russia, but this claim is demonstrably false. Papadopoulos joined the Centre before he had even talked to the Trump Campaign about the possibility of becoming an advisor. The group's trip to Rome was pre-planned. Papadopoulos's madcap plan to organize a meeting between Trump and Putin was entirely his own scheme.

After Trump won the November 8 election, Mifsud sent Papadopoulos a congratulatory message in which he also reminded him of an upcoming talk at the European Council of Foreign Relations.[54] The Council had invited Papadopoulos via Mifsud on October 19. It is not known whether Papadopoulos ended up giving the talk, but it is notable that Mifsud's post-election email focused on such a benign issue. If Russia had used Mifsud and Papadopoulos to help elect Trump, surely the two men would have had more urgent matters to discuss.

All of these communications reinforce that Papadopoulos was a young man eager to impress and nothing more. Mueller's office was aware of all of Papadopoulos's emails. In fact, they were compiled for Mueller's case against Papadopoulos. Despite knowing the truth, Mueller's office told the public a very different story, suggesting that Papadopoulos and Mifsud were intermediaries in a supposed scheme that connected the Trump campaign with the Kremlin.

In the days after Papadopoulos entered into a plea deal with Mueller's office in October 2017, Mifsud gave two interviews. The first was given to the Italian newspaper *La Repubblica*.[55] When asked whether he had told Papadopoulos about Russian "dirt" on Hillary Clinton, Mifsud replied: "This is nonsense. Papadopoulos doesn't tell the truth. The only thing I did was to facilitate contacts between official and unofficial sources to resolve a crisis. It is usual business everywhere. I put think tanks in contact, groups of experts with other groups of experts." Mifsud added: "I strongly deny any discussion of mine about secrets concerning Hillary Clinton. I swear it on my daughter. I don't know anyone belonging to the Russian government: the only Russian I know is Ivan Timofeev." Mifsud also spoke to *The Telegraph* newspaper. When he was asked whether he had told Papadopoulos that the Russians had "dirt" on Hillary Clinton, Mifsud replied: "absolutely this is not true."[56]

Perhaps the most significant evidence that Mifsud did not tell Papadopoulos anything of significance is the absence of a reaction from Papadopoulos. Sherlock Holmes would call it "the dog that didn't bark." Papadopoulos was constantly reaching out to Trump campaign officials to demonstrate his supposed value to the campaign. But although he bragged about being connected to various foreign dignitaries, he did not boast about

Mifsud, let alone about what Mifsud supposedly told him about Hillary Clinton's emails. Lead investigator Peter Strzok claimed in his 2020 book that the dog didn't bark, either because Papadopoulos did not want to put this information in writing or because he wanted to keep it secret "as leverage to increase the campaign's interest in him."[57] These excuses are laughable, bordering on preposterous. First, there is no evidence that Papadopoulos ever informed the campaign about stolen emails, either orally or in writing. In fact, there isn't even a suggestion that this happened. Second, Papadopoulos could not have used the stolen email story as leverage if he was the only one who knew about it.

In truth, it is simply not believable that a known self-promoter like Papadopoulos would not have told someone on the campaign about such explosive information if he had received it. It is even less believable that Papadopoulos would have bragged about a secret message from Russia to a diplomat in London that he had never met before but not said a word to anyone on the campaign. In contrast, it is very plausible that Papadopoulos informed the foreign diplomat, Downer, about what he had seen on Fox News the night before. If that were the case, he would not have needed to inform the campaign because everyone on the campaign watched Fox News without needing to be reminded by Papadopoulos. In fact, after being sentenced in September 2018, Papadopoulos admitted to CNN's Jake Tapper that Mifsud "was simply repeating gossip and rumors . . . I never heard something that wasn't already rumored to be."[58] That should have been the end of the false narrative that Papadopoulos had been offered Hillary Clinton's emails, but it wasn't. The Mueller Report, which was published eight months after Papadopoulos's CNN interview, maintained that Papadopoulos had indeed been offered secret information.

Another aspect of the deceptions spun by Mueller's office regarding Mifsud that has not received much attention is that the first time Papadopoulos ever mentioned the term "dirt" or, for that matter, Hillary Clinton's emails, was in an FBI interview in January 2017.[59] The story told by the media, and the general perception among the public, is that Papadopoulos had said these things during the campaign. In fact, Papadopoulos never mentioned dirt or emails to Downer, or to anyone else. Although the full transcript of Papadopoulos's January 2017 FBI interview has never been released, Papadopoulos's sentencing memorandum—this is the document that outlined Mueller's recommendation on what Papadopoulos's penalty should be—reveals that Papadopoulos was pressured by FBI agents to come up with a scapegoat. As Mueller's office acknowledged, Papadopoulos was asked a "series of specific questions about when the defendant first learned about Russia's disclosure of information related to the campaign and whether the defendant had ever 'received any information or anything like that from a [] [*sic*] Russian government official.'"⁶⁰ At first, and despite intense pressure from the FBI, Papadopoulos insisted that no one had told him about Hillary Clinton's emails. Instead of Papadopoulos trying to hide something, it appears as if he simply did not know what the FBI was talking about. After additional pressure was brought to bear, Papadopoulos eventually mentioned Mifsud but insisted that he had met Mifsud before joining the Trump campaign. Finally, Papadopoulos, who at this point must have started doubting his own sanity, told the FBI what they wanted to hear: that Mifsud had told him about the emails. Foolishly, Papadopoulos thought that by falsely implicating Mifsud, his problems would go away. Instead, they became a lot worse.

Mueller eventually charged Papadopoulos with lying about when he first met Mifsud. Papadopoulos claimed it was before he joined the Trump campaign, but according to Mueller, it was after. The truth is that Papadopoulos had his interview with Clovis about joining the campaign on March 7, 2016,⁶¹ but he was not announced as a campaign advisor until two weeks later, on March 21.⁶² Furthermore, Papadopoulos did not meet anyone from the campaign until March 31.⁶³ Papadopoulos met Mifsud for the first time on March 14, right in the middle of the process of joining the campaign.⁶⁴ In other words, Papadopoulos's skepticism of the theory that the FBI was trying to implant in his head was well-founded. How could Mifsud have played the role of a Russian intermediary in giving Papadopoulos secret information if they met before it was publicly known that Papadopoulos was going to join the Trump campaign? It was not possible.

It was this realization, specifically the fact that Papadopoulos had pleaded guilty to a crime he did not commit, that was my personal gateway into Russiagate. It simply did not make any sense. That is when I started searching the internet to see if anyone else had encountered this anomaly, which is how I first met Stephen McIntyre. Both of us had independently stumbled into the same issue. When we met a few weeks later, we spent several hours brainstorming various theories as to why Papadopoulos would admit to a crime of which he was not guilty.

Stephen and I could see how perplexing the situation must have been from Papadopoulos's point of view. He did not know that Downer had misinterpreted something Papadopoulos had said nine months earlier. To Papadopoulos, it had been a completely innocuous meeting that he had probably long forgotten about. He also did not know that Downer had gone to the FBI. He did not even know that the FBI interview was about Downer. In contrast, he did know that the media had embarked on a massive Russia collusion push. The Steele dossier had just been published. There were smear stories about Michael Flynn. Sergei Millian was being disparaged by the *Wall Street Journal* as the link between Trump and the Kremlin. And suddenly, the FBI was at his house, asking him questions that implied he was part of a purported Trump-Russia collusion plot. Given this frame of reference, it is perhaps not surprising that Papadopoulos scapegoated Mifsud.

Incidentally, Papadopoulos would have been much better off if he had just listened to his mother, who had answered the door when the FBI came calling. She told her son not to answer any questions. But he did not listen, a fact which Peter Strzok and an unnamed FBI agent were soon snickering about in their text messages. Right after the interview, the agent texted Strzok: "His mom wasn't going to let him go to the FBI office to talk, but he went anyway. :-)," to which Strzok responded: "That's what you get for not listening to your mom . . . ;)."[65]

In truth, Mifsud was not a conduit for the Russian government. He was a wandering professor who, like Papadopoulos, lived and worked through networking. There are conference circuits within academia that are filled with people like Mifsud. Not all academics are part of these networks, but some are incredibly prolific. The circuit is their workplace. Mifsud was in that group. I spent some time on the arbitration conference circuit but quickly found it too tiresome. You move from conference to conference, traveling from London to Brussels to Dubai and back to London, often sharing the stage with the same individuals. You are constantly networking and seeking consulting opportunities to supplement your academic income. As if to underline this point, when the FBI asked Mifsud whether he had told Papadopoulos about Hillary Clinton's emails, Mifsud was in Washington, DC for one of the conferences on his circuit. The story that he told the FBI was completely unremarkable. He had met Papadopoulos through the London Centre of International Law Practice, introduced Papadopoulos to Timofeev, and confirmed that he had no prior knowledge that Russia was in possession of DNC emails.[66] It's notable that the FBI asked Mifsud about the DNC's emails instead of Hillary Clinton's emails, which had been their initial story. It appears as if the FBI conveniently changed their story after the event, particularly when it became evident that no one had Clinton's emails, or that, in any case, those emails never surfaced.

While his activities were completely routine and consistent with those of a roving academic, there is one oddity about Mifsud that ought to be mentioned. Up until the announcement by Mueller's office on October 30, 2017, of Papadopoulos's plea deal with Mueller, Mifsud contentedly lived his life on the conference circuit. He attended conferences across the globe, including one in Washington, DC, where he would hardly have traveled voluntarily if he had been a Russian agent who manipulated the 2016 election in favor of Trump. But that life came to an abrupt end after October 2017. Mifsud stopped participating in the conference circuit and withdrew from public life. This has been suggested by some to be a sign of guilt. But that is nonsense. If he had been guilty of anything, he would have disappeared on February 11, 2017, immediately after the FBI interrogated him about whether he had made an offer to Papadopoulos involving stolen emails from Russia. But he did not. He continued to be highly visible. But nine months later Papadopoulos made his plea deal, and Mifsud was caught in a bind. He could continue his public life, but that would mean getting dragged down into the mud. It was his word against that of Papadopoulos. But, as we have seen, the entire foundation of the fraudulent Crossfire Hurricane investigation was based on Papadopoulos having been told about Clinton's stolen emails. The FBI, Mueller, and everyone else who participated in the fraud needed that story to be true, and it could only be true if Mifsud had told Papadopoulos about stolen emails. There was no way Mifsud could win.

It was hopeless, and Mifsud chose to lie low. He chose wisely. Other innocent bystanders had their lives ruined by Mueller's office. Businessman Ekim Alptekin spent millions of dollars on legal fees but still got indicted by Mueller for allegedly conspiring to act as an agent of a foreign government.[67] The only reason why Alptekin got in Mueller's crosshairs was that he had once hired Michael Flynn's consulting firm. Alptekin's situation had nothing to do with Russia. But that did not stop Mueller's team, who wanted to use Alptekin to go after Flynn, and ultimately Trump. Many others were dragged through the mud at huge personal expense, as well as at the expense of their liberty. Most of those were not able to lie low because they lived in the United States and were at the mercy of Mueller's mob. Political strategist Michael Caputo, who had helped the Trump campaign with communications, was targeted by Mueller because he had lived in Russia in the 1990s.[68] He had done nothing wrong and was never charged with anything, but by the end of the Mueller inquisition in 2019, his health and finances were ruined.

The nefarious behavior did not start with Mueller's office. While the Papadopoulos emails portray him as a young man who was completely out of his depth, the FBI could have assessed the insignificance of Downer's tip without any knowledge of these emails. As previously noted, the simple fact of the matter was that Papadopoulos and Downer met before many of the DNC's emails, which ended up with WikiLeaks, had been written. That should have been the end of the inquiry. The fact that Downer's contemporaneous statement, which the FBI had, explicitly stated that Papadopoulos may have simply been discussing publicly available information, coupled with the fact that Fox News had reported the same information the night before Papadopoulos met Downer, were the final pieces of evidence that should have ended any conspiracy investigation before it even started. But it did not. The FBI assumed the worst, and when the facts did not pan out that way, they just made things up.

As would become a disturbing pattern in the months and years ahead, the FBI disregarded the facts and instead forged ahead with only one goal. Like a dog with a bone, they were singularly focused on getting Trump.

After Downer's tip reached FBI leadership, Deputy Director Andrew McCabe instructed the counterespionage chief, Peter Strzok, to initiate the Crossfire Hurricane investigation into the alleged Trump-Russia collusion. McCabe would later also open an investigation into Trump himself.[69] The fact that FBI leadership orchestrated the initiation of Crossfire Hurricane is perfectly exemplified by the formal document used to initiate investigations. This document, known as an electronic communication in FBI terminology, was authored, approved, and sent by Strzok himself.[70]

Immediately after opening the investigation, Strzok flew to London to interview Downer. It did not seem to have occurred to FBI leadership that perhaps they ought to have talked to Downer first and opened their investigation later. In any case, if Strzok did not already realize it, the interview would have made it abundantly clear that whatever Downer was talking about, it could not have had any relevance to the alleged hacking of the DNC. The dates and timeline of Downer's story simply did not match the allegation that Papadopoulos had advance knowledge of the WikiLeaks email release. But whereas an honest law enforcement officer would have shut down the investigation, Strzok had other plans in mind. Confronted with the fact that Downer's account did not match the allegation that Trump or his campaign knew anything about the WikiLeaks emails, Strzok fabricated a false story about Downer.

Downer visited the US embassy in London on July 26, 2016, after reading news reports about the alleged hacking, which the Clinton campaign had attributed to Russia. The Clinton campaign further claimed that Russia had hacked the emails to assist Trump in getting elected. It was a preposterous allegation. True to his style, the very next day, Trump ridiculed the accusations with an off-the-cuff joke at an impromptu press conference at his Doral golf club in Miami: "Russia, if you're listening, I hope you're able to find the 30,000 emails that are missing," Trump said. "I think you will probably be rewarded mightily by our press."[71]

But in a stunning act of dishonesty, the media reported that Trump had been serious. The statement was twisted and used as the foundation for insinuations of collusion with Russia.[72] *Politico* reported: "Trump urges Russia to hack Clinton's email."[73] Trump had done no such thing. Instead, he had made a sarcastic remark about the Clinton campaign's smear against him. But by that point, the media had stopped caring about the truth. The deceptive reporting provided Strzok with a perfect cover story. The true story, which was that Downer came forward after hearing about the alleged hacking of the DNC, was weak because the timelines didn't match. Additionally, it meant that Downer's report to the US embassy had not been triggered by anything that Papadopoulos said, but instead had been triggered by the Clinton campaign's smear. Strzok knew that this was not a solid basis for opening an investigation, so he created a new narrative out of thin air. Strzok falsely claimed that Downer came forward after he heard Trump's "Russia, if you're listening" remark on July 27. Strzok's lie did not resolve the problem that Papadopoulos could not have known about emails that hadn't yet been written, but it redirected the attention away from Clinton and toward Trump. Strzok's false narrative also implied that Downer believed Trump was colluding with Russia. In truth, Downer has steadfastly maintained that this was not what he thought, and that Papadopoulos never even suggested any such thing.[74]

Strzok injected this lie wherever he could, including during briefings at the Department of Justice (DOJ).[75] So cocky was Strzok that he memorialized his lie in his 2020 book, where he wrote that "[i]n Downer's recounting, Trump's words jarred his memory of a series of conversations months earlier."[76] Not only had he fabricated the story, but he was also falsely attributing his own lie to Downer. On September 6, 2020, Strzok repeated his lie once again, this time to CBS's national security correspondent, David Martin.[77] As appears to be typical for members of the media, Martin appeared to be clueless about the facts and did not challenge Strzok. But I did. I immediately tweeted at Martin and CBS, pointing out that Downer had provided his tip before Trump spoke.[78] A few days later, Strzok nonchalantly conceded that his story was not true: "So, I got that wrong."[79] Strzok blamed the purported error on not having his notes when he wrote his book. That too was a lie. Strzok was now lying about lying.

We know from notes taken during a briefing that Strzok gave to the DOJ on February 16, 2017, that he told the department the exact same falsehood he later included in his book.[80] The lie was repeated in a March 6, 2017 briefing for the then-acting attorney general.[81] Trump associates such as Flynn, Papadopoulos, and Stone were prosecuted for lying. Despite being caught red-handed, Peter Strzok has faced no consequences. Instead of facing justice for a highly significant lie that strikes at the core of the justification for initiating the Crossfire Hurricane investigation, he has been rewarded with a position as a commentator on MSNBC.

But the lies did not stop with Trump's quip about WikiLeaks. Strzok further claimed in his 2020 book that, according to Downer's account of his meeting with Papadopoulos, "the Russian government had offered to assist the Trump campaign through a coordinated release of material."[82] Once again, the problem is that Downer did not say this. In fact, we know of at least three instances where Downer refuted the false narrative that Papadopoulos had mentioned collusion. First, the contemporaneous note that Downer's colleague, Erika Thompson, had written about their meeting with Papadopoulos stated that Papadopoulos had "suggested the Trump team had received some kind of suggestion from Russia that it could assist this process with the anonymous release of information during the campaign that would be damaging to Mrs[.] Clinton (and President Obama)."[83] It is not known why Papadopoulos would have said such a thing, but it may have been part of his usual method of feigning importance and connections, as he did with his false claims about having met the Russian ambassador in the United Kingdom, as well as Putin's niece. However, even if we assume that Papadopoulos was not bragging, a "suggestion of a suggestion" does not amount to a "coordinated release of material." What is more, the contemporaneous note does not include any mention of the hacking of the DNC or even of any emails. It does, however, claim that the information Papadopoulos allegedly provided was damaging to both Hillary Clinton and President Obama. That should have been another red flag that whatever Papadopoulos was talking about had nothing to do with the alleged hacking of the DNC. Second, Downer told Strzok on August 2, 2016 that he "did not get the sense Papadopoulos was the middle-man to coordinate with the

How Did Crossfire Hurricane Begin?

Russians."[84] Third, Downer confirmed in 2019 that there "was no suggestion that there was collusion between Donald Trump or between Donald Trump's campaign and the Russians."[85] Fourth, when Downer spoke to Durham in 2019, he acknowledged that the wording of the original contemporaneous note, which had been drafted by his assistant, was not phrasing he would have chosen. Downer again confirmed that "Papadopoulos made no mention of Clinton emails, dirt or any specific approach by the Russian government to the Trump campaign team with an offer or suggestion of providing assistance." According to Downer, Papadopoulos simply stated, "the Russians have information, and that was all."[86]

While we only have access to some snippets of what Downer told Strzok during their meeting in London on August 2, 2016, it is unlikely to have been significantly different from what he has consistently stated since then. In any case, regardless of the exact words Downer might have used, Strzok faced an insurmountable obstacle. Papadopoulos, as a matter of logic, could not have known anything about hacked emails that had not yet been written.

However, Strzok was too engrossed in his anti-Trump agenda to heed logic. Instead of accurately portraying Downer's tip, Strzok fabricated a misleading narrative, which led to an escalation in the investigation. Subsequently, the focus shifted from Papadopoulos to include Trump campaign manager Paul Manafort, campaign advisor Michael Flynn, and campaign aide Carter Page. The significant increase in intensity, stemming from a flimsy tip, lacked any justifiable rationale. Moreover, even if the tip had some validity, it pertained solely to Papadopoulos.

Strzok's seemingly reckless and irrational actions can only be understood in the context of what was going on at FBI headquarters and between Strzok and his FBI colleague Lisa Page in the weeks before Downer came forward. In truth, the FBI's investigation of Trump began before the opening of Crossfire Hurricane on July 31, 2016. As we would later learn from a text message exchanged between Strzok and his alleged mistress, Lisa Page, who was counsel to FBI Deputy Director Andrew McCabe, the FBI had an open investigation into Trump before anyone in the FBI had heard of Alexander Downer. On July 28, Strzok texted Page about "our open CI [counterintelligence] investigations relating to Trump's Russian connections."[87] The official document used to open the Crossfire Hurricane investigation on July 31 states that the investigation was initiated based on information that the FBI received on July 29. That information was Downer's tip. Thus, Strzok's reference to an open counterintelligence investigation before July 29 conflicts with the official opening of the probe. To date, the

FBI has not acknowledged the existence of a secret investigation into Trump that occurred before both the official commencement of the investigation and the official predicate—Downer's tip—for initiating the investigation. Soon after Crossfire Hurricane was officially opened, Page texted Strzok: "Trump's not ever going to become president, right? Right?!" Strzok replied: "No. No he's not. We'll stop it."[88]

The question remains: What prompted the initial Trump investigation that Strzok and Page discussed in their text messages? There are several possibilities. Steele had been passing his reports to the FBI since early July. While it remains unclear who dealt with those reports and at what level, they present one possible reason why there may have been an unofficial investigation before Crossfire Hurricane was initiated. There is also the fact that the FBI had been investigating Carter Page since April 2016 "based on his continued contacts with Russian intelligence officers."[89] Curiously, that investigation opened shortly after Trump identified Carter Page as one of his five foreign policy advisers.[90] Perhaps in his text message to Lisa Page, Strzok meant the Carter Page investigation. One problem with that interpretation is that the alleged contacts that Page had with Russian intelligence officers predated his involvement with the Trump campaign by several years. Another problem is the fact that the Horowitz Report states that "there was limited investigative activity" in the Page matter.[91] Another possibility is the Paul Manafort investigation, which was also ongoing. The DOJ's Money Laundering and Asset Recovery Section had been investigating Trump's then-campaign manager since at least 2014.[92] The investigation focused on Manafort's role as a lobbyist for the political party of Viktor Yanukovych, the former president of Ukraine who was ousted in the US-backed coup in 2014. However, since this investigation was initiated before Manafort's involvement in the Trump campaign by at least two years, it is improbable that Strzok was specifically alluding to the Manafort investigation when he mentioned "our open CI [counterintelligence] investigations relating to Trump's Russian connections." Both the Page and Manafort investigations were merged into Crossfire Hurricane and later incorporated into Mueller's special counsel investigation.

The most straightforward explanation for Strzok's acknowledgment that there were open counterintelligence investigations appears to be a combination of all the factors mentioned. One strong hint supporting this conclusion is that Crossfire Hurricane was initiated as an "enterprise investigation."[93] Enterprise investigation is a term of art in the FBI's Domestic Investigations and Operations Guide.[94] The threshold for opening such investigations is very high and requires an "articulable factual basis" that an organization is engaged in a pattern of racketeering, terrorism, or furthering political goals through violence. The official predication of the Crossfire Hurricane investigation, based on hearsay regarding a "suggestion of a suggestion" from Papadopoulos, does not meet this standard. While FBI leadership threw out the rulebook when opening Crossfire Hurricane, they may have chosen to initiate an enterprise investigation to consolidate all four parts—namely, the Steele dossier, Manafort, Page, and Papadopoulos—under one umbrella. In other words, when Downer's tip about Papadopoulos arrived on July 29, FBI leadership viewed it as an opportunity to formalize and streamline their previously undisclosed investigations of the Trump campaign.

Contrary to the conclusions reached in the Horowitz Report, the opening of Crossfire Hurricane on July 31 was not the beginning of the investigation; it was the formalization of an investigation that was already in full swing, albeit unofficially. It did not matter how threadbare Downer's tip was or that it fell apart under even minimal scrutiny. FBI leadership used Downer as a pretext to initiate an official investigation and to conceal the existence of a prior unofficial investigation.

CHAPTER 10

Spying on the Trump Campaign

Immediately after Strzok formally opened the Crossfire Hurricane investigation, he and FBI supervisory special agent Joe Pientka flew to London to talk to Downer. Pientka was Strzok's sidekick who later accompanied Strzok to the White House ambush interview of Michael Flynn. The London trip was a facade. Whatever Downer had told them would not change the path that Comey, McCabe, and Strzok had embarked on—the path to trip up Trump. If they had a genuine interest in listening to what Downer had to say, they wouldn't have initiated a full enterprise investigation into a presidential campaign without even speaking to him first. At the time Crossfire Hurricane was initiated, FBI leadership had only received a quadruple hearsay account that originated with Papadopoulos and passed from Downer to Dibble and Haspel, then to an FBI agent, and ultimately to FBI leadership.

To make matters worse, the original story was completely insignificant. Downer later told an Australian journalist that Papadopoulos had mentioned that "he thought the Russians might release information that could be damaging to Hillary Clinton's campaign at some stage before the election."[1] This was merely a watered-down version of what many people were speculating about at the time. Yet, FBI leadership turned an innocuous encounter into a pernicious plot by suggesting that Papadopoulos had learned about stolen emails that Russia and the Trump campaign were planning to release. The narrative was entirely fabricated by FBI leadership.

An early indication that the narrative was fabricated and that the FBI was aware of this was that neither Strzok nor anyone else bothered to investigate how Papadopoulos might have obtained such sensitive information.

If he had indeed been aware that Russia had acquired Hillary Clinton's emails, it would have constituted a pressing national security concern requiring prompt intervention. However, no such action was taken. As discussed in the previous chapter, Mueller's special counsel office was forced to retrospectively do what the FBI had not done; i.e., construct a narrative explaining how Papadopoulos was supposed to have learned about Russia having Clinton's emails. But that was years later when the needs were different. Mueller's task was to retroactively legitimize what the FBI had done. In 2016, the FBI had a very different task, which was to keep the investigation going as long as possible in order to maximize the chances of tripping up Trump. For this reason, the FBI did not bother to interview Papadopoulos in 2016, when he would very likely have told them that he only shared with Downer what he had heard on Fox News the night before. FBI leadership could not afford to have him say that and risk losing their false investigative predicate just as the investigation was getting started. In fact, they only interviewed Papadopoulos six months later, on January 27, 2017, when the investigation was well established. But even then, they never asked him directly about Downer.

Instead of treating the Papadopoulos matter as a national security crisis, the FBI instructed an undercover operative to deceive him. The purpose was not to find out what he knew—after all, they knew that he knew nothing—but to make him say things that could be used against Trump. The operative in question was Stefan Halper, a foreign policy scholar who had served in the Nixon and Reagan administrations. Allegedly, Halper has also conducted a questionable opposition research campaign against then-President Jimmy Carter.[2] As discussed in an earlier chapter, the FBI assigned Halper to entice Papadopoulos to London by offering him $3,000 to write a paper. While in London, the plan was to get Papadopoulos drunk with the assistance of a female agent who claimed to be Halper's assistant. The agent introduced herself as Azra Turk, but no such person exists. One of the first things that became apparent when the transcript of Halper's secret recording of Papadopoulos was released in March 2020 was that Halper did not ask Papadopoulos about Downer.[3] Just as with Papadopoulos's FBI interview in 2017, there was no effort to find out what Papadopoulos had allegedly told Downer. Instead, Halper's questions were designed to entrap Papadopoulos by coaxing him into saying things that the FBI could distort. For instance, Halper tried to get Papadopoulos to comment on hypothetical scenarios, such as whether it would be advantageous if Russia provided the Trump campaign with information that could be used against Hillary

Clinton. Papadopoulos did not take the bait. Instead, he said that it would be illegal, much to the disappointment of FBI agents who were listening in on the conversation.

Incredibly, since Papadopoulos had not said anything that could be manipulated and utilized against him or Trump, the FBI chose to conceal the transcript of his exchanges with Halper. But this was not the FBI's choice to make. Every word that Papadopoulos uttered in the thirty-seven-page transcript was exculpatory. This meant that the FBI had a duty to inform the Foreign Intelligence Surveillance Court (FISC) of the transcript when they sought the Carter Page warrant. When Inspector General Horowitz asked why this had not happened, the FBI's excuse was that Papadopoulos's "response to the direct questions seemed weird" to the Crossfire Hurricane team because it "seemed rehearsed and almost rote."[4] They also claimed that Papadopoulos gave "a canned answer, which he was probably prepped to say when asked" and that he had "been coached by a legal team." The FBI was trying to have it both ways. If Papadopoulos had said something that could be twisted and used against Trump, they would have immediately pounced on it. But since he only said exculpatory things, they dismissed it as being rehearsed. It was a lose-lose situation for Papadopoulos and Trump.

But even if the FBI truly believed that Papadopoulos had been coached, and there is no indication in the transcript that this was the case, they still had a duty to inform the FISC. The FBI never gave the FISC an opportunity to make its own assessment. What is more, it appears that after Papadopoulos was arrested in July 2017 for an alleged innocuous lie about when he first met Joseph Mifsud, the entire Halper saga was concealed from Papadopoulos and his legal team. Given the exculpatory nature of his statements, Mueller was under a duty to share the transcripts with Papadopoulos's lawyers before Papadopoulos was pressured into pleading guilty. But this did not happen. In fact, when Papadopoulos pleaded guilty to lying about Mifsud in October 2017, he was still blissfully unaware that there had even been an attempt to entrap him. For all he knew, Stefan Halper was a bona fide academic who genuinely wanted to seek his input on international affairs. It wasn't until March 2018 that, with the help of journalist Chuck Ross, Papadopoulos was able to start putting the pieces together.[5] By that point, it had become known that Halper had also targeted Carter Page, which made Papadopoulos recall his own interactions with Halper. The bottom line is that Papadopoulos was pressured into pleading guilty to trivial matters without ever knowing that he had been subjected to an FBI entrapment scheme.

But the Halper plot was not the only entrapment scheme to which Papadopoulos was subjected. There was another scheme that not even Papadopoulos knew about until April 2020 when a whopping 173 pages' worth of transcripts and surveillance photos were released.[6] The transcripts involved Papadopoulos and an old college friend of his. As soon as the transcripts were released, Walkafyre from our research group immediately identified the friend as Jeffrey Wiseman. Walkafyre remembered that some of the exchanges described in the transcript aligned with what Papadopoulos had written in his 2019 book, *Deep State Target: How I Got Caught in the Crosshairs of the Plot to Bring Down President Trump*.[7] In his book, Papadopoulos recalls Wiseman texting him to alert him that the FBI had questioned Wiseman about Papadopoulos. Wiseman also mentioned that the FBI knew that the two of them had been at a casino. The trip to the casino was a giveaway as part of the FBI's secret recording of Papadopoulos took place at a casino.

That's how we knew who the FBI's source was. When Wiseman informed Papadopoulos about the FBI's inquiries, Wiseman was attempting to create a decoy. Papadopoulos believed him. Incredibly, when he wrote his book, which was after he pleaded guilty and served his sentence, Papadopoulos still had no idea that Wiseman had spied on him at the behest of the FBI. As with the Halper entrapment scheme, Papadopoulos should have been informed about the Wiseman scheme before being pressured into pleading guilty. Also, just as with the Halper scheme, Wiseman had not been instructed to talk about Downer. For all we know, Wiseman may not even have been told about Downer. Instead, the plan appears to have been to get Papadopoulos to brag or say things that could be used against Trump. Even though Papadopoulos spent far more time with Wiseman than with Halper, and even though their interactions were far more casual, Papadopoulos did not utter a single word that the FBI could use against him or Trump.

Wiseman even attempted another approach to encourage Papadopoulos to say something that could be manipulated and exaggerated by FBI leadership. Wiseman pretended to endorse the notion that Russia was heavily involved in this election, hoping that Papadopoulos would agree. Papadopoulos pushed back, stating, "That's all bullshit" and "conspiracy theories." Papadopoulos went on to explain that no one knew who hacked the Democratic National Committee's (DNC) emails, suggesting that it could have been "the Chinese, could be the Iranians, it could be some Bernie [Sanders] supporters."[8]

Papadopoulos was so unsuspecting that during the course of one afternoon, the two men used the words "fuck" and "fucking" over 430 times, as meticulously documented in the FBI's transcript. Papadopoulos also made disparaging remarks about Trump supporters, once again confirming that he was perfectly at ease talking to his old friend Wiseman. Papadopoulos was completely unguarded and unsuspecting, yet he said nothing noteworthy. Once again, the FBI concealed the entire entrapment scheme when it should have informed the FISC about it, specifically that Papadopoulos's interactions with Wiseman were both innocuous and exculpatory.

Whatever was thrown at him at the FBI's behest, Papadopoulos would not bite. At no point did the FBI's undercover operatives Halper and Wiseman ask Papadopoulos about his conversation with Downer. All their efforts were based on indirect allusions and innuendo. If they had asked him, he would probably have told them that whatever he told Downer was just something he had heard on Fox News. Yet, despite never having been given an opportunity to directly confront the false accusation against him, everything that Papadopoulos told the operatives was exculpatory. The obvious question is why Papadopoulos would spill the beans about Russia collusion in a half-hour meeting with a foreign diplomat whom he had never met but say absolutely nothing of the sort while spending an entire day with an old friend?

Just as bad as the failure to inform Papadopoulos of the mountains of exculpatory evidence was the failure to inform the FISC. The court operates on an ex parte basis. The Latin phrase "ex parte," which means "from the party," is legal terminology used when the court only hears one side of the story. In the case of the FISC, this represents the FBI's perspective. Naturally, if the subject of a FISA warrant application were aware of being targeted, they might begin to dispose of the evidence. This makes sense, but the ability to use ex parte proceedings comes with an obligation to present all facts, including those that are unfavorable to a warrant application. In the case of Carter Page, this was not done. Specifically, the Page FISA warrant application claimed that the investigation had started with Papadopoulos—falsely, as explained in the previous chapter. This very fact meant that the FBI had a duty to tell the court everything about Papadopoulos, including his numerous exculpatory statements.

It was not enough to claim to have privately concluded, as the FBI later informed Inspector General Horowitz, that Papadopoulos had been coached. That was for the court to decide. Not only did the FBI keep the court in the dark, but they also escalated their actions by reapplying for three additional FISA warrants against Page. Each time they falsely claimed that during his meeting with Downer, Papadopoulos had disclosed the existence of a secret plot and that Page was the campaign's connection to the Russian side in this alleged scheme. Even if we were to assume, for argument's sake, that Papadopoulos had disclosed the existence of a plot—something that is emphatically denied by Downer—there was never any evidence of any kind that Page had anything to do with such a supposed plot. And yet, that is what FBI leadership secretly told a federal court, knowing that, due to the way FISA warrant applications are administered, only the judge would have access to their fabricated accusations, making it impossible for anyone else to see or contest them.

Halper was also assigned to spy on Carter Page. This was not spying authorized by the FISC but in addition to the FISA warrant, which only became active in late October 2016. Unlike the clumsy plan the FBI had hatched to entrap Papadopoulos, this time they came up with a more cautious approach: Halper's task was to befriend Page with the aim of eliciting potentially incriminating statements from him. Meanwhile, the FBI's surveillance team would be recording their conversations. However, once more, the operation resulted in a total failure for the FBI. Page did not say anything significant. Despite this, the FBI breathlessly asserted to the FISC that Page had hinted at an "October Surprise" in his discussions with Halper. In truth, that was nothing out of the ordinary; every presidential campaign has an October Surprise. In 2016, there was the disclosure of Trump's *Access Hollywood* tape and the release of Clinton campaign chief John Podesta's emails. In 2020, revelations emerged indicating that during his tenure as vice president, Joe Biden had encounters with Ukrainian business associates of his son, Hunter Biden, as evidenced by data retrieved from Hunter's abandoned laptop. This was something Biden had always denied. In Carter Page's case, the conversation about an October Surprise was academic. Halper and Page were comparing the 1980 October Surprise, an allegation that Ronald Reagan's campaign had made a secret deal with Iran to delay the release of American hostages until after the election, to a potential 2016 October Surprise. Page also jokingly added that he would not mind if the "conspiracy theory" about Hillary Clinton's 33,000 missing emails turned out to be part of the next email dump. The FBI falsely informed the FISC that this implied Page had prior knowledge of an upcoming email leak. In fact, anyone who was remotely interested in politics was having conversations about Clinton's missing emails resurfacing.

When the Halper-Page transcripts were declassified in 2021, they revealed that while Page was blissfully unaware of being spied on, he enjoyed sharing his stories with Halper.[9] Most of those stories were about completely irrelevant matters, such as a recent trip to South Africa. An honest reading of the transcripts leaves one with the distinct impression that Page genuinely thought of Halper as a friend. Such was the cruelty of the FBI's scheme. Despite Halper's attempts to get Page to say something that could be twisted and used against Trump, Page did not make any such statements. When asked about Trump campaign manager Paul Manafort, Page told Halper that he had "literally never met" Manafort, that he had "never said one word to him," and that Manafort had not responded to any of Page's emails. As with Papadopoulos, the exculpatory evidence of Halper's interactions with Page was not shared with the FISC.

As if two failed entrapment operations were not enough, Halper was also tasked with spying on Trump's foreign policy coordinator, Sam Clovis. Clovis was not under formal investigation, but the FBI decided to target him anyway. Their cover story was the most audacious one yet. Halper was supposed to pretend to be interested in joining the Trump campaign.[10] Nothing came of the operation. Clovis did not divulge any incriminating secrets because there were no such secrets. Years later, when Clovis found out that Halper had been sent by the FBI to spy on him, he angrily exclaimed that the FBI attempted to compromise the Trump campaign: "What they tried to do was nothing short of attempting to overturn the results of a duly conducted election, and that is a despicable, shameful set of events."[11] In truth, it was even worse than that. Halper spoke to Clovis on September 1, 2016, under the pretense of wanting to help the Trump campaign. The timing is notable as the campaign had just entered the final stretch. Despite this, the FBI tasked Halper with asking Clovis about highly sensitive information— information that would have been very valuable to the Clinton campaign. For instance, mirroring his conversation with Page, Halper asked Clovis whether the Trump campaign was planning an October Surprise.[12] Halper also queried Clovis about "Trump's immigration strategy, efforts to reach out to minority groups and the impact of those efforts, and the campaign's strategies for responding to questions about Trump's decision not to release his tax returns."[13] Halper even got Clovis to reveal the "internal structure, organization, and functioning of the Trump campaign."[14]

Imagine the media outcry if the FBI, under President Trump, had sent an undercover operative to gather information about the Biden campaign's internal strategies, pretending to offer assistance to Biden. It would have been the scandal of the decade, and yet hardly anyone knows that the FBI under Obama did exactly that to Trump.

Although all three entrapment operations had turned out to be failures, the FBI concealed both their existence and the copious amount of exculpatory information they received. The FISC never found out about these facts officially. The FBI also concealed that Halper's fourth operation, if it can be called that, proved to be completely bogus. Halper had reported to the FBI that Cambridge historian Svetlana Lokhova was purportedly engaged in a romantic relationship with General Michael Flynn.[15] The story was completely false, a fact that the FBI acknowledged when they shut down the investigation into Flynn on January 4, 2017.[16] FBI Director Comey later reopened the case against Flynn out of animosity toward Trump, famously boasting that he had dispatched two agents, Peter Strzok and Joe Pientka, to the White House to ensnare Flynn. In doing so, Comey had circumvented all protocols and later claimed that this was something he "probably wouldn't have done or maybe gotten away with in a more organized administration."[17]

However, regardless of Comey's actions, nothing changes the fact that Lokhova was an entirely innocent bystander. She, like Sergei Millian, was targeted solely because she had a Russian name, spoke with a Russian accent, and had attended a dinner function in 2014 where Flynn happened to be a guest of honor in his capacity as the director of the Defense Intelligence Agency at that time. Yet, even though, as per its own document closing the Flynn investigation on January 4, 2017, the FBI knew that Halper's smears against Lokhova were baseless, they never informed the FISC of any of this. This omission was doubly bad because if it had been disclosed that the story about Lokhova and Flynn was bogus, it would have destroyed Halper's credibility and, thus, anything else he claimed.

Right from the start of the Crossfire Hurricane investigation, the FBI decided to focus on four individuals: Papadopoulos, Flynn, Page, and Manafort. In many ways, Manfort was the odd one out because he did have actual skeletons in his closet, which made him vulnerable to being pressured into fabricating stories. He was also by far the most visible and senior individual targeted. Papadopoulos and Page were unpaid volunteers. Flynn was an advisor. Manafort was the campaign manager.

Manafort's first foray into politics was as a delegate coordinator for then-President Gerald Ford at the 1976 Republican convention. He was later given a role on the Reagan campaign in 1979 and managed to secure a White House job as the associate director of the Presidential Personnel

Office. He then turned to lobbying, founding the lobbying firm Black, Manafort & Stone, together with Charles Black Jr. and long-time Trump confidante Roger Stone. Even in the early 1980s, Stone was already an established political operator in Republican circles. He would later become a friend and informal counselor to Donald Trump long before Trump ran for president. It was that friendship that attracted the attention of Mueller's special counsel operation. Mueller tightened the screws on Stone in hopes of getting him to provide information about his close friend, Donald Trump.

And so it was with Manafort as well. He was on the initial FBI Crossfire Hurricane target list, presumably because he was the then-campaign manager and was known to have engaged in shady lobbying, or at least lobbying for questionable individuals. But things were about to change quickly. When the *New York Times* ran a smear piece targeting Manafort, Trump fired him.[18] He was replaced by Kellyanne Conway. This was less than three weeks after the official start of Crossfire Hurricane. But it had nothing to do with Crossfire Hurricane, as Trump did not know about the investigation until Comey announced its existence in March 2017, a full seven months later.[19] Manafort was fired after the *New York Times* claimed to have received a copy of a "black ledger."[20] The ledger allegedly detailed undeclared cash payments that Manafort had allegedly received from the party of Viktor Yanukovych, who had been the president of Ukraine until the US-led coup in February 2014. In 2019, it was revealed that the black ledger was most likely fake.[21] Notably, the ledger was never entered into evidence when Special Counsel Robert Mueller prosecuted Manafort for various financial crimes. Valentin Nalyvaichenko, the former head of the Security Service of Ukraine (SBU), expressed doubts about the ledger's authenticity, noting that only one section was leaked and no handwriting analysis had been conducted. He described it as "crazy" that Manafort was investigated based on the ledger. Manafort has consistently claimed that the ledger is not authentic.[22]

In 2020, a tape recording between Petro Poroshenko, Yanukovych's replacement, and Vice President Joe Biden surfaced.[23] In the recording, which was made in August 2016, Poroshenko can be heard bragging about his government leaking the "black ledger." Both Biden and Poroshenko can then be heard laughing about the demise of Manafort, which was caused by the ledger. Although the revelations about Biden's phone call were only made in 2020, the warnings were already there for everyone to see. That is because while Manafort was being targeted by the FBI in 2016, Valentyn Nalyvaichenko, the head of Ukraine's Security Service (SBU), openly called the ledger suspicious and pointed out that there had been no handwriting analysis.²⁴ That should have cast a big cloud of doubt over the ledger, but as with all their other targets, the FBI did not care. There is also the fact that Biden, the then-sitting vice president, was intimately involved in the coordinated takedown of Trump's campaign manager. If it had been Trump laughing with a foreign leader who had just taken down Biden's campaign manager, he would have been impeached in a millisecond.

The ledger story had been concocted to harm Trump. Indeed, Ukrainian officials were very keen to prevent Trump from becoming president. Ostensibly, this was because he had already indicated that he would seek to improve relations with Russia, a prospect that the Ukrainian government did not desire. How different things would have turned out if Trump had been given a chance to fulfill his promise. But he was never allowed to, as Russiagate effectively criminalized diplomacy with Russia.

One intriguing aspect of Ukrainian election interference is the question of whether it was prompted by the CIA. According to revelations made in February 2024, the CIA and its then-director, John Brennan, became heavily involved in Ukraine following the February 2014 coup.²⁵ One of the first things that the aforementioned head of Ukraine's SBU, Nalyvaichenko, did on the night of the coup was to contact the local CIA representative. Brennan arrived in Kiev a few days later, and the two sides, namely the CIA and SBU, collaborated on constructing twelve secret bases near the Russian border. Leaving aside the issue that this was unlikely to have been viewed kindly by Russia, the CIA's deep involvement in Ukraine raises the question of whether the CIA was engaged in activities beyond constructing secret bases. Ukrainian officials, including President Poroshenko, who bragged about publicizing the Manafort ledger, were highly involved in trying to undermine Trump's 2016 campaign. The Ukrainian ambassador in the United States, Valeriy Chaly, openly chastised Trump,²⁶ as did the former Ukrainian Prime Minister Arsenyi Yatseniuk, who was appointed by Victoria Nuland as her handpicked leader of post-coup Ukraine.²⁷ Ukraine's interior minister, Arsen Avakov, referred to Trump as a "dangerous misfit" who was "dangerous both for Ukraine and for the United States to the same extent."²⁸

All of these attacks took place in August 2016, just before the release of the Manafort ledger by Ukraine. While it is not known whether the CIA or anyone else in the United States government encouraged Ukraine to criticize Trump, it is certainly highly unusual for high-ranking officials from a foreign country to be so overtly hostile to a presidential nominee. At a minimum, it is very unwise because, as it turned out in 2016, the person being targeted might end up becoming president. As Nalyvaichenko admitted after the 2016 election, Ukraine's government had in fact "intervened in the presidential campaign" when it leaked the Manafort ledger.[29]

The results of Ukraine's interference were immediate. Whether the ledger was real or not, Trump had no choice but to fire Manafort. While the ledger pertained to payments dating back several years, Manafort had become too much of a liability. Trump was in the final stretch of the 2016 campaign, and he could hardly afford to be distracted by a stream of revelations about his campaign manager's past dealings in Ukraine. One immediate consequence of Manafort being fired was that while the FBI intensified its pursuit of Page and Papadopoulos, they appear to have lost interest in Manafort. While he was Trump's campaign manager, he was a valuable target. However, once he was gone, he was no longer useful to the Crossfire Hurricane team. The fact that they lost interest in Manafort demonstrates once more that the FBI's focus was on getting Trump rather than uncovering any real crimes. The FBI was guided by a short-term view in this situation. Their main task during the 2016 campaign was to ensure the election of Hillary Clinton. As Strzok had promised his paramour Lisa Page, "We'll stop it," by which he meant that the FBI would stop Trump from becoming president.[30] Once this objective was achieved, the investigation would be ended and memory-holed.

But it did not turn out this way, which is why Manafort became a target again after the election. The reason is simple. By targeting Manafort, the FBI hoped to get Trump. Ironically, just like Manafort, most individuals targeted by the FBI's Crossfire Hurricane team would have personally been much better off if Hillary Clinton had won. In Manafort's case, the FBI's and later Special Counsel Mueller's attention would focus on his foreign lobbying and tax problems. Manafort had failed to register as a foreign agent, which he attempted to rectify retroactively in 2017.[31] Additionally, he apparently did not pay taxes on his substantial income. The plan appears to have been to use those problems as leverage to get Manafort to fabricate stories about Trump. But Manafort held firm. He was eventually tried and convicted for financial crimes that were completely unrelated to Trump or his campaign.[32] The original ledger accusation that led to Manafort's dismissal, alleging that he had received substantial amounts of cash from Ukrainian sources, turned out to be false. There were no cash payments.

As for Steele and Danchenko, the originators of the dossier, the FBI showed little interest in them. As noted earlier, Danchenko was not interviewed until after Trump became president. When he disavowed the dossier in that interview, the FBI buried both his admission and Danchenko's existence. A March 2017 memo prepared by top FBI officials for the Gang of Eight, the eight Congressional leaders who are briefed on classified intelligence matters, promoted Steele and his dossier, as if Danchenko had never disavowed it. The FBI also falsely claimed that Danchenko was Russian-based, and that the FBI had "no control" over him, even though he was on their payroll.[33] Similarly, the FBI made no attempt to seriously question Steele. The only known pre-election meeting between Steele and anyone from the Crossfire Hurricane team took place in Rome, Italy, on October 3, 2016. As we would only find out six years later, it was at that meeting that the FBI offered Steele one million dollars to corroborate his dossier claims.[34] Instead of seizing the opportunity for a huge payday, Steele became uncooperative. Steele refused to provide the names of his sources and did not offer any useful information.

If the accumulation of prior investigative dead ends and red flags was not sufficient, the Rome meeting should have been the final straw. But it wasn't. A mere eighteen days after Steele proved, through his recalcitrance and million-dollar rejection that he could not be trusted, the FBI filed an application with the FISC to spy on Carter Page. The basis of the application was the Steele dossier. FBI Deputy Director McCabe later admitted that without Steele, there would have been no FISA warrant: "No surveillance warrant would have been sought from the FISC without the Steele dossier information."[35]

Despite depending on Steele's information, the FBI did not conduct a purportedly serious interview with him until September 2017, which was well into Trump's presidency. The FBI's Form 302, which memorialized Steele's interview, was completely redacted when it was finally released years later. Every single one of the twenty-six pages of interview notes had been blacked out.[36] It wasn't until Trump's last day in office on January 20, 2021, that we got to see a less redacted version of Steele's FBI debriefing.[37] Trump had attempted to release an entire bundle of declassified Russiagate documents but inexplicably, his White House chief of staff, Mark Meadows, decided to send the declassified documents back to the Department of Justice (DOJ). Apparently, he was told they wanted to make additional redactions. But the notion that Meadows would have expected a Biden DOJ to then re-release the documents is absurd. And so it turned out. The DOJ never re-released the bundle. The only reason we got to see Steele's 302 is that journalist John Solomon obtained a copy of it before Meadows sent the bundle back to the DOJ.

In the end, the FBI needn't have tried so hard to conceal Steele's Form 302 as it only reaffirms what we already knew: Steele was recalcitrant, and the FBI failed to press him on his fabrications. For instance, Steele insisted that the "primary subsource has sub-sources with serious access." The FBI knew this to be untrue because, nine months earlier, Danchenko had informed them that those sub-sources were his drinking buddies who merely shared gossip in jest. Steele also appears to have stuck with his story that Millian was the main source for most of the dossier's accusations. Again, the FBI did not question him about the impossibility of this, as Danchenko had already confessed that he never spoke to Millian. It was the same story over and over. Despite the FBI knowing that the Steele story was fabricated, they continued to rely on it to pursue Trump. Every time additional deceptions were revealed, the FBI escalated the investigation instead of shutting it down. To this day, no one has been held accountable for these acts of fraud on the American people.

CHAPTER 11

The Alfa Bank Hoax

Unbeknownst to almost everyone until 2021, the Steele dossier wasn't the only component of Clinton's project. The campaign's Swiftboat offensive had a second prong, the Alfa Bank hoax. This part of the plan was executed in parallel to the Steele dossier but received far less attention, both at the time it was being implemented and after Trump became president. While it was known that accusations had been made during the campaign that Trump had a secret communications channel with the Kremlin through Alfa Bank, those allegations did not gain much traction.[1] Both the *New York Times* and *Vox*, not exactly known as Trump-friendly outlets, reported that the Alfa Bank story did not amount to much.[2] Stories of lurid sex tapes tend to capture the imagination more effectively than technical hoaxes related to the internet's Domain Name System, also known as DNS.

Those who saw through the con game probably assumed that the smears linking Trump to Alfa Bank were an extension of the dossier's allegations and not a separate element of the Swiftboat campaign. After all, Steele himself wrote a dossier report on the Alfa Bank story. The report was dated September 14, 2016, and it was made public, along with most of the dossier, when BuzzFeed published photos of it on January 10, 2017.[3] The details of the Alfa Bank hoax and its connection to the Swiftboat campaign did not surface until September 19, 2021, when Michael Sussmann, a lawyer for the Clinton campaign, was charged with lying to the FBI about his involvement in promoting the Alfa Bank hoax.[4] The Sussmann indictment, for the first time, revealed the extent to which Clinton campaign operatives had gone to concoct Trump-Alfa Bank links. It also revealed, for the first time, the existence of previously unknown participants in this scheme, including tech executive Rodney Joffe and IT researchers at Georgia Tech.

An article from 2018 in the *New Yorker* alluded to the presence of these additional players, but it did not provide specific details.[5] The purpose of the article seems to have been to resurrect the Alfa Bank hoax, possibly in response to Alfa Bank's legal actions aimed at uncovering the truth behind the hoax. The article's author, Dexter Filkins, wrote another piece in 2020 that overtly aimed to undermine Alfa Bank's legal efforts.[6] The legal efforts were initiated with a lawsuit in 2017 against Christopher Steele's employers, Fusion GPS. Two further lawsuits were subsequently filed against unknown "John Does." Ironically, the 2018 article in the *New Yorker* fueled the John Doe lawsuits. Filkins mentioned that he had spoken to a source who claimed to have been involved in the effort to link Trump to Alfa Bank. The source identified himself as Max, which was later revealed to be a false name. Initially, all that Alfa Bank had to go on was a 2016 article in *Slate* magazine that cited a pseudonymous individual referring to themselves as "Tea Leaves" who claimed to have discovered a "bank in Moscow that kept irregularly pinging a server registered to the Trump Organization on Fifth Avenue."[7] It was Filkins who provided Alfa Bank with the lead on "Max," prompting the bank's lawyers to initiate legal processes to identify both "Tea Leaves" and "Max." While it is often assumed that the Sussmann indictment led to the identification of "Tea Leaves" as internet security researcher April Lorenzen and "Max" as Rodney Joffe, our group had made those identifications earlier using obscure legal filings in the various Alfa Bank cases.[8] But more on that later.

The Alfa Bank hoax was far more complex, involving many more moving parts, than the dossier hoax. The dossier was a fabricated document that attributed false stories to a former intelligence official from America's closest ally, which were then disseminated to the FBI and the media. It was a devious scheme but fairly simple in its basic outline. In contrast, the Alfa Bank plan required real-world data that needed to be traceable on the internet, allowing third parties, including the FBI, to access it. The plan was to create the appearance of internet traffic between the servers at Trump Tower and the servers of Alfa Bank. The existence of such alleged traffic could then be reported to the FBI to trigger an investigation of Trump. Once the investigation was triggered, the fact that there was an investigation would be disseminated through the media. The snag was that with this hoax, Steele's say-so wasn't sufficient. There needed to be actual data that anyone could find online.

The Alfa Bank Hoax

The details of when and how the Alfa Bank plan was hatched remain unknown. Perhaps it was part of the original Swiftboat project discussed by Clinton Communications Director Jennifer Palmieri in February 2016. By mid-April, it was evident that Trump would almost certainly secure the Republican nomination for president. Around that time, Sussmann and Rodney Joffe, the IT executive identified by Walkafyre and Fool Nelson through a review of Alfa Bank's legal filings,[9] began implementing the Alfa Bank plan. Coincidentally, or not, by late April, the Democratic National Committee (DNC) suspected that it had been hacked. Amy Dacey, the committee's CEO, called Sussmann, who provided legal services for the committee.[10] What was unusual is that the timing of the alleged discovery of the hacking activity perfectly coincided not only with the beginnings of the Alfa Bank plot but also with the hiring of Fusion GPS by the Clinton campaign. What was also unusual is that the committee called Sussmann first, instead of an IT specialist. It was Sussmann who subsequently contacted a specialist, Shawn Henry, from a firm called CrowdStrike.

On May 3, a few days after Sussmann enlisted Henry, Trump secured the Republican Party's presidential nomination by winning the Indiana primary. On May 4, the following day, a team of IT researchers working for Sussmann and Joffe started compiling—or creating, as the exact nature is unclear—information that allegedly connected the Trump Organization to Alfa Bank. The data consisted of DNS lookups that purportedly demonstrated Trump's covert communication with Alfa Bank. A DNS lookup is the process by which a server finds another server on the internet. It is like looking up a phone number in a phone book. The main allegation was that Alfa Bank's server and the Trump Organization's server were communicating with each other. More specifically, it was also alleged that Trump used a Russian-made Yota phone in various locations, which had been tracked with the help of DNS data.

In truth, the DNS data was either completely incidental or fabricated. The charitable view is that an old account managed by a company that conducted marketing campaigns for the Trump Organization's hotels was sending spam to tens of thousands of email accounts, including some in Russia. The less charitable view is that the old account that had previously been associated with the hotel marketing firm had been spoofed. In either case, there was no secret communication. It was all made up, just like the Yota phone story, which was based on the same absurd assumption that any online interactions or searches must have been malicious. In the case of the Yota phone, there were millions of searches for Yota phones originating from US-based internet addresses.[11] That is not surprising, considering that Yota phones were sold in the United States for a number of years. The fact that one of the millions of Yota phone lookups might have originated from a Trump Tower internet address means absolutely nothing. For all we know, it could have been a Russian businessman using Wi-Fi at the Starbucks on the second floor. Despite the lack of robust data, the scheme to tie Trump to Alfa Bank still moved forward.

Sussmann's and Joffe's data curation was completed on July 29. This happened to be the same day when Steele traveled to Washington, DC to meet Sussmann. It was the first meeting between the two men in charge of their respective parts of the Swiftboat plan and marked the convergence of the two prongs of the scheme. The meeting took place at the offices of Sussmann's law firm, Perkins Coie. Also in attendance were Marc Elias, the attorney of record for the Clinton campaign, and key figures from Fusion GPS, including the company's owner, Glenn Simpson.

When Steele was later sued in London by the owners of Alfa Bank, he testified that the meeting at Perkins Coie's office was the first time he had ever heard of the Alfa Bank story.[12] Steele also testified that he was instructed by Fusion's Simpson to write a dossier report about Alfa Bank. This is one of the key pieces of evidence that shows that Steele, according to his own testimony, wrote customized reports for the Clinton campaign.

The meeting on July 29 involving the key figures in the Swiftboat campaign occurred at a crucial juncture. Clinton's campaign manager, Robbie Mook, publicly initiated the operation a few days earlier when he appeared on CNN and asserted that Russia had hacked the DNC with the specific intention of assisting Trump.[13] Early dossier reports, which Steele had shared with the FBI's Michael Gaeta, had, by that point, also reached the highest levels of the FBI.[14]

Most importantly, the FBI was about to open its Crossfire Hurricane investigation into the Trump campaign. While Elias, Sussmann, Steele, and the others probably did not know that this was about to happen, they must have expected it. After all, the main objective of the Swiftboat project was to prompt the FBI to investigate Trump. As became known in 2020, when incriminating text messages between lead Trump investigator Peter Strzok and his paramour Lisa Page were released, the FBI had ongoing counterintelligence investigations relating to Trump's Russian connections before Crossfire Hurricane was opened.[15] It is possible that the Swiftboat conspirators knew about these early investigations.

The Alfa Bank Hoax

In the weeks following the July 29 meeting of the Swiftboat campaign's main operatives, the Alfa Bank side of the project appears to have been put on the backburner. Instead, the Clinton campaign prioritized the broader message that Trump was somehow involved with Vladimir Putin. On August 6, Hillary Clinton sent out a tweet asking, "Seriously, what is going on with Trump and Russia?"[16] The tweet included a video with media clips questioning Trump's conciliatory tone toward Putin.

Of course, there was nothing to wonder about. Trump had made it clear from the start of his campaign that he would seek improved relations with Russia. As Trump explained at the time, it is better to have nonbelligerent relations with the world's biggest nuclear power than to keep sliding toward war. But those facts were ignored by the media, which started parroting the Clinton campaign's Trump-Russia messaging.

On August 7, Hillary Clinton sent another tweet about Trump's alleged closeness with the Kremlin.[17] This time, she attached a press release. She sent a similar tweet on August 15.[18] While the Alfa Bank angle was not being emphasized by the campaign at this time, the Manafort angle was. Paul Manafort had become Trump's convention manager in March and his campaign manager in June. This provided new material for the Swiftboat schemers. Manafort had a history of advising dubious politicians worldwide. One of these individuals was the former Ukrainian President, Viktor Yanukovych. Ukraine isn't Russia, but it was close enough for the Clinton campaign. They ran an ad using footage of Michael Isikoff, a journalist with Yahoo News who was willing to promote Clinton talking points, to insinuate that Manafort was connected to Putin.[19]

The trigger was pulled on Manafort on August 14 when the *New York Times* ran a story with the headline: "Secret Ledger in Ukraine Lists Cash for Donald Trump's Campaign Chief."[20] The article alleged that Manafort had received $12 million from Yanukovych's political party from 2007 to 2012. What that had to do with Trump remains the Clinton campaign's secret. For its part, the *New York Times* made sure to mention Putin and Russia repeatedly in an article that had nothing to do with Russia. Perhaps unsurprisingly, one of the co-authors of the *New York Times* piece was Isikoff's associate Barry Meier. The *New York Times* also made sure to mention that Manafort had business dealings with Oleg Deripaska, whom they claimed to be a close ally of Putin. What they did not mention was that Deripaska was a client of dossier author Christopher Steele. As noted earlier, the anti-Manafort ledger proved to be false, evidently fabricated by Ukrainian operatives who were working overtime to prevent a Trump presidency.[21] But it did not matter. The damage was done, and Manafort was fired on August 19.

In the short run, it was a wise move on Trump's part. Regardless of Manafort's guilt or innocence, Trump was aware that the allegations would continue to be used against his campaign as long as Manafort was involved. Cutting him loose helped kill the story—at least for a while. In the long run, it was a bad move as it showed Trump's enemies that he would fire loyal staffers in response to media hit pieces—a weakness that was exploited early in Trump's presidency when he fired General Michael Flynn after a false leak about a conversation Flynn had with the Russian ambassador appeared in the *Washington Post*.

After Manafort's departure, the Clinton campaign intensified its advertising efforts by accusing Trump of being closely associated with the Kremlin. The seed had been so firmly planted that even Senate Minority Leader Harry Reid started demanding an investigation into Trump's alleged ties to Putin.[22]

With everyone primed, it was time to unleash the Alfa Bank hoax. Steele's made-to-order report on Alfa Bank was completed on September 14, five days before Sussmann pulled the trigger with James Baker, the FBI's general counsel. On September 15, the lead lawyer for Clinton, Marc Elias, communicated with Clinton's top three advisers regarding the Alfa Bank scheme. Among those three were Communications Director Palmieri, Campaign Manager Mook, and Foreign Policy Adviser Jake Sullivan. It is not known what they discussed.

Steele's Alfa Bank report, titled Report 112, consisted of the usual fabricated fantasies.[23] However, unlike Steele's other reports, we know the details of its creation. During his visit to Washington, DC on July 29, Steele received an order from Sussmann to write a story linking Alfa Bank to the Kremlin and Putin. Without such a link, the alleged communications between Trump and Alfa Bank would be meaningless. Following the July meeting, Steele asked Danchenko to establish connections between Putin and Alfa Bank. Luckily for both, Alfa Bank had long been an interest of Danchenko's dating back to his days at the Brookings Institution. There has been speculation that, given his pre-existing interest, it was Danchenko who injected the Alfa Bank hoax into the dossier. But the facts do not support that claim. The Steele dossier never mentioned Alfa Bank until Sussmann commissioned Steele to write Report 112.

The story that Steele and Danchenko finally settled on was that a former Alfa Bank employee, Oleg Govorun, was the conduit between Alfa

Bank and Putin. This linkage allegedly occurred while Putin was the deputy mayor of St. Petersburg in the 1990s. Steele wrote in Report 112: "According to the top level Russian government official, during the 1990s GOVORUN had been Head Of Government Relations at Alpha Group and in reality, the 'driver' and 'bag carrier' used by FRIDMAN and AVEN to deliver large amounts of illicit cash to the Russian president, at that time deputy Mayor of St Petersburg."24

Steele also claimed that a "top level Russian government official described the PUTIN-Alpha relationship as both carrot and stick. Alpha held 'kompromat' on PUTIN and his corrupt business activities from the 1990s whilst although not personally overly bothered by Alpha's failure to reinvest the proceeds of its TNK oil company sale into the Russian economy Since, the president was able to use pressure on this count from senior Kremlin colleagues as a lever on FRIDMAN and AVEN to make them do his political bidding."25

In essence, Steele's narrative suggests that twenty years ago, the owners of Alfa Bank—Mikhail Fridman, Peter Aven, and German Khan—allegedly bribed Putin. This alleged bribery granted Putin influence over them, enabling him to manipulate their actions ever since. Like many of Steele's stories, this one made no sense. It was complete gibberish.

Leaving the logical flaws aside, and also disregarding Danchenko's admission that Steele had no "top level Russian government official" sources, the story also falls apart because Govorun's role at Alfa Bank and Putin's mayorship in St. Petersburg never overlapped. Putin left St. Petersburg in June 1996. Govorun took up his position at Alfa Bank in March 1997.

Interestingly, an archived version of Govorun's Wikipedia page contains incorrect dates, giving the impression of an overlap. The false Wikipedia entry was cleaned up in January 2022, after Stephen McIntyre and I pointed out the problem.26 Despite his previously professed interest in all things Alfa Bank, it appears that Steele and Danchenko constructed their false narrative based on an inaccurate Wikipedia entry. Further evidence of their sloppy work can be seen in the misspelling of "Alfa" as "Alpha" in the dossier. Such elementary errors should have been seen as a significant red flag, but the FBI had other plans.

The plans became clear in the days following Sussmann's presentation of the fabricated Alfa Bank story to his friend, the FBI's general counsel, James Baker, on September 19. Sussmann had texted Baker the previous evening to inform him that he would be visiting Baker's office the next day with some information. This detail was crucial to Sussmann's eventual indictment because he explicitly stated that he was not representing any client. Sussmann allegedly repeated the claim when he showed up in Baker's office the next day. In truth, Sussmann was representing the Clinton campaign and the DNC. Baker would have assumed this both as Sussmann's friend and from Sussmann's media appearances. That is why it was so important for Sussmann to lie and claim that, in this particular instance, he did not represent any Democrats.

The legal standard for determining whether someone can be prosecuted for lying to the FBI is whether the lie is material, meaning it could potentially affect an investigation. This standard was met in this case because the lie may well have diverted attention from the Clinton campaign. However, when Special Counsel Durham prosecuted Sussmann for his lie, the only direct evidence was Baker's statement about what Sussmann had said at their September 19, 2016 meeting, namely that he was just there as a Good Samaritan. Durham did not have Sussmann's text message from September 18 until shortly before Sussmann's trial was set to begin. That is when Baker supposedly found the message on an old phone and gave it to Durham. The text message read: "Jim—it's Michael Sussmann. I have something time-sensitive (and sensitive) I need to discuss. Do you have availability for a short meeting tomorrow? I'm coming on my own—not on behalf of a client or company—want to help the Bureau. Thanks."[27] Due to its late submission, the text message was not admissible as evidence in the trial. The smoking gun evidence was excluded.

But our focus should be on Baker. How did the FBI's chief lawyer fail to understand the necessity of turning over all the evidence? How did he forget the most crucial evidence? The likely answer is that he did not forget, but rather that he was protecting Sussmann. Not only did Baker wait for a few months before turning over the text message to Durham, but he also waited just long enough for the statute of limitations to expire. In other words, Baker timed things so that there was an insurance policy. Sussmann could not be charged with a superseding indictment because more than five years had passed since the text message was sent. Baker ensured that Sussmann was protected both in relation to the trial he was facing and any potential future charges.

In fact, Sussmann's lie about not representing Clinton was both material and critical. It was intended to mislead the FBI into thinking that the Alfa Bank data was genuine and not in any way connected to the Clinton campaign. It should be noted that, unbeknownst to the Swiftboat collaborators, the CIA had learned of their scheme. On July 28, 2016, then-CIA

Director John Brennan secretly briefed President Obama on an intercepted communication that revealed Hillary Clinton's campaign had a plan "to vilify Donald Trump by stirring up a scandal claiming interference by the Russian security service."[28] The stated purpose of the plan was to distract the public from her private email server scandal. The fact that Brennan and Obama knew about the Swiftboat plan only came to light in September 2020 when the director of National Intelligence, John Ratcliffe, revealed that they had been aware of the plan since July 2016.[29] A few days later, Ratcliffe also released a redacted version of Brennan's notes that he had used when briefing Obama.[30]

On September 7, the CIA passed the information about Clinton's Swiftboat plan to FBI Director James Comey and the lead Crossfire Hurricane investigator, Peter Strzok.[31] This was a mere twelve days before Sussmann showed up at the FBI with the phony Alfa Bank data. The two events should have been immediately connected. The Clinton campaign had a plan to vilify Trump by falsely linking him to Putin. Supposedly coincidentally, Clinton's campaign lawyer walked into FBI headquarters with alleged data connecting Trump to Putin. The scheme could not have been more obvious. But the FBI ignored the evidence that was right in front of their noses. Once again, in a pattern that can be observed throughout the entire saga, the FBI buried inconvenient facts and continued with their agenda to pursue Trump. When, four years later, Comey was confronted with the fact that he had ignored the existence of a Clinton plan to falsely accuse Trump of Russia collusion, he told the Senate Judiciary Committee that he claimed not to remember receiving this information: "That doesn't ring any bells with me."[32]

Baker knew that the FBI covered up the fact that the Clinton campaign seeded the Alfa Bank hoax. He also knew he could save his friend Sussmann while at the same time washing his own hands. It was a classic case of having your cake and eating it. Without documentary evidence of Sussmann's guilt, the jury decided to acquit him of lying to Baker about not representing any client. The media then misportrayed the acquittal as evidence that Sussmann—and by extension, the Clinton campaign—had done nothing wrong. In truth, Sussmann's text message provides powerful evidence of the depth of the Clinton campaign's scheming and the FBI's cover-up of that scheming.

In the end, Sussmann need not have sent the text message at all. The FBI had his back, just as they had Danchenko's and Steele's backs. As events unfolded in the days after Sussmann brought the fake Alfa Bank data to

Baker, it became clear that FBI leadership could not have cared less about the authenticity of the data. All they saw was another fake scandal to hang around Trump's neck.

The data that Sussmann gave Baker purported to show that the Trump Organization was secretly communicating with Alfa Bank. Steele's report, which was delivered to the FBI on the same day as the Alfa Bank data, September 19,[33] aimed to establish a parallel narrative linking Alfa Bank to Putin and, consequently, to Trump. Sussmann had given Baker the phony data on a USB stick. The data was immediately passed to FBI Special Agent Scott Hellman, a cybercrime specialist at the Washington, DC office. It did not take Hellman very long to figure out that the data was useless at best. As revealed in FBI text messages, which were released years later in 2022, within two hours of receiving the USB stick and Sussmann's accompanying notes, Hellman texted his unit chief, Nate Batty: "The more I read this thing . . . it feels a little 5150ish."[34] "5150ish" is law enforcement jargon for something crazy. The name originated from the California law code that permits the psychiatric commitment of individuals who pose a danger to themselves or others. During Sussmann's trial, Hellman testified that his mention of "5150ish" indicated that the person who wrote Sussmann's notes "was suffering from some mental disability."[35] A short time later, Hellman told his boss, Batty, that the data was "intended to overwhelm and confuse the reader." Hellman then sent Batty a series of text messages that proves beyond any doubt that the FBI knew they were dealing with a hoax: "0 activity until [the] NIGHT before the author started investigating," "awfully strange to have a domain created in 2009, and the investigator just HAPPENED to start looking up EVERY domain belonging to trump that looks like a mail server," "and LO AND BEHOLD then," "they send more requests and do another pull."[36]

In other words, the alleged communications between Trump and Alfa Bank started right when Sussmann's team began searching for them. It would have been obvious to a child that this was a setup. But that wasn't the only problem. The next significant red flag was that Trump allegedly used a domain with his own name to conduct his secret communications with the Kremlin. Hellman texted his superior again, this time using a markedly sarcastic tone:

"Nate," "I need to talk to you. . . . privately. . . . I want to make sure NO ONE knows I'm contacting you. . . . I will ONLY send you emails from a server set to ONLY communicate with you," "don't worry . . . this idea is bulletproof," "I've registered the domain under mail1.scott.hellman-email.com," "NO ONE WILL FIND OUT."[37]

The Alfa Bank Hoax

It was completely obvious from day one that the Alfa Bank story was a hoax. But that is not what the FBI leadership wanted to hear. Instead of following the standard procedure of questioning Sussmann about the fabricated data, Deputy Assistant Director Eric Sporre decided to remove the case from Hellman's jurisdiction.[38] Hellman was honest and had consequently become a problem. After removing Hellman from the case, FBI leadership sent the data to agents outside of Washington, DC and instructed them to open a full investigation. Those agents, who were located in Chicago, were more compliant than Hellman had been. They pretended that the Alfa Bank data might be meaningful. Thus the issue was kept alive.

As if the timing of all of that wasn't bad enough, there was even more evidence that Sussmann was part of a scheme to trigger the FBI into investigating Trump. In the three months leading up to Sussmann taking the USB stick with the phony data to Baker, he exchanged at least forty-five emails with his regular cyber contacts at the FBI. FBI leadership knew this, but no one seems to have asked Sussmann why he took the Alfa Bank data to Baker, who knew nothing about DNS data, instead of discussing it with the cybersecurity specialists with whom he was already in constant contact. The answer can only be that the goal was to deliver the data to FBI leadership, a scenario that would likely not have occurred if Sussmann had given the USB stick to a lower-level analyst. Sussmann's actions, in turn, provide additional evidence of the malicious nature of his scheme. Sussmann did not want the data to be debunked by a cyber analyst. He wanted to help FBI leadership strengthen their false narrative that Trump was colluding with Russia. And it worked like a charm. As expected, the cyber analysts, Hellman and Batty, immediately debunked the data's premise. But because Sussmann had gone through FBI leadership, he ensured that would not be the end of the road.

Meanwhile, Clinton's Swiftboat team had enlisted its media partners to promote the story in the public eye. Sussmann had met with the *New York Times*' Eric Lichtblau shortly before meeting with Baker.[39] While Lichtblau was eager to run the Alfa Bank story, his colleague Steven Lee Myers was less enthusiastic. A few days after Sussmann delivered the phony data to Baker, Lichtblau and Myers asked the FBI about the story. The two reporters were asked to meet with FBI officials. During the meeting, FBI leadership requested that the *New York Times* refrain from publishing anything about Alfa Bank while the allegations were being investigated. While it might at first appear that the FBI was assisting Trump by keeping the story out of the news, the opposite is true. By this point, FBI leadership knew that their own cyber agents had exposed the story as a hoax. But instead of acknowledging this fact, they used the excuse of delaying publication to keep the hoax alive. FBI leadership may also have been concerned that, despite Lichtblau's enthusiasm, the story might poke holes in the Alfa Bank narrative. In that sense too, it was safer for the FBI that nothing was published. It is hard to believe from today's perspective, but the *New York Times* of 2016 wasn't yet completely unhinged. When the *New York Times* finally published its article on Alfa Bank on October 31, eight days before the 2016 election, the FBI's concerns, if they existed, were confirmed.[40] The article effectively dismissed the Alfa Bank story as insignificant. Citing unnamed FBI sources, the *New York Times* concluded "that there could be an innocuous explanation" for the Alfa Bank data, "like a marketing email or spam, for the computer contacts."

Clinton campaign operatives also attempted to promote the story to Reuters, targeting a reporter named Mark Hosenball. Like Lichtblau, Hosenball was willing, but he faced resistance within his organization. Emails uncovered years later in Alfa Bank's lawsuit against Fusion GPS reveal that Hosenball expressed to Fusion's Peter Fritsch his concern that Reuters' in-house cybersecurity team was not convinced of the story's accuracy.[41] Like the FBI's Hellman, they probably saw right through the hoax. That only made Fritsch angrier. On October 18, less than three weeks before the election, he commanded Hosenball to "do the fucking alfa bank secret comms story. It is hugely important."[42] But Reuters did not bite.

While their efforts with Reuters and the *New York Times* were unsuccessful, Clinton campaign operatives achieved success with at least one other outlet: *Slate* magazine. On October 31, that outlet published an article by Franklin Foer titled "Was a Trump Server Communicating With Russia?"[43] Foer parroted the fake Alfa Bank story in all its glory without a hint of suspicion or even inquisitiveness.

The following day, FBI lawyer Lisa Page texted her boss, Andrew McCabe, saying, "the alphabank story is in slate," as if this was something they had been anticipating. McCabe sent a one-word reply: "Awesome."[44]

What might have felt awesome to McCabe was, in truth, an incredibly dishonest hit piece. Like the *New York Times* and Reuters, *Slate* needed someone to corroborate the Clinton campaign's false accusations. However, unlike the *New York Times* and Reuters, *Slate* found that someone in Paul Vixie, an acclaimed computer scientist who pioneered DNS. *Slate* wrote that "[i]n the world of DNS experts, there's no higher authority. Vixie wrote central strands of the DNS code that makes the internet work." With that level of expertise in the exact area at issue, it probably took Vixie no more than a few seconds to figure out that the Alfa Bank data was completely meaningless. It would have been like asking Steven Spielberg whether *E.T.* was real.

But even though he must have quickly realized that the data was, at best, meaningless, Vixie told *Slate* a very different story. Indeed, he went into full tinfoil hat mode and claimed that "[t]he parties were communicating in a secretive fashion. The operative word is secretive. This is more akin to what criminal syndicates do if they are putting together a project." Vixie also stated that "[t]he data has got the right kind of fuzz growing on it . . . If you look at those time stamps, they are not simulated . . . This passes the reasonable person test." Finally, Vixie exclaimed that "[n]o reasonable person would come to the conclusion other than the one I've come to."

This was a remarkable conclusion considering that the FBI's in-house expert reached the exact opposite conclusion—that the data was the work of a lunatic. Fortunately, we know who was right. And we know it straight from the horse's mouth. Unbeknownst to the general public, the highest echelons of the cybersecurity world have a secret chat group called Crimeware. The existence of this chat group came to light during Alfa Bank's defamation case. On the day Foer's *Slate* article was published, the chat group lit up, with one expert criticizing Foer's piece: "this looks to be absolutely terrible 'journalism'" and "there's literally zero reasonable reason to think there's any actual connection to Trump. Much more likely this is some random email marketing shit setup by a hospitality company than something being used to surreptitiously communicate between Trump and the Ruskies."[45] In a follow-up email, the same tech executive sarcastically noted that "maybe Vixie's behind it all—clearly DNS is the link between all of this, so Vixie is directly tied to Russia and China. Both are known users of DNS!!!!!"[46]

Another of Vixie's peers commented that the story "was terrible analysis with insane leaps based on statements that could not be validated . . . It was as if the journalists involved already had their story and just wanted quotes from industry."[47] Yet, another executive tried to help Vixie save face by sharing that "[w]e all get burned from time to time by 'enterprising' journalists. I think we all understand that everyone's quotes were taken out of context and used for a 'non-technical' purpose (to put it diplomatically)."[48]

Some others believed that the *Slate* article must have been a case of Foer having gone rogue. It was only at this point that Vixie chimed in with a one-liner: "you're even more right than you may know."[49] After having seen the *Slate* piece torn to shreds by his peers, Vixie obviously decided it was best to blame the reporter. But not everyone on the secret chat board bought that explanation. After he was pressed by another participant, Vixie gave his mea culpa: "i should not have spoken with certainty. other interpretations are possible, and i should have said so. also, i should not have spoken out on a politics-related matter unless it was a clearly nonpartisan act—for example, only referring to a party or candidate i am known to support. there was no upside from speaking on this story . . . i ought to have known better and i don't mind getting spanked for it . . . feel free to spank further if there's some important lesson you think i haven't yet taken to heart."[50]

Vixie's professed mea culpa raises the question of why he did not publicly speak up, or at least walk back the extravagant quotes that he had given *Slate* magazine. The answer appears to be identical to the reason why Vixie deceived *Slate* readers in the first place. He wanted Hillary Clinton to be president. Luckily for Vixie, most, if not all, participants on the secret Crimeware chat board were Clinton supporters. One member of the chat group offered some conciliatory advice: "Moral of the story: Even security researchers have partisan biases."[51] Another participant tried to humorously pivot the discussion to Trump: "Everyone knows his covert channel involves the encoding of his hairpiece."[52]

Most of the individuals in the Crimeware group are prominent tech executives. Yet not a single participant spoke up in public to debunk the false claims, not even after Clinton lost. This is yet another symptom of an industry heavily occupied by Democrat partisans. Politics over truth.

The publication of the *Slate* hit piece was accompanied by a tweet from candidate Clinton herself: "Computer scientists have apparently uncovered a covert server linking the Trump Organization to a Russian-based bank."[53] Clinton did not mention that those computer scientists worked for her Swiftboat team. Nor did she mention that the brainchild behind the scheme, Joffe, was allegedly offered a high-ranking position in a Clinton administration.[54]

Clinton not only concealed the fact that her designated cyber specialist Joffe had been front and center of the entire Alfa Bank scheme but also failed to mention that the IT specialists who had helped Sussmann and Joffe to curate the Alfa Bank data had huge misgivings about what they had been asked to do. In private messages that were unearthed by Special Counsel John Durham, the IT specialists called the allegation of a secret communications channel "a red herring."[55] The group, which had been convened by Joffe, was well aware of the purpose of their task. One member messaged the group: "Being able to provide evidence of *anything* that shows an attempt to behave badly in relation to this, the VIPs would be happy. They're looking for a true story that could be used as the basis for closer examination."⁵⁶ The goal was to find any kind of real-world data that could be used to create a narrative to prompt the FBI into investigating the matter. Special counsel Durham concluded that the VIPs to be pleased were Sussmann, Elias, and the Clinton campaign.⁵⁷

At least one member of the group had serious misgivings about the scheme: "Lets [sic] for a moment think of the best case scenario, where we are able to show (somehow) that DNS [] [sic] communication exists between Trump and R[ussia]. How do we plan to defend against the criticism that this is not spoofed [] [sic] traffic we are observing?" What this person was saying is that anyone could concoct fake DNS lookups involving a server associated with the Trump Organization. How could the existence of such a lookup constitute anything meaningful? It could not. The IT researchers acknowledged this: "There is no answer to that." He also questioned Joffe about what would happen if they could trick someone into thinking the data was both real and meaningful: "Let's assume again that they are not smart enough to refute our 'best case' scenario. [Joffe], you do realize that we will have to expose every trick we have in our bag to even make a very weak association? Lets [sic] all reflect upon that for a moment." The researchers concluded by saying that "we cannot technically make any claims that would fly public scrutiny" and that the "only thing that drives us at this point is that we just do not like [Trump]. This will not fly in eyes of public scrutiny. Folks, I am afraid we have tunnel vision. Time to regroup?"⁵⁸

It was not just the FBI's Hellman who knew that the data was, at best, meaningless. The Swiftboat team's own researcher knew it too. But the Clinton campaign had no shame and no scruples. This is evident from the fact that on the day the *Slate* article was published, Clinton's foreign policy adviser, Jake Sullivan, issued the following statement:

> This could be the most direct link yet between Donald Trump and Moscow. Computer scientists have apparently uncovered a covert server linking the Trump Organization to a Russian-based bank. This secret hotline may be the key to unlocking the mystery of Trump's ties to Russia. It certainly seems the Trump Organization felt it had something to hide, given that it apparently took steps to conceal the link when it was discovered by journalists. This line of communication may help explain Trump's bizarre adoration of Vladimir Putin and endorsement of so many pro-Kremlin positions throughout this campaign. It raises even more troubling questions in light of Russia's

masterminding of hacking efforts that are clearly intended to hurt Hillary Clinton's campaign. We can only assume that federal authorities will now explore this direct connection between Trump and Russia as part of their existing probe into Russia's meddling in our elections.⁵⁹

Sullivan's statement, particularly the last sentence, perfectly captures the intended purpose of the Alfa Bank hoax. Clinton's Swiftboat operatives knew from day one that the data would never pass muster. As revealed by their text messages, which were later uncovered by Durham, Joffe and his team were fully aware that anyone with basic technical knowledge would realize that the data was entirely meaningless. The Swiftboat team would also have known that the FBI would reach that same conclusion very quickly. Consequently, the Clinton campaign was not looking to trigger a comprehensive investigation. Rather, the timing of their push with both the media and the FBI indicates that the campaign was seeking an opportunity for the media to report on the FBI investigating a secret communications channel between Trump and Putin. The strategic juxtaposition of the terms "Trump," "Putin," and "secret communications channel" would have the desired impact on the voting public. Once Clinton won the election, everyone would move on, and none of this would ever be looked at again.

But Clinton lost, and the Alfa Bank story did not fade. Counterintuitively, it was not us Russiagate researchers, nor Special Counsel Durham, who rekindled it. It was Clinton campaign lawyer Sussmann. For reasons that are still not fully understood, in February 2017, Sussmann took the phony Alfa Bank data to the CIA, presenting the same pitch he had made to Baker five months earlier. According to the CIA agents who received the information, Sussmann once again claimed that he was not representing a client, reiterating his earlier falsehood to the FBI. The reason why Sussmann was only charged with lying to Baker but not charged with lying to the CIA remains unknown. The CIA analyzed Sussmann's claims and arrived at the same conclusion as the FBI and members of the Crimeware chat group. They determined that the data were "user created" and not "technically plausible."⁶⁰

The story was revived when the owners of Alfa Bank filed a defamation lawsuit against Fusion GPS on October 3, 2017.⁶¹ This case provided our group and Russiagate researchers with a first glimpse of Clinton's Alfa Bank scheme. At the time the owners of Alfa Bank—Fridman, Aven, and Khan—filed their lawsuit, very little was known about the Swiftboat plot, let alone the Alfa Bank aspect. It was not even known that the Clinton campaign was behind the Steele dossier. The information only became known weeks after Alfa Bank filed its lawsuit.[62] At the time of filing, the owners of Alfa Bank knew they had been defamed by Steele as Putin's bagmen. That is all they knew.

Fridman, Aven, and Khan spent the next five years peeling away the layers of the onion. Unfortunately, they were derailed by the Ukraine War in 2022 when the sanctions imposed against them made it impossible to continue with the case. It was an incredibly fortunate break for the Swiftboat conspirators. Danchenko was about to be deposed, and the depositions of the various individuals involved in orchestrating the Alfa Bank scam were already underway. Fusion's Peter Fritsch was so afraid of being grilled about the Alfa Bank plot in a deposition that, according to court documents, he struck an Alfa Bank process server with his car.[63] The Alfa Bank case probably presented the best opportunity to hold someone accountable. But in the end, it was all for nothing. The Swiftboat plotters and their helpers all walked away scot-free.

CHAPTER 12

The Media Strategy

Just before the Alfa Bank prong of Clinton's Swiftboat attack was set in motion in late July 2016, another part of the project was kicked off: the media strategy. On July 24, Clinton campaign manager Robby Mook went on CNN and boldly declared that Russia had hacked the Democratic National Committee's (DNC) emails to assist Donald Trump. With that, the idea of Russian collusion was planted. The messaging was perfectly executed.

Mook's exact words were, "experts are telling us that Russian state actors broke into the DNC, stole these emails. And other experts are now saying that the Russians are releasing these emails for the purpose of actually helping Donald Trump."[1] What Mook didn't mention was that those experts were part of his own in-house team, Sussmann and Joffe. One was Clinton's campaign lawyer, and the other had been promised a high-level government job in the event of a Clinton presidency.[2]

Mook went on to say "that Trump and his allies made changes to the Republican platform to make it more pro-Russian. And we saw him talking about how NATO shouldn't intervene to defend—necessarily should intervene to defend our Eastern European allies if they are attacked by Russia. So, I think, when you put all this together, it's a disturbing picture. And I think voters need to reflect on that."

Mook's statement about Trump and his allies making the Republican platform more pro-Russian referred to a specific incident during the 2016 Republican National Convention in Cleveland. At that time, a delegate for Ted Cruz proposed an amendment to the platform advocating for the provision of "lethal defensive weapons" to Ukraine.[3] The proposal was not adopted. Mook's claim was plainly false. The platform wasn't changed at all. The only thing that happened was that a pugnacious proposal from a Cruz delegate was not adopted. In fact, Obama himself had insisted on not providing Ukraine with any weapons or other lethal aid due to a long-standing concern that arming Ukraine would lead to a proxy war between the United States and Russia. This is the proxy war we are currently engaged in. This was due in no small part to Clinton's Swiftboat smear campaign, which led to the effective criminalization of diplomacy with Russia.

The false story about Trump changing the Republican platform was, wittingly or unwittingly, seeded by Josh Rogin in an opinion article that was published in the *Washington Post* on July 18, 2017.[4] It is not known why Rogin ran the piece or if anyone put him up to it. However, it is noteworthy that the article appeared in the same paper that, a month earlier, had alleged, without any evidence, that Russia had hacked the DNC's emails. "Russian government hackers penetrated the computer network of the Democratic National Committee and gained access to the entire database of opposition research on GOP presidential candidate Donald Trump," claimed Ellen Nakashima of the *Washington Post* on June 14.[5] Citing unnamed DNC officials and security experts, Nakashima added that "the intruders so thoroughly compromised the DNC's system they also were able to read all e-mail and chat traffic."

While Nakashima did not disclose the identity of these security experts, her article mentioned Clinton campaign lawyer Michael Sussmann as being involved in the response to the alleged hacking. The article also quoted Shaun Henry, the CEO of CrowdStrike, the cybersecurity firm that was called in to deal with the situation. Henry was quoted as saying that he thought the alleged hack was so sophisticated that it must have been perpetrated by a state actor.[6] Henry exclaimed, "[W]e're perceived as an adversary of Russia," noting that "[Russia's] job when they wake up every day is to gather intelligence against the policies, practices and strategies of the U.S. government." The fact that Henry felt the need to prop up his technical analysis with geopolitical opinions implies that the hack attribution was not as cut and dried as suggested. A year later, in 2017, Henry was finally called to testify before Congress. During his testimony, all he would say under oath was "that, as it relates to the DNC, we have indicators that data was exfiltrated from the DNC, but we have no indicators that it was actually exfiltrated."[7] In other words, despite his boasts to the *Washington Post* a year earlier that he knew that the Russian government had hacked the DNC, he actually had no idea who, how, or even if anything was exfiltrated from the

DNC. Henry then said, "There are times when we can see data exfiltrated, and we can say conclusively. But in this case, it appears it was set up to be exfiltrated, but we just don't have the evidence that says it actually left." Henry emphasized this point repeatedly, stating, "There's no evidence that they were actually exfiltrated. There's circumstantial evidence but no evidence that they were actually exfiltrated."

In a press release issued years later in June 2020—which, unlike Henry's testimony, was not subject to perjury laws—CrowdStrike claimed to have proof of Russian hacking.[8] But CrowdStrike did not provide any evidence for their statement. Instead, CrowdStrike immediately pivoted to claiming that their assessment was supported by the Senate Intelligence Committee, the Intelligence Community Assessment, and Special Counsel Mueller. The problem is that the DNC never handed over its servers to the FBI. Instead, the FBI and everyone else had to rely on what CrowdStrike had found, which made CrowdStrike's repeated name-dropping of the other groups circular and meaningless. That bears repeating: The only authorities cited by CrowdStrike to support its claim of Russian hacking were agencies that were solely dependent on CrowdStrike's assertions. It was the ultimate circle jerk.

Despite the facts not aligning with the *Washington Post*'s headline that "Russian government hackers penetrated DNC," Nakashima's article soon became widely regarded as the gospel truth. Russia hacked the DNC. Nakashima's article also laid the foundations for Mook's statement on July 24 that Russia was helping to elect Trump.

While it is not known who fed Nakashima a story that perfectly aligned with the Swiftboat project in terms of content and timing, Sussmann's appearance in the article is conspicuous. Rogin's July article, on the other hand, appears to have been sourced from the Cruz delegate herself. The delegate, Diana Denman, not only supported Trump's opponent but had also spent time in Ukraine as an election observer in the 1990s. In 2017, she told Congressional investigators that she felt very strongly about the issue of Ukraine.[9] Perhaps her attempt to change the Republican platform had more to do with her personal agenda than with Clinton or Trump. If that is indeed the case, and there is no compelling evidence to believe otherwise, then the Rogin article may simply have come as a stroke of good fortune for the Swiftboat conspirators.

Whether or not the Swiftboat conspirators seeded the Rogin story, there is no doubt that they immediately seized on it. Not only did Mook bring it up when he unveiled the Russia collusion narrative on July 24, but Steele also promptly included it in his Report 95 a few days later. But there is more. Steele did not just cite the *Washington Post*. Instead, he spun an entire tale out of Rogin's tidbit. Steele claimed that Sergei Millian had confessed that "the TRUMP team had agreed to sideline Russian intervention in Ukraine as a campaign issue and to raise defence commitments in the Baltics and Eastern Europe to deflect attention away from Ukraine" as a favor to Putin, who "needed to cauterise the subject."[10] Millian had allegedly admitted that by doing this, Trump was repaying Putin for leaking the hacked DNC emails to WikiLeaks.

Once again, Steele's modus operandi is evident: taking a minor piece of public information—for instance, an opinion piece from the *Washington Post*—and amplifying it into an elaborate conspiracy theory. What is noteworthy is that on this occasion Steele wasn't the only one doing it. Soon after, the FBI took a page out of Steele's playbook and used the Rogin article to also spin a wild tale of collusion: Carter Page changed the Republican platform in exchange for the DNC's emails. The FBI later presented this narrative to the Foreign Intelligence Surveillance Court (FISC) to obtain a surveillance warrant for Carter Page. To make matters worse, Rogin's piece was an opinion piece and was marked as such. It did not even pretend to be a news piece. The FBI, however, disregarded this fact and instead misrepresented the story to the FISC by claiming that a "news organization reported" that the Trump campaign had covertly ensured that the Republican "platform would not call for giving weapons to Ukraine to fight Russian and rebel forces."[11] The FBI proceeded to insert verbatim excerpts from the Steele dossier into their FISA application, asserting to the court that the Trump campaign "agreed to sideline Russian intervention in Ukraine as a campaign issue and to raise U.S./NATO defense commitments in the Baltics and Eastern Europe to deflect attention away from Ukraine."[12] While the FBI recognized in its FISA warrant application that the information in question was sourced from Steele, it sought to validate its credibility by asserting that Carter Page participated in the alleged collusion between Trump and the Kremlin. This collusion was purportedly aimed at diminishing the significance of Ukraine as a campaign topic in return for the publication of the WikiLeaks email dump. The FBI lacked any evidence to substantiate its assertions.

While it remains unknown whether Clinton campaign operatives seeded the Nakashima or Rogin stories, we know from emails unearthed as part of Alfa Bank's lawsuit against Fusion GPS that, around the same time as the other stories, Fusion corresponded with a *Washington Post* reporter about promoting another one of their false narratives. The reporter was Tom Hamburger. On July 29, the same day that the main protagonists of the Swiftboat project met at the offices of Perkins Coie, Simpson was attempting to persuade Hamburger to publish a story about Carter Page meeting Igor Sechin and Sergei Ivanov in Moscow.[13] Sechin was, and remains, the CEO of Rosneft, one of the world's largest oil companies. The Steele dossier falsely alleged that Page was in line to receive a substantial payout from Rosneft. Ivanov was Putin's chief of staff at the time. The idea that Carter Page simply flew into Moscow and met these two men was ludicrous on its face. The *Washington Post* thought so too. "It's bullshit," "Impossible," Hamburger wrote to Simpson, citing the *Post*'s own reporters in Moscow.[14]

Julia Ioffe, writing in *Politico* on September 23, was less circumspect. Ioffe cited Yahoo News in claiming that "U.S. intelligence believes Page had an audience with top Russian officials—including Rosneft head Igor Sechin—during a summer trip to Moscow."[15] Ioffe added that "[f]rom what I could find about him, it's hard to imagine he could have secured those meetings without that mention by Trump." Instead of casting doubt on a wild and unsubstantiated claim, Ioffe exacerbated the situation by implicating Trump personally in the scheme. It was reckless reporting. It was also yet another circle jerk. The article Ioffe relied on came from Michael Isikoff, who had, in turn, received his information from Steele, whom Isikoff described as "a well-placed Western intelligence source."[16]

The Swiftboat campaign's media strategy kicked into full gear in August 2016. On August 3, 2016, a few days after the Swiftboat campaign principals had met in Washington, DC, an article appeared in *Politico* claiming that Trump had changed his stance on Ukraine shortly after Paul Manafort joined the campaign.[17] Apparently, Manafort's hiring caused Trump to adopt a "far milder tone" toward Russia. The *Politico* article, written by Michael Crowley, suggested that Manafort had triggered a sudden interest in making peace with Russia. It stated that Trump "might recognize Crimea as Russian territory and lift punitive U.S. sanctions against Russia." This echoed Steele's claims in Report 94 from July 19, where he alleged that Carter Page had assured Russian leaders of the "lifting of Western sanctions against Russia over Ukraine." The FBI later referenced the *Politico* article in its FISA warrant application against Carter Page.[18] In fact, an entire section from the article was copied and pasted almost verbatim into the FISA application: "While the reason for his shift is not clear, Trump's more conciliatory words—which contradict his own party's official platform—follow his recent association with several people sympathetic to Russian influence in Ukraine. They include his campaign manager Paul Manafort, who has worked for Ukraine's deposed pro-Russian president, [and] his foreign policy adviser Carter Page." This information was then used as allegedly independent verification of Page's involvement in the collusion scheme. But it was all nonsense. Since the beginning of his campaign in 2015, Trump's entire foreign policy perspective had been guided by the belief that enhanced relations with Russia would be in the long-term interest of everyone.[19] Manafort had nothing to do with it. Crowley, who previously worked for the far-left *New Republic*, also appears on far-left networks such as PBS, NPR, and MSNBC. While it is not known whether any Swiftboat operatives planted the story with Crowley—he was not part of the usual group of Fusion GPS's media operatives—he did fit the bill of a Clinton-friendly reporter. It would not be surprising if the article had been seeded by someone in the Clinton camp, similar to how Isikoff's article, which was also used as supposedly independent corroboration by the FBI, originated with Steele.

On August 14, the *New York Times* published its infamous hit piece on Trump campaign manager Paul Manafort.[20] The article alleged that Manafort had received $12 million from the party of then-Ukrainian president Viktor Yanukovych between 2007 and 2012. What that had to do with Trump remains the Clinton campaign's secret. The *New York Times* made sure to mention Putin and Russia repeatedly in the article, even though neither of them had anything to do with Russia. The article discussed Manafort's work for the president of Ukraine. Even though, as discussed more extensively in previous chapters, the article's premise of a ledger supplied by Ukraine turned out to be false, Trump had no choice but to fire Manafort. It was a clear case of Ukraine interfering in the 2016 presidential election.

But it wasn't just Ukraine that had a role in the story. The Manafort hit piece was one of the first instances in which we can definitively prove that Clinton operatives were involved. Ironically, the reason we know this is that in 2021, the article's co-author, Barry Meier, got into an argument with Fusion GPS's owners, Glenn Simpson and Peter Fritsch. Meier had written a book in which he criticized political operatives, such as Fusion GPS, for promoting the fake Russia collusion scam.[21] Despite being involved in seeding the Russia collusion narrative through the Manafort article, Meier absolved himself of any wrongdoing. Fusion GPS was not happy about being thrown under the bus by their former ally, so they published email exchanges with Meier. In one email dated August 2, twelve days before the *New York Times* article was published, Meier asked Fusion

The Media Strategy

for help in locating documents for the article.[22] That is how we know that Swiftboat operatives were directly involved in seeding the Manafort hit. In a post on the blogging site Medium, Simpson and Fritsch also claimed that Fusion GPS had provided Meier with the link connecting Manafort and Russian oligarch Oleg Deripaska.[23] The link was prominently featured in Meier's *New York Times* article. While the *New York Times* highlighted Manafort's alleged business dealings with Oleg Deripaska, whom they claimed to be a close ally of Putin, they failed to mention that Deripaska was an associate of dossier author Christopher Steele. They also failed to mention that they had worked with paid operatives of Clinton when writing the article.

After the success of the *New York Times* story in getting Manafort fired, the Swiftboat team's media strategy became more aggressive. While news stories over the summer had focused on the broader theme of Putin wanting to help Trump, September saw the public emergence of the collusion narrative. At the same time, the FBI was preparing to spy on the Trump campaign through the Carter Page FISA warrant. The official reason was that they suspected Page of being a Russian spy. The real purpose was to find out what opposition research Trump's team had on Clinton. But the FBI was struggling to obtain the warrant. The draft warrant application they submitted to the Foreign Intelligence Surveillance Court (FISC) remained weak. The only evidence they had was a "suggestion of a suggestion" from Papadopoulos, an entirely uncorroborated dossier from Steele, and a few articles from the *Washington Post*. While getting past the FISA warrant hurdle is not particularly onerous—between the inception of the FISC in 1978 and 2012, only eleven out of 33,900 warrant applications were rejected[24]—there were still boxes that needed to be ticked. The search was on for something more solid that could be sold to the FISC as evidence of collusion.

Fortuitously, Michael Isikoff of Yahoo News published an article about Page at a most opportune time. The article was titled "U.S. Intel Officials Probe Ties Between Trump Adviser and Kremlin" and detailed how Page had been in Moscow in July to meet with top Putin associates.[25] According to Isikoff, Page had traveled to Moscow to discuss the lifting of economic sanctions against Russia if Trump were to become president. Isikoff claimed that he had multiple sources, but it appears that he only had one: Christopher Steele. Both of the article's main claims, that "Page met with Igor Sechin, a longtime Putin associate and former Russian deputy prime minister" and that "Page met with another top Putin aide while in

Moscow—Igor Diveykin," were attributed to "a well-placed Western intelligence source," a.k.a. Steele.

By September 2016, FBI Director James Comey and counterespionage chief Peter Strzok had been informed by the CIA that the entire Trump-Russia collusion story was a dirty trick orchestrated by the Clinton campaign.[26] On top of that, they had a copy of the dossier and would have immediately noticed that Steele's claims were eerily similar to Isikoff's. They would have also noticed that Isikoff's "well-placed Western intelligence source" sounded a lot like Steele. Incredibly, both the original FISA application and subsequent renewals state that the FBI did not believe that Steele had provided the story to Isikoff, although they did acknowledge that the law firm that hired Steele might have done so.[27] They failed to inform the FISC that the law firm in question was Perkins Coie, the legal representatives for Hillary Clinton.

The FBI further informed the FISC that Steele had received $95,000 from the FBI and that the FBI was unaware of any negative information about Steele. That, too, was a lie. During an October 3 meeting with Steele, which took place before the FISA warrant application, the FBI proposed offering Steele up to $1 million for any evidence supporting his dossier claims.[28] Steele failed (or was unable) to provide such evidence. This was at least the fourth time that the investigation into Trump should have been halted. The other occasions were when the FBI discovered Clinton's Swiftboat plan on September 7, when Papadopoulos denied any insinuation of Russia collusion on September 15, and when Carter Page personally wrote to Comey on September 25[29] to disavow the allegations in the Isikoff article. Instead, the FBI forged ahead.

As far as the Trump campaign was concerned, they were spooked by Isikoff's article and issued this statement: "[Carter Page] was announced as an informal adviser in March. Since then he has had no role or official contact with the campaign. We have no knowledge of activities past or present and he now officially has been removed from all lists etc."[30]

It was exactly what the Clinton campaign and the FBI had hoped for. By throwing Carter Page under the bus, the Trump campaign made itself look guilty. After Manafort, this was the second time in a month that a news article planted by Swiftboat operatives resulted in significant repercussions for the Trump campaign. In truth, the Trump campaign probably knew very little about Carter Page and was just playing it safe. Like Papadopoulos, Page was an unpaid volunteer, hired because no one else was available. By the time Super Tuesday arrived on March 1, Trump was the odds-on favorite to become the Republican nominee. But he lacked the campaign infrastructure that traditional campaigns typically possess. After Trump's success on Super Tuesday, the campaign's foreign policy coordinator, Sam Clovis, quickly organized a small group to demonstrate that the campaign did have a foreign policy team. The team included novices and unknown individuals, such as Page and Papadopoulos. Page was essentially a warm body when the campaign needed more people. Even then, when a photo opportunity was arranged in late March, Page could not make it. In the following months, Page was careful to separate his work-related activities from his campaign activities, which, in any case, were almost nonexistent. When Page traveled to Moscow for the commencement address at the New Economic School in July, he made sure to note that he was not there representing the campaign.

But it didn't matter. For the FBI and the media, everything that Page did was for the campaign. The Trump campaign's panic played right into Special Counsel Mueller's hands. In his report, Mueller highlighted that "Manafort was asked to resign amid media coverage scrutinizing his ties to a pro-Russian political party in Ukraine and links to Russian business," adding that "when the media published stories about Page's connections to Russia in September 2016, Trump Campaign officials terminated Page's association with the Campaign and told the press that he had played 'no role' in the Campaign."[31] Mueller failed to mention that both media stories had been seeded by Clinton operatives.

While Meier, the co-author of the Manafort article, is less well-known, Isikoff is no stranger to controversy. In 1998, while working for *Newsweek*, Isikoff was about to break the story that President Clinton had an affair with an intern, Monica Lewinsky. At the last second, Isikoff was scooped by the Drudge Report. The incident marked the launch of Matt Drudge, whose website had been largely unknown up to that point. Isikoff's role in the Lewinsky scandal was memorialized in the TV miniseries *American Crime Story*. In 2005, Isikoff reported in *Newsweek* that interrogators at Guantanamo Bay had "flushed a Qur'an down a toilet."[32] The article caused massive anti-US protests and riots in Afghanistan and elsewhere. Isikoff's name was later removed from the byline.

More recently, Isikoff became one of the very few journalists to disavow the dossier. In 2018, he acknowledged that Steele's claims were likely false.[33] In 2021, he admitted that he was never able to verify the contents of the dossier.[34] He now claims that he published his September 2016 story because the FBI was investigating Page. According to Isikoff, being informed that the FBI was investigating Page implied that there must have been some substance to the investigation. In reality, the FBI was investigating Page for the same reason that Isikoff was writing about him: Steele. While Isikoff now claims to have thought that the FBI obtained its information from independent sources, they actually received it from the same person Isikoff did. In 2021, Isikoff also belatedly admitted that Fusion GPS's Simpson was a very good friend of his, whom he'd frequently hang out and party with.[35]

But Isikoff's mea culpa came far too late. The damage was done. The FBI copied and pasted sections of Isikoff's article into the Page FISA application, creating the impression that Isikoff had acquired the information about Page independently. It was more like circular reporting, a pattern that was often replayed during the Russiagate saga. This approach was a central tenet not only of the FBI's strategy but also of the Swiftboat strategy: leveraging the FBI's investigations to generate media coverage, which in turn fueled further investigations. In fact, this was one of the foundations upon which the entire Swiftboat project was built. The fact that it was all a house of cards was irrelevant to the functioning of the plan, the sole purpose of which was to get Clinton elected. Once that was achieved, all the smear stories about Trump would be forgotten.

The day before Isikoff's article was published was also significant for the Swiftboat plotters' media strategy. On the morning of September 22, ABC aired a clip from its unaired interview with Sergei Millian. As mentioned previously, the interview was organized by Matthew Mosk, an individual associated with Fusion GPS, who was employed by ABC at the time. Mosk is now the director of CBS News's Investigative Unit. The segment aired on ABC's *Good Morning America* and featured Millian discussing how Trump had received "hundreds of millions of dollars" from Russian businessmen. There was nothing inherently wrong about those transactions, nor about Millian mentioning that fact. Trump has sold thousands of properties throughout his career, including to Russians. But it was presented in the most nefarious way possible. Within a few hours, the Clinton campaign, which potentially had received a heads-up from Mosk that the clip was going to be aired, featured the clip as the centerpiece of a new attack ad against Trump. Clinton herself tweeted the ad that same afternoon, asking, "The man who could be your next president may be deeply indebted to another country. Do you trust him to run ours?"[36] It is not known whether *Good Morning America* host George Stephanopoulos had a role in the scheme to provide the Clinton campaign with dirt on Trump through his show. In the 1990s, Stephanopoulos

The Media Strategy

served as the White House communications director and senior advisor to President Clinton.

Millian immediately realized that he had been set up. It had been two months since Mosk and his ABC colleague Brian Ross interviewed him. Initially, he had wondered why the interview never aired, but he had almost forgotten about it by the time *Good Morning America* ran the clip. It had been planned this way all along, and Millian knew it. His reaction was swift. He messaged Mosk: "You know you fabricated my original story, twisted and changed my words, cut and pasted questions and answers and now you feel proud of your work?! I told you I was a broker of Trump Hollywood. Why in the world did you switch it to the Trump Organization? You totally managed to destroy my reputation nationwide. Shame on you for working like this. You maliciously lied to me." Millian continued: "You did not do the interview you told me you will do."[37]

Neither Mosk nor Ross has ever been held accountable for their involvement in colluding with the Clinton campaign to set up Millian, an American citizen. Ross was fired by ABC in 2017 for another Russiagate smear. Ross had falsely claimed that candidate Trump had instructed Michael Flynn to establish contacts with Russia.[38] The story was entirely made up, but that didn't stop it from causing a brief stock market crash. ABC later informed viewers that Trump's instructions to Flynn occurred after he was elected president, not before, as Ross had claimed. It was a perfectly normal instruction to give an incoming national security advisor. Ross's producer at ABC, Rhonda Schwartz, left ABC at the same time that Ross did. In one of the stranger anecdotes of Russiagate, Ross and Schwartz befriended George Papadopoulos. When Papadopoulos married Simona Mangiante on March 2, 2018, Ross and Schwartz were the only people in attendance. Whether that was by coincidence or design has never been resolved.

One of the least well-known aspects of the Swiftboat campaign's media strategy was that it included personal briefings by Steele. While it has been well understood for many years that Steele provided Isikoff with his story on Page, the extent to which Steele was also briefing reporters from other outlets only became known when emails between those reporters and Fusion GPS were uncovered as part of Alfa Bank's lawsuit.[39] Steele had last been in Washington, DC at the end of July for a meeting of Swiftboat operatives at the offices of Perkins Coie. He then returned to Washington, DC on September 21, just two days after Sussmann had initiated the Alfa Bank aspect of the Swiftboat campaign, and two days before Isikoff published the article that the FBI required for their FISA warrant on Carter Page. For the morning of September 22, Fusion had arranged for Steele to give a talk at the Tabard Inn to a group of friendly reporters, which included Mosk, Isikoff, Jane Mayer of the *New Yorker*, and Eric Lichtblau and David Sanger of the *New York Times*.

Located only a few blocks from the White House, the Tabard Inn is one of Washington's oldest hotels. It was bought in 1974 by a former *Washington Post* reporter, Edward Cohen, and his wife, Fritzi. Perhaps that is the reason why it is popular with the capital's press corps. It should have been big news in and of itself that Clinton campaign operatives had invited a group of media allies to meet Steele. But the public was kept in the dark until Mayer finally admitted in 2018 that such a meeting had taken place.[40] Significantly, Mayer added that she knew her hosts were working for the Clinton campaign. The fact that Mayer and her fellow Clinton-friendly reporters knew that the Clinton campaign was behind the meeting only reinforces the significance of the absence of any disclosures at the time. Hillary Clinton's Swiftboat operatives were parading a washed-out British spy to her favored reporters, and everyone remained silent about this fact, even after Trump became president. Even worse, it took Devin Nunes and his investigators more than a year to uncover the connection between Steele and Clinton. During this time, Trump was relentlessly pursued with false accusations and subjected to a special counsel investigation. Yet, while a presidency was being destroyed over a litany of lies, not one of the so-called journalists who had been at the Tabard Inn in 2016 had the honesty or integrity to speak up and tell the world that Steele was working for Clinton.

The same must be said with respect to the *Washington Post*. Although they did not attend the Tabard Inn meeting, they received something even better. To emphasize the unique role that Fusion assigned to the *Washington Post*, on the day of the Tabard Inn meeting, Steele gave the *Post*'s Tom Hamburger and Dana Priest their own personal briefing.[41]

While the *Washington Post*'s Nakashima had kicked things off with her article on June 14 blaming the DNC hack on Russia, it was Hamburger who followed up on June 17 with an article titled "Inside Trump's Financial Ties to Russia and His Unusual Flattery of Vladimir Putin."[42] Priest then managed to secure an interview with Michael Flynn, which led to the publication of two very unflattering articles in August. The first article was titled "Trump Adviser Michael T. Flynn on His Dinner with Putin and Why Russia Today Is Just Like CNN."[43] The second ridiculed Flynn for his alleged fall from grace. It was titled: "He was one of the most respected intelligence officers of his generation. Now he's leading 'Lock her up' chants."[44]

But they weren't done yet. On September 5, Nakashima, Hamburger, and Priest teamed up to produce yet another article that promoted the Russia collusion narrative: "Intelligence community investigating covert Russian influence operations in the United States."[45] But apparently the spin wasn't quite good enough. By the evening of September 5, the *Washington Post* had, without acknowledgment, rewritten their headline to say something altogether more nefarious: "U.S. investigating potential covert Russian plan to disrupt November elections."[46] The article itself reinforced the narrative that Putin was trying to undermine Clinton. In October, Priest and Hamburger collaborated on yet another article, this time with an even more ominous heading: "Trump refusal to accept government assessments on Russian hacks dismays former officials."[47] In the span of a few months, three *Washington Post* reporters had published six articles all promoting the Trump-Russia narrative. What is even more stunning is that they did so despite the fact that Hamburger had called out Fusion GPS in July for promoting a false story about Carter Page meeting Putin's chief of staff. Again and again, journalistic standards were disregarded due to animosity toward Trump. It is not surprising that Fusion's Simpson and Fritsch were so eager for Steele to provide personal briefings to the *Washington Post*.

In October, the Swiftboat operatives made a renewed push to publicize the phony Alfa Bank story, but only *Slate*'s Franklin Foer cooperated as Fusion desired.[48] Another angle that was being revisited was the Millian story. On the same day as the *Slate* story, the *Financial Times* published a critical article about Sergei Millian titled "The shadowy Russian émigré touting Trump."[49] Millian was neither shadowy nor Russian. He wasn't touting Trump either. The piece was written by Catherine Belton, who is a close friend of Steele's. When Belton first approached Millian, he told her that he couldn't talk because he was in South Korea on a business trip. Within a few days, Steele had incorporated this tidbit into a new dossier chapter, Report 139. But he did not stop there. In typical fashion, Steele added lies and attributed Millian's trip to South Korea to him having "been forced to lie low abroad following his exposure in Western media." Incredibly, Steele also claimed that Millian "was being paid, by implication by the Russian regime, not to return to the US or talk to Western journalists."[50] It was another breathtaking display of dishonesty. Millian later realized that Belton must have told Steele that Millian was traveling, and that Steele used that information to fabricate Report 139, which astonishingly also claimed that "MILLIAN had played a specific role for the Kremlin in shaping TRUMP's protectionist policy stance (especially relating to TPP and TIPP which the

Russian leadership strongly opposed)." All of a sudden, Millian, who had never spoken to either Steele or Danchenko, nor had any role of any kind in the Trump campaign, was supposed to have shaped Trump's foreign policy to suit Putin. Once again, it was all made up out of whole cloth. In fact, Trump's disapproval of multilateral trade treaties dates back many decades.

As a side note, Report 139, along with Reports 132 and 137, was never published. Our small group of researchers eventually managed to assemble a more comprehensive picture by consolidating various pieces of information that were gradually released. In 2019, the Senate Committee on Homeland Security and Governmental Affairs released an FBI matrix from 2016. The matrix aimed to visualize how the different Steele reports had reached FBI headquarters.[51] The information was disseminated through three channels: journalist David Corn, who provided copies of some reports to FBI General Counsel James Baker; Fusion's Glenn Simpson, who shared some reports with the Department of Justice's Bruce Ohr; and directly from Steele. The three unpublished reports all came directly from Steele. A significant source of information was the acting director of National Intelligence, Richard Grenell, who, in April 2020, released a document containing unredacted footnotes from the Horowitz Report. Another source of information was a spreadsheet released to Senate investigators in October 2020.[52] The spreadsheet tracked the FBI's alleged efforts to verify the Steele dossier. While nothing other than publicly known facts were ever validated, the spreadsheet did at least provide some insight into Steele's unpublished reports, which were selectively quoted.

When Belton again confronted Millian with Steele's false accusations, he responded, "Hi Catherine, I can recommend a good psychologist in NYC or London to anyone who came to these conclusions."[53] Millian did not hear from Belton again.

The Millian smears by the Clinton camp once more exposed the Trump campaign's tendency to distance itself from its own supporters. They had done so with Manafort and Page, and now it was Millian's turn. This was understandable. Trump's team knew even less about Millian than it did about Page. Trump campaign spokeswoman Hope Hicks informed Belton that Trump had "met and spoken" with Millian only "on one occasion almost a decade ago at a hotel opening."[54] Trump's then-personal lawyer and self-styled campaign surrogate, Michael Cohen, told Belton that Millian's claim of once selling Trump condominiums—which was accurate—was "nothing more than a weak attempt to align himself with Mr Trump's overwhelmingly successful brand."[55]

While these various attempts to distance the campaign from potential problems are readily understandable, the media spun the denials into evidence of nefarious acts. While Trump was able to overcome this issue during the campaign, the firing of Michael Flynn in response to media pressure was a significant mistake that haunted Trump's entire presidency.

Belton was later sued by the owners of Alfa Bank after she wrote a book claiming that they were connected to the KGB. Belton and her publisher, HarperCollins, lost the case in London's High Court. The judgment was handed down in November 2021.[56] HarperCollins issued an apology and was forced to rewrite portions of Belton's book. If the case had been delayed, Belton might have gotten away with it, just like Fusion GPS did when Alfa Bank had to abandon their case against them in March 2022 due to Western sanctions against Russia.

The *Slate* and *Financial Times* pieces marked both the high point and the endpoint of the Swiftboat campaign's media strategy. A few days later, Clinton lost the election. This, however, did not mean the end of the media campaign; it simply meant that it would be carried out by a broader range of individuals, all sharing one goal: to ruin Trump's presidency.

CHAPTER 13

The Intelligence Community Assessment

The transition from the Clinton campaign's Swiftboat strategy to a broader anti-Trump strategy was seamless. But instead of the Clinton campaign being the driving force, it was the federal government under Obama that took the reins. The groundwork for the takeover of the Swiftboat project by a vehemently anti-Trump federal bureaucracy had been established even before Trump's unexpected victory on November 8. On October 7, the Department of Homeland Security and the Office of the Director of National Intelligence on Election Security released a joint statement asserting that the United States Intelligence Community was

> confident that the Russian Government directed the recent compromises of e-mails from US persons and institutions, including from US political organizations. The recent disclosures of alleged hacked e-mails on sites like DCLeaks.com and WikiLeaks and by the Guccifer 2.0 online persona are consistent with the methods and motivations of Russian-directed efforts. These thefts and disclosures are intended to interfere with the US election process. Such activity is not new to Moscow—the Russians have used similar tactics and techniques across Europe and Eurasia, for example, to influence public opinion there. We believe, based on the scope and sensitivity of these efforts, that only Russia's senior-most officials could have authorized these activities.[1]

The Department of Homeland Security and the director of National Intelligence had no basis for making their statement. As their own words betray, they had no evidence. All they had was a vague belief that Russia might have hacked the DNC because that is something Russia would, in their opinion, do. It was a ludicrous statement on its face. Its sole purpose seemed to be to reinforce Clinton campaign talking points. In other words, the Obama administration was using the machinery of the federal government to promote Clinton campaign rhetoric. There was an additional advantage to releasing this statement during the campaign. If Clinton were to lose the election, this statement could be repurposed as an early reference point for the narrative that Trump was elected solely due to Russian interference. And that is exactly how the statement would be used in the months and years ahead.

When Trump won on November 8, panic ensued in the FBI, the wider intelligence community, and all of Washington, DC for that matter. Clinton wasn't supposed to lose. At first, various factors, ranging from disgruntled Bernie Sanders voters to FBI Director James Comey, were blamed. Ten days before the election, Comey briefly reopened the Clinton email investigation. What is often overlooked is that Comey had no intention of reopening the investigation or ever discussing the subject again. A few months earlier, on July 5, Comey had committed insubordination by giving a nationally televised speech in which he absolved Clinton of her email cover-up.[2] Like many, I remember precisely where I was and what I was doing that morning. In my case, it was having breakfast at a hotel in Houston with everyone glued to the TV. Comey started by listing all of Clinton's misdeeds, only to conclude that no reasonable prosecutor would bring a case against her. There was a stunned silence in the room. The entire speech was about Clinton's guilt; however, at the last minute, Comey absolved her.

Comey's speech provided insights into his deceptive thought process. It wasn't just that the speech did not match the conclusion. There was also the issue of Comey changing the legal standard surreptitiously. Comey stated that Clinton's behavior had been "extremely careless." However, the legal standard for mishandling classified documents is gross negligence.[3] Under any reasonable definition, there is no difference whatsoever between being extremely careless and being grossly negligent. By avoiding the use of the appropriate legal term and replacing it with a term that is functionally identical, Comey had attempted to mislead the public. In 2017, it was revealed that the first draft of Comey's speech had included the term "grossly negligent," implying that she had violated federal law.[4] Comey later changed the wording to "extremely careless," leaving no doubt that he had corruptly let Clinton off the hook. Furthermore, it was not Comey's responsibility to make any decisions regarding prosecution. That was a matter for the attorney general, Loretta Lynch.

Comey faced criticism for his actions, and he would have been the last person on Earth to want to reopen the entire affair. However, Anthony Weiner, the sex offender and husband of Clinton's top aide Huma Abedin, threw a monkey wrench into the works. A field agent in the FBI's New York office discovered a cache of Clinton's State Department emails—the ones she kept on her unauthorized server—on Weiner's laptop.[5] At the time, Weiner was being investigated for sexting with a fifteen-year-old girl from North Carolina, and his devices had been seized. But rather than reopening the case, FBI leadership buried it. This prompted an FBI field agent to inform his superior that no action was being taken regarding Clinton's emails on Weiner's laptop. The superiors later informed the inspector general that the field agent believed that "somebody was trying to bury this." Comey had to get ahead of the story. This is why he announced the reopening of the investigation. Of course, he had made plans to ensure that things would not go in an unwelcome direction. In just a few days, the FBI reportedly reviewed 650,000 emails, a task that Trump described as impossible. Subsequently, Comey announced that all was well and that he would not change his conclusions from his July 5 speech.[6]

While Comey's actions may have helped Trump in the final days of the election, they were not voluntary. Blaming Comey, or Bernie Sanders supporters for that matter, for Clinton's election loss would have been a bad strategy for the expanding anti-Trump coalition. Those excuses would have simply highlighted that Clinton was a poor candidate with lots of baggage. What was needed was a strategy that shifted the blame to external forces, forces beyond the control of Clinton or the Democratic Party. It soon became obvious who the bogeyman would be: Russia. Clinton's Swiftboat campaign had pioneered the path; all that needed to be done was for the federal government to weaponize that strategy.

On November 9, the day after the election, Strzok and Lisa Page resumed scheming through text messages. Page suggested convening a meeting of what she referred to as the "secret society." Strzok replied, "Too hard to explain here. Election related. Which is also godawful bad."[7] The next day, November 10, Strzok, Page, and the FBI's head of counterintelligence, Bill Priestap, met to strategize about election-related matters. The details of what they plotted remain unknown, but from what followed in the weeks ahead, it appears that the overarching goal was to establish a narrative that Russia had helped Trump win. Up to that point, most of the investigative activity was limited to the FBI, but in early December, the CIA joined the investigation. A December 9 *Washington Post* article co-authored by Ellen Nakashima—the same reporter who had been wittingly or unwittingly influencing the Swiftboat campaign's media messaging—claimed that the CIA had "concluded in a secret assessment that Russia intervened in the 2016 election to help Donald Trump win the presidency, rather than just to undermine confidence in the U.S. electoral system."[8] Nakashima also reported that the CIA had briefed "key Senators" on its conclusions.

Just as the Nakashima article in June was used to establish the narrative that the Russian government hacked the DNC to the exclusion of anyone else, her December article was used to establish the narrative that Trump owed his presidency to Putin. At the same time that Lisa Monaco, the White House Homeland Security and Counterterrorism adviser, stated that the "President has directed the Intelligence Community to conduct a full review of what happened during the 2016 election process," Nakashima, citing anonymous officials, claimed to already know the outcome, that Putin had helped Trump. Nakashima would later also be instrumental, wittingly or unwittingly, in seeding false narratives about Flynn and Carter Page.[9] Monaco, who appears to have been the White House's coordinator of the effort to undermine the incoming Trump administration through the intelligence community review, later became the deputy attorney general in the Biden administration. In this role, she supervises highly politicized cases, including the investigation of Trump for allegedly mishandling classified documents and the prosecution of individuals linked to the January 6 protests.

The media often repeated the claim that "all 17 intelligence agencies" had concluded that Putin helped Trump get elected. Even months later, in June 2017, the *New York Times* claimed that "[t]he latest presidential tweets were proof to dismayed members of Mr. Trump's party that he still refuses to acknowledge a basic fact agreed upon by 17 American intelligence agencies that he now oversees: Russia orchestrated the attacks, and did it to help get him elected."[10] Anyone with a functioning brain would have known that even if the specifics of the claim were true, and they were not, agencies such as the National Geospatial-Intelligence Agency, the National Reconnaissance Office, or US Coast Guard Intelligence would have had no input on the issue. Yet, they are part of the much-vaunted seventeen intelligence agencies. As an aside, with the establishment of Space Force in 2019, there are now eighteen intelligence agencies. Of course, just as US Coast Guard Intelligence has no special insight into Putin's thinking, intelligence officers in the Space Force don't either.

In truth, only three agencies were tasked with writing up the assessment that Putin had helped Trump get elected: the CIA, the FBI, and the National Security Agency. Within twenty-five days, these agencies would magically conjure up an Intelligence Community Assessment (ICA) titled "Assessing Russian Activities and Intentions in Recent US Elections."[11] This was completely unheard of. No self-respecting community of intelligence professionals would deem it appropriate to produce a report of this magnitude and importance within a few weeks. By comparison, the similarly dishonest intelligence community report on the origin of COVID-19, which consists of a paltry 5,497 words and only eighteen pages, took three months to complete.[12] When Biden issued a statement upon the completion of that report in August 2021, he praised the intelligence community for finishing the report in what he referred to as a "90-day sprint."[13] The ICA on alleged Russia collusion was completed in about a quarter of the time. It was never meant to be a sincere or serious document but rather a political one. And yet, it was the ICA that altered the course of national and international politics for generations to come.

Unusually, the ICA had no written terms of reference. Allegedly, Obama had given verbal instructions to "include everything."[14] James Clapper, Obama's director of National Intelligence (DNI) who was part of the ICA effort, later informed the Senate that "there was no document memorializing this presidential direction."[15] Clapper also admitted that without Obama's directions, the three agencies would not have undertaken the effort they did. Some might argue that Obama was trying to safeguard against the possibility that there really was collusion between Trump and the Kremlin. But that assertion does not pass the smell test. First, if he truly believed so, he should have allowed the FBI to proceed with its investigation covertly instead of effectively informing Trump that his scheme had been uncovered. But there is also a second, far more significant reason why Obama's ICA ploy was a deliberate attempt to sabotage his successor. As discussed earlier, in July 2016, US intelligence services intercepted communications indicating that Hillary Clinton had approved "a plan concerning U.S. presidential candidate Donald Trump and Russian hackers hampering U.S. elections as a means of distracting the public from her use of a private email server."[16] Someone had obtained details of Clinton's Swiftboat project, and the CIA got hold of that information. The individuals behind the intercepted communications remain unidentified, but the seriousness of the information prompted then-CIA Director John Brennan to brief President Obama in the Oval Office on July 28, 2016. Brennan's notes from that meeting reveal that Clinton had approved "a proposal from one of her foreign policy advisers to vilify Donald Trump by stirring up a scandal claiming interference by the Russian security service."[17]

The date of the briefing was just three days before Strzok formally opened the Crossfire Hurricane investigation into Trump. In a just world, he would have opened an investigation into Clinton for framing Trump. While it is likely that Comey was in attendance at the July 28 White House briefing, this is not known with certainty. However, it is known that Brennan formally shared the intelligence about Clinton's Swiftboat project with the FBI on September 7, just before the FBI escalated its investigation of Trump, including setting up an entrapment scheme for Papadopoulos, spying on Carter Page, and playing along with Sussmann's Alfa Bank hoax.[18] Instead of persisting with the Trump investigation, the FBI should have promptly initiated an investigation into Clinton. But this did not happen.

This takes us back to Obama. While he may not have known the details of what the FBI or its Swiftboat companions were up to, he did know that his own CIA director had warned him that Clinton had a plan to vilify Trump by stirring up a false scandal involving the Kremlin. This fact alone dispels the myth that Obama had good intentions when he ordered the ICA. Instead, Obama's intention was to severely undermine Trump before he was even inaugurated.

By all accounts, there were very few deliberations or internal debates about the ICA, which was sold to the public as the gold standard of intelligence assessments. There was broad agreement among the three agencies from the beginning that the entire effort was aimed at creating an official intelligence community document that attributed interference in the 2016 election to Russia in general, and Putin in particular, to assist Trump. It was understood by all that the ICA would be used as a political weapon to delegitimize the incoming Trump administration. To underline this point, Russia experts with decades of experience were excluded from the effort altogether.[19] The ICA plotters could not afford to be derailed by individuals with actual knowledge. The CIA's top two experts on Russia were so upset by what was unfolding that they twice wrote to then-CIA Director Brennan, bitterly complaining that there was no evidence whatsoever that Putin wanted to help elect Trump.[20]

According to a senior intelligence official who came forward in 2020 after one of the authors of the ICA had gone on CBS's *60 Minutes* to promote her work, "It was not an intelligence assessment."[21] The Brennan associate, CIA analyst Andrea Kendall-Taylor, had told *60 Minutes* that "the Russian government aspired to help President-elect Trump's election chances," adding that the ICA "was based on a large body of evidence that demonstrated not only what Russia was doing, but also its intent" and that "it's based on a number of different sources, collected human intelligence, technical intelligence."[22] Not only is there no evidence of any such sources or intelligence, but the whistleblower, who has not been named, asserted that the ICA was written by "just a small group of people selected and driven by Brennan himself" and that "Brennan did the editing." The source added that it "wasn't 17 agencies and it wasn't even a dozen analysts from the three agencies who wrote the assessment"; "It was just five officers of the CIA who wrote it, and Brennan hand-picked all five."

The whistleblower's claims, which were first publicized in 2020, were confirmed by former CIA director Mike Pompeo in his 2023 book, *Never Give an Inch*. Pompeo claims to have personally seen emails in which CIA officials, who had long careers specializing in Russia, bitterly complained to his predecessor, Brennan, about the flimsiness of the ICA:

> In February 2017, a senior career analyst and his colleague approached me to say that they had formally and vigorously objected in writing to two of the central features of the ICA. Their objections were twofold. First, it was their judgment that there was no basis for the claim that Putin had sought to undermine Hillary Clinton and support Donald Trump. Second, they believed that the ICA's mere mention of the unvetted, lie-ridden document known as the Steele dossier—which instigated a raft of unlawful FBI spying on the Trump campaign—was analytic malpractice.[23]

During his tenure as the CIA director, Pompeo saw no evidence that Putin wanted to help Trump get elected, let alone that they had colluded.

Both the whistleblower's and Pompeo's accounts align with the known facts. The published version of the ICA claims at the outset that "Putin and the Russian Government developed a clear preference for President-elect Trump." However, it fails to make the case that Putin favored Trump. The extremely short timespan for producing the ICA does not speak for its credibility or accuracy. But there are even more important reasons to believe the whistleblower. The Federal Security Service (FSB) was accused by Steele of being responsible for Russia's hacking activities, but the ICA attributed the blame to GRU, Russia's military intelligence service. Likewise, Mueller's special counsel office exclusively blamed the GRU. However, GRU is not mentioned in any Steele report. If the dossier was important enough to include in the ICA, why wasn't this inconsistency mentioned, let alone discussed? As we have seen in Report 86, Steele described a plot in which the FSB recruited Jewish American IT executives to spy on American citizens by embedding Trojan viruses in their software. Steele even claimed that this plot was a "significant operational success." Why was this not discussed in the ICA? Surely, such co-opting of American citizens by Russia's security services would have been a huge national security problem? Why did Brennan cherry-pick Steele's collusion allegations but ignore the arguably much bigger issue of millions of Americans being targeted by Russian malware?

In truth, the ICA was a political hit job. Putin did not have a favored candidate, let alone a candidate with whom he was colluding. One does not need to be a genius to come to this conclusion. Clinton was leading by wide margins in the polls and was widely expected to win. It was extremely unlikely that, even if there had been any interference by Russia, this could have influenced the outcome of the race. In comparison, the week-long media onslaught against Trump following the leak of the *Access Hollywood* tape would have had a far greater impact than anything Russia could have done. The most Putin could expect to achieve—assuming he had the intention of interfering in the election—was to create a bit of mischief. In fact, before the Russia collusion narrative gained traction, it had been widely assumed that if Russia was involved in anything, it was trying to sow discord, rather than support one or the other candidate. But after the election, that narrative was no longer useful to those who were intent on harming Trump. Adam Schiff, who was the top Democrat on the House Intelligence Committee at the time, acknowledged in an NBC interview, "Plainly, they were after discord and in this they were spectacularly successful."[24] However, with Trump's victory needing to be explained, Schiff had a new narrative. Russia wanted more than just to "sow discord"; they wanted to elect Trump: "They had a candidate with pro-Putin, pro-Russian views who belittled NATO, who was willing to potentially remove sanctions on Russia and by contrast they had in Secretary Clinton a candidate very tough on Russia."[25] The *Washington Post* made the same pivot. In a December 9, 2016 article, an unnamed intelligence official was cited as claiming that there was a consensus that Russia wanted to help elect

Trump. Purportedly, a new threshold had been crossed, indicating that Russia was not merely interested in meddling but actively seeking to have its preferred candidate elected.[26]

The main—and apparently only—point of contention between Brennan's handpicked ICA drafters and DNI James Clapper on one side and FBI leadership on the other side was how exactly to incorporate the Steele dossier into the ICA. The FBI leadership advocated for the dossier to be included in the main body, while Brennan and Clapper preferred it to be in an annex. Ironically, things turned out in favor of the FBI when Comey lost that fight. But more on that in a moment.

In typical Comey fashion, he evaded the issue when questioned by the Senate Judiciary Committee, stating, "I don't remember whether it was Brennan, I was told that the group's view was [the Steele dossier] was significant enough and consistent enough with the other intelligence that it ought to be included but it wasn't sufficiently corroborated to be in the body of the Intelligence Community Assessment so they put a brief summary of it in an annex."[27]

It does not take a genius to figure out why the FBI wanted to give the dossier maximum prominence. The FBI had spied on a presidential campaign, attempted to entrap presidential campaign advisors, and disregarded an intercepted communication that showed the opposing presidential campaign had orchestrated the entire scheme. Furthermore, nearly all of the FBI's actions were based on the Steele report. At the time, and to this day, Steele was the only person who had explicitly alleged collusion between Trump and Russia. Everyone else had merely raised the specter of collusion. But Steele said it was a fact. It was crucially important for FBI leadership to keep Steele's lies alive. If Steele was exposed as a liar, everything the FBI had done would collapse like a house of cards. Anyone who had touched the dossier would have had to resign or be fired. For this reason, the dossier needed to be made credible. The FBI leadership intended to achieve this by incorporating Steele's falsehoods in the ICA. It helped that Brennan wanted the same thing.[28]

It was a solid plan. If a formal intelligence community report cited Steele, the assumption among the media and the public would be that Steele's claims had been corroborated. And this is exactly how it played out.

On December 19, Strzok sent the following text message to an unnamed person: "Hey [redacted] need to talk, hit me here when you can. BLUF [bottom line up front]—I need to talk to [redacted] at the [redacted] about using his sh*t in the report POTUS has asked for."[29] It is not known who the unnamed person was but it is very clear that Strzok was talking about the ICA. It might have been Page's boss, McCabe, who was himself a big proponent of incorporating the dossier in the ICA.

The following day, the FBI finally identified Steele's primary sub-source, Igor Danchenko.[30] This created many new problems. Danchenko was not a well-connected Kremlin mole. He had no connections to the Kremlin and did not even live in Russia. In fact, he lived just a few miles from the FBI's headquarters. It was a catastrophe that the FBI leadership covered up by designating Danchenko as a confidential human source, thereby removing him from scrutiny and providing complete protection from any investigations, including congressional inquiries. Incredibly, the fact that corrupt FBI leaders hid Danchenko from view isn't even the worst part of this story. What is even worse is when they decided to do so. Buried deep inside thousands of trial documents from the case brought by Special Counsel John Durham against Danchenko is a reference to an FBI email dated January 12, 2017, which discussed the FBI's plan to make Danchenko a confidential human source.[31] The problem with this is that on January 12, the FBI had not yet spoken to Danchenko. Why would the FBI hire a confidential human source about whom they knew nothing? The only possible answer is that FBI leadership already knew that the Steele dossier was a bunch of lies and that the only way to perpetuate the dossier hoax was to hide the purported source. As we now know, the FBI's devious plan worked. It took us almost four years to finally bring Danchenko to light.

But the FBI had an even more immediate problem after they identified Danchenko in December 2016. They could not afford to let the Danchenko identification get in the way of incorporating Steele's dossier in the ICA. The way they accomplished this was to delay talking to Danchenko. Had they done so immediately, and had Danchenko told them then what he told them a month later, which is that the dossier was based on stories his friends told him in jest at a bar, it would have been more difficult to include the dossier. According to documents revealed years later by the Senate Intelligence Committee, FBI leadership pushed hard for the inclusion of the dossier. Their main argument was that since Obama had directed that the ICA "include everything," the dossier needed to be included.[32] The same argument was used to set aside the usual requirement that all information used in official assessments needed to be corroborated. In a December 17 phone call with Clapper, Comey falsely vouched for Steele, claiming he was a "credible person with a source and sub-source network in position to report on such things."[33] Comey also pleaded for the dossier to be included in the ICA: "we thought it important to bring it forward to the IC effort." Comey did not mention that three months earlier, Steele had been offered $1 million for any information that would corroborate his dossier claims, but he did not do so. The FBI also concealed this information from Congress, congressional inquiries, Trump officials, and the courts. Comey also failed to update the ICA group when, three days later, Danchenko was identified, and it became evident that he was a former Washington, DC think tank staffer who did not have any access to Kremlin insiders.

The CIA's representatives on the ICA group were not convinced. They maintained that the Steele dossier should not be in the main part of the report and "recommended that it be moved to an appendix."[34] Brennan later informed the Senate Intelligence Committee that "so as long as [the Steele dossier] was separated from the ICA's substance and judgments and as long as it was not going to be part of the formal briefing we gave on the ICA, we felt, ok, Jim [Comey], you want to do it, okay. We're not going to object."[35]

FBI Deputy Director Andrew McCabe disagreed. In a December 28 email to Clapper, McCabe wrote, "I would also like to speak with you tomorrow about my concerns about where the [Steele] references will appear in the joint report, notwithstanding the fact that it is officially part of the assessment. We oppose CIA's current plan to include it as an appendix; there are a number of reasons why I feel strongly that it needs to appear in some fashion in the main body of the reporting, and I would welcome the chance to talk to you about it tomorrow."[36] When questioned about his push to promote the dossier to the main section of the ICA, McCabe informed Inspector General Horowitz that he had three reasons for doing so. First, Obama had asked for "everything you have relevant to this topic of Russian influence." Second, he stated that the FBI had "confidence in" Steele. Third, McCabe asserted that "he felt strongly that the Steele election reporting belonged in the body of the ICA, because he feared that placing it in an appendix was 'tacking it on' in a way that would 'minimiz[e]' the information and prevent it from being properly considered."[37]

Comey's and McCabe's efforts failed. When the ICA was presented to Obama on January 5, the Steele dossier, or a summary of it, was featured in an annex and not the main body. What Comey and McCabe did not know at the time was that demoting the Steele dossier to an annex turned out to be a significant victory for the FBI. The reason for this was because of how the media interpreted the fact that the dossier was in an annex. In retrospect, it was probably predictable that things would turn out this way. The inclusion of the dossier in an annex meant that it was not part of the publicly released version of the ICA.[38] That version was published on January 6. In the following days, one or more people leaked the fact that a synopsis of the dossier was included in an annex. The media's angle in reporting this was that Trump had been briefed on the dossier. CNN's headline on January 10 read: "Intel chiefs presented Trump with claims of Russian efforts to compromise him."[39] The article, which featured Evan Perez, Jim Sciutto, Jake Tapper, and Carl Bernstein of Watergate fame in the byline, claimed that "the synopsis was considered so sensitive it was not included in the classified report about Russian hacking that was more widely distributed, but rather in an annex only shared at the most senior levels of the government: President Obama, the President-elect, and the eight Congressional leaders." Thus, the prevailing media narrative quickly became that the dossier had been placed in an annex not because of its inherent flaws but because it contained extremely sensitive intelligence. Placing the dossier in the annex greatly enhanced its power, rather than downgrading it. Was this Comey's and McCabe's work? Had they leaked the annex story to Tapper or Bernstein in an effort to turn a loss into a win? We never found out who leaked the information, but things could not have turned out better for the FBI or the others in the ICA group, for that matter. From the moment the CNN story was published, the entire focus of the Trump-Russia collusion narrative centered on the phony dossier.

To this day, the classified version of the ICA remains under lock and key. But this probably does not matter much. If the classified sections contained damning evidence of Trump-Russia collusion, or even just of Putin meddling to help Trump, we would most likely have found out by now. After all, Mueller, the media, Democrats, and other anti-Trump forces would have liked nothing more than such evidence. But there is no evidence of collusion or meddling.

The public version of the ICA comprises fifteen pages, most of which are either blank or insignificant. The main section comprises only five pages of text with very generous spacing. This section broadly asserts that: "By their nature, Russian influence campaigns are multifaceted and designed to be deniable because they use a mix of agents of influence, cutouts, front organizations, and false-flag operations." The sole piece of evidence provided for this sweeping assertion is that "Moscow demonstrated this during the Ukraine crisis in 2014, when Russia deployed forces and advisers to eastern Ukraine and denied it publicly."[40] Even if, for the sake of argument, we were to accept that Russia did what the ICA accuses it of in 2014, how does that prove that Putin helped elect Trump? It doesn't.

The Intelligence Community Assessment

Another point highlighted by the ICA as proof of a malign influence campaign is that the international Russian news broadcaster RT aired negative stories about Hillary Clinton. Even if, for argument's sake, we were to accept this claim, how much influence would that amount to? A study from the United Kingdom revealed that 76 percent of the public gets its news from the BBC, whereas only 2 percent watched RT.[41] The figure is now at zero percent after the United Kingdom and other European countries banned RT in 2022 following the Ukraine war.[42] The BBC, of course, was highly influential in promoting Russiagate.[43] It does not appear as if Brennan's ICA group even attempted to assess negative reporting about Trump on RT or to compare the ratio of negative RT reporting on Clinton to negative reporting on Trump overall.

The ICA also states that a journalist claimed that Russian trolls who opposed the 2014 coup in Ukraine were assisting Trump on social media. Leaving aside the folly of attributing an intelligence community assessment to a single journalist, who was likely biased from the start, we now know from Elon Musk's Twitter Files revelations that Twitter, under its previous Democrat-friendly leadership, investigated these claims of Russian trolls but was unable to substantiate them.[44]

As ridiculous as these assertions are, they do not even come close to the ICA's coup de grâce, which is its focus on RT's coverage of the 2012 presidential election. The ICA claims that RT's reporting in 2012 was designed to "fuel discontent" in the United States. Aside from the fact that the 2012 election does not tell us anything about how Putin feels about Trump, there had been a broad consensus—at least before the hype surrounding Russia collusion started in late 2016—that if Russia was doing anything at all, it was trying to sow discontent.

Further evidence that undermines the ICA can be found in the fact that the House Intelligence Committee was briefed in early December 2016—before the ICA was commissioned—indicating that there was no consensus on Putin's motivations: "In terms of favoring one candidate over another, you know, the evidence is a little bit unclear."[45] The briefing was conducted by Julia Gurganus, a national intelligence officer on Russia working in Clapper's DNI office. An FBI official, whose identity remains unknown, was similarly uncertain about the Kremlin's intentions.[46] Perhaps that person, who might have worked for Peter Strzok, had not received the memo about the new narrative. Brennan's ICA group had received the memo, and miraculously, within a few weeks, ICA drafters claimed to know precisely what Putin had been doing all along. Clapper later told the House

Intelligence Committee that Gurganus did not have access to "very, very sensitive information" when she gave her briefing.[47] No such information has emerged in the past eight years. This suggests that Clapper was referring to the Steele dossier or that he fabricated his story about "very, very sensitive information."

The ICA was completed on or just before January 5, 2017, when it was presented to Obama. Brennan, Clapper, Comey, and NSA Director Michael Rogers personally briefed Obama at the White House that day. During this briefing, then-Vice President Joe Biden, who was also present, advised Comey to pursue General Michael Flynn on Logan Act charges.[48] The Logan Act is a law from 1799 that makes it illegal for private citizens to discuss official government business with foreign officials. It has never been used in any prosecution. Biden's suggestion came in light of information that Flynn had talked on the phone to Sergei Kislyak, the then-Russian ambassador in Washington, DC, even though it was Flynn's job as the incoming National Security Advisor to talk to foreign officials. Flynn's conversation was later used as a pretext by Comey to have Flynn fired. Using the conversation with Kislyak as a pretext, Comey sent Strzok to the White House to conduct an ambush interview with Flynn.[49] Despite Flynn accurately stating that he had not discussed sanctions with Kislyak, he was still accused of having done so. Consequently, Flynn was fired. The truth only came to light four years later when the transcripts of his conversations with Kislyak were made public.[50]

On January 6, the same briefers met President-elect Trump and his national security team at Trump Tower to present them with the ICA. After the meeting, Comey stayed behind to tell Trump about the dossier in private.[51] As he would later claim, the purpose of briefing Trump in this manner was that Comey could gauge Trump's reaction when told about the salacious dossier stories about Trump's alleged sexual exploits. In fact, by that point, the FBI had identified Igor Danchenko and knew that he was not in a position to know what Steele claimed he knew. Comey did not tell Trump about this, nor about the fact that nothing in the dossier had been corroborated.

A few hours later, the fact that the dossier had been included in the ICA and that Trump had been briefed on it was leaked to the media. Because nothing in the dossier had ever been corroborated, and because the media in 2016 still had slightly higher standards than it does nowadays, there had been very little reporting on the dossier up to that point. What was needed was a veneer of legitimacy, as well as a news hook. Inclusion of the dossier in the ICA provided legitimacy, and Trump being briefed provided the news hook. On January 10, CNN's Tapper and his colleagues ran the aforementioned article that seeded the notion that the dossier was included in an annex because it was extremely sensitive, rather than because it was completely unverified. The dossier of lies had been officially legitimized. From that day on, hardly a day passed during the next four years without the media whining about Trump-Russia collusion.

Not even a last-minute snag could stop the floodgates. Tapper's plan had been to create a daily drip effect by leaking dossier stories one by one instead of releasing the entire document. This was not only good for the news cycle but probably necessary, as anyone presented with the full dossier would likely have realized that the entire document was bogus. Panic ensued when, a day after Tapper's CNN story was released, Ken Bensinger of BuzzFeed News published the entire dossier.[52] Tapper was extremely angry and lashed out at Bensinger, stating, "I think your move makes the story less serious and credible," and adding that Bensinger had "damaged [the dossier's] impact."[53] But Tapper needn't have worried. While some observers, such as Paul Gregory from the Hoover Institution writing in *Forbes* magazine, immediately recognized that the dossier was a hoax, most people were far more credulous and trusting.[54] And who can blame them? An average citizen does not have the time or patience to examine Steele's thirty-five-page dossier. Most people simply want the bottom line, and the bottom line that the media fraudulently presented was that, because the intelligence community had supposedly validated the dossier, Trump stood credibly accused of colluding with Russia to get elected.

This was likely the true purpose of the ICA, and it could not have worked out more perfectly. It was a significant victory for Obama, who had commissioned the ICA, but it marked only the beginning of the establishment's attack on Trump's presidency. What followed were four years of investigations and daily smears regarding Russia collusion. The fallout continues to this day. When FBI informant Alexander Smirnov was arrested in February 2024 for allegedly lying to the FBI about Joe Biden receiving a bribe from Ukrainian energy company Burisma, Department of Justice prosecutors successfully invoked the ICA to deny Smirnov bail.[55] There was no connection between the ICA and Smirnov, but prosecutors convinced a judge that since the ICA had determined that Putin had assisted in Trump's election in 2016, he would likely do the same in 2024 unless Smirnov was detained pending trial. It was laughable, but it underlined how incredibly successful the ICA hoax was in entrenching a false narrative.

EPILOGUE

The Butterfly Effect

Mueller's special counsel operation lasted for 742 days, which is more than half of Trump's presidency. Throughout this entire period, the media reporting was predominantly focused on Trump and his alleged collusion with Russia. It was the defining topic of the news cycle from 2017 until 2019. Not a day passed without another sensational story about the mounting pressure on Trump. In the end, there was no Russia collusion. There never was, as Mueller and the FBI knew all along. The entire effort was aimed at sabotaging Trump's presidency and ruining his prospects of negotiating peaceful relations with the world's largest nuclear power. Looking back at this period of time, one can only conclude that the effort was wildly successful.

Trump had run on a platform of putting America first. During his 2016 campaign, he frequently pointed out that the United States was bearing most of the cost of the NATO alliance while its supposed allies were freeloading. Trump also questioned the wisdom of constantly feuding with Russia instead of trying to make peace.

Trump's wise words and ideas did not sit well with the Washington, DC establishment, who thought that "America First" was a retreat from the geopolitical playground they had dominated since World War II. What raised particular concern was Trump's stance on Crimea, the peninsula that was annexed by Russia in February 2014, right after the Obama State Department assisted in organizing a coup d'état in Ukraine.

According to a leaked phone call from State Department official Victoria Nuland in early February 2014, the Ukraine coup was approved by then-Vice President Biden. Much about the events surrounding the US-backed coup remains shrouded in mystery, including the identity of the snipers who shot and killed scores of protesters in Maidan Square in Ukraine's capital, Kiev. The massacre on February 20 directly led to the downfall of Ukraine's President Viktor Yanukovych on February 22. Russia annexed Crimea on February 27. Yanukovych was replaced by Arseniy Yatsenyuk, the same man whom Nuland had anointed as her chosen leader of Ukraine in her phone call a few weeks earlier.

While the Maidan massacre was immediately blamed on police working on behalf of Yanukovych, a very different picture has emerged over the past year. Even a Ukrainian court has now found that the Maidan protesters were likely massacred by snipers directed by protest leaders, such as the far-right Svoboda party, and not by the police led by Yanukovych.[1]

The idea that a Trump presidency could expose the real roots of the 2014 Ukraine coup was unsettling for the Washington, DC establishment as a whole. It was especially concerning for supporters of Ukraine, such as Nuland and a Democratic Party operative named Alexandra Chalupa.

Chalupa is the daughter of Ukrainian immigrants with connections to the Ukrainian diaspora in America and to the US Embassy in Ukraine. She also worked for the DNC. During the 2016 election, she lobbied the Ukrainian embassy in Washington to take action regarding candidate Trump and was at the forefront of efforts to tarnish Trump's campaign manager, Paul Manafort, whom she called "Putin's political brain for manipulating U.S. foreign policy and elections."[2] Ukraine's ambassador in Washington, DC, Valeriy Chaly, subsequently published an op-ed in *The Hill*, criticizing Trump for even considering the idea of recognizing Russia's annexation of Crimea. What is often forgotten is that the Crimean peninsula had always been Russian before it was transferred to the Ukrainian Soviet Socialist Republic in 1954 by Soviet leader Nikita Khrushchev, who had himself grown up in Eastern Ukraine.

While the annexation of Crimea can be debated, it is not as straightforward a case as portrayed by the media and the Washington, DC establishment. By the time Trump commented on the issue, Russia had already held the territory for two years and showed no intention of returning it. It wasn't as if Trump could magically turn back the clock. In fact, anyone with a modicum of common sense knew that Russia was not going to relinquish Crimea, no matter what. Trump's open-mindedness regarding the issue was highly sensible, but it only made him appear more threatening to the establishment. If Trump were to reset relations with Russia, it would undermine the establishment's foreign policy hegemony. Normalizing relations with

Russia would also have reduced the significance of NATO. The establishment's long-held dream of extending the NATO alliance to Ukraine and Georgia would have been dead in the water.

While it is no secret that the combined forces of the establishment were deeply opposed to Trump, it was unprecedented for a foreign country's ambassador to intervene in the US presidential race with an op-ed aimed at undermining one of the leading candidates. But things were only getting started with Ambassador Chaly's intervention. Former Prime Minister Yatseniuk wrote on Facebook that candidate Trump "challenged the very values of the free world."[3] This was more than hypocritical coming from the man whom Nuland had handpicked as Ukraine's post-coup leader. Ukraine's interior minister, Arsen Avakov, also criticized Trump, referring to him as a "clown" and asserting that Trump posed "an even bigger danger to the US than terrorism."[4]

Ukrainian operatives and officials did not stop there. Words are one thing, but they let actions follow. Out of the blue, a handwritten ledger surfaced in Ukraine in August 2016. The ledger purported to show that Trump's campaign manager had received millions of off-the-books payments from Yanukovych's party. The stunt killed two birds with one stone. Manafort was fired, and Trump was damaged. Ukraine's then-president, Petro Poroshenko, bragged in an August 2016 phone call with Biden that his government had released the ledger. Both men snickered about Manafort's fate. As it turned out later, the ledger was likely fake, which does not mean that Manafort was innocent.[5] His numerous tax issues resurfaced later during the Mueller investigation. The Ukrainians had correctly identified a weak link in Trump's campaign and successfully undermined him. The fact that Manafort was replaced by the highly affable and competent Kellyanne Conway was likely a blessing in disguise for Trump. Manafort's firing did not turn out as the Ukrainians had intended.

One of the key figures behind these efforts to tarnish Trump was Chalupa, who later confessed that the Ukrainian Embassy in Washington "worked directly with reporters researching Trump, Manafort, and Russia to point them in the right directions."[6] Chalupa also collaborated with Michael Isikoff, a reporter from Yahoo News, who later fueled the media's narrative of Russian collusion against Trump by inaccurately claiming that Carter Page had ties to the Kremlin.[7]

As a paid Democratic Party operative, Chalupa was very likely informed about the broader scheme to link Trump to Russia. But the ferocity of her efforts to thwart Trump, as well as the efforts of Ukrainian officials, had less to do with supporting Clinton than with an aversion to Trump's pragmatic approach to relations with Russia. The intelligence agencies and foreign policy establishment shared that aversion, regardless of supporting Clinton.

Ukrainian officials likely saw Trump as an existential threat to the survival of their country. It was a giant miscalculation. Despite all his flaws, Trump projected strength in foreign policy, both on the question of Ukraine and more broadly. Despite fake media reports claiming the opposite, Trump was tough on Russia, even tougher than Obama, under whose watch Crimea was annexed. The Trump administration imposed multiple rounds of sanctions on Russia. Trump even imposed sanctions on Russian officials and citizens to penalize them for alleged election interference in 2016.[8] The Ukrainian officials who had demonstrably tried to interfere in the election—and later admitted to doing so—were not sanctioned.[9]

Unlike Obama, Trump was also the first president to supply Ukraine with lethal weapons. Contrary to what legacy media now claims, that decision was not the result of Trump's first impeachment after he had been accused in 2019 of pressuring Ukrainian President Volodymyr Zelenskyy to investigate the Bidens. That decision was made by Trump in 2017, long before most people even knew that Hunter Biden had used his father's position to secure a profitable no-show job from a Ukrainian oligarch.[10]

The countless false narratives about Trump cannot conceal the fact that the Russiagate plot caused tremendous damage not only to Trump but also to the country and the world as a whole. The US-led coup in 2014 firmly set the Western alliance on a path toward a new Cold War with Russia, or worse. Trump, the candidate, recognized this and sensibly asked whether this was a good idea or if there were any alternatives. He also recognized that China was the main threat to the Western alliance, especially since the ascension of Xi Jinping in 2012. But the combined forces of the Clinton campaign, the Washington establishment, and the media threw a spanner in the works by fraudulently linking Trump to Russia.

In one fell swoop, the plot defeated all of Trump's good intentions. Clinton's Swiftboat project, which was later adopted by the Washington establishment, successfully undermined Trump to the extent that diplomatic relations with Russia were essentially criminalized. Trump found himself being pushed into the opposite corner, where he felt compelled to appease the Russiagate skeptics with symbolic actions like imposing sanctions on Yevgeny Prigozhin, a figure referred to by the corporate media as "Putin's chef."[11] Prigozhin, who died in a 2023 plane crash near Moscow, was the owner of Concord Management and Consulting, a firm that operates restaurants in Russia.[12] Mueller's special counsel operation accused Concord of financially supporting a group known as the Internet Research Agency. Allegedly, that group interfered in the 2016 election by reportedly purchasing three thousand Facebook ads. Prigozhin was sanctioned in early 2018 by Trump's Treasury Department, which was overseen by Steve Mnuchin. It was a classic case of "shoot first, ask questions later." More sanctions were imposed on Prigozhin in September 2019, just as Ukraine impeachment proceedings against Trump were beginning.[13] It was likely yet another effort to appease Trump's enemies, and, just like previous attempts, it would fail.

The sad fact is that there should not have been so much appeasement, and there should have been a lot more resistance. The Concord case proves that not only could this have been done, but it also needed to happen. Concord was unique in that it decided to mount a counteroffensive against the charges brought by Mueller. And they were proven right when, in March 2020, the DOJ, which had taken over the case from Mueller, decided to drop all charges.[14] While Mueller's team utilized its indictments against several Russian nationals for media and PR purposes, they never anticipated any of these Russians to actually appear and defend the charges. Concord unexpectedly fought back. Their defense attorney, Eric Dubelier, successfully argued that there was no evidence whatsoever that Prigozhin's company, Concord, had done anything wrong, and that the entire case was political. He was correct, and the DOJ abandoned the case altogether before Dubelier could expose Mueller's misdeeds in public. The government's official excuse for dropping all charges was that moving the case to trial would bring "risk of exposure of law enforcement's tools and techniques," but that only reinforces that the case was a political stunt from the start.[15] After all, if you are unable to bring a case to trial, you should not bring it at all. In a strange twist of irony, the Concord case was dismissed on March 16, 2020, a day that will live in infamy for a very different reason. It was the day when Trump fatefully announced, "15 Days to Slow the Spread," which almost certainly doomed his re-election prospects.[16] It's almost as if fate has decided that any significant victory for Trump must immediately be followed by a major blunder. The exact same situation happened in 2019 when Trump had his infamous phone call with the Ukrainian president just a few hours after Robert Mueller had absolved him of colluding with Russia.

The Concord case makes one wonder about what might have happened if other accused Russians had appeared to defend themselves against the spurious charges brought by Mueller's team, including those accused of hacking the DNC. The alleged DNC hack stands out as the holy grail of

Russiagate. It is the one narrative that has stuck, even as the dossier and other hoaxes, such as the Alfa Bank hoax, have fallen apart. Once one realizes that the Steele dossier was entirely fabricated and that there was no Russia collusion, what is left? The only thing left is that Russia hacked the DNC. That is what we have all been told so many times that there is seemingly no room for doubt. And yet, no one has ever presented a shred of evidence that that actually happened. The FBI never even got to examine the DNC's servers.[17] Instead, they had to rely on the say-so of a private company whose sworn statements sharply contrast with its public pronouncements. Even *Slate* magazine, which ran the phony Alfa Bank story, had to admit that any conclusions about the DNC hack are hard to trust, considering that the FBI was never allowed to access the DNC's server.[18]

While the false Russiagate accusations prevented Trump from pursuing diplomacy with Russia, he compounded the problem by attempting to appease his detractors, thereby exacerbating the situation. There can be little doubt that without the Clinton Swiftboat project, the public perception of Russia as a mortal enemy would never have become so deeply entrenched. The Democratic Party itself underwent a significant shift from seeking potential diplomatic solutions with Russia to viewing Russia as the world's greatest pariah. A few years before the Swiftboat smear, Obama was caught on an open microphone telling the then-Russian president, Dmitry Medvedev, that he would have "more flexibility" to negotiate with Russia after the 2012 presidential election.[19] But suddenly, all that was gone. Suddenly, the Democratic Party aligned itself with warmongers and neocons. The party that had stood for distrust of the intelligence agencies became their biggest apologist and promoter. The Democratic Party's foreign policy became bellicose, marking a departure from its historical stance. Suddenly, it was Trump and a faction of the Republican Party that became the doves, while the Democratic Party aligned with the neocons as hawks.

By 2016, the deterioration of relations with Russia had been going on for some time. But there was still time to reverse the trend. In fact, this had been one of Trump's stated goals when he ran for president. What none of us knew at the time was that the inception of Clinton's Swiftboat project in February 2016 ensured that things could only get worse. This was when the butterfly first flapped its wings. A couple of people at Clinton's campaign headquarters had the idea of creating a fake narrative linking Trump to Russia. They probably didn't have grand geopolitical strategies in mind; they were simply creating a plan for a rainy day.

They knew their candidate had used a private email server while serving as secretary of state. They further knew that thirty thousand of the emails on the private server were missing and that they were probably not all about yoga and Chelsea's wedding, as the candidate had claimed. They were unsure if someone had hacked or otherwise obtained those emails and needed an action plan in case the emails were leaked in the lead-up to the election. Using Russia as the bogeyman in the Swiftboat campaign was perfect. By blaming Russia for any potential leaks of Clinton's emails, the campaign aimed to shift focus away from the content of those emails.

In the end, Clinton's emails were never leaked. But the fact that the strategy was nevertheless effective was proven four years later when it was used by the Biden campaign. When the contents of Hunter Biden's laptop were disclosed three weeks ahead of the 2020 election, Biden blamed Russia.[20] It worked, and Joe Biden was inaugurated as president despite the laptop demonstrably proving that he had lied when he claimed he didn't know anything about his son's overseas business dealings.[21]

We will never know what would have happened if Clinton's thirty thousand emails had been leaked. But we did find out, to our collective detriment, what would happen if her Swiftboat plan went into action, as it did in late July 2016 in response to DNC emails being released by WikiLeaks. The process took some time to unfold. The emails in question were not particularly revealing, and the notion that Russia posed an existential threat to life on Earth was not as deeply ingrained as it is today. Most importantly, Clinton's campaign did not push the issue as hard as it might have if Clinton had not been far ahead in the polls. Additionally, if the subject matter had been Clinton's emails instead of random DNC emails, the campaign's approach might have been different.

And so it came to be that the idea of Trump as a Manchurian candidate controlled by Russia only gained momentum after Trump's unexpected victory. If Trump had not won, we probably would never have heard of Russia collusion again. Despite having seeded the Russia collusion hoax, it is possible that Clinton herself, after having bungled her first attempt in 2009, might have tried to reset relations with Russia.[22]

But Trump did win, and the Washington, DC establishment immediately and fully co-opted what had begun as a dirty tricks campaign to shackle Trump and specifically prevent him from engaging in diplomacy with Russia. An added bonus—one that the collusion plotters could not necessarily have expected—was that by attempting to appease his detractors, Trump adopted a tough stance on Russia. Four years of Russia collusion hysteria contributed to firmly establishing the idea among the general public that Russia was the number one enemy. Trump's detractors had achieved the best of both worlds. Not only was Trump prevented from pursuing peace with Russia, but he was also inadvertently fulfilling many wishes of his adversaries.

As mentioned, it is not without irony that on the day after the Russiagate hoax formally ended with Robert Mueller's congressional testimony, Trump carelessly ignited the next hoax by talking on the phone to Ukraine's Zelenskyy about Biden corruption while a dozen or more people from the permanent bureaucracy—who all hated Trump—including the now-infamous Alexander Vindman, were listening in.

It's not so much that Trump did anything objectively wrong; he did not. He had every right to inquire about the role, if any, that Joe Biden might have played in facilitating the firing of the Ukrainian general prosecutor who was targeting Hunter Biden's patron. The problem was that Trump said what he said at the most inopportune time and in the most unfavorable circumstances.

Throughout 2021, the world came to recognize Zelenskyy as a staunch opponent of Russia. But it wasn't always like this. Zelenskyy, a television actor who had portrayed an ordinary man unexpectedly becoming the president of Ukraine, found himself in the actual role of the president of Ukraine, this time for real. He won the 2019 presidential election by a landslide by running on a platform of making peace with Russia. But that ambition was quickly undermined both by domestic anti-Russian pressure, as well as through international pressure.

Trump's impeachment issue in Ukraine had a lot to do with the latter. While the media portrayed the entire situation as a quid pro quo, there was never any evidence of that. First, in his now-infamous phone call, Trump simply asked for Zelenskyy's cooperation with the Biden investigation.[23] He did not coerce Zelenskyy, nor did he make any threats. Second, Ukraine received the Javelin missiles, which were the supposed object of the extortion plot, on time. Other than being exceedingly clumsy, Trump did nothing wrong. During the latter part of 2019, the effort to remove Trump due to the phone call gained momentum. It was a given that a compliant media would do the Democrats' bidding. But they would have done that for any allegation or impeachment attempt. The choice of Ukraine as the topic of Trump's first impeachment was deliberate. Just as one of the objectives and effects of the Russiagate hoax was to criminalize diplomacy with Russia, one of the main objectives of the Ukraine impeachment hoax was to further reinforce the criminalization of diplomacy with Russia.

The result of all this was that Trump was neutralized as a potential peace envoy in Zelenskyy's stated intentions to make peace with Russia. By the time Zelenskyy and Putin met in December 2019, any prospects of peace had been ruined.[24] Trump couldn't talk to Putin because that would have immediately been regarded as selling out to Russia. But he couldn't talk to Zelenskyy either because anything he said or did would be perceived as an attempt to mitigate the impeachment situation or as advancing the alleged quid pro quo. For his part, Zelenskyy couldn't be seen as making any concessions to Putin. Had he done so, he might have been accused of doing Trump's bidding as part of an imaginary quid pro quo. The fact that Trump was in the process of being impeached over delaying weapons shipments to Ukraine had made it clear who the boss was. It wasn't Trump. The situation was completely intractable. There would be no peace; there wouldn't even be peace talks.

By perpetrating both the Russiagate scam and the Ukraine impeachment scam, the Washington, DC establishment had successfully thwarted any possibility of a resolution to Ukraine-Russia hostilities, which began in 2014, not in 2022. The revelation that the CIA has been secretly constructing bases along the Ukraine-Russia border since 2014 only underscores why the Washington establishment could not afford to let Trump act as a peace broker or investigate what was truly happening in Ukraine.[25] The same applies to the fact that Joe Biden fired the prosecutor who was investigating his son's Ukrainian firm.[26] Short of a Trump win in 2020—with the political capital that a victory would have brought—the path toward a full-scale war between Russia and Ukraine was set in motion with the Russiagate hoax and solidified with Trump's first impeachment.

To be sure, there were many reasons for Trump's loss in 2020. He should not have let Anthony Fauci publicly undermine him for so many months. He should have insisted on moving forward with the presidential commission of inquiry into the origin of the pandemic instead of allowing Treasury Secretary Steve Mnuchin and National Economic Council Director Larry Kudlow to dissuade him. He should have seen to it much earlier that Republicans countered the election law maneuvers promoted by the Democratic super lawyer Marc Elias, the same man who masterminded the Swiftboat hoax. There is a lot more that could be added to this list. However, it is beyond doubt that if the true story about Hunter Biden's laptop had become known to voters, the election—which was decided in the electoral college by less than forty-four thousand voters across three states—would have had a different outcome. The laptop proved that Joe

Biden had been involved in his son's shady business dealings and that he had repeatedly lied about his involvement. The reason the story was successfully suppressed is due to the original Russiagate hoax. When the laptop story first emerged, social media giants shut it down, claiming that it was Russian disinformation. It is inconceivable that such an obvious lie would have had so much success without everyone being conditioned by years of Russia collusion claims. As we would later discover, social media companies had been warned about the impending Hunter Biden laptop leak by the FBI, which had never ceased its efforts to undermine Trump's presidency.[27] The FBI's actions in falsely prebunking the laptop scandal to protect Joe Biden were simply a continuation of their Russia collusion scam.

During the second presidential debate on October 22, 2020, Biden himself claimed that the laptop story was a Russian plot.[28] More than fifty former intelligence officials, including five former CIA directors—John Brennan, Michael Hayden, John McLaughlin, Michael Morell, and Leon Panetta—wrote a letter falsely insinuating that the entire laptop had been fabricated by Russia.[29] However, anyone with an internet connection could have easily verified the contents of the laptop by matching emails with other parties on email chains. This was one of the first things that Stephen McIntyre and I did, and the emails matched. There were also numerous audio files of Hunter and various other individuals in conversation, many of which were deeply distressing and could not have been fabricated.

However, by that point, the minds of the general public and the media had been so thoroughly conditioned that any mention of Russian disinformation immediately discredited whatever was labeled as such. Without four years of Russia collusion hysteria, no one would have believed the ridiculous excuses for Hunter Biden's laptop.

Soon after the election, it was confirmed that Hunter Biden was indeed under FBI investigation in connection with crimes documented on the laptop.[30] In 2023, he was indicted based on information found on his laptop.[31] A post-election poll found that if voters had known about the FBI's Hunter Biden investigation in connection with the laptop, Trump would have easily won.[32]

As for Biden, despite all his rhetoric about standing up to Russia, the Ukraine war occurred during his presidency. His catastrophic handling of the Afghanistan withdrawal emboldened adversaries worldwide. His bellicose tone, falsely blaming Russia for fabricating a laptop documenting his family's very real corruption woes, made reconciliation impossible. And then, to top it all off, Biden exacerbated the situation when he offered

NATO membership to Ukraine in December 2021, at a time when tensions were already at a breaking point.[33] This was a well-known significant red line for Russia, as had been confirmed by William Burns, CIA chief under Biden: "Ukrainian entry into NATO is the brightest of all redlines for the Russian elite (not just Putin). In more than two and a half years of conversations with key Russian players, from knuckle-draggers in the dark recesses of the Kremlin to Putin's sharpest liberal critics, I have yet to find anyone who views Ukraine in NATO as anything other than a direct challenge to Russian interests."[34] Biden appeared to be either blissfully unaware of this red line, he didn't care, or perhaps his cognitive abilities are too impaired to have understood what he was doing.

Be that as it may, Biden's actions have pushed Russia into the welcoming embrace of China, forming a new and formidable alliance that will fundamentally reshape the geopolitical landscape for generations to come. In just a few short years, we have transitioned from the post-World War II paradigm to something much more perilous and unstable.

In the end, it was a scam orchestrated by a few operatives at the Clinton campaign headquarters that initiated a process that has brought us to the brink of World War III. Long after we are all gone, Hillary Clinton's Swiftboat hoax will be remembered as the greatest geopolitical sabotage of all time.

Notes

Foreword
1. Examination of the FBI's Crossfire Hurricane Investigation, U.S. Department of Justice, December 9, 2019, p. 188, https://www.justice.gov/storage/120919-examination.pdf.
2. "Newly Declassified Document Indicates FBI Misled Congress on Reliability of Steele Dossier," Senate Judiciary Committee, August 19, 2020, https://www.judiciary.senate.gov/press/rep/releases/newly-declassified-document-indicates-fbi-misled-congress-on-reliability-of-steele-dossier.

Introduction
1. Report on the Investigation into the FBI's Crossfire Hurricane Investigation, U.S. Department of Justice, August 2023, p. 53, https://www.justice.gov/storage/durham report.pdf.
2. Stephen McIntyre and Ross McKitrick, "Hockey Sticks, Principal Components, and Spurious Significance," Geophysical Research Letters 32, no. 2 (February 2005): 1-4, https://doi.org/10.1029/2004GL021750.
3. Dave McKinney, "DePaul Professor: George Papadopoulos Was 'Zealous And A Bit Simple'," WBEZ, October 30, 2017, https://www.wbez.org/stories/depaul-professor-george-papadopoulos-was-zealous-and-a-bit-simple/51c0334a-8f92-452a-8158-11fde4450f49.
4. The Trump-Russia Dossier as Released by BuzzFeed, Scribd, January 10, 2017, https://www.scribd.com/document/336226994/The-Trump-Russia-Dossier-as-Released-By-Buzzfeed.
5. Tom Lobianco, "How the Anti-Trump Dossier Came to Be," interview by Hari Sreenivasan, NewsHour, PBS, October 28, 2017, https://www.pbs.org/newshour/show/conservative-site-was-original-funder-of-anti-trump-dossier.
6. Glenn Simpson and Peter Fritsch, Crime in Progress (New York: Random House, 2019), chap. 6, Kindle.
7. Ken Bensinger, Miriam Elder, and Mark Schoofs, "These Reports Allege Trump Has Deep Ties To Russia," Buzzfeed, January 10, 2017, https://www.buzzfeednews.com/article/kenbensinger/these-reports-allege-trump-has-deep-ties-to-russia.

8 Nick Gass, "Trump has spent years courting Hillary and other Dems," Politico, June 16, 2015, https://www.politico.com/story/2015/06/donald-trump-donations-democrats-hillary-clinton-119071.
9 Zeke Miller, "When Donald Trump Praised Hillary Clinton," Time, July 17, 2015, https://time.com/3962799/donald-trump-hillary-clinton/.
10 Matt Taibbi, "In the Year of Trump, the Joke Was On Us," Rolling Stone, December 29, 2015, https://www.rollingstone.com/politics/politics-news/in-the-year-of-trump-the-joke-was-on-us-60847/.
11 "Special Counsel John Durham Testifies on Investigation of the FBI," C-SPAN, June 21, 2023, video, 2:05:12, https://www.c-span.org/video/?528789-1/special-counsel-john-durham-testifies-investigation-fbi-part-1. Durham states: "There is not a single substantive piece of information in the dossier that has ever been corroborated by the FBI, or to my knowledge anyone else."
12 Examination of the FBI's Crossfire Hurricane Investigation, U.S. Department of Justice, December 9, 2019, https://www.justice.gov/storage/120919-examination.pdf.
13 Chuck Grassley, "Debunked Anti-Trump Dossier Sub-Source Who Sought to Traffic Classified Information Remained on FBI Payroll Until Late 2020," Senator Chuck Grassley, October 5, 2023, https://www.grassley.senate.gov/news/news-releases/debunked-anti-trump-dossier-sub-source-who-sought-to-traffic-classified-information-remained-on-fbi-payroll-until-late-2020.
14 Lee Smith, The Plot Against the President: The True Story of How Congressman Devin Nunes Uncovered the Biggest Political Scandal in U.S. History (New York: Center Street, 2019).
15 Chad Day, "Ex-Trump campaign adviser sentenced to 14 days in prison," Associated Press, September 8, 2018, https://apnews.com/33b41dfa67164c9b973784248c3f90f6/Ex-Trump-campaign-adviser-sentenced-to-14-days-in-prison.
16 Report on the Investigation into Russian Interference in the 2016 Presidential Election, Special Counsel's Office, U.S. Department of Justice, March 22, 2019, https://www.justice.gov/archives/sco/file/1373816/download.
17 Office of the Director of National Intelligence to Senator Chuck Grassley, May 29, 2020, https://www.grassley.senate.gov/imo/media/doc/2020-05-29%20ODNI%20to%20CEG%20RHJ%20(Flynn%20Transcripts).pdf.
18 Office of the Director of National Intelligence to Senator Chuck Grassley, May 29, 2020, p. 15, https://www.grassley.senate.gov/imo/media/doc/2020-05-29%20ODNI%20to%20CEG%20RHJ%20(Flynn%20Transcripts).pdf.
19 Katelyn Polantz, "Transcript released of Flynn voicemail from Trump lawyer showing possible attempt to obstruct," CNN, May 31, 2019, https://www.cnn.com/2019/05/31/politics/michael-flynn-john-dowd-voicemail/index.html
20 Report on the Investigation into Russian Interference in the 2016 Presidential Election, Special Counsel's Office, U.S. Department of Justice, March 22, 2019, p. 81, https://www.justice.gov/archives/sco/file/1373816/download.
21 The Bolt Report (@theboltreport), "Former Foreign Minister Alexander Downer," Twitter, May 9, 2019, https://twitter.com/theboltreport/status/1126422767820087297.
22 Report on the Investigation into the FBI's Crossfire Hurricane Investigation, U.S. Department of Justice, May 2023, p. 53, https://www.justice.gov/storage/durhamreport.pdf. The report states: "According to Downer, Papadopoulos made no mention of Clinton emails, dirt or any specific approach by the Russian government to the Trump

campaign team with an offer or suggestion of providing assistance. Rather, Downer's recollection was that Papadopoulos simply stated 'the Russians have information' and that was all."

23 Volume 5 of the Senate Intelligence Committee Report on Russian Active Measures, U.S. Senate Select Committee on Intelligence, August 18, 2020, p. 476, https://www.intelligence.senate.gov/sites/default/files/documents/report_volume5.pdf.

24 Hans Mahncke (@HansMahncke), "302s of Trump Foreign Policy Meeting Attendees," Twitter, June 1, 2020, https://twitter.com/HansMahncke/status/1267541776241434629.

25 Assessment on Russian Activities and Intentions in Recent US Elections, Office of the Director of National Intelligence, January 6, 2017, https://www.dni.gov/files/documents/ICA_2017_01.pdf.

26 "Read Newly Released Russia Probe Transcripts from the House Intelligence Committee," PBS NewsHour, May 7, 2020, https://www.pbs.org/newshour/politics/read-newly-released-russia-probe-transcripts-from-the-house-intelligence-committee.

27 Michael Isikoff and David Corn, Russian Roulette: The Inside Story of Putin's War on America and the Election of Donald Trump (New York: Twelve, 2018), 98-110.

28 Michael Isikoff, "U.S. Intel Officials Probe Ties Between Trump Adviser and Kremlin," Yahoo News, September 23, 2016, https://news.yahoo.com/u-s-intel-officials-probe-ties-between-trump-adviser-and-kremlin-175046002.html.

29 Erik Wemple, "David Corn and the Steele dossier: Just checking the facts!," Washington Post, January 10, 2020, https://www.washingtonpost.com/opinions/2020/01/10/david-corn-steele-dossier-just-checking-facts/.

30 Michael Isikoff and David Corn, Russian Roulette: The Inside Story of Putin's War on America and the Election of Donald Trump, (New York: Twelve, 2018), 99.

31 Glenn Simpson and Peter Fritsch, Crime in Progress (New York: Random House, 2019), chap. 13, Kindle.

32 Electronic Communication, February 9, 2017, https://www.judiciary.senate.gov/imo/media/doc/February%209,%202017%20Electronic%20Communication.pdf.

33 Examination of the FBI's Crossfire Hurricane Investigation, U.S. Department of Justice, December 9, 2019, https://www.justice.gov/storage/120919-examination.pdf.

34 Jeremy Diamond and Nicole Gaouette, "Donald Trump unveils foreign policy advisers," CNN, March 21, 2016, https://www.cnn.com/2016/03/21/politics/donald-trump-foreign-policy-team/index.html.

35 Carter Page HPSCI Hearing Transcript, November 2, 2017, p. 122, https://intelligence.house.gov/uploadedfiles/carter_page_hpsci_hearing_transcript_nov_2_2017.pdf.

36 FISA Warrant Application for Carter Page, U.S. Senate Judiciary Committee, https://www.judiciary.senate.gov/imo/media/doc/FISA%20Warrant%20Application%20for%20Carter%20Page.pdf.

37 Examination of the FBI's Crossfire Hurricane Investigation, U.S. Department of Justice, December 9, 2019, https://www.justice.gov/storage/120919-examination.pdf.

38 Examination of the FBI's Crossfire Hurricane Investigation, U.S. Department of Justice, December 9, 2019, p. 215, https://www.justice.gov/storage/120919-examination.pdf.

39 Examination of the FBI's Crossfire Hurricane Investigation, U.S. Department of Justice, December 9, 2019, p. 190, https://www.justice.gov/storage/120919-examination.pdf.

40 Examination of the FBI's Crossfire Hurricane Investigation, U.S. Department of Justice, December 9, 2019, footnote 389, https://www.justice.gov/storage/120919-examination.pdf.

41. Examination of the FBI's Crossfire Hurricane Investigation, U.S. Department of Justice, December 9, 2019, footnote 389, https://www.justice.gov/storage/120919-examination.pdf. The footnote states: "Email communications reflect that in March 2017-after the first FISA application and first renewal were filed and before the last two renewals-the Supervisory Intel Analyst reviewed the first FISA application and the first renewal at OGC's request to assist with potential redactions before the Department responded to Congressional information requests. The Supervisory Intel Analyst 1 provided comments to the OGC Attorney, including advising him that the Primary Sub-source was not [REDACTED] as stated in the FISA applications, and asking whether a correction should be made. The Supervisory Intel Analyst did not provide any other comments relating to the Primary Sub-source, and he told us that he did not notice anything else potentially inaccurate or incomplete in the applications at that time."

42. Electronic Communication, February 9, 2017, https://www.judiciary.senate.gov/imo/media/doc/February%209,%202017%20Electronic%20Communication.pdf.

43. Kevin Clinesmith Indictment, U.S. District Court for the District of Columbia, August 14, 2020, https://www.documentcloud.org/documents/7036421-Kevin-Clinesmith-Indictment.

44. Electronic Communication, February 9, 2017, https://www.judiciary.senate.gov/imo/media/doc/February%209,%202017%20Electronic%20Communication.pdf.

45. Report on the Investigation into the FBI's Crossfire Hurricane Investigation, U.S. Department of Justice, August 2023, p. 14, https://www.justice.gov/storage/durhamreport.pdf.

46. Electronic Communication, February 9, 2017, p. 14, https://www.judiciary.senate.gov/imo/media/doc/February%209,%202017%20Electronic%20Communication.pdf.

47. Electronic Communication, February 9, 2017, p. 13, https://www.judiciary.senate.gov/imo/media/doc/February%209,%202017%20Electronic%20Communication.pdf.

48. Tim Mak and Katie Zavadski, "Meet The Man Who Is Spinning For Donald Trump In Russia," Daily Beast, September 8, 2016, https://www.thedailybeast.com/meet-the-man-who-is-spinning-for-donald-trump-in-russia; Catherine Belton, "The shadowy Russian émigré touting Trump," Financial Times, November 1, 2016, https://www.ft.com/content/ea52a678-9cfb-11e6-8324-be63473ce146; Jennifer Rubin, "Trump's Russia problem," Washington Post, September 26, 2016, https://www.washingtonpost.com/blogs/right-turn/wp/2016/09/26/trumps-russia-problem/.

49. Alexey Kovalev et al., "Meduza spoke to all the likely sources behind the 'Steele dossier.' The report that forever transformed Donald Trump into a 'Russian agent' looks less and less convincing," Meduza, November 3, 2020, https://meduza.io/en/feature/2020/11/03/raw-intelligence.

50. Fridman v. Bean LLC, U.S. District Court for the District of Columbia, June 21, 2021, https://storage.courtlistener.com/recap/gov.uscourts.dcd.189930/gov.uscourts.dcd.189930.153.4.pdf, https://storage.courtlistener.com/recap/gov.uscourts.dcd.189930/gov.uscourts.dcd.189930.153.5.pdf, https://storage.courtlistener.com/recap/gov.uscourts.dcd.189930/gov.uscourts.dcd.189930.153.6.pdf, https://storage.courtlistener.com/recap/gov.uscourts.dcd.189930/gov.uscourts.dcd.189930.153.7.pdf, https://storage.courtlistener.com/recap/gov.uscourts.dcd.189930/gov.uscourts.dcd.189930.153.8.pdf, https://storage.courtlistener.com/recap/gov.uscourts.dcd.189930/gov.uscourts.dcd.189930.153.9.pdf.

51. "May Harvard CAPS/Harris Poll: Trump Now Beats Biden by 7 Points in 2024 Presidential Matchup," PR Newswire, May 23, 2024, https://www.prnewswire.com

/news-releases/may-harvard-caps—harris-poll-trump-now-beats-biden-by-7-points-in-2024-presidential-matchup-301829894.html.

52 "Merrick Garland testifies at Senate Judiciary Committee Confirmation Hearing," C-SPAN, February 22, 2021, video, 01:29:07, https://www.c-span.org/video/?508877-1/attorney-general-confirmation-hearing-day-1.

Chapter 1

1 Marshall Cohen, "Hillary Clinton personally approved plan to share Trump-Russia allegation with the press in 2016, campaign manager says," CNN, May 20, 2022, https://www.cnn.com/2022/05/20/politics/hillary-clinton-robby-mook-fbi/index.html.
2 "Email from John Podesta," WikiLeaks, February 26, 2016, archived November 10, 2016, https://web.archive.org/web/20161110001858/https://wikileaks.org/podesta-emails/emailid/56595.
3 "Bucharest Summit Declaration," North Atlantic Treaty Organization, NATO, April 3, 2008, https://www.nato.int/cps/en/natolive/official_texts_8443.htm.
4 Katharina Wagner, "Das große Rätsel um Genschers angebliches Versprechen," Frankfurter Allgemeine, April 19, 2014, https://www.faz.net/aktuell/politik/ost-erweiterung-der-nato-was-versprach-genscher-12902411.html.
5 Jonathan Marcus, "Ukraine crisis: Transcript of leaked Nuland-Pyatt call," BBC, February 7, 2014, https://www.bbc.com/news/world-europe-26079957.
6 "Statement Regarding Russian and Belarusian Individuals at The Championships 2022," Wimbledon, April 20, 2022, https://www.wimbledon.com/en_GB/news/articles/2022-04-20/statement_regarding_russian_and_belarusian_individuals_at_the_championships_2022.html.
7 Guo Shipeng and Ben Blanchard, "China signs border demarcation pact with Russia," Reuters, July 21, 2008, https://www.reuters.com/article/us-china-russia-border/china-signs-border-demarcation-pact-with-russia-idUKPEK29238620080721.
8 Alexander Burns, "Donald Trump Reaffirms Support for Warmer Relations With Putin," New York Times, August 1, 2016, https://www.nytimes.com/2016/08/02/us/politics/donald-trump-vladimir-putin-russia.html.
9 Erhard Dagi, The NATO Strategy and the New Security Environment, NATO Defense College, July 1999, https://www.nato.int/acad/fellow/99-01/dagi.pdf.
10 Donald Trump, The America We Deserve (Los Angeles: Renaissance Books, 2000), 142.
11 Mike Allen, "TRUMP to Chuck Todd, on his military advisers: 'Well, I, watch the shows' – On whether to admit Ukraine to NATO: 'I would not care that much, to be honest'—May soon rule out third-party bid," Politico, August 16, 2015, https://www.politico.com/tipsheets/playbook/2015/08/trump-to-chuck-todd-on-his-military-advisers-well-i-watch-the-shows-on-whether-to-admit-ukraine-to-nato-i-would-not-care-that-much-to-be-honest-may-soon-rule-out-third-party-bid-212543.
12 Nick Gass, "Donald Trump's 11 worst foreign policy gaffes," Politico, September 4, 2015, https://www.politico.com/story/2015/09/donald-trump-foreign-policy-gaffes-2016-213345.
13 G. Mitchell Reyes, "The Swift Boat Veterans for Truth, the Politics of Realism, and the Manipulation of Vietnam Remembrance in the 2004 Presidential Election," Rhetoric and Public Affairs 9, no. 4 (Winter 2004): 571-600, https://www.jstor.org/stable/41940103.

Chapter 2

1. Glenn Simpson and Peter Fritsch, Crime in Progress (New York: Random House, 2019), chap. 4, Kindle.
2. Ryan Mills and Tobias Hoonhout, "Democratic Legal Activist Marc Elias Has Spent a Career Preparing for the 2020 Election Fight," National Review, November 3, 2020, https://www.nationalreview.com/news/democratic-legal-activist-marc-elias-has-spent-a-career-preparing-for-the-2020-election-fight/.
3. Molly Ball, "The Secret History of the Shadow Campaign That Saved the 2020 Election," Time, February 4, 2021, https://time.com/5936036/secret-2020-election-campaign/.
4. "Perkins Coie and Its Political Law Group Announce the Formation of the Independent Firm Elias Law Group LLP," Perkins Coie, August 2, 2023, https://www.perkinscoie.com/en/news-insights/perkins-coie-and-its-political-law-group-announce-the-formation-of-the-independent-firm-elias-law-group-llp.html.
5. Conciliation Agreement, Federal Election Commission, March 29, 2022, https://static1.squarespace.com/static/6243b3f8b001843f2379a673/t/624486ac6da88f37bd43e98d/1648658094980/MUR+7449+closing+letter+to+Coolidge+Reagan+Foundation.pdf.
6. United States v. Michael Sussmann, U.S. District Court for the District of Columbia, Indictment September 16, 2021, https://www.justice.gov/sco/press-release/file/1433511/download.
7. "IN PERSON: Christopher Steele: Former MI6 Officer," YouTube video, posted by Oxford Union, March 1, 2022, https://www.youtube.com/watch?v=fLVQfwwN_r8. Steele states that the dossier "was actually a series of single source intelligence reports," shifting the blame to Danchenko.
8. ABC set up an interview with Millian under false pretenses. The interview never aired, however, footage from the interview was later used in a Clinton campaign ad: Hillary Clinton (@HillaryClinton), "Indebted to Russia?," Twitter, September 22, 2016, https://twitter.com/HillaryClinton/status/779055195607166977; The Wall Street Journal, where Fusion GPS's founders previously worked, ran a baseless smear piece against Millian: Mark Maremont, "Key Claims in Trump Dossier Said to Come From Head of Russian-American Business Group", Wall Street Journal, January 24, 2017, http://www.wsj.com/articles/key-claims-in-trump-dossier-came-from-head-of-russian-american-business-group-source-1485253804.
9. Glenn Simpson and Peter Fritsch, Crime in Progress (New York: Random House, 2019), chap. 5, Kindle.
10. Glenn Simpson and Peter Fritsch, Crime in Progress (New York: Random House, 2019), chap. 5, Kindle.
11. Lee Smith, "New Documents Suggest The Steele Dossier Was A Deliberate Setup For Trump," The Federalist, January 2, 2019, https://thefederalist.com/2019/01/02/new-documents-suggest-steele-dossier-deliberate-setup-trump/.
12. Rowan Scarborough, "Cody Shearer, Sidney Blumenthal emerge in Russia dossier case," Washington Times, January 31, 2018, https://www.washingtontimes.com/news/2018/jan/31/cody-shearer-sidney-blumenthal-emerge-russia-dossi/.
13. Jane Mayer, "Christopher Steele, the Man Behind the Trump Dossier," The New Yorker, March 5, 2018, https://www.newyorker.com/magazine/2018/03/12/christopher-steele-the-man-behind-the-trump-dossier; Lee Smith, "Unpacking the Other Clinton-Linked Russia Dossier," Real Clear Investigations, April 26, 2018; https://www

Notes

.realclearinvestigations.com/articles/2018/04/25/test.html; Volume 5 of the Senate Intelligence Committee Report on Russian Active Measures, U.S. Senate Select Committee on Intelligence, August 18, 2020, p. 891, https://www.intelligence.senate.gov/sites/default/files/documents/report_volume5.pdf.

14. Volume 5 of the Senate Intelligence Committee Report on Russian Active Measures, U.S. Senate Select Committee on Intelligence, August 18, 2020, p. 846, https://www.intelligence.senate.gov/sites/default/files/documents/report_volume5.pdf.

15. Lee Smith, "New Documents Suggest The Steele Dossier Was A Deliberate Setup For Trump," The Federalist, January 2, 2019, https://thefederalist.com/2019/01/02/new-documents-suggest-steele-dossier-deliberate-setup-trump/.

16. Lee Smith, "Unpacking the Other Clinton-Linked Russia Dossier," Real Clear Investigations, April 26, 2018, https://www.realclearinvestigations.com/articles/2018/04/25/test.html.

17. Lee Smith, "Unpacking the Other Clinton-Linked Russia Dossier," Real Clear Investigations, April 26, 2018, https://www.realclearinvestigations.com/articles/2018/04/25/test.html.

18. Steele Dossier, DocumentCloud, Report 112, https://www.documentcloud.org/documents/21200685-steele-dossier.

19. Fridman v. Bean LLC, U.S. District Court for the District of Columbia, June 21, 2021, https://storage.courtlistener.com/recap/gov.uscourts.dcd.189930/gov.uscourts.dcd.189930.153.4.pdf, https://storage.courtlistener.com/recap/gov.uscourts.dcd.189930/gov.uscourts.dcd.189930.153.5.pdf, https://storage.courtlistener.com/recap/gov.uscourts.dcd.189930/gov.uscourts.dcd.189930.153.6.pdf, https://storage.courtlistener.com/recap/gov.uscourts.dcd.189930/gov.uscourts.dcd.189930.153.7.pdf, https://storage.courtlistener.com/recap/gov.uscourts.dcd.189930/gov.uscourts.dcd.189930.153.8.pdf, https://storage.courtlistener.com/recap/gov.uscourts.dcd.189930/gov.uscourts.dcd.189930.153.9.pdf.

20. Robert Baer, "Putin Will Be All Over Twitter if There's No Regulations on This Fake Accounts," Newsroom, CNN, November 25, 2022, video, https://grabien.com/story.php?id=403007.

21. Zachary Stieber, "Reporters Worked Closely With Fusion GPS on Trump–Russia Stories, Emails Show," Epoch Times, April 26, 2022, https://www.theepochtimes.com/article/reporters-worked-closely-with-fusion-gps-on-trump-russia-stories-emails-show-4428926.

22. Fusion GPS Emails, DocDroid, accessed August 5, 2024, https://www.docdroid.net/YLaEg5W/searchpage4-pdf#page=409.

23. Franklin Foer, "The Quiet American," Slate, April 28, 2016, https://slate.com/news-and-politics/2016/04/paul-manafort-isnt-a-gop-retread-hes-made-a-career-of-reinventing-tyrants-and-despots.html.

24. Franklin Foer, "Putin's Puppet," Slate, July 4, 2016, https://www.slate.com/articles/news_and_politics/cover_story/2016/07/vladimir_putin_has_a_plan_for_destroying_the_west_and_it_looks_a_lot_like.html.

25. Glenn Simpson and Peter Fritsch, Crime in Progress (New York: Random House, 2019), chap. 7, Kindle.

26. Jeremy Herb, "Mook suggests Russians leaked DNC emails to help Trump," Politico, July 24, 2016, https://www.politico.com/story/2016/07/robby-mook-russians-emails-trump-226084.

27 Alana Abramson and Shushannah Walshe, "The 4 Most Damaging Emails From the DNC WikiLeaks Dump," ABC, July 25, 2016, https://abcnews.go.com/Politics/damaging-emails-dnc-wikileaks-dump/story?id=40852448.
28 Michael Crowley, "Why Putin hates Hillary," Politico, July 25, 2016, https://www.politico.com/story/2016/07/clinton-putin-226153.
29 Letter to Sen. Graham Regarding Declassification of FBI's Crossfire Hurricane Investigations, September 29, 2020, https://www.judiciary.senate.gov/imo/media/doc/09-29-20_Letter%20to%20Sen.%20Graham_Declassification%20of%20FBI%27s%20Crossfire%20Hurricane%20Investigations_20-00912_U_SIGNED-FINAL.pdf.
30 Jeremy Herb, "Hillary Clinton Campaign Manager Robby Mook Testifies FBI Was Told about Trump-Russia Allegations," CNN, May 20, 2022, https://www.cnn.com/2022/05/20/politics/hillary-clinton-robby-mook-fbi/index.html.
31 Glenn Simpson and Peter Fritsch, Crime in Progress (New York: Random House, 2019), chap. 6, Kindle.
32 Greg Miller, "As Russia reasserts itself, U.S. intelligence agencies focus anew on the Kremlin," Washington Post, September 14, 2016, https://www.washingtonpost.com/world/national-security/as-russia-reasserts-itself-us-intelligence-agencies-focus-anew-on-the-kremlin/2016/09/14/cc212c62-78f0-11e6-ac8e-cf8e0dd91dc7_story.html
33 Electronic Communication, February 9, 2017, https://www.judiciary.senate.gov/imo/media/doc/February%209,%202017%20Electronic%20Communication.pdf.
34 "Trump Advisor quoted Putin in response to a question about sanctions," TVC News, July 7, 2016, translated by author, https://www.tvc.ru/news/show/id/96031; "Famous Economist Carter Page Delivered a Speech to NES Graduates," New Vedomosti, July 8, 2016, translated by author, https://nvdaily.ru/info/80347.html.
35 Durham Reporter Email List, Scribd, April 25, 2022, https://www.scribd.com/document/571730091/2022-04-25-HUGE-Durham-Reporter-Email-List.
36 FISA Warrant Application for Carter Page, U.S. Senate Judiciary Committee, https://www.judiciary.senate.gov/imo/media/doc/FISA%20Warrant%20Application%20for%20Carter%20Page.pdf.
37 Stephen Bierman, "Russian Government Backs Sale of 19.5% Rosneft Stake Next Year," Bloomberg, July 3, 2014, https://www.bloomberg.com/news/articles/2014-07-03/russian-government-backs-sale-of-19-5-rosneft-stake-next-year.
38 Natasha Bertrand, "Memos: CEO of Russia's state oil company offered Trump adviser, allies a cut of huge deal if sanctions were lifted," Business Insider, January 27, 2017, https://www.businessinsider.com/carter-page-trump-russia-igor-sechin-dossier-2017-1.
39 "Special Counsel John Durham Testifies at the House Judiciary Committee," C-SPAN, June 21, 2023, video, 2:05:12, https://www.c-span.org/video/?528789-1/special-counsel-john-durham-testifies-investigation-fbi-part-1. Durham states: "There is not a single substantive piece of information in the dossier that has ever been corroborated by the FBI, or to my knowledge anyone else."
40 FOOL_NELSON (@FOOL_NELSON), "Danchenko List," Twitter, August 6, 2020, https://twitter.com/FOOL_NELSON/status/1291791519939207169.
41 Hans Mahncke (@HansMahncke), "It appears that Danchenko," Twitter, July 20, 2020, https://twitter.com/HansMahncke/status/1285237810027532288.

Notes

42. Report on the Investigation into the FBI's Crossfire Hurricane Investigation, U.S. Department of Justice, May 2023, p. 129, https://www.justice.gov/storage/durham report.pdf.
43. Report on the Investigation into the FBI's Crossfire Hurricane Investigation, U.S. Department of Justice, May 2023, p. 133, https://www.justice.gov/storage/durham report.pdf.

Chapter 3

1. Electronic Communication, February 9, 2017, https://www.judiciary.senate.gov/imo/media/doc/February%209,%202017%20Electronic%20Communication.pdf.
2. Electronic Communication, February 9, 2017, https://www.judiciary.senate.gov/imo/media/doc/February%209,%202017%20Electronic%20Communication.pdf.
3. Letter from the Attorney General to Chairman Graham Regarding Declassification of Crossfire Hurricane Investigations, Senate Judiciary Committee, September 24, 2020, https://www.judiciary.senate.gov/imo/media/doc/AG%20Letter%20to%20Chairman%20Graham%209.24.2020.pdf.
4. Redacted FBI Witness Interview, December 20, 2017, p. 18, https://s3.documentcloud.org/documents/6887584/Redacted-FBI-Witness-Dec-20-2017.pdf.
5. Hans Mahncke (@HansMahncke), "Mook on CNN," Twitter, September 29, 2020, https://twitter.com/HansMahncke/status/1311030611843461123.
6. Redacted FBI Witness Interview, December 20, 2017, p. 31, https://s3.documentcloud.org/documents/6887584/Redacted-FBI-Witness-Dec-20-2017.pdf.
7. Redacted FBI Witness Interview, December 20, 2017, p. 29, https://s3.documentcloud.org/documents/6887584/Redacted-FBI-Witness-Dec-20-2017.pdf.
8. Report on the Investigation into the FBI's Crossfire Hurricane Investigation, U.S. Department of Justice, May 2023, p. 245, https://www.justice.gov/storage/durham report.pdf.
9. Report on the Investigation into the FBI's Crossfire Hurricane Investigation, U.S. Department of Justice, May 2023, p. 246, https://www.justice.gov/storage/durham report.pdf.
10. Report on the Investigation into the FBI's Crossfire Hurricane Investigation, U.S. Department of Justice, May 2023, p. 247, https://www.justice.gov/storage/durham report.pdf.
11. Report on the Investigation into the FBI's Crossfire Hurricane Investigation, U.S. Department of Justice, May 2023, p. 94, https://www.justice.gov/storage/durhamreport.pdf.
12. Ben Feuerherd and Bruce Golding, "FBI agent mocked Trump-Russia tale pushed by Clinton camp as '51-50ish'," New York Post, May 17, 2022, https://nypost.com/2022/05/17/fbi-agent-mocked-trump-russia-tale-pushed-by-clinton-camp/.
13. Report on the Investigation into the FBI's Crossfire Hurricane Investigation, U.S. Department of Justice, May 2023, p. 111, https://www.justice.gov/storage/durhamreport.pdf.
14. Sussmann was eventually acquitted by a Washington, D.C. jury. Josh Gerstein, "Sussmann Acquitted on Charge Brought by Special Counsel Durham," Politico, May 31, 2022, https://www.politico.com/news/2022/05/31/sussmann-acquitted-trump-special-counsel-00036033.

15 United States v. Michael Sussmann, U.S. District Court for the District of Columbia, Indictment, September 16, 2021, p. 13, https://www.justice.gov/sco/press-release/file/1433511/download.
16 United States v. Michael Sussmann, U.S. District Court for the District of Columbia, Indictment, September 16, 2021, p. 14, https://www.justice.gov/sco/press-release/file/1433511/download.
17 Hans Mahncke (@HansMahncke), "Fake Alfa Dossier," Twitter, April 7, 2022, https://twitter.com/HansMahncke/status/1512156287832047617.
18 Steele Dossier, DocumentCloud, Report 80, https://www.documentcloud.org/documents/21200685-steele-dossier.
19 Kevin Liptak, Kaitlan Collins, and Jeremy Diamond, "Led by notorious germaphobe, West Wing braces for coronavirus," CNN, March 3, 2020, https://www.cnn.com/2020/03/03/politics/donald-trump-germaphobe-coronavirus/index.html
20 Examination of the FBI's Crossfire Hurricane Investigation, U.S. Department of Justice, December 9, 2019, p. 95, https://www.justice.gov/storage/120919-examination.pdf.
21 James B. Comey, "Statement by FBI Director James B. Comey on the Investigation of Secretary Hillary Clinton's Use of a Personal E-Mail System," Federal Bureau of Investigation, July 5, 2016, https://www.fbi.gov/news/press-releases/statement-by-fbi-director-james-b-comey-on-the-investigation-of-secretary-hillary-clinton2019s-use-of-a-personal-e-mail-system.
22 Examination of the FBI's Crossfire Hurricane Investigation, U.S. Department of Justice, December 9, 2019, p. 85, https://www.justice.gov/storage/120919-examination.pdf.
23 Ken Bensinger, Red Card: How the U.S. Blew the Whistle on the World's Biggest Sports Scandal (New York: Simon & Schuster, 2018), 19; Steele Dossier, DocumentCloud, Report 94, https://www.documentcloud.org/documents/21200685-steele-dossier.
24 Ken Bensinger, Red Card: How the U.S. Blew the Whistle on the World's Biggest Sports Scandal (New York: Simon & Schuster, 2018), 19.
25 https://s3.documentcloud.org/documents/6887584/Redacted-FBI-Witness-Dec-20-2017.pdf, p. 29
26 Steele Dossier, DocumentCloud, Report 80, https://www.documentcloud.org/documents/21200685-steele-dossier.
27 Steele Dossier, DocumentCloud, Report 97, https://www.documentcloud.org/documents/21200685-steele-dossier.
28 Steele Dossier, DocumentCloud, Report 113, https://www.documentcloud.org/documents/21200685-steele-dossier.
29 Steele Dossier, DocumentCloud, Reports 80, 101, and 130, https://www.documentcloud.org/documents/21200685-steele-dossier.
30 Ken Bensinger, Miriam Elder, and Mark Schoofs, "These Reports Allege Trump Has Deep Ties To Russia," Buzzfeed, January 10, 2017, https://www.buzzfeednews.com/article/kenbensinger/these-reports-allege-trump-has-deep-ties-to-russia
31 Paul Roderick Gregory, "The Trump Dossier Is Fake—And Here Are The Reasons Why," Forbes, January 13, 2017, https://www.forbes.com/sites/paulroderickgregory/2017/01/13/the-trump-dossier-is-false-news-and-heres-why
32 Assessing Russian Activities and Intentions in Recent US Elections, Office of the Director of National Intelligence, January 6, 2017, https://www.dni.gov/files/documents/ICA_2017_01.pdf.

Notes

33 Public Statement on the Hunter Biden Emails, Politico, October 19, 2020, https://www.politico.com/f/?id=00000175-4393-d7aa-af77-579f9b330000.

34 Michael Flynn Resignation Letter, February 13, 2017, https://s3.documentcloud.org/documents/3461411/Michael-Flynn-Resignation-Letter.pdf.

35 Steele Dossier, DocumentCloud, Report 101, https://www.documentcloud.org/documents/21200685-steele-dossier.

36 Robert Windrem, "Guess Who Came to Dinner With Flynn and Putin," NBC, April 18, 2017, https://www.nbcnews.com/news/world/guess-who-came-dinner-flynn-putin-n742696.

37 Malia Zimmerman, "Hillary Clinton sided with Russia on sanctions as Bill made $500G on Moscow speech," Fox News, July 18, 2017, https://www.foxnews.com/politics/hillary-clinton-sided-with-russia-on-sanctions-as-bill-made-500g-on-moscow-speech.

38 Michael Schmidt, Mark Mazzetti, and Matt Apuzzo, "Trump Campaign Aides Had Repeated Contacts With Russian Intelligence," New York Times, February 14, 2017, https://www.nytimes.com/2017/02/14/us/politics/russia-intelligence-communications-trump.html.

39 "George W. Bush on Trump and Russia: 'We all need answers'," Associated Press, February 27, 2017, https://apnews.com/article/fb5ab4c8ff58440490c7139a31cc5802.

40 "HPSCI Hearing on Russian Active Measures Investigation," Federal Bureau of Investigation, March 20, 2017, https://www.fbi.gov/news/testimony/hpsci-hearing-titled-russian-active-measures-investigation.

41 Rod Rosenstein Letter Appointing Robert Mueller Special Counsel, May 17, 2017, https://www.documentcloud.org/documents/3726408-Rosenstein-letter-appointing-Mueller-special.

42 Greg Miller and Greg Jaffe, "Trump revealed highly classified information to Russian foreign minister and ambassador," Washington Post, May 15, 2017, https://www.washingtonpost.com/world/national-security/trump-revealed-highly-classified-information-to-russian-foreign-minister-and-ambassador/2017/05/15/530c172a-3960-11e7-9e48-c4f199710b69_story.html.

43 Alison Rourke, "'Putin's poodle': newspapers declare Trump a traitor after Helsinki summit," The Guardian, July 17, 2018, https://www.theguardian.com/us-news/2018/jul/17/putins-poodle-newspapers-declare-trump-a-traitor-after-helsinki-summit.

44 James Masters, "Trump-Putin Summit: European Newspapers React," CNN, July 17, 2018, https://www.cnn.com/2018/07/17/europe/trump-putin-summit-newspaper-reaction-intl/index.html.

45 Brooke Singman, "Durham: CIA Concluded Data Alleging Trump-Russia Connection Not Technically Plausible, User-Created," Fox News, August 2, 2023, https://www.foxnews.com/politics/durham-cia-concluded-data-alleging-trump-russia-connection-not-technically-plausible-user-created.

46 Clare Foran, "Trump-Putin Soccer Ball 'Chip' Claim Is a Conspiracy Theory, Experts Say," CNN, July 25, 2018, https://www.cnn.com/2018/07/25/politics/trump-putin-soccer-ball-chip-transmitter/index.html.

47 "Trump-Ukraine Transcript (Unclassified)," September 2019, https://s3.documentcloud.org/documents/6429028/Trump-Ukraine-Transcript-Unclassified-09-2019.pdf.

48 "Special Counsel Robert Mueller Testifies at the House Intelligence Committee," C-SPAN, July 24, 2019, video, https://www.c-span.org/video/?462629-1/robert-mueller-testifies-house-intelligence-committee.

Chapter 4

1. Charles Creitz, "Graham: Steele Dossier Source Played Role in Russian Intelligence," Fox News, August 1, 2023, https://www.foxnews.com/media/graham-steele-dossier-source-played-russian-intelligence.
2. "Electronic Communication," February 9, 2017, p. 11, https://www.judiciary.senate.gov/imo/media/doc/February%209,%202017%20Electronic%20Communication.pdf.
3. "Trump Campaign Press Release: Donald J. Trump Announces Campaign Convention Manager Paul J. Manafort," The American Presidency Project, April 6, 2016, https://www.presidency.ucsb.edu/documents/trump-campaign-press-release-donald-j-trump-announces-campaign-convention-manager-paul-j.
4. "Trump Campaign Announces Expanded Role for Paul Manafort," ABC News, August 19, 2016, https://abcnews.go.com/Politics/trump-campaign-announces-expanded-role-paul-manafort/story?id=39231973.
5. "Electronic Communication," February 9, 2017, p. 11, https://www.judiciary.senate.gov/imo/media/doc/February%209,%202017%20Electronic%20Communication.pdf.
6. "Electronic Communication," February 9, 2017, p. 12, https://www.judiciary.senate.gov/imo/media/doc/February%209,%202017%20Electronic%20Communication.pdf.
7. Hans Mahncke (@HansMahncke), "Text of the letter from DOJ to the House Judiciary Committee regarding the Steele dossier," Twitter, March 12, 2022, https://twitter.com/HansMahncke/status/1502705901244985344.
8. Jaap Titulaer (@JaapTitulaer), "Screenshot of Danchenko's LinkedIn Page," Twitter, November 4, 2021, https://twitter.com/JaapTitulaer/status/1456339818355609602/photo/1.
9. Fiona Hill and Clifford G. Gaddy, Mr. Putin: Operative in the Kremlin (Washington, DC: Brookings Institution Press, 2015), 296.
10. Tobias Hoonhout, "Fiona Hill Details Relationship with Christopher Steele, Disparages Steele Dossier," National Review, August 7, 2023, https://www.nationalreview.com/news/fiona-hill-details-relationship-with-christopher-steele-disparages-steele-dossier/.
11. "Letter from Attorney General William Barr to Chairman Lindsey Graham," September 24, 2020, https://repository.library.georgetown.edu/bitstream/handle/10822/1060488/AG%20Letter%20to%20Chairman%20Graham%209.24.2020.pdf?sequence=3&isAllowed=y.
12. "Letter from Attorney General William Barr to Chairman Lindsey Graham," September 24, 2020, https://repository.library.georgetown.edu/bitstream/handle/10822/1060488/AG%20Letter%20to%20Chairman%20Graham%209.24.2020.pdf?sequence=3&isAllowed=y.
13. "Electronic Communication," February 9, 2017, p. 11, https://www.judiciary.senate.gov/imo/media/doc/February%209,%202017%20Electronic%20Communication.pdf.
14. Examination of the FBI's Crossfire Hurricane Investigation, U.S. Department of Justice, December 9, 2019, footnote 336, https://www.justice.gov/storage/120919-examination.pdf.
15. Examination of the FBI's Crossfire Hurricane Investigation, U.S. Department of Justice, December 9, 2019, footnote 336, https://www.justice.gov/storage/120919-examination.pdf.
16. Natasha Bertrand, "FBI Texts Reveal Officials' Criticism of Trump, Mueller Probe," Politico, February 8, 2018, https://www.politico.com/story/2018/02/08/fbi-texts-officials-resign-400533.

Notes

[17] "Biden Document," DocumentCloud, https://s3.documentcloud.org/documents/24476201/biden1-copy.pdf; "Biden Document 2," DocumentCloud, https://s3.documentcloud.org/documents/24476203/biden-2-copy.pdf.

[18] Charles Creitz, "Graham: Steele Dossier Source Played Role in Russian Intelligence," Fox News, August 1, 2023, https://www.foxnews.com/media/graham-steele-dossier-source-played-russian-intelligence.

[19] "Letter from Attorney General William Barr to Chairman Lindsey Graham," September 24, 2020, https://repository.library.georgetown.edu/bitstream/handle/10822/1060488/AG%20Letter%20to%20Chairman%20Graham%209.24.2020.pdf?sequence=3&isAllowed=y.

[20] Report on the Investigation into the FBI's Crossfire Hurricane Investigation, U.S. Department of Justice, May 2023, p. 14, https://www.justice.gov/storage/durhamreport.pdf.

[21] "Electronic Communication," February 9, 2017, p. 5, https://www.judiciary.senate.gov/imo/media/doc/February%209,%202017%20Electronic%20Communication.pdf.

[22] "Jerry Dunleavy, Report: FBI Agent Linked to Steele Dossier 'Worried' About Trump Campaign," Washington Examiner, August 29, 2023, https://www.washingtonexaminer.com/?p=2351302.

[23] "Electronic Communication," February 9, 2017, p. 12, https://www.judiciary.senate.gov/imo/media/doc/February%209,%202017%20Electronic%20Communication.pdf.

[24] "Electronic Communication," February 9, 2017, p. 7, https://www.judiciary.senate.gov/imo/media/doc/February%209,%202017%20Electronic%20Communication.pdf.

[25] "Electronic Communication," February 9, 2017, p. 7, https://www.judiciary.senate.gov/imo/media/doc/February%209,%202017%20Electronic%20Communication.pdf.

[26] "Electronic Communication," February 9, 2017, p. 9, https://www.judiciary.senate.gov/imo/media/doc/February%209,%202017%20Electronic%20Communication.pdf.

[27] "Nunes Memo," DocumentCloud, February 2, 2018, https://www.documentcloud.org/documents/4365338-Nunes-memo.

[28] Emily Tillett, "Victoria Nuland Says Obama State Dept. Informed FBI of Reporting from Steele Dossier," CBS News, May 10, 2023, https://www.cbsnews.com/news/victoria-nuland-says-obama-state-dept-informed-fbi-of-reporting-from-steele-dossier/.

[29] Shane Harris, "When Carter Page Met Stefan Halper," Wall Street Journal, May 22, 2018, https://www.wsj.com/articles/when-carter-page-met-stefan-halper-1527029988.

[30] Sean Davis, "What We Learned Sunday from Spygate Insider Steven Schrage," The Federalist, August 10, 2020, https://thefederalist.com/2020/08/10/what-we-learned-sunday-from-spygate-insider-steven-schrage/.

[31] Transcript of George Papadopoulos and FBI Confidential Human Source, declassified March 13, 2020, https://www.judiciary.senate.gov/imo/media/doc/2020-3-13%20FISA%20Senate%20-%20Transcript%20of%20George%20Papadopoulos%20and%20FBI%20Confidential%20Human%20Source%20declassified%20March%2013%202020.pdf.

[32] "Donald Trump on Russia & Missing Hillary Clinton Emails," YouTube video, posted by C-SPAN, July 27, 2016, https://www.youtube.com/watch?v=3kxG8uJUsWU.

[33] Ladar Levison, "The FBI's Secret Warrant to Surveil Carter Page Should Scare Us All," NBC News, April 3, 2019, https://www.nbcnews.com/think/opinion/fbi-s-secret-warrant-surveil-carter-page-should-scare-all-ncna852131.

34 Assessing Russian Activities and Intentions in Recent US Elections, Office of the Director of National Intelligence, January 6, 2017, https://www.dni.gov/files/documents/ICA_2017_01.pdf.
35 Assessing Russian Activities and Intentions in Recent US Elections, Office of the Director of National Intelligence, January 6, 2017, p. 4, https://www.dni.gov/files/documents/ICA_2017_01.pdf.
36 U.S. House Permanent Select Committee on Intelligence, "Russia Investigation," accessed August 5, 2024, https://democrats-intelligence.house.gov/russiainvestigation/.
37 "This Week Transcript: Kellyanne Conway, Rep. Adam Schiff, and More," ABC News, February 21, 2019, https://abcnews.go.com/Politics/week-transcript-21-19-kellyanne-conway-rep-adam/story?id=62525364.
38 Zachary Cohen and Jeremy Herb, "House Intelligence Committee Releases Russia Probe Interview Transcripts," CNN, May 6, 2020, https://www.cnn.com/2020/05/06/politics/house-intelligence-russia-probe-interview-transcript-release/index.html.
39 Examination of the FBI's Crossfire Hurricane Investigation, U.S. Department of Justice, December 9, 2019, p. 177, https://www.justice.gov/storage/120919-examination.pdf.
40 Caitlin Oprysko, "McCabe says he opened investigations into Trump to put Russia probe 'on solid ground'," Politico, February 14, 2019, https://www.politico.com/story/2019/02/14/fbi-investigation-trump-russia-1169846.
41 "Second 2020 Presidential Debate," YouTube video, posted by C-SPAN, October 22, 2020, 1:36:19, https://www.youtube.com/live/bPiofmZGb8o?si=nWakDFtSpRQKhNbB.
42 Public Statement on the Hunter Biden Emails, Politico, October 19, 2020, https://www.politico.com/f/?id=00000175-4393-d7aa-af77-579f9b330000.
43 In a January 2024 court filing in a federal gun charges case brought against Hunter Biden, prosecutors revealed that they had obtained a warrant for Hunter Biden's iCloud account with Apple and that the data on Hunter Biden's abandoned laptop matched the iCloud data: United States v. Robert Hunter Biden, U.S. District Court for the District of Delaware, Document 68, January 16, 2024, https://storage.courtlistener.com/recap/gov.uscourts.ded.82797/gov.uscourts.ded.82797.68.0.pdf; In June 2024, Hunter Biden's abandoned laptop was entered into evidence during Hunter Biden's gun charges trial without objection: United States v. Robert Hunter Biden, U.S. District Court for the District of Delaware, Document 227, June 11, 2024, https://storage.courtlistener.com/recap/gov.uscourts.ded.82797/gov.uscourts.ded.82797.227.0.pdf.

Chapter 5

1 Hollie McKay, "Stefan Halper: The Trump-Russia Hoax," Fox News, December 15, 2020, https://www.foxnews.com/politics/stefan-halper-russiagate-trump-russia-hiding-why; Matt Taibbi, "Our Man in Cambridge," Racket News, August 9, 2020, https://www.racket.news/p/our-man-in-cambridge-93f.
2 Jane Mayer, "Christopher Steele: The Man Behind the Trump Dossier," The New Yorker, March 5, 2018, https://www.newyorker.com/magazine/2018/03/12/christopher-steele-the-man-behind-the-trump-dossier.
3 John Solomon, "Russian Oligarch's Story Could Spell Trouble for Team Mueller," The Hill, July 2, 2019, https://thehill.com/opinion/white-house/451413-russian-oligarchs-story-could-spell-trouble-for-team-mueller/.

4. John Solomon, "Russian Oligarch, Justice Department, and a Clear Case of Collusion," The Hill, August 28, 2018, https://thehill.com/hilltv/rising/404061-russian-oligarch-justice-department-and-a-clear-case-of-collusion/.
5. Bruce Ohr Interview Transcript, House Judiciary Committee, August 28, 2018, https://archive.is/MR9lq.
6. "Mueller Files," TheMYEFiles, accessed August 5, 2024, https://themyefiles.knack.com/mueller-files/#home/?view_6_per_page=1000&view_6_page=1.
7. John Solomon, "Mueller May Have a Conflict, and It Leads Directly to a Russian Oligarch," The Hill, May 14, 2018, https://thehill.com/opinion/white-house/387625-mueller-may-have-a-conflict-and-it-leads-directly-to-a-russian-oligarch/.
8. State Department Emails, Senate Committee on Homeland Security and Governmental Affairs, accessed August 5, 2024, https://www.hsgac.senate.gov/wp-content/uploads/imo/media/doc/STATE_combined.pdf.
9. Jonathan Marcus, "Ukraine crisis: Transcript of leaked Nuland-Pyatt call," BBC, February 7, 2014, https://www.bbc.com/news/world-europe-26079957.
10. Victoria Thompson et al., "Exclusive: Hiding in Plain Sight? Hunter Biden Defends Foreign Business Dealings," ABC News, October 15, 2019, https://abcnews.go.com/Politics/exclusive-hiding-plain-sight-hunter-biden-defends-foreign/story?id=66275416.
11. United States v. Alexander Smirnov, U.S. District Court for the District of Nevada, February 20, 2024, p. 23, https://storage.courtlistener.com/recap/gov.uscourts.nvd.167064/gov.uscourts.nvd.167064.15.0.pdf.
12. "Biden Tells Story of Ukraine Prosecutor Being Fired," C-SPAN, October 15, 2019, video, https://www.c-span.org/video/?c4820105/user-clip-biden-tells-story-ukraine-prosecutor-fired.
13. State Department Emails, Senate Committee on Homeland Security and Governmental Affairs, accessed August 5, 2024, https://www.hsgac.senate.gov/wp-content/uploads/imo/media/doc/STATE_combined.pdf.
14. Volume 5 of the Senate Intelligence Committee Report on Russian Active Measures, U.S. Senate Select Committee on Intelligence, August 18, 2020, p. 853, https://www.intelligence.senate.gov/sites/default/files/documents/report_volume5.pdf.
15. Durham Reporter Email List, Scribd, April 25, 2022, https://www.scribd.com/document/571730091/2022-04-25-HUGE-Durham-Reporter-Email-List.
16. Mark Hosenball, "Former MI6 Spy Known to U.S. Agencies Is Author of Reports on Trump in Russia," Reuters, January 12, 2017, https://www.reuters.com/article/us-usa-trump-steele-idUSKBN14W0HN/.
17. Moyer Interview, House Committee on the Judiciary and the House Committee on Oversight and Government Reform, October 23, 2018, p. 176, https://www.justsecurity.org/wp-content/uploads/2019/08/10.23.18-Moyer-Interview_Redacted-DJ.pdf.
18. Complaint from Fridman Against Steele and Orbis, D.C. Superior Court, April 16, 2018, https://cdn.cnn.com/cnn/2018/images/04/20/complaint.from.fridman.against.steele.orbis.in.dc.superior.court.pdf.
19. State Department Emails, Senate Committee on Homeland Security and Governmental Affairs, accessed August 5, 2024, p. 66, https://www.hsgac.senate.gov/wp-content/uploads/imo/media/doc/STATE_combined.pdf.
20. State Department FOIA Production, Judicial Watch, July 24, 2019, https://www.judicialwatch.org/wp-content/uploads/2019/08/JW-DCNF-v-State-Steele-prod-9-00968.pdf.

21. Ken Dilanian, "Justice Department Ends Investigation into Tony Podesta and Vin Weber Without Charges," NBC News, October 8, 2019, https://www.nbcnews.com/politics/justice-department/justice-department-ends-investigation-tony-podesta-vin-weber-without-charges-n1058306.
22. Glenn Simpson and Peter Fritsch, Crime in Progress (New York: Random House, 2019), chap. 6, Kindle.
23. Report on Russian Activity, Intelligence and Security Committee of Parliament, United Kingdom, July 21, 2020, https://isc.independent.gov.uk/wp-content/uploads/2021/03/CCS207_CCS0221966010-001_Russia-Report-v02-Web_Accessible.pdf.
24. Anne Applebaum, "The Case for Trump-Russia Collusion: We're Getting Very, Very Close," The Washington Post, September 8, 2017, https://www.washingtonpost.com/news/global-opinions/wp/2017/09/08/the-case-for-trump-russia-collusion-were-getting-very-very-close/.
25. Regina Mouradian, The Hermitage Effect: How Bill Browder Went from Ally to Enemy of Russia (Outskirts Press, 2020).
26. Paul Roderick Gregory, "Vladimir Putin and Hillary Clinton's Emails," Forbes, February 12, 2016, https://www.forbes.com/sites/paulroderickgregory/2016/02/12/vladimir-putin-hillary-clinton-emails/.
27. Jacob Sullum, "Hillary Clinton's False Hopes," Reason, March 3, 2016, https://reason.com/2016/03/03/hillary-clintons-false-hopes/.
28. SeekerOTL (@SeekerOTL), "Judge Napolitano on Fox News," Twitter, May 24, 2020, https://twitter.com/SeekerOTL/status/1264675836076179456.
29. Hans Mahncke (@HansMahncke), "Judge Napolitano on Fox News," Twitter, December 14, 2019, https://twitter.com/HansMahncke/status/1205930771346862083.
30. Report on the Investigation into Russian Interference in the 2016 Presidential Election, Special Counsel's Office, U.S. Department of Justice, March 22, 2019, p. 81, https://www.justice.gov/archives/sco/file/1373816/download.

Chapter 6

1. "Sergei Millian: Donald Trump will improve relations with Russia," RIA Novosti, April 13, 2016, translated by author, https://ria.ru/20160413/1409790646.html.
2. "Sergei Millian talks to Maria Bartiromo about the Ukraine Crisis in 2014," YouTube video, posted by Sergei Millian, February 17, 2017, https://www.youtube.com/watch?v=3DYoiXc69nk.
3. "Sergei Millian: Donald Trump will improve relations with Russia," RIA Novosti, April 13, 2016, translated by author, https://ria.ru/20160413/1409790646.html.
4. Sergei Millian, interview with the author, March 27, 2022.
5. Glenn Simpson and Peter Fritsch, Crime in Progress (New York: Random House, 2019), chap. 6, Kindle.
6. Petr Aven, Mikhail Fridman, and German Khan v. Orbis Business Intelligence Limited, transcript, March 16, 2020, https://justthenews.com/sites/default/files/2021-10/SteeleLegalArgumentsBritishCase.pdf.
7. Glenn Simpson and Peter Fritsch, Crime in Progress (New York: Random House, 2019), chap. 6, Kindle.
8. Ohr, Steele Messages, Scribd, January 2017, https://www.scribd.com/document/385703667/Ohr-Steele-Text-Messages-January-2017.

9. Stephen McIntyre (@ClimateAudit), "Danchenko Email," August 12, 2020, https://twitter.com/ClimateAudit/status/1293622656231780353.
10. Stephen McIntyre (@ClimateAudit), "Danchenko Email," August 12, 2020, https://twitter.com/ClimateAudit/status/1293622656231780353.
11. Report on the Investigation into the FBI's Crossfire Hurricane Investigation, U.S. Department of Justice, May 2023, p. 174, https://www.justice.gov/storage/durham report.pdf.
12. Ben Feuerherd and Mark Lungariello, "FBI Brass Were Fired Up About Now-Debunked Trump-Russia Ties: Texts, Testimony," New York Post, May 24, 2022, https://nypost.com/2022/05/24/fbi-brass-were-fired-up-about-now-debunked-trump-russia-ties-texts-testimony/.
13. Brian Steinberg, "Brian Ross, who aired erroneous Trump report, to leave ABC," Reuters, July 2, 2018, https://www.reuters.com/article/idUSKBN1JT08J/
14. Michael Isikoff and David Corn, "Russian Roulette: The Real Story Behind the Steele Dossier," Australian Financial Review, March 17, 2018, https://www.afr.com/life-and-luxury/arts-and-culture/russian-roulette-the-real-story-behind-the-steele-dossier-20180315-h0xj4g.
15. Glenn Simpson and Peter Fritsch, Crime in Progress (New York: Random House, 2019), chap. 7, Kindle.
16. Good Morning America, ABC, September 22, 2016, https://archive.org/details/KGO_20160922_140000_Good_Morning_America.
17. Hillary Clinton (@HillaryClinton), "The man who could be your next president," Twitter, September 22, 2016, https://twitter.com/HillaryClinton/status/779055195607166977.
18. Interview of Glenn Simpson, Permanent Select Committee On Intelligence, U.S. House Of Representatives, November 14, 2017, 46, https://docs.house.gov/meetings/IG/IG00/20180118/106796/HMTG-115-IG00-20180118-SD002.pdf.
19. Tim Mak and Katie Zavadski, "Meet The Man Who Is Spinning For Donald Trump In Russia," Daily Beast, September 8, 2016, https://www.thedailybeast.com/meet-the-man-who-is-spinning-for-donald-trump-in-russia.
20. Catherine Belton, "The shadowy Russian émigré touting Trump," Financial Times, November 1, 2016, https://www.ft.com/content/ea52a678-9cfb-11e6-8324-be63473ce146.
21. Luke Harding, "Roman Abramovich Settles Libel Claim over Putin Biography," The Guardian, December 22, 2021, https://www.theguardian.com/world/2021/dec/22/roman-abramovich-settles-libel-claim-over-putin-biography.
22. Steele Deposition, Scribd, March 17, 2020, https://www.scribd.com/document/458992503/Steele-deposition.
23. Codyave (@codyave), "Screenshot of Belton Message," Twitter, May 5, 2022, https://twitter.com/codyave/status/1522098089317650432/photo/1.
24. Millian to Hicks, November 2, 2016, on file with author.
25. Mark Maremont, "Key Claims in Trump Dossier Said to Come From Head of Russian-American Business Group", Wall Street Journal, January 24, 2017, https://www.wsj.com/articles/key-claims-in-trump-dossier-came-from-head-of-russian-american-business-group-source-1485253804.
26. Matthew Mosk and Brian Ross, "U.S. Russian Businessman Is Source for Key Trump Dossier Claims," ABC News, January 30, 2017, https://abcnews.go.com/Politics/us-russian-businessman-source-key-trump-dossier-claims/story?id=45019603.

27. Laurie P. Cohen et al., "Bush's Financial War on Terrorism Includes Strikes at Islamic Charities," The Wall Street Journal, September 25, 2001, https://www.wsj.com/articles/SB1001368124216698720.
28. Glenn Simpson and Peter Fritsch, Crime in Progress (New York: Random House, 2019), chap. 8, Kindle.
29. Report of Investigation of Certain Allegations Relating to Former FBI Deputy Director Andrew McCabe, U.S. Department of Justice, February 2018, https://oig.justice.gov/reports/2018/o20180413.pdf.
30. Matthew Mosk and Brian Ross, "U.S. Russian Businessman Is Source for Key Trump Dossier Claims," ABC News, January 30, 2017, https://abcnews.go.com/Politics/us-russian-businessman-source-key-trump-dossier-claims/story?id=45019603.
31. Glenn Simpson and Peter Fritsch, Crime in Progress (New York: Random House, 2019), chap. 6, Kindle.
32. Electronic Communication, February 9, 2017, https://www.judiciary.senate.gov/imo/media/doc/February%209,%202017%20Electronic%20Communication.pdf.
33. Fridman v. Bean LLC, U.S. District Court for the District of Columbia, Docket, October 3, 2017, https://www.courtlistener.com/docket/6163126/fridman-v-bean-llc/.
34. Aven v. Orbis Business Intelligence Ltd, High Court of Justice, July 8, 2020, https://www.bailii.org/ew/cases/EWHC/QB/2020/1812.html.
35. The Trump-Russia Dossier as Released by BuzzFeed, Scribd, January 10, 2017, p. 35, https://www.scribd.com/document/336226994/The-Trump-Russia-Dossier-as-Released-By-Buzzfeed.
36. Gubarev v. Orbis Business Intelligence Ltd, High Court of Justice, October 30, 2020, https://www.judiciary.uk/wp-content/uploads/2020/10/Gubarev-v-Orbis-judgment.pdf.
37. Gubarev v. BuzzFeed Inc., U.S. District Court for the Southern District of Florida, December 19, 2018, https://casetext.com/case/gubarev-v-buzzfeed-inc-2.
38. Trump v. Orbis Business Intelligence Ltd, High Court of Justice, February 1, 2024, https://www.judiciary.uk/wp-content/uploads/2023/06/Trump-v-Orbis-Judgment.pdf.
39. Gubarev v. BuzzFeed Inc., High Court of Justice, March 21, 2018, https://www.judiciary.uk/wp-content/uploads/2018/03/gubarev-v-buzzfeed.pdf.
40. Aven v. Orbis Business Intelligence Ltd, High Court of Justice, July 8, 2020, https://www.bailii.org/ew/cases/EWHC/QB/2020/1812.html.
41. Steele Deposition, Scribd, March 17, 2020, https://www.scribd.com/document/458992503/Steele-deposition.
42. Chuck Ross, "Book Provides New Details About Major Steele Dossier Source," The Daily Caller, March 13, 2018, https://dailycaller.com/2018/03/13/russian-roullette-book-steele-dossier-source/.
43. Samuel Chamberlain, "Anti-Trump Harvard Law Prof. Laurence Tribe Falsely Claims Dossier Source Killed in Russia Plane Crash," Fox News, February 12, 2018, https://www.foxnews.com/us/anti-trump-harvard-law-prof-laurence-tribe-falsely-claims-dossier-source-killed-in-russia-plane-crash.

Chapter 7

1. Steele Dossier, DocumentCloud, Report 80, https://www.documentcloud.org/documents/21200685-steele-dossier.

Notes

2   Steele Dossier, DocumentCloud, Report 97, https://www.documentcloud.org/documents/21200685-steele-dossier.
3   Electronic Communication, February 9, 2017, p. 14, https://www.judiciary.senate.gov/imo/media/doc/February%209,%202017%20Electronic%20Communication.pdf.
4   Steele Deposition, Scribd, March 17, 2020, https://www.scribd.com/document/458992503/Steele-deposition.
5   FOOL_NELSON (@FOOL_NELSON), "Danchenko List," Twitter, August 7, 2020, https://twitter.com/FOOL_NELSON/status/1291791519939207169.
6   Fridman v. Bean LLC, U.S. District Court for the District of Columbia, June 21, 2021, https://storage.courtlistener.com/recap/gov.uscourts.dcd.189930/gov.uscourts.dcd.189930.153.9.pdf.
7   "Archived Page on Indian Embassy," archived at Wayback Machine, accessed August 5, 2024, https://web.archive.org/web/20070714122417/http://www.india.mid.ru/2.html.
8   Fridman v. Bean LLC, U.S. District Court for the District of Columbia, June 21, 2021, https://storage.courtlistener.com/recap/gov.uscourts.dcd.189930/gov.uscourts.dcd.189930.153.9.pdf.
9   Transcript of George Papadopoulos and FBI Confidential Human Source, declassified March 13, 2020, https://www.judiciary.senate.gov/imo/media/doc/2020-3-13%20FISA%20Senate%20-%20Transcript%20of%20George%20Papadopoulos%20and%20FBI%20Confidential%20Human%20Source%20declassified%20March%2013%202020.pdf.
10 Examination of the FBI's Crossfire Hurricane Investigation, U.S. Department of Justice, December 9, 2019, p. 331, https://www.justice.gov/storage/120919-examination.pdf.
11 Electronic Communication, February 9, 2017, p. 39, https://www.judiciary.senate.gov/imo/media/doc/February%209,%202017%20Electronic%20Communication.pdf.
12 Rachel Sandler, "DOJ Says Two Wiretap Warrants Against Former Trump Aide Carter Page Are Invalid," Forbes, January 23, 2020, https://www.forbes.com/sites/rachelsandler/2020/01/23/doj-says-two-wiretap-warrants-against-former-trump-aide-carter-page-are-invalid/?sh=717b85b6581a.
13 Fridman v. Bean LLC, U.S. District Court for the District of Columbia, June 21, 2021, https://storage.courtlistener.com/recap/gov.uscourts.dcd.189930/gov.uscourts.dcd.189930.153.6.pdf.
14 Bari Weiss (@bariweiss), "One of the accounts," Twitter, December 8, 2022, https://twitter.com/bariweiss/status/1601018810495995904 Matt Novak, "Elon Musk Says US Gov't Had Full Access to Private Twitter DMs," Forbes, April 17, 2023, https://www.forbes.com/sites/mattnovak/2023/04/17/elon-musk-says-us-govt-had-full-access-to-private-twitter-dms/.
15 Ari Blaff, "My Jaw Dropped: Explosive Musk Biography Reveals Why Ex-FBI Lawyer Jim Baker Was Fired from Twitter," National Review, September 12, 2023, https://www.nationalreview.com/news/my-jaw-dropped-explosive-musk-biography-reveals-why-ex-fbi-lawyer-jim-baker-was-fired-from-twitter/.
16 Lee Smith, "New Documents Suggest Steele Dossier a Deliberate Setup Against Trump," The Federalist, January 2, 2019, https://thefederalist.com/2019/01/02/new-documents-suggest-steele-dossier-deliberate-setup-trump/.
17 United States v. Igor Danchenko, U.S. District Court for the Eastern District of Virginia, Indictment, November 3, 2021, https://storage.courtlistener.com/recap/gov.uscourts.vaed.515692/gov.uscourts.vaed.515692.1.0_5.pdf.

18. Adam Goldman and Charlie Savage, "Authorities Arrest Analyst Who Contributed to Steele Dossier," The New York Times, November 4, 2021, https://www.nytimes.com/2021/11/04/us/politics/igor-danchenko-arrested-steele-dossier.html.
19. Alexey Kovalev et al., "Meduza spoke to all the likely sources behind the 'Steele dossier.' The report that forever transformed Donald Trump into a 'Russian agent' looks less and less convincing," Meduza, November 3, 2020, https://meduza.io/en/feature/2020/11/03/raw-intelligence.
20. Fridman v. Bean LLC, U.S. District Court for the District of Columbia, June 21, 2021, https://storage.courtlistener.com/recap/gov.uscourts.dcd.189930/gov.uscourts.dcd.189930.153.9.pdf.
21. Fridman v. Bean LLC, U.S. District Court for the District of Columbia, June 21, 2021, https://storage.courtlistener.com/recap/gov.uscourts.dcd.189930/gov.uscourts.dcd.189930.153.6.pdf.
22. Examination of the FBI's Crossfire Hurricane Investigation, U.S. Department of Justice, December 9, 2019, p. 163, https://www.justice.gov/storage/120919-examination.pdf.
23. Report on the Investigation into the FBI's Crossfire Hurricane Investigation, U.S. Department of Justice, May 2023, p. 118, https://www.justice.gov/storage/durham report.pdf.
24. "Miss Universe Pageant 2013," Chicago Tribune, November 9, 2013, http://galleries.apps.chicagotribune.com/chi-miss-universe-pageant-2013-20131109/.
25. Stephen McIntyre (@ClimateAudit), "Exhibit 0243 (Sussmann)," Twitter, June 3, 2023. https://twitter.com/ClimateAudit/status/1664969809711202305; Exhibit 0243, DocumentCloud, June 4, 2022, https://www.documentcloud.org/documents/22046223-0243.
26. Exhibit DX-563, DocumentCloud, June 4, 2022, https://www.documentcloud.org/documents/22046174-dx-563.

Chapter 8

1. Alana Abramson and Shushannah Walshe, "The 4 Most Damaging Emails From the DNC WikiLeaks Dump," ABC, July 25, 2016, https://abcnews.go.com/Politics/damaging-emails-dnc-wikileaks-dump/story?id=40852448.
2. Daniel Strauss and Bianca Padró Ocasio, "Debbie Wasserman Schultz once called Sanders' campaign manager a 'damn liar'," Politico, July 22, 2016, https://www.politico.com/story/2016/07/debbie-wasserman-schultz-jeff-weaver-226032.
3. Euan McKirdy, "Assange Defends WikiLeaks in Interview with Hannity," CNN, January 4, 2017, https://www.cnn.com/2017/01/04/politics/assange-wikileaks-hannity-intv/index.html.
4. Blair Guild, "Clinton Campaign Chief: Russians Used Trump to Promote Pro-Russian Platform," ABC News, July 24, 2016, https://abcnews.go.com/ThisWeek/clinton-campaign-chief-russians-trump-pro-russian-platform/story?id=40824946.
5. "Mook on DNC E-Mail Leak: Experts Are Now Saying That the Russians Are Releasing These E-Mails for the Purpose of Actually Helping Donald Trump," CNN Press Room, July 24, 2016, https://cnnpressroom.blogs.cnn.com/2016/07/24/mook-on-dnc-e-mail-leak-experts-are-now-saying-that-the-russians-are-releasing-these-e-mails-for-the-purpose-of-actually-helping-donald-trump/.

Notes

6   Josh Rogin, "Trump Campaign Guts GOP's Anti-Russia Stance on Ukraine," The Washington Post, July 18, 2016, https://www.washingtonpost.com/opinions/global-opinions/trump-campaign-guts-gops-anti-russia-stance-on-ukraine/2016/07/18/98adb3b0-4cf3-11e6-a7d8-13d06b37f256_story.html.
7   Examination of the FBI's Crossfire Hurricane Investigation, U.S. Department of Justice, December 9, 2019, p. 264, https://www.justice.gov/storage/120919-examination.pdf.
8   Alec Schemmel, "Jury Foreperson Claims Sussmann Case Was 'Waste of Time' Following Not Guilty Verdict," WPDE, June 1, 2022, https://wpde.com/news/nation-world/jury-foreperson-claims-sussmann-case-was-waste-of-time-following-not-guilty-verdict.
9   Ben Feuerherd and Bruce Golding, "Judge allows Hillary, AOC donors in jury pool for ex-Clinton-lawyer's Russia trial," New York Post, May 16, 2022, https://nypost.com/2022/05/16/hillary-aoc-donors-among-jury-pool-in-ex-clinton-lawyers-trial/.
10   Michael Sussmann, Testimony before the U.S. House Permanent Select Committee on Intelligence, December 18, 2017, p. 75, https://intelligence.house.gov/uploadedfiles/michael_sussman_testimony_dec_18_2017.pdf.

Chapter 9

1   Emily Tillett, "Victoria Nuland Says Obama State Dept. Informed FBI of Reporting from Steele Dossier," CBS News, February 4, 2018, https://www.cbsnews.com/news/victoria-nuland-says.
2   Michael Gaeta, Testimony before the U.S. House Permanent Select Committee on Intelligence, December 20, 2017, p. 29, https://s3.documentcloud.org/documents/6887584/Redacted-FBI-Witness-Dec-20-2017.pdf.
3   Report on the Investigation into the FBI's Crossfire Hurricane Investigation, U.S. Department of Justice, May 2023, p. 110, https://www.justice.gov/storage/durhamreport.pdf.
4   "Statement by Attorney General William P. Barr on the Inspector General's Report on the Review of Four FISA Applications," U.S. Department of Justice, December 9, 2019, https://www.justice.gov/opa/pr/statement-attorney-general-william-p-barr-inspector-generals-report-review-four-fisa.
5   "Statement by U.S. Attorney John H. Durham," U.S. Department of Justice, December 9, 2019, https://www.justice.gov/usao-ct/pr/statement-us-attorney-john-h-durham.
6   Examination of the FBI's Crossfire Hurricane Investigation, U.S. Department of Justice, December 9, 2019, p. 188, https://www.justice.gov/storage/120919-examination.pdf.
7   Paul Roderick Gregory, "Vladimir Putin and Hillary Clinton's Emails," Forbes, February 12, 2016, https://www.forbes.com/sites/paulroderickgregory/2016/02/12/vladimir-putin-hillary-clinton-emails/; Jacob Sullum, "Hillary Clinton's False Hopes," Reason, March 3, 2016, https://reason.com/2016/03/03/hillary-clintons-false-hopes/.
8   Hans Mahncke (@HansMahncke), "Judge Napolitano on Fox News," Twitter, October 21, 2019, https://twitter.com/HansMahncke/status/1186344815010766848.
9   Examination of the FBI's Crossfire Hurricane Investigation, U.S. Department of Justice, December 9, 2019, p. 52, https://www.justice.gov/storage/120919-examination.pdf.
10   Report on the Investigation into the FBI's Crossfire Hurricane Investigation, U.S. Department of Justice, May 2023, p. 53, https://www.justice.gov/storage/durhamreport.pdf.

11 Hans Mahncke (@HansMahncke), "Judge Napolitano on Fox News," Twitter, December 14, 2019, https://twitter.com/HansMahncke/status/1205930771346862083.
12 Examination of the FBI's Crossfire Hurricane Investigation, U.S. Department of Justice, December 9, 2019, p. 52, https://www.justice.gov/storage/120919-examination.pdf.
13 Sharon Lafraniere, Mark Mazzetti And Matt Apuzzo, "How the Russia Inquiry Began: A Campaign Aide, Drinks and Talk of Political Dirt," The New York Times, December 30, 2017, https://www.nytimes.com/2017/12/30/us/politics/how-fbi-russia-investigation-began-george-papadopoulos.html.
14 T.A. Frank, "The Surreal Life of George Papadopoulos," The Washington Post, May 20, 2019, https://www.washingtonpost.com/news/magazine/wp/2019/05/20/feature/the-surreal-life-of-george-papadopoulos.
15 Hans Mahncke (@HansMahncke), "Papadopoulos Talking to Greek Media," Twitter, August 26, 2019, https://twitter.com/HansMahncke/status/1165836470676008960.
16 Email from Erika Thompson to George Papadopoulos, May 9, 2024, 1:00 PM, on file with author.
17 Daniel W. Drezner, "Let's Give George Papadopoulos Some Free Advice," The Washington Post, October 24, 2018, https://www.washingtonpost.com/outlook/2018/10/24/lets-give-george-papadopoulos-some-free-advice/.
18 Report on the Investigation into Russian Interference in the 2016 Presidential Election, U.S. Department of Justice, March 22, 2019, p. 81, https://www.justice.gov/archives/sco/file/1373816/download.
19 Report on the Investigation into Russian Interference in the 2016 Presidential Election, U.S. Department of Justice, March 22, 2019, p. 84, https://www.justice.gov/archives/sco/file/1373816/download.
20 "Mueller Files," TheMYEFiles, accessed August 5, 2024, https://themyefiles.knack.com/mueller-files/#home/view-mueller-302-details/5f6f91a689a78b067b3054c8/
21 "Mueller Files," TheMYEFiles, accessed August 5, 2024, https://themyefiles.knack.com/mueller-files/#home/view-mueller-302-details/5f6f91a689a78b067b3054c6/
22 "Mueller Files," TheMYEFiles, accessed August 5, 2024, https://themyefiles.knack.com/mueller-files/#home/view-mueller-302-details/5f6f91a689a78b067b3054c8/
23 "Mueller Files," TheMYEFiles, accessed August 5, 2024, https://themyefiles.knack.com/mueller-files/#home/view-mueller-302-details/5f6f91a689a78b067b3054c6/
24 "Mueller Files," TheMYEFiles, accessed August 5, 2024, https://themyefiles.knack.com/mueller-files/#home/view-mueller-302-details/5f6f91a689a78b067b3054c8/
25 Email from Ivan Timofeev to George Papadopoulos, April 29, 2016, 9:45 AM, on file with author.
26 "Donald Trump Delivers a Foreign Policy Speech at the Mayflower Hotel—April 27, 2016," Vimeo, February 3, 2020, video, https://vimeo.com/389036268.
27 Email from George Papadopoulos to Ivan Timofeev, April 29, 2016, 9:51 AM, on file with author.
28 Haley Britzky, "Report: Papadopoulos Played a Critical Role in the Russia Investigation," Axios, December 30, 2017, https://www.axios.com/2018/01/05/report-papadopoulos-played-a-critical-role-in-the-russia-investigation-1515110919; Sabrina Siddiqui, "Trump aide told Australian diplomat Russia had dirt on Clinton—report," The Guardian, December 31, 2017, https://www.theguardian.com/us-news/2017/dec/30/donald-trump-russia-inquiry-george-papadopoulos-australian-diplomat.

Notes

[29] Sharon Lafraniere, Mark Mazzetti And Matt Apuzzo, "How the Russia Inquiry Began: A Campaign Aide, Drinks and Talk of Political Dirt," The New York Times, December 30, 2017, https://www.nytimes.com/2017/12/30/us/politics/how-fbi-russia-investigation-began-george-papadopoulos.html.

[30] Email from George Papadopoulos to Joseph Mifsud, April 30, 2016, 9:12 AM, on file with author.

[31] Report on the Investigation into Russian Interference in the 2016 Presidential Election, Special Counsel's Office, U.S. Department of Justice, March 22, 2019, p. 81, https://www.justice.gov/archives/sco/file/1373816/download.

[32] Report on the Investigation into Russian Interference in the 2016 Presidential Election, Special Counsel's Office, U.S. Department of Justice, March 22, 2019, p. 193, https://www.justice.gov/archives/sco/file/1373816/download.

[33] "Valdai Club Discusses Main Trends and Scenarios of the Global Energy Development," Valdai Club, accessed August 5, 2024, https://valdaiclub.com/events/posts/articles/valdai-club-discusses-main-trends-and-scenarios-of-the-global-energy-development-/.

[34] Email from Joseph Mifsud to George Papadopoulos, April 21, 2016, 11:41 PM, on file with author.

[35] Email from Joseph Mifsud to George Papadopoulos, April 28, 2016, 00:10 AM, on file with author.

[36] United States v. George Papadopoulos, U.S. District Court District of Columbia, Statement of Offense, p. 2, https://storage.courtlistener.com/recap/gov.uscourts.dcd.189898/gov.uscourts.dcd.189898.19.0_2.pdf.

[37] Email from George Papadopoulos to Joseph Mifsud, April 24, 2016, 10:26 AM, on file with author.

[38] Email from George Papadopoulos to Joseph Mifsud, April 27, 2016, 6:24 PM, on file with author

[39] Email from Joseph Mifsud to George Papadopoulos and Ivan Timofeev, April 18, 2016, 7:04 AM, on file with author.

[40] Email from George Papadopoulos to Joseph Mifsud and Ivan Timofeev, April 18, 2016, 10:34 AM, on file with author.

[41] Email from Sam Clovis to Walid Phares, Joseph Schmitz, Carter Page, Chuck Kubic, George Papadopoulos, Bert Mizusawa and Keith Kellogg, March 21, 2016, 4:54 PM, on file with author.

[42] Email from Sam Clovis to George Papadopoulos, March 24, 2016, 7:55 AM, on file with author.

[43] Hans Mahncke (@HansMahncke), "Times Front Page" Twitter, April 27, 2019, https://twitter.com/HansMahncke/status/1122338733724880896.

[44] Email from Sam Clovis to George Papadopoulos, May 5, 2016, 5:40 PM, on file with author.

[45] Email from Sam Clovis to George Papadopoulos, May 19, 2016, 1:14 PM, on file with author.

[46] Email from George Papadopoulos to Paul Manafort, May 21, 2016, 1:20 PM, on file with author.

[47] Email from Paul Manafort to Rick Gates May 21, 2016, 1:20 PM, on file with author.

[48] Email from George Papadopoulos to Corey Lewandowski, June 1, 2016, 2:08 PM, on file with author.

[49] Email from Corey Lewandowski to George Papadopoulos, June 1, 2016, 2:20 PM, on file with author.

50. Email George Papadopoulos to Sam Clovis, June 1, 2016, 2:29 PM, on file with author.
51. Email Rick Dearborn to George Papadopoulos, June 24, 2016, 9:56 AM, on file with author.
52. Email Sam Clovis to George Papadopoulos, July 14, 2016, 1:20 PM, on file with author.
53. United States v. George Papadopoulos, U.S. District Court District of Columbia, Sentencing Memorandum, p. 4, https://storage.courtlistener.com/recap/gov.uscourts.dcd.189898/gov.uscourts.dcd.189898.44.0_3.pdf; Jeremy Diamond and Nicole Gaouette, "Donald Trump Unveils Foreign Policy Advisers," CNN, March 21, 2016, https://www.cnn.com/2016/03/21/politics/donald-trump-foreign-policy-team/index.html.
54. Email Joseph Mifsud to George Papadopoulos, November 10, 2:01 AM, on file with author.
55. Paolo G. Brera, "Russiagate: Mystery Professor Joseph Mifsud Speaks Out: 'Dirt on Hillary Clinton? Nonsense,'" La Repubblica, November 1, 2017, https://www.repubblica.it/esteri/2017/11/01/news/russiagate_mystery_professor_joseph_mifsud_speaks_out_dirt_on_hillary_clinton_nonsense_-179948962/.
56. Ben Riley-Smith, "Exclusive: Mysterious professor at heart of Trump-Russia scandal heard for the first time," The Telegraph, February 13, 2020, https://www.telegraph.co.uk/news/2020/02/13/joseph-mifsud-mysterious-professor-trump-russia-scandal-heard-crossfire/.
57. Peter Strzok, Compromised: Counterintelligence and the Threat of Donald J. Trump (New York: Houghton Mifflin Harcourt, 2020), 85.
58. "CNN Special Report: Transcript of September 7, 2018," CNN, September 7, 2018, https://transcripts.cnn.com/show/csr/date/2018-09-07/segment/01.
59. United States v. George Papadopoulos, U.S. District Court District of Columbia, Statement of Offense, p. 6-7, https://storage.courtlistener.com/recap/gov.uscourts.dcd.189898/gov.uscourts.dcd.189898.19.0_2.pdf.
60. United States v. George Papadopoulos, U.S. District Court District of Columbia, Sentencing Memorandum, p. 4, https://storage.courtlistener.com/recap/gov.uscourts.dcd.189898/gov.uscourts.dcd.189898.44.0_3.pdf.
61. Email from George Papadopoulos to Sam Clovis, March 7, 2016, 5:34 PM, on file with author.
62. Jeremy Diamond and Nicole Gaouette, "Donald Trump Unveils Foreign Policy Advisers," CNN, March 21, 2016, https://www.cnn.com/2016/03/21/politics/donald-trump-foreign-policy-team/index.html.
63. Donald J. Trump (@realDonaldTrump), "National Security Meeting," Twitter, March 31, 2016, https://twitter.com/realDonaldTrump/status/715725628465680386.
64. United States v. George Papadopoulos, U.S. District Court District of Columbia, Sentencing Memorandum, p. 4, https://storage.courtlistener.com/recap/gov.uscourts.dcd.189898/gov.uscourts.dcd.189898.44.0_3.pdf.
65. Chuck Grassley and Ron Johnson, Submission Regarding Hunter Biden and the Biden Family's Influence Peddling, December 18, 2020, https://media.washtimes.com/media/misc/2020/12/18/Johnson-Grassley_Submission.pdf.
66. "Mueller Files," TheMYEFiles, accessed August 5, 2024, https://themyefiles.knack.com/mueller-files/#home/view-mueller-302-details/5f6f91b589a78b067b3057a0/.
67. Matthew Mosk and Ali Dukakis, "Turkish businessman who hired Flynn says neither of them worked for Turkish government," ABC News, May 22, 2017, https://abcnews

Notes

.go.com/International/turkish-businessman-hired-flynn-refuses-comment-investigation/story?id=47569093.

68. Michael Caputo, "The Mueller Investigation: Michael Caputo on the Trump Campaign from the Inside," Politico Magazine, March 28, 2019, https://www.politico.com/magazine/story/2019/03/28/mueller-investigation-michael-caputo-trump-first-person-226336/.

69. Caitlin Oprysko, "McCabe says he opened investigations into Trump to put Russia probe 'on solid ground'," Politico, February 14, 2019, https://www.politico.com/story/2019/02/14/fbi-investigation-trump-russia-1169846.

70. Crossfire Hurricane Opening Electronic Communication, Judicial Watch, March 17, 2020, https://www.judicialwatch.org/wp-content/uploads/2020/05/JW-v-DOJ-reply-02743.pdf

71. "Donald Trump Asks Russia to Find Hillary Clinton's Emails," C-SPAN, July 27, 2016, video, https://www.c-span.org/video/?c4615538/donald-trump-asks-russia-find-hillary-clintons-emails.

72. Ashley Parker and David Sanger, "Donald Trump Calls on Russia to Find Hillary Clinton's Missing Emails," The New York Times, July 27, 2016, https://www.nytimes.com/2016/07/28/us/politics/donald-trump-russia-clinton-emails.html; Z. Byron Wolf, "Trump Asked Russians to Get Clinton Emails. They Immediately Started Trying," CNN, July 13, 2018, https://www.cnn.com/2018/07/13/politics/trump-asked-russians-to-get-clinton-emails-they-immediately-started-trying-/index.html; Ali Vitali, "Trump Calls on Russia to Help Find Missing Clinton Emails," NBC News, July 27, 2016, https://www.nbcnews.com/politics/2016-election/trump-calls-russia-help-find-missing-clinton-emails-n617846.

73. Michael Crowley and Tyler Pager, "Trump urges Russia to hack Clinton's email,'" Politico, July 27, 2016, https://www.politico.com/story/2016/07/trump-putin-no-relationship-226282.

74. Hans Mahncke (@HansMahncke), "Downer has been consistent," Twitter, December 14, 2019, https://twitter.com/HansMahncke/status/1205930845476970496.

75. FOIA-Processed Documents: Fusion GPS, U.S. Department of Justice, February 10, 2020, https://www.justice.gov/oip/foia-library/foia-processed/general_topics/fusion_gps_02_10_2020_interim/download.

76. Peter Strzok, Compromised: Counterintelligence and the Threat of Donald J. Trump (New York: Houghton Mifflin Harcourt, 2020), 109.

77. "His Side: Peter Strzok Speaks," CBS News, September 6, 2020, video, https://www.cbsnews.com/video/his-side-peter-strzok-speaks/.

78. Hans Mahncke (@HansMahncke), "Hi @CBSDavidMartin," Twitter, September 6, 2020, https://twitter.com/HansMahncke/status/1302674506453078017.

79. Jerry Dunleavy, "I Got That Wrong: Peter Strzok Admits He Botched Timeline on Opening of Trump-Russia Investigation," Washington Examiner, September 9, 2020, https://www.washingtonexaminer.com/news/1015131/i-got-that-wrong-peter-strzok-admits-he-botched-timeline-on-opening-of-trump-russia-investigation/.

80. FOIA-Processed Documents: Fusion GPS, U.S. Department of Justice, February 10, 2020, https://www.justice.gov/oip/foia-library/foia-processed/general_topics/fusion_gps_02_10_2020_interim/download.

81. United States v. Michael Sussmann, U.S. District Court for the District of Columbia, Document 123-1, May 8, 2022, https://storage.courtlistener.com/recap/gov.uscourts.dcd.235638/gov.uscourts.dcd.235638.123.1_1.pdf.

82. Peter Strzok, Compromised: Counterintelligence and the Threat of Donald J. Trump (New York: Houghton Mifflin Harcourt, 2020), 109.
83. Examination of the FBI's Crossfire Hurricane Investigation, U.S. Department of Justice, December 9, 2019, p. 52, https://www.justice.gov/storage/120919-examination.pdf.
84. Report on the Investigation into the FBI's Crossfire Hurricane Investigation, U.S. Department of Justice, May 2023, p. 54, https://www.justice.gov/storage/durhamreport.pdf.
85. Hans Mahncke (@HansMahncke), "Downer has been consistent," Twitter, December 14, 2019, https://twitter.com/HansMahncke/status/1205930845476970496.
86. Report on the Investigation into the FBI's Crossfire Hurricane Investigation, U.S. Department of Justice, May 2023, p. 53, https://www.justice.gov/storage/durhamreport.pdf.
87. FBI Text Messages, Senate Homeland Security and Governmental Affairs Committee, December 9, 2020, https://www.hsgac.senate.gov/wp-content/uploads/imo/media/doc/Johnson-Grassley%20Submission%202020-12-09.pdf.
88. Examination of the FBI's Crossfire Hurricane Investigation, U.S. Department of Justice, December 9, 2019, p. 67, https://www.justice.gov/storage/120919-examination.pdf.
89. Examination of the FBI's Crossfire Hurricane Investigation, U.S. Department of Justice, December 9, 2019, p. 62, https://www.justice.gov/storage/120919-examination.pdf.
90. https://www.nytimes.com/2016/03/23/us/politics/donald-trump-foreign-policy-advisers.html
91. Examination of the FBI's Crossfire Hurricane Investigation, U.S. Department of Justice, December 9, 2019, p. 62, https://www.justice.gov/storage/120919-examination.pdf.
92. Examination of the FBI's Crossfire Hurricane Investigation, U.S. Department of Justice, December 9, 2019, p. 292, https://www.justice.gov/storage/120919-examination.pdf.
93. Report on Russian Active Measures, House Permanent Select Committee on Intelligence, March 22, 2018, p. 2, https://intelligence.house.gov/uploadedfiles/final_russia_investigation_report.pdf.
94. FBI's Domestic Investigations and Operations Guide, FBI Vault, 2008, https://vault.fbi.gov/FBI%20Domestic%20Investigations%20and%20Operations%20Guide%20%28DIOG%29/fbi-domestic-investigations-and-operations-guide-diog-2008-version/FBI%20Domestic%20Investigations%20and%20Operations%20Guide%20%28DIOG%29%20Part%201%20of%201/view.

Chapter 10

1. Hans Mahncke (@HansMahncke), "Downer has been consistent," Twitter, December 14, 2019, https://twitter.com/HansMahncke/status/1205930845476970496.
2. Leslie H. Gelb, "Reagan Aides Describe Operation to Gather Inside Data on Carter," The New York Times, July 7, 1983, https://www.nytimes.com/1983/07/07/us/reagan-aides-describe-operation-to-gather-inside-data-on-carter.html.
3. Transcript of George Papadopoulos and FBI Confidential Human Source, declassified March 13, 2020, https://www.judiciary.senate.gov/imo/media/doc/2020-3-13%20FISA%20Senate%20-%20Transcript%20of%20George%20Papadopoulos%20and%20FBI%20Confidential%20Human%20Source%20declassified%20March%2013%202020.pdf.

Notes

4. Examination of the FBI's Crossfire Hurricane Investigation, U.S. Department of Justice, December 9, 2019, p. 332, https://www.justice.gov/storage/120919-examination.pdf.
5. Chuck Ross, "George Papadopoulos and the London Emails," Daily Caller, March 25, 2018, https://dailycaller.com/2018/03/25/george-papadopoulos-london-emails/.
6. Transcript of George Papadopoulos and FBI Confidential Human Source, Senate Judiciary Committee, April 3, 2020, https://www.judiciary.senate.gov/imo/media/doc/2020-04-03%20Submission%20SJC%20SSCI%20-%20Transcript%20of%20George%20Papadopoulos%20and%20FBI%20Confidential%20Human%20Source%20declassified%20on%20April%201%202020.pdf.
7. George Papadopoulos, Deep State Target: How I Got Caught in the Crosshairs of the Plot to Bring Down President Trump (New York: Diversion Books, 2019).
8. Transcript of George Papadopoulos and FBI Confidential Human Source, Senate Judiciary Committee, April 3, 2020, https://www.judiciary.senate.gov/imo/media/doc/2020-04-03%20Submission%20SJC%20SSCI%20-%20Transcript%20of%20George%20Papadopoulos%20and%20FBI%20Confidential%20Human%20Source%20declassified%20on%20April%201%202020.pdf.
9. Transcript of Carter Page and FBI Confidential Human Source, November 16, 2016, https://justthenews.com/sites/default/files/2021-01/HalperPageIntercept11-2016.pdf.
10. Meeting with FBI Confidential Human Source to discuss Crossfire Hurricane, August 15, 2016, https://justthenews.com/sites/default/files/2021-02/Halper%20Source%20Documents_final.pdf.
11. Ben Riley-Smith, "Spies, Lies and Secret Recordings: How a Cambridge Professor Snooped on Trump Campaign Advisers," The Telegraph, March 5, 2020, https://www.telegraph.co.uk/news/2020/03/05/spies-lies-secret-recordings-cambridge-professor-snooped-trump/.
12. Examination of the FBI's Crossfire Hurricane Investigation, U.S. Department of Justice, December 9, 2019, p. 328, https://www.justice.gov/storage/120919-examination.pdf.
13. Examination of the FBI's Crossfire Hurricane Investigation, U.S. Department of Justice, December 9, 2019, p. 329, https://www.justice.gov/storage/120919-examination.pdf.
14. Examination of the FBI's Crossfire Hurricane Investigation, U.S. Department of Justice, December 9, 2019, p. 328-9, https://www.justice.gov/storage/120919-examination.pdf.
15. Lokhova v. Halper, U.S. District Court for the Eastern District of Virginia, Docket, March 23, 2019, https://www.courtlistener.com/docket/15671580/lokhova-v-halper/.
16. FBI Closing Communication, January 4, 2017, https://storage.courtlistener.com/recap/gov.uscourts.dcd.191592/gov.uscourts.dcd.191592.198.2_1.pdf.
17. "New James Comey Revelations On Flynn, Trump Legal Jeopardy, Blackmail Concerns," YouTube video, posted by MSNBC, December 10, 2018, https://www.youtube.com/watch?v=NxNhjFrjXqI.
18. Andrew E. Kramer, Mike McIntire, and Barry Meier, "Secret Ledger in Ukraine Lists Cash for Donald Trump's Campaign Chief," The New York Times, August 14, 2016, https://www.nytimes.com/2016/08/15/us/politics/what-is-the-black-ledger.html.
19. "FBI Director James Comey testifies at House Select Intelligence Committee Hearing," C-SPAN, March 20, 2017, video, https://www.c-span.org/video/?425087-1/russian-election-interference.
20. Andrew E. Kramer, Mike McIntire, and Barry Meier, "Secret Ledger in Ukraine Lists Cash for Donald Trump's Campaign Chief," The New York Times, August 14, 2016, https://www.nytimes.com/2016/08/15/us/politics/what-is-the-black-ledger.html.

21. John Solomon, "FBI Warned Early and Often That Manafort File Might Be Fake, Used It Anyway," The Hill, June 19, 2019, https://thehill.com/opinion/white-house/449206-fbi-warned-early-and-often-that-manafort-file-might-be-fake-used-it-anyway/.
22. Kenneth P. Vogel and David Stern, "Ukraine's Sabotage of Trump Backfires," Politico, January 11, 2017, https://www.politico.com/story/2017/01/ukraine-sabotage-trump-backfire-233446.
23. "Biden and Poroshenko Discuss Publishing the So-Called Black Book," Bitchute, August 19, 2016, video, https://www.bitchute.com/video/7veGywPluRSz/.
24. Kenneth P. Vogel and David Stern, "Ukraine's Sabotage of Trump Backfires," Politico, January 11, 2017, https://www.politico.com/story/2017/01/ukraine-sabotage-trump-backfire-233446.
25. Adam Entous and Michael Schwirtz, "The Spy War: How the C.I.A. Secretly Helps Ukraine Fight Putin," The New York Times, February 25, 2024, https://www.nytimes.com/2024/02/25/world/europe/the-spy-war-how-the-cia-secretly-helps-ukraine-fight-putin.html.
26. Amb. Valeriy Chaly, "Ukraine's Ambassador: Trump's Comments Send Wrong Message to Ukraine," The Hill, August 4, 2016, https://thehill.com/blogs/pundits-blog/international/290411-ukraines-ambassador-trumps-comments-send-wrong-message-to/.
27. Arseniy Yatsenyuk, "Donald Trump's statement about Crimea and Putin went beyond any framework of a domestic political campaign," Facebook, July 31, 2016, https://web.archive.org/web/20161109102827/https://www.facebook.com/yatsenyuk.arseniy/posts/696167553870716.
28. Arsen Avakov, "The shameless statement by US presidential candidate Trump," Facebook, July 31, 2016, https://www.facebook.com/photo.php?fbid=1096263383797100&set=a.382483715175074.91896.100002403454361&type=3&theater.
29. Kenneth P. Vogel and David Stern, "Ukraine's Sabotage of Trump Backfires," Politico, January 11, 2017, https://www.politico.com/story/2017/01/ukraine-sabotage-trump-backfire-233446.
30. Examination of the FBI's Crossfire Hurricane Investigation, U.S. Department of Justice, December 9, 2019, p. 67, https://www.justice.gov/storage/120919-examination.pdf.
31. Tom Hamburger and Rosalind S. Helderman, "Former Trump Campaign Chairman Paul Manafort Files as Foreign Agent for Ukraine Work," The Washington Post, June 27, 2017, https://www.washingtonpost.com/politics/former-trump-campaign-chairman-paul-manafort-files-as-foreign-agent-for-ukraine-work/2017/06/27/8322b6ac-5b7b-11e7-9fc6-c7ef4bc58d13_story.html.
32. Darren Samuelsohn, Josh Gerstein and Matthew Choi, "Manafort Gets 47 Months in Prison for Financial Fraud," Politico, March 7, 2019, https://www.politico.com/story/2019/03/07/manafort-gets-47-months-in-prison-for-financial-fraud-1210786.
33. Exhibit DX-563, DocumentCloud, June 4, 2022, p. 16, https://www.documentcloud.org/documents/22046174-dx-563.
34. "Republicans Blast Report That FBI Offered Steele $1 Million for Proof of Dossier," House Judiciary Committee, October 12, 2022, https://judiciary.house.gov/media/in-the-news/republicans-blast-report-that-fbi-offered-steele-1-million-for-proof-of-dossier.
35. "Nunes Memo," DocumentCloud, February 2, 2018, https://www.documentcloud.org/documents/4365338-Nunes-memo.

Notes

36. Hans Mahncke (@HansMahncke), "Christopher Steele interview," Twitter, December 14, 2020, https://twitter.com/HansMahncke/status/1338631561135132672.
37. FBI Debriefing of Steele, November 9, 2017, https://justthenews.com/sites/default/files/2021-01/Steele2017FBIDebriefing.pdf.

Chapter 11

1. Franklin Foer, "Was a Trump Server Communicating With Russia?" Slate, October 31, 2016, https://www.slate.com/articles/news_and_politics/cover_story/2016/10/was_a_server_registered_to_the_trump_organization_communicating_with_russia.html.
2. Eric Lichtblau and Steven Lee Myers, "Investigating Donald Trump, F.B.I. Sees No Clear Link to Russia," The New York Times, October 31, 2016, https://www.nytimes.com/2016/11/01/us/politics/fbi-russia-election-donald-trump.html; Timothy B. Lee, "That explosive story about Trump's secret server for talking to Russia doesn't add up," Vox, November 1, 2016, https://www.vox.com/policy-and-politics/2016/11/1/13484340/trump-russia-secret-server.
3. The Trump-Russia Dossier as Released by BuzzFeed, Scribd, January 10, 2017, https://www.scribd.com/document/336226994/The-Trump-Russia-Dossier-as-Released-By-Buzzfeed.
4. United States v. Michael Sussmann, U.S. District Court for the District of Columbia, Indictment, September 16, 2021, https://storage.courtlistener.com/recap/gov.uscourts.dcd.235638/gov.uscourts.dcd.235638.1.0_13.pdf.
5. Dexter Filkins, "Was There a Connection Between a Russian Bank and the Trump Campaign?" The New Yorker, October 8, 2018, https://www.newyorker.com/magazine/2018/10/15/was-there-a-connection-between-a-russian-bank-and-the-trump-campaign.
6. Dexter Filkins, "The Contested Afterlife of the Trump-Alfa Bank Story," The New Yorker, October 7, 2020, https://www.newyorker.com/news/news-desk/the-contested-afterlife-of-the-trump-alfa-bank-story.
7. Franklin Foer, "Was a Trump Server Communicating With Russia?" Slate, October 31, 2016, https://www.slate.com/articles/news_and_politics/cover_story/2016/10/was_a_server_registered_to_the_trump_organization_communicating_with_russia.html.
8. Margot Cleveland, "Spygate Figure Whose Attorney Outed Him to The New York Times Now Wants His Name Hidden in Court Documents," The Federalist, March 4, 2022, https://thefederalist.com/2022/03/04/spygate-figure-whose-attorney-outed-him-to-the-new-york-times-now-wants-his-name-hidden-in-court-documents/.
9. @FOOL_NELSON, "Joffe is a good candidate," Twitter, September 15, 2021, https://twitter.com/FOOL_NELSON/status/1438214296035545088.
10. Daniel Strauss, "Russian Government Hackers Broke Into DNC Servers and Stole Trump Opposition Research," Politico, June 14, 2016, https://www.politico.com/story/2016/06/russian-government-hackers-broke-into-dnc-servers-stole-trump-oppo-224315.
11. United States v. Michael Sussmann, U.S. District Court for the District of Columbia, Document 35, February 11, 2022, p. 4, https://storage.courtlistener.com/recap/gov.uscourts.dcd.235638/gov.uscourts.dcd.235638.35.0_1.pdf.
12. Steele Deposition, Scribd, March 17, 2020, https://www.scribd.com/document/458992503/Steele-deposition.

13. Eric Bradner, "Clinton's campaign manager: Russia helping Trump," CNN, July 24, 2016, https://www.cnn.com/2016/07/24/politics/robby-mook-russia-dnc-emails-trump/index.html.
14. Report on the Investigation into the FBI's Crossfire Hurricane Investigation, U.S. Department of Justice, May 2023, p. 110, https://www.justice.gov/storage/durham report.pdf.
15. FBI Text Messages, Senate Homeland Security and Governmental Affairs Committee, December 9, 2020, https://www.hsgac.senate.gov/wp-content/uploads/imo/media/doc/Johnson-Grassley%20Submission%202020-12-09.pdf.
16. Hillary Clinton (@HillaryClinton), "Seriously, what is going on with Trump and Russia?," Twitter, August 6, 2016, https://twitter.com/HillaryClinton/status/762059962101198848.
17. Hillary Clinton (@HillaryClinton), "We have some questions about @realDonaldTrump's cozy relationship with Russia," Twitter, August 7, 2016, https://twitter.com/HillaryClinton/status/762452870553702401.
18. Hillary Clinton (@HillaryClinton), "We have some questions about Donald Trump's cozy relationship with Russia," Twitter, August 15, 2016, https://twitter.com/HillaryClinton/status/765288353419890688.
19. Hillary Clinton (@HillaryClinton), "We have some questions about Donald Trump's cozy relationship with Russia," Twitter, August 15, 2016, https://twitter.com/HillaryClinton/status/765288353419890688
20. Andrew E. Kramer, Mike McIntire, and Barry Meier, "Secret Ledger in Ukraine Lists Cash for Donald Trump's Campaign Chief," The New York Times, August 14, 2016, https://www.nytimes.com/2016/08/15/us/politics/what-is-the-black-ledger.html.
21. Kenneth P. Vogel and David Stern, "Ukraine's Sabotage of Trump Backfires," Politico, January 11, 2017, https://www.politico.com/story/2017/01/ukraine-sabotage-trump-backfire-233446; John Solomon, "FBI Warned Early and Often That Manafort File Might Be Fake, Used It Anyway," The Hill, June 19, 2019, https://thehill.com/opinion/white-house/449206-fbi-warned-early-and-often-that-manafort-file-might-be-fake-used-it-anyway/.
22. Letter from Harry Reid to James Comey, DocumentCloud, August 27, 2016, https://www.documentcloud.org/documents/3035844-Reid-Letter-to-Comey.
23. Steele Dossier, DocumentCloud, Report 112, https://www.documentcloud.org/documents/21200685-steele-dossier.
24. Steele Dossier, DocumentCloud, Report 112, https://www.documentcloud.org/documents/21200685-steele-dossier.
25. Steele Dossier, DocumentCloud, Report 112, https://www.documentcloud.org/documents/21200685-steele-dossier.
26. "Oleg Govorun: Revision history," Wikipedia, accessed August 5, 2024, https://en.wikipedia.org/w/index.php?title=Oleg_Govorun&action=history.
27. United States v. Michael Sussmann, U.S. District Court for the District of Columbia, Document 61, April 4, 2022, https://pacer-documents.s3.amazonaws.com/36/235637/04519147331.pdf.
28. Brennan Notes, DocumentCloud, October 6, 2020, https://www.documentcloud.org/documents/22049825-enclosure_1__brennan_notes__u.
29. Letter to Sen. Graham Regarding Declassification of FBI's Crossfire Hurricane Investigations, September 29, 2020, https://www.judiciary.senate.gov/imo/media/doc

/09-29-20_Letter%20to%20Sen.%20Graham_Declassification%20of%20FBI%27s%20Crossfire%20Hurricane%20Investigations_20-00912_U_SIGNED-FINAL.pdf.

30. Brennan Notes, DocumentCloud, October 6, 2020, https://www.documentcloud.org/documents/22049825-enclosure_1__brennan_notes__u.

31. Chairman Graham Releases Information from DNI Ratcliffe on FBI's Handling of Crossfire Hurricane, Senate Judiciary Committee, September 29, 2020, https://www.judiciary.senate.gov/press/rep/releases/chairman-graham-releases-information-from-dni-ratcliffe-on-fbis-handling-of-crossfire-hurricane.

32. "James Comey Testimony on Russia Investigation," C-SPAN, September 30, 2020, video, 37:37, https://www.c-span.org/video/?475947-1/fbi-director-james-comey-testimony-russia-investigation.

33. Examination of the FBI's Crossfire Hurricane Investigation, U.S. Department of Justice, December 9, 2019, p.77, https://www.justice.gov/storage/120919-examination.pdf.

34. Sussmann Trial Transcript: Scott Hellman and Steve DeJong, May 17, 2022, https://irp.cdn-website.com/5be8a42f/files/uploaded/sussmann-trial-517-Scott%20Hellman%20Steve%20DeJong%20.pdf.

35. Sussmann Trial Transcript: Scott Hellman and Steve DeJong, May 17, 2022, https://irp.cdn-website.com/5be8a42f/files/uploaded/sussmann-trial-517-Scott%20Hellman%20Steve%20DeJong%20.pdf.

36. Exhibit DX-513, DocumentCloud, September 16, 2021, https://www.documentcloud.org/documents/22029046-dx-513#document/p2/a2262573.

37. Sussmann Trial Transcript: Scott Hellman and Steve DeJong, May 17, 2022, https://irp.cdn-website.com/5be8a42f/files/uploaded/sussmann-trial-517-Scott%20Hellman%20Steve%20DeJong%20.pdf.

38. Sussmann Trial Transcript: Scott Hellman and Steve DeJong, May 17, 2022, https://irp.cdn-website.com/5be8a42f/files/uploaded/sussmann-trial-517-Scott%20Hellman%20Steve%20DeJong%20.pdf.

39. Report on the Investigation into the FBI's Crossfire Hurricane Investigation, U.S. Department of Justice, May 2023, p. 250, https://www.justice.gov/storage/durham report.pdf.

40. Eric Lichtblau and Steven Lee Myers, "Investigating Donald Trump, F.B.I. Sees No Clear Link to Russia," The New York Times, October 31, 2016, https://www.nytimes.com/2016/11/01/us/politics/fbi-russia-election-donald-trump.html.

41. Durham Reporter Email List, Scribd, April 25, 2022, https://www.scribd.com/document/571730091/2022-04-25-HUGE-Durham-Reporter-Email-List.

42. Durham Reporter Email List, Scribd, April 25, 2022, https://www.scribd.com/document/571730091/2022-04-25-HUGE-Durham-Reporter-Email-List.

43. Franklin Foer, "Was a Trump Server Communicating With Russia?" Slate, October 31, 2016, https://www.slate.com/articles/news_and_politics/cover_story/2016/10/was_a_server_registered_to_the_trump_organization_communicating_with_russia.html.

44. Andrew McCabe Lynch Text Messages, Senate Committee on the Judiciary, October 9, 2020, https://www.grassley.senate.gov/imo/media/doc/2020-10-09-14%20%20Andrew%20McCabe%20Lync_text%20messages%20from%206-8-15%20to%203-14-18.pdf.

45. "Crimeware" Message Board Post, Ops-Trust.net, November 1, 2016, 12:33 AM, on file with author.

46. "Crimeware" Message Board Post, Ops-Trust.net, November 1, 2016, 1:13 AM, on file with author.
47. "Crimeware" Message Board Post, Ops-Trust.net, November 1, 2016, 6:33 AM, on file with author.
48. "Crimeware" Message Board Post, Ops-Trust.net, November 1, 2016, 8:39 AM, on file with author.
49. "Crimeware" Message Board Post, Ops-Trust.net, November 1, 2016, 2:39 PM, on file with author.
50. "Crimeware" Message Board Post, Ops-Trust.net, November 3, 2016, 7:58 PM, on file with author.
51. "Crimeware" Message Board Post, Ops-Trust.net, November 1, 2016, 12:15 PM, on file with author.
52. "Crimeware" Message Board Post, Ops-Trust.net, November 1, 2016, 10:55 AM, on file with author.
53. Hillary Clinton (@HillaryClinton), "Computer scientists have apparently uncovered," Twitter, October 31, 2016, https://twitter.com/HillaryClinton/status/793250312119263233.
54. United States v. Michael Sussmann, U.S. District Court for the District of Columbia, Indictment, September 16, 2021, p. 5, https://www.justice.gov/sco/press-release/file/1433511/download.
55. United States v. Michael Sussmann, U.S. District Court for the District of Columbia, Indictment, September 16, 2021, p. 13, https://www.justice.gov/sco/press-release/file/1433511/download.
56. United States v. Michael Sussmann, U.S. District Court for the District of Columbia, Indictment, September 16, 2021, p. 12, https://www.justice.gov/sco/press-release/file/1433511/download.
57. Report on the Investigation into the FBI's Crossfire Hurricane Investigation, U.S. Department of Justice, May 2023, p. 246, https://www.justice.gov/storage/durhamreport.pdf.
58. United States v. Michael Sussmann, U.S. District Court for the District of Columbia, Indictment, September 16, 2021, p. 13, https://www.justice.gov/sco/press-release/file/1433511/download.
59. Hillary Clinton Campaign Press Release: Statement from Jake Sullivan on New Report Exposing Russian Interference, October 31, 2016, https://www.presidency.ucsb.edu/documents/hillary-clinton-campaign-press-release-statement-from-jake-sullivan-new-report-exposing.
60. United States v. Michael Sussmann, U.S. District Court for the District of Columbia, Document 70, April 15, 2022, https://storage.courtlistener.com/recap/gov.uscourts.dcd.235638/gov.uscourts.dcd.235638.70.0_3.pdf
61. Fridman v. Bean LLC, U.S. District Court for the District of Columbia, Complaint, October 3, 2017, https://storage.courtlistener.com/recap/gov.uscourts.dcd.189930/gov.uscourts.dcd.189930.1.0_2.pdf.
62. Adam Entous, Devlin Barrett and Rosalind S. Helderman, "Clinton Campaign, DNC Paid for Research That Led to Russia Dossier," The Washington Post, October 24, 2017, https://www.washingtonpost.com/world/national-security/clinton-campaign-dnc-paid-for-research-that-led-to-russia-dossier/2017/10/24/226fabf0-b8e4-11e7-a908-a3470754bbb9_story.html?utm_term=.4a456a51d134.

63 AO Alfa Bank v John Doe, Superior Court of the District of Columbia, Seago Motion, August 3, 2021, https://www.scribd.com/document/754378364/Seago-Motion.

Chapter 12

1   "Interview with Hillary Clinton's Campaign Manager Robby Mook," CNN, July 24, 2016, https://transcripts.cnn.com/show/sotu/date/2016-07-24/segment/02.
2   United States v. Michael Sussmann, U.S. District Court for the District of Columbia, Indictment, September 16, 2021, p. 5, https://www.justice.gov/sco/press-release/file/1433511/download.
3   Diane Denman, Testimony before the U.S. House Permanent Select Committee on Intelligence, December 5, 2017, p. 52, https://d3i6fh83elv35t.cloudfront.net/static/2020/05/dd12.pdf.
4   Josh Rogin, "Trump Campaign Guts GOP's Anti-Russia Stance on Ukraine," The Washington Post, July 18, 2016, https://www.washingtonpost.com/opinions/global-opinions/trump-campaign-guts-gops-anti-russia-stance-on-ukraine/2016/07/18/98adb3b0-4cf3-11e6-a7d8-13d06b37f256_story.html.
5   Ellen Nakashima, "Russian Government Hackers Penetrated DNC, Stole Opposition Research on Trump," The Washington Post, June 14, 2016, https://www.washingtonpost.com/world/national-security/russian-government-hackers-penetrated-dnc-stole-opposition-research-on-trump/2016/06/14/cf006cb4-316e-11e6-8ff7-7b6c1998b7a0_story.html.
6   While it remains unknown whether the alleged hack was perpetrated by a state actor, there is a potential trail leading to Israeli operatives that has not been extensively investigated. Lee Smith, "How Russiagate Became Israelgate," Tablet Magazine, June 8, 2018, https://www.tabletmag.com/sections/news/articles/how-russiagate-became-israelgate.
7   Shawn Henry, Testimony before the U.S. House Permanent Select Committee on Intelligence, December 5, 2017, p. 75, https://www.dni.gov/files/HPSCI_Transcripts/2020-05-04-Shawn_Henry-MTR_Redacted.pdf.
8   "CrowdStrike's work with the Democratic National Committee: Setting the record straight," CrowdStrike, June 5, 2020, https://www.crowdstrike.com/blog/bears-midst-intrusion-democratic-national-committee/.
9   Diane Denman, Testimony before the U.S. House Permanent Select Committee on Intelligence, December 5, 2017, p. 44, https://d3i6fh83elv35t.cloudfront.net/static/2020/05/dd12.pdf.
10 The Trump-Russia Dossier as Released by BuzzFeed, Scribd, January 10, 2017, p. 8, https://www.scribd.com/document/336226994/The-Trump-Russia-Dossier-as-Released-By-Buzzfeed.
11 FISA Warrant Application for Carter Page, U.S. Senate Judiciary Committee, p. 21, https://www.judiciary.senate.gov/imo/media/doc/FISA%20Warrant%20Application%20for%20Carter%20Page.pdf.
12 Steele Dossier, DocumentCloud, Report 95, https://www.documentcloud.org/documents/21200685-steele-dossier.; FISA Warrant Application for Carter Page, U.S. Senate Judiciary Committee, p. 20, https://www.judiciary.senate.gov/imo/media/doc/FISA%20Warrant%20Application%20for%20Carter%20Page.pdf.
13 Durham Reporter Email List, Scribd, April 25, 2022, p. 16 https://www.scribd.com/document/571730091/2022-04-25-HUGE-Durham-Reporter-Email-List.

14. Durham Reporter Email List, Scribd, April 25, 2022, p. 16, https://www.scribd.com/document/571730091/2022-04-25-HUGE-Durham-Reporter-Email-List.
15. Julia Ioffe, "Who Is Carter Page? The mystery of Trump's man in Moscow," Politico, September 23, 2016, https://www.politico.com/magazine/story/2016/09/the-mystery-of-trumps-man-in-moscow-214283/.
16. Michael Isikoff, "U.S. Intel Officials Probe Ties Between Trump Adviser and Kremlin," Yahoo News, September 23, 2016, https://news.yahoo.com/u-s-intel-officials-probe-ties-between-trump-adviser-and-kremlin-175046002.html.
17. Michael Crowley, "Trump Changed Views on Ukraine After Hiring Paul Manafort as Campaign Manager," Politico EU, August 3, 2016, https://www.politico.eu/article/trump-changed-views-on-ukraine-after-hiring-paul-manafort-campaign-manager-russia-vladimir-putin/.
18. FISA Warrant Application for Carter Page, U.S. Senate Judiciary Committee, p. 21, https://www.judiciary.senate.gov/imo/media/doc/FISA%20Warrant%20Application%20for%20Carter%20Page.pdf.
19. Alexander Burns, "Donald Trump Reaffirms Support for Warmer Relations With Putin," The New York Times, August 1, 2016, https://www.nytimes.com/2016/08/02/us/politics/donald-trump-vladimir-putin-russia.html; Molly O'Toole, "The World According to Trump: Super Tuesday's Big Winner," Foreign Policy, March 1, 2016, https://foreignpolicy.com/2016/03/01/the-world-according-to-trump-super-tuesdays-big-winner/.
20. Andrew E. Kramer, Mike McIntire, and Barry Meier, "Secret Ledger in Ukraine Lists Cash for Donald Trump's Campaign Chief," The New York Times, August 14, 2016, https://www.nytimes.com/2016/08/15/us/politics/what-is-the-black-ledger.html.
21. Barry Meier, Spooked: The Trump Dossier, Black Cube, and the Rise of Private Spies (New York: Harper, 2021).
22. Email from Barry Meier to Fusion GPS, August 2, 2016, https://miro.medium.com/v2/1*Ildh1sphSa4QWeO2vgDDiw.jpeg.
23. Statement by Fusion GPS, Medium, May 20, 2021, https://fusion-gps.medium.com/barry-meiers-spooked-ef502cceb1c.
24. Evan Perez, "Secret Court's Oversight Gets Scrutiny," The Wall Street Journal, June 9, 2013, https://www.wsj.com/articles/SB10001424127887324904004578535670310514616.
25. Michael Isikoff, "U.S. Intel Officials Probe Ties Between Trump Adviser and Kremlin," Yahoo News, September 23, 2016, https://news.yahoo.com/u-s-intel-officials-probe-ties-between-trump-adviser-and-kremlin-175046002.html.
26. Chairman Graham Releases Information from DNI Ratcliffe on FBI's Handling of Crossfire Hurricane, Senate Judiciary Committee, September 29, 2020, https://www.judiciary.senate.gov/press/rep/releases/chairman-graham-releases-information-from-dni-ratcliffe-on-fbis-handling-of-crossfire-hurricane.
27. FISA Warrant Application for Carter Page, U.S. Senate Judiciary Committee, p. 23, https://www.judiciary.senate.gov/imo/media/doc/FISA%20Warrant%20Application%20for%20Carter%20Page.pdf.
28. Report on the Investigation into the FBI's Crossfire Hurricane Investigation, U.S. Department of Justice, May 2023, p. 118, https://www.justice.gov/storage/durhamreport.pdf.

Notes

29 Carter Page Letter to James Comey, September 25, 2016, https://www.washingtonpost.com/r/2010-2019/WashingtonPost/2016/09/26/Editorial-Opinion/Graphics/2016.09.25_FBI_letter.pdf.

30 Report on the Investigation into Russian Interference in the 2016 Presidential Election, Special Counsel's Office, U.S. Department of Justice, March 22, 2019, p. 102, https://www.justice.gov/archives/sco/file/1373816/download.

31 Report on the Investigation into Russian Interference in the 2016 Presidential Election, Special Counsel's Office, U.S. Department of Justice, March 22, 2019, p. 20, https://www.justice.gov/archives/sco/file/1373816/download.

32 John Barry, "Gitmo: The SOUTHCOM Showdown," Newsweek, May 8, 2005, http://www.newsweek.com/2005/05/08/gitmo-southcom-showdown.html.

33 William Cummings, "Reporter who broke Steele dossier story says ex-British agent's claims 'likely false'," USA Today, December 18, 2018, https://www.usatoday.com/story/news/politics/2018/12/18/steele-dossier-michael-isikoff/2347833002.

34 "Michael Isikoff Talks to Barry Meier," YouTube video, posted by Montclair Public Library, May 20, 2021, https://www.youtube.com/watch?v=K54J4qiXRcA.

35 "Michael Isikoff Talks to Barry Meier," YouTube video, posted by Montclair Public Library, May 20, 2021, 13:46, https://www.youtube.com/watch?v=K54J4qiXRcA.

36 Hillary Clinton (@HillaryClinton), "The man who could be your next president may be deeply indebted to another country," Twitter, September 22, 2016, https://twitter.com/hillaryclinton/status/779055195607166977.

37 Sergei Millian (@SergeiMillian), "ABC interview - Behind the scenes," Twitter, April 28, 2022, https://twitter.com/SergeiMillian/status/1519708950685536256.

38 Brian Steinberg, "Brian Ross, who aired erroneous Trump report, to leave ABC," Reuters, July 2, 2018, https://www.reuters.com/article/idUSKBN1JT08J/.

39 Durham Reporter Email List, Scribd, April 25, 2022, https://www.scribd.com/document/571730091/2022-04-25-HUGE-Durham-Reporter-Email-List.

40 Jane Mayer, "Christopher Steele, the Man Behind the Trump Dossier," The New Yorker, March 5, 2018, https://www.newyorker.com/magazine/2018/03/12/christopher-steele-the-man-behind-the-trump-dossier.

41 Glenn Simpson and Peter Fritsch, Crime in Progress (New York: Random House, 2019), chap. 9, Kindle; Peter Fritsch Deposition, DocumentCloud, February 13, 2022, https://www.documentcloud.org/documents/21274481-220218-alfa-motion-for-extension#document/p244/a2085714.

42 Tom Hamburger, Rosalind S. Helderman and Michael Birnbaum, "Inside Trump's Financial Ties to Russia and His Unusual Flattery of Vladimir Putin," The Washington Post, June 17, 2016, https://www.washingtonpost.com/politics/inside-trumps-financial-ties-to-russia-and-his-unusual-flattery-of-vladimir-putin/2016/06/17/dbdcaac8-31a6-11e6-8ff7-7b6c1998b7a0_story.html.

43 Dana Priest, "Trump Adviser Michael T. Flynn on His Dinner with Putin and Why Russia Today Is Just Like CNN," The Washington Post, August 15, 2016, https://www.washingtonpost.com/news/checkpoint/wp/2016/08/15/trump-adviser-michael-t-flynn-on-his-dinner-with-putin-and-why-russia-today-is-just-like-cnn/.

44 Dana Priest and Greg Miller, "He was one of the most respected intel officers of his generation. Now he's leading 'Lock her up' chants," The Washington Post, August 15, 2016, https://www.washingtonpost.com/world/national-security/nearly-the-entire-national-security-establishment-has-rejected-trumpexcept-for-this-man/2016/08/15/d5072d96-5e4b-11e6-8e45-477372e89d78_story.html.

45 Dana Priest, Ellen Nakashima and Tom Hamburger, "Intelligence Community Investigating Covert Russian Influence Operations in the United States," The Washington Post, September 5, 2016, https://archive.is/1ErxB.
46 Dana Priest, Ellen Nakashima and Tom Hamburger, "U.S. investigating potential covert Russian plan to disrupt November elections," The Washington Post, September 5, 2016, https://archive.is/s38jq.
47 Dana Priest and Tom Hamburger, "Trump's Refusal to Accept Government Assessments on Russian Hacks Dismays Former Officials," The Washington Post, October 14, 2016, https://www.washingtonpost.com/politics/trump-refusal-to-accept-government-assessments-on-russian-hacks-dismays-former-officials/2016/10/14/6d1c7f60-8fc4-11e6-9c52-0b10449e33c4_story.html.
48 Franklin Foer, "Was a Trump Server Communicating With Russia?" Slate, October 31, 2016, https://www.slate.com/articles/news_and_politics/cover_story/2016/10/was_a_server_registered_to_the_trump_organization_communicating_with_russia.html.
49 Catherine Belton, "The shadowy Russian émigré touting Trump," Financial Times, November 1, 2016, https://www.ft.com/content/ea52a678-9cfb-11e6-8324-be63473ce146.
50 "Steele Spreadsheet," Senate Judiciary Committee, accessed August 5, 2024, p. 68, https://www.scribd.com/document/479781400/Steele-Spreadsheet-1.
51 "DOJ Documents Combined," Senate Committee on Homeland Security and Governmental Affairs, accessed August 5, 2024, https://www.hsgac.senate.gov/wp-content/uploads/imo/media/doc/DOJ%20Docs%20Combined.pdf.
52 "Steele Spreadsheet," Senate Judiciary Committee, accessed August 5, 2024, p. 68, https://www.scribd.com/document/479781400/Steele-Spreadsheet-1.
53 Codyave (@codyave), "Screenshot of Belton Message," Twitter, May 5, 2022, https://twitter.com/codyave/status/1522098089317650432/photo/1.
54 Catherine Belton, "The shadowy Russian émigré touting Trump," Financial Times, November 1, 2016, https://www.ft.com/content/ea52a678-9cfb-11e6-8324-be63473ce146.
55 Catherine Belton, "The shadowy Russian émigré touting Trump," Financial Times, November 1, 2016, https://www.ft.com/content/ea52a678-9cfb-11e6-8324-be63473ce146.
56 Abramovich v. HarperCollins Judgment, High Court of Justice, London, United Kingdom, November 24, 2021, https://www.judiciary.uk/wp-content/uploads/2022/07/Abramovich-v-HarperCollins-judgment-241121.pdf.

Chapter 13

1 Joint Statement from the Department of Homeland Security and the Office of the Director of National Intelligence, Department of Homeland Security, October 7, 2016, https://www.dhs.gov/news/2016/10/07/joint-statement-department-homeland-security-and-office-director-national.
2 "FBI Director James Comey News Conference on Clinton Email," C-SPAN, video, July 5, 2016, https://www.c-span.org/video/?412231-1/fbi-director-james-comey-news-conference-clinton-email.
3 "18 U.S. Code § 793 - Gathering, Transmitting or Losing Defense Information," Cornell Law School, accessed August 5, 2024, https://www.law.cornell.edu/uscode/text/18/793.

4. John Solomon, "Early Comey Memo Accused Clinton of 'Gross Negligence' on Emails," The Hill, November 6, 2017, https://thehill.com/homenews/senate/358982-early-comey-memo-accused-clinton-of-gross-negligence-on-emails/.
5. Strzok Dismissal Report, Federal Bureau of Investigation, August 8, 2018, https://media.washtimes.com/media/misc/2019/12/05/Strzok_firing_letter.pdf.
6. Eric Bradner, Pamela Brown and Evan Perez, "FBI Clears Clinton - Again," CNN, November 6, 2016, https://www.cnn.com/2016/11/06/politics/comey-tells-congress-fbi-has-not-changed-conclusions/index.html.
7. Strzok-Page Text Messages, Department of Justice, JustSecurity, August 2019, https://www.justsecurity.org/wp-content/uploads/2019/08/McCabe-Preistap-and-Comey-emails-regarding-Clinton-Email-investigation-and-Strzok-Page-Text-Messages_Part-2.pdf.
8. Adam Entous, Ellen Nakashima and Greg Miller, "Secret CIA assessment says Russia was trying to help Trump win White House," The Washington Post, December 9, 2016, https://www.washingtonpost.com/world/national-security/obama-orders-review-of-russian-hacking-during-presidential-campaign/2016/12/09/31d6b300-be2a-11e6-94ac-3d324840106c_story.html.
9. Greg Miller, Adam Entous and Ellen Nakashima, "National Security Adviser Flynn Discussed Sanctions with Russian Ambassador Despite Denials, Officials Say," The Washington Post, February 9, 2017, https://www.washingtonpost.com/world/national-security/national-security-adviser-flynn-discussed-sanctions-with-russian-ambassador-despite-denials-officials-say/2017/02/09/f85b29d6-ee11-11e6-b4ff-ac2cf509efe5_story.html; Ellen Nakashima, Devlin Barrett and Adam Entous, "FBI Obtained FISA Warrant to Monitor Former Trump Adviser Carter Page," The Washington Post, April 11, 2017, https://www.washingtonpost.com/world/national-security/fbi-obtained-fisa-warrant-to-monitor-former-trump-adviser-carter-page/2017/04/11/620192ea-1e0e-11e7-ad74-3a742a6e93a7_story.html.
10. Maggie Haberman, "Trump's Deflections and Denials on Russia Frustrate Even His Allies," The New York Times, June 25, 2017, https://www.nytimes.com/2017/06/25/us/politics/trumps-deflections-and-denials-on-russia-frustrate-even-his-allies.html.
11. Assessing Russian Activities and Intentions in Recent US Elections, Office of the Director of National Intelligence, January 6, 2017, https://www.dni.gov/files/documents/ICA_2017_01.pdf.
12. Declassified Assessment on COVID-19 Origins, Office of the Director of National Intelligence, March 2023, https://www.dni.gov/files/ODNI/documents/assessments/Declassified-Assessment-on-COVID-19-Origins.pdf.
13. Statement by President Joe Biden on the Investigation into the Origins of COVID-19, The White House, August 27, 2021, https://www.whitehouse.gov/briefing-room/statements-releases/2021/08/27/statement-by-president-joe-biden-on-the-investigation-into-the-origins-of-covid-%E2%81%A019/.
14. Volume 4 of the Senate Intelligence Committee Report on Russian Active Measures, U.S. Senate Select Committee on Intelligence, April 2020, p. 26, https://www.intelligence.senate.gov/sites/default/files/documents/Report_Volume4.pdf.
15. Volume 4 of the Senate Intelligence Committee Report on Russian Active Measures, U.S. Senate Select Committee on Intelligence, April 2020, p. 27, https://www.intelligence.senate.gov/sites/default/files/documents/Report_Volume4.pdf.

16. Letter to Senator Graham Regarding Declassification of FBI's Crossfire Hurricane Investigations, Senate Committee on the Judiciary, September 29, 2020, https://www.judiciary.senate.gov/imo/media/doc/09-29-20_Letter%20to%20Sen.%20Graham_Declassification%20of%20FBI's%20Crossfire%20Hurricane%20Investigations_20-00912_U_SIGNED-FINAL.pdf.
17. Brennan Notes, DocumentCloud, October 6, 2020, https://www.documentcloud.org/documents/22049825-enclosure_1__brennan_notes__u.
18. Chairman Graham Releases Information from DNI Ratcliffe on FBI's Handling of Crossfire Hurricane, Senate Judiciary Committee, September 29, 2020, https://www.judiciary.senate.gov/press/rep/releases/chairman-graham-releases-information-from-dni-ratcliffe-on-fbis-handling-of-crossfire-hurricane.
19. Paul Sperry, "Secret Report: How CIA's Brennan Overruled Dissenting Analysts Who Thought Russia Favored Hillary," RealClearInvestigations, September 24, 2020, https://www.realclearinvestigations.com/articles/2020/09/24/secret_report_how_cias_brennan_overruled_dissenting_analysts_who_thought_russia_favored_hillary_125315.html.
20. Mike Pompeo, Never Give an Inch: Fighting for the America I Love (New York: HarperCollins, 2023), 115-16.
21. Paul Sperry, "Secret Report: How CIA's Brennan Overruled Dissenting Analysts Who Thought Russia Favored Hillary," RealClearInvestigations, September 24, 2020, https://www.realclearinvestigations.com/articles/2020/09/24/secret_report_how_cias_brennan_overruled_dissenting_analysts_who_thought_russia_favored_hillary_125315.html.
22. Scott Pelley, "Why President Trump asked Ukraine to look into a DNC "server" and CrowdStrike," CBS News, February 16, 2020, https://www.cbsnews.com/news/trump-crowdstrike-ukraine-server-conspiracy-theory-60-minutes-2020-02-16/.
23. Mike Pompeo, Never Give an Inch: Fighting for the America I Love (New York: HarperCollins, 2023), 115.
24. "Meet The Press 12/11/16," NBC News, December 11, 2016, video, https://www.nbcnews.com/meet-the-press/meet-press-12-11-16-n694576.
25. "Meet The Press 12/11/16," NBC News, December 11, 2016, video, https://www.nbcnews.com/meet-the-press/meet-press-12-11-16-n694576.
26. Adam Entous, Ellen Nakashima and Greg Miller, "Secret CIA assessment says Russia was trying to help Trump win White House," The Washington Post, December 9, 2016, https://www.washingtonpost.com/world/national-security/obama-orders-review-of-russian-hacking-during-presidential-campaign/2016/12/09/31d6b300-be2a-11e6-94ac-3d324840106c_story.html.
27. "FBI Director James Comey Testimony on Russia Investigation," C-SPAN, June 8, 2017, video, 1:08:40, https://www.c-span.org/video/?475947-1/fbi-director-james-comey-testimony-russia-investigation.
28. Rand Paul (@RandPaul), "BREAKING: A high-level source tells me it was Brennan," Twitter, March 27, 2019, https://twitter.com/RandPaul/status/1110987950605680642.; Rowan Scarborough, "John Brennan endorsed anti-Trump Steele dossier: Bob Woodward," The Washington Times, September 11, 2018, https://www.washingtontimes.com/news/2018/sep/11/john-brennan-endorsed-anti-trump-steele-dossier-bo/.

Notes

29 McCabe and Strzok Text Messages, Senate Committee on Homeland Security and Governmental Affairs, JustTheNews, March 2021, https://justthenews.com/sites/default/files/2021-03/messages.pdf.

30 USA v. Danchenko, U.S. District Court for the Eastern District of Virginia, Document 113, October 12, 2022), p. 119, https://storage.courtlistener.com/recap/gov.uscourts.vaed.515692/gov.uscourts.vaed.515692.113.0.pdf.

31 USA v. Danchenko, U.S. District Court for the Eastern District of Virginia, Document 130-3, October 18, 2022, https://storage.courtlistener.com/recap/gov.uscourts.vaed.515692/gov.uscourts.vaed.515692.130.3_2.pdf.

32 Volume 5 of the Senate Intelligence Committee Report on Russian Active Measures, U.S. Senate Select Committee on Intelligence, August 18, 2020, p. 927, https://www.intelligence.senate.gov/sites/default/files/documents/report_volume5.pdf.

33 Examination of the FBI's Crossfire Hurricane Investigation, U.S. Department of Justice, December 9, 2019, p. 178, https://www.justice.gov/storage/120919-examination.pdf.

34 Examination of the FBI's Crossfire Hurricane Investigation, U.S. Department of Justice, December 9, 2019, p. 178, https://www.justice.gov/storage/120919-examination.pdf.

35 Volume 4 of the Senate Intelligence Committee Report on Russian Active Measures, U.S. Senate Select Committee on Intelligence, April 2020, p. 42, https://www.intelligence.senate.gov/sites/default/files/documents/Report_Volume4.pdf.

36 Examination of the FBI's Crossfire Hurricane Investigation, U.S. Department of Justice, December 9, 2019, p. 178-9, https://www.justice.gov/storage/120919-examination.pdf.

37 Examination of the FBI's Crossfire Hurricane Investigation, U.S. Department of Justice, December 9, 2019, p. 179, https://www.justice.gov/storage/120919-examination.pdf.

38 ODNI Statement on Declassified Intelligence Community Assessment of Russian Activities and Intentions in Recent U.S. Elections, Office of the Director of National Intelligence, January 6, 2017, https://www.intelligence.senate.gov/publications/assessing-russian-activities-and-intentions-recent-us-elections.

39 Evan Perez et al., "Intel chiefs presented Trump with claims of Russian efforts to compromise him," CNN, January 10, 2017, https://www.cnn.com/2017/01/10/politics/donald-trump-intelligence-report-russia/index.html.

40 Assessing Russian Activities and Intentions in Recent US Elections, Office of the Director of National Intelligence, January 6, 2017, p. 2, https://www.dni.gov/files/documents/ICA_2017_01.pdf.

41 UK News Consumption 2019 Report, Ofcom, United Kingdom, July 2019, https://www.ofcom.org.uk/__data/assets/pdf_file/0027/157914/uk-news-consumption-2019-report.pdf.

42 Mark Thompson, "Britain bans Russian state TV channel RT," CNN, March 18, 2022, https://www.cnn.com/2022/03/18/media/uk-bans-russia-rt-tv/index.html.

43 Paul Wood, "Trump Russia dossier key claim 'verified'," BBC News, March 31, 2017, https://www.bbc.com/news/world-us-canada-39435786; Gordon Corera, "Christopher Steele: Ex-spy says more must be done to stop Russian interference," BBC News, August 6, 2020, https://www.bbc.com/news/uk-53685051; "Fusion GPS dossier author 'feared Trump was blackmail target'," BBC News, January 9, 2018, https://www.bbc.com/news/world-us-canada-42628347.

44 Matt Taibbi (@mtaibbi), "Twitter Files #14," Twitter post, January 12, 2023, https://twitter.com/mtaibbi/status/1613589031773769739.

45 James Clapper, Testimony before the U.S. House Permanent Select Committee on Intelligence, July 17, 2017, p. 16, https://web.archive.org/web/20200507215144/https://intelligence.house.gov/uploadedfiles/jc7.pdf.

46 Ellen Nakashima and Adam Entous, "FBI and CIA Give Differing Accounts to Lawmakers on Russia's Motives in 2016 Hacks," The Washington Post, December 10, 2016, https://www.washingtonpost.com/world/national-security/fbi-and-cia-give-differing-accounts-to-lawmakers-on-russias-motives-in-2016-hacks/2016/12/10/c6dfadfa-bef0-11e6-94ac-3d324840106c_story.html.

47 James Clapper, Testimony before the U.S. House Permanent Select Committee on Intelligence, July 17, 2017, p. 17, https://web.archive.org/web/20200507215144/https://intelligence.house.gov/uploadedfiles/jc7.pdf.

48 United States v. Michael Flynn, U.S. District Court for the District of Columbia, Document 231-1, June 24, 2020, https://storage.courtlistener.com/recap/gov.uscourts.dcd.191592/gov.uscourts.dcd.191592.231.1_1.pdf.

49 "New James Comey Revelations On Flynn, Trump Legal Jeopardy, Blackmail Concerns," YouTube video, posted by MSNBC, YouTube, December 10, 2018, https://www.youtube.com/watch?v=NxNhjFrjXqI.

50 Declassified Flynn Transcripts: Part 1, Scribd, May 29, 2020, https://www.scribd.com/document/463583097/Declassified-Flynn-Transcripts-Part-1; Declassified Flynn Transcripts: Part 2, Scribd, May 29, 2020, https://www.scribd.com/document/463583107/Declassified-Flynn-Transcripts-Part-2.

51 Report on the Investigation into Russian Interference in the 2016 Presidential Election, Special Counsel's Office, U.S. Department of Justice, March 22, 2019, p. 27, https://www.justice.gov/archives/sco/file/1373816/download.

52 Ken Bensinger, Miriam Elder, and Mark Schoofs, "These Reports Allege Trump Has Deep Ties To Russia," Buzzfeed, January 10, 2017, https://www.buzzfeednews.com/article/kenbensinger/these-reports-allege-trump-has-deep-ties-to-russia.

53 Chuck Ross, "Emails: Jake Tapper Tore Into 'Irresponsible' BuzzFeed Editor For Publishing The Steele Dossier," The Daily Caller, February 8, 2019, https://dailycaller.com/2019/02/08/jake-tapper-buzzfeed-dossier/.

54 Paul Roderick Gregory, "The Trump Dossier Is False News — And Here's Why," Forbes, January 13, 2017, https://www.forbes.com/sites/paulroderickgregory/2017/01/13/the-trump-dossier-is-false-news-and-heres-why/.

55 United States v. Alexander Smirnov, U.S. District Court for the District of Nevada, February 20, 2024, p. 20, https://storage.courtlistener.com/recap/gov.uscourts.nvd.167064/gov.uscourts.nvd.167064.15.0.pdf.

Epilogue

1 Ivan Katchanovski, "The 'Snipers' Massacre' on the Maidan in Ukraine," Journal of Media and Communication Studies 11, no. 2 (2023), https://doi.org/10.1080/23311886.2023.2269685.

2 Kenneth P. Vogel and David Stern, "Ukraine's Sabotage of Trump Backfires," Politico, January 11, 2017, https://www.politico.com/story/2017/01/ukraine-sabotage-trump-backfire-233446.

3 "Ukrainian Politicians Denounce Trump's Readiness to Legitimize Putin's Crimean Anschluss," Euromaidan Press, August 2, 2016, https://euromaidanpress.com/2016/08/02

Notes

/ukrainian-politicians-denounce-trumps-readiness-to-legitimize-putins-crimean-anschluss-euromaidan-press/.

4. Arsen Avakov, "The shameless statement by US presidential candidate Trump," Facebook, July 31, 2016, https://www.facebook.com/photo.php?fbid=1096263383797100&set=a.382483715175074.91896.100002403454361&type=3&theater.
5. John Solomon, "FBI Warned Early and Often That Manafort File Might Be Fake, Used It Anyway," The Hill, June 19, 2019, https://thehill.com/opinion/white-house/449206-fbi-warned-early-and-often-that-manafort-file-might-be-fake-used-it-anyway/.
6. Kenneth P. Vogel and David Stern, "Ukraine's Sabotage of Trump Backfires," Politico, January 11, 2017, https://www.politico.com/story/2017/01/ukraine-sabotage-trump-backfire-233446.
7. John Solomon, "Ukrainian Embassy Confirms DNC Contractor Solicited Trump Dirt in 2016," The Hill, May 2, 2019, https://thehill.com/opinion/white-house/441892-ukrainian-embassy-confirms-dnc-contractor-solicited-trump-dirt-in-2016/.
8. Ryan Lucas and Tamara Keith, "U.S. Imposes New Sanctions on Russia Over Election Interference, Cyberattacks," NPR, March 15, 2018, https://www.npr.org/2018/03/15/593895383/us-imposes-new-sanctions-on-russia-over-election-interference-cyberattacks.
9. Kenneth P. Vogel and David Stern, "Ukraine's Sabotage of Trump Backfires," Politico, January 11, 2017, https://www.politico.com/story/2017/01/ukraine-sabotage-trump-backfire-233446.; Valentyn Nalyvaichenko, "Ukraine Will Get the Truth on Corruption," The Wall Street Journal, October 10, 2019, https://www.wsj.com/articles/ukraine-will-get-the-truth-on-corruption-11570745983.
10. "U.S. Officials Say Lethal Weapons Headed to Ukraine," CNBC, December 23, 2017, https://www.cnbc.com/2017/12/23/us-officials-say-lethal-weapons-headed-to-ukraine.html.
11. Amanda Macias, "Treasury Sanctions Putin's Chef, Other Russians Over Cyber-Related Threats," CNBC, March 15, 2018, https://www.cnbc.com/2018/03/15/treasury-sanctions-putins-chef-other-russians-over-cyber-related-threats.html.
12. Yaroslav Trofimov and Thomas Grove, "Plane Carrying Wagner Owner Prigozhin Crashes in Russia; All Aboard Killed," The Wall Street Journal, August 23, 2023, https://www.wsj.com/world/russia/plane-carrying-wagner-owner-prigozhin-crashes-in-russia-all-aboard-killed-82d25f1e.
13. Treasury Sanctions Russian Individuals and Entities for Malicious Cyber Activity, U.S. Department of the Treasury, September 30, 2019, https://home.treasury.gov/news/press-releases/sm787.
14. C. Ryan Barber, "'It's Not Croquet': In Dropped Mueller Case, Reed Smith's Eric Dubelier Didn't Pull Punches Defending Russian Firm," The National Law Journal, March 18, 2020, https://www.law.com/nationallawjournal/2020/03/18/its-not-croquet-in-dropped-mueller-case-reed-smiths-eric-dubelier-didnt-pull-punches-defending-russian-firm/?slreturn=20240211210302.
15. USA v. Concord Management and Consulting LLC, et al., U.S. District Court for the District of Columbia, Document 381, March 16, 2020, p. 9, https://storage.courtlistener.com/recap/gov.uscourts.dcd.193580/gov.uscourts.dcd.193580.381.0.pdf.
16. 15 Days to Slow the Spread, The White House, March 16, 2020, https://trumpwhitehouse.archives.gov/articles/15-days-slow-spread/.

17. Evan Perez and Daniella Diaz, "FBI: DNC rebuffed request to examine computer servers," CNN, January 5, 2017, https://www.cnn.com/2017/01/05/politics/fbi-russia-hacking-dnc-crowdstrike/index.html.
18. Josephine Wolff, "The FBI Relied on a Private Firm's Investigation of the DNC Hack—Which Makes the Agency Harder to Trust," Slate, May 9, 2017, https://slate.com/technology/2017/05/the-fbi-is-harder-to-trust-on-the-dnc-hack-because-it-relied-on-crowdstrikes-analysis.html.
19. Matt Spetalnick and Steve Holland, "Obama tells Russia's Medvedev more flexibility after election," Reuters, March 26, 2012, https://www.reuters.com/article/idUSBRE82P0JI/.
20. "Second 2020 Presidential Debate," YouTube video, posted by C-SPAN, October 22, 2020, 1:36:19, https://www.youtube.com/live/bPiofmZGb8o?si=nWakDFtSpRQKhNbB.
21. "Joe Biden Met Nearly Every Foreign Associate Funneling His Family Millions," House Committee on Oversight and Accountability, February 14, 2024, https://oversight.house.gov/blog/joe-biden-met-nearly-every-foreign-associate-funneling-his-family-millions%EF%BF%BC/.
22. "US Gift to Russia," YouTube video, posted by The Associated Press, March 6, 2009, https://www.youtube.com/watch?v=0GdLClHAMB0.
23. Transcript of the July 25, 2019, Phone Call Between President Donald J. Trump and President Volodymyr Zelensky, DocumentCloud, September 2019, https://s3.documentcloud.org/documents/6429028/Trump-Ukraine-Transcript-Unclassified-09-2019.pdf.
24. "Vladimir Putin Sits Down with Ukraine President Zelensky for the First Time Today," CBS News, December 9, 2019, https://www.cbsnews.com/news/vladimir-putin-sits-down-with-ukraine-president-zelensky-for-the-first-time-today-2019-12-09/.
25. Adam Entous and Michael Schwirtz, "The Spy War: How the C.I.A. Secretly Helps Ukraine Fight Putin," The New York Times, February 25, 2024, https://www.nytimes.com/2024/02/25/world/europe/the-spy-war-how-the-cia-secretly-helps-ukraine-fight-putin.html.
26. "Joe Biden on Defending Democracy," YouTube video, posted by Council on Foreign Relations, January 23, 2018, 52:59, https://www.youtube.com/watch?v=Q0_AqpdwqK4.
27. "Testimony Reveals FBI Employees Who Warned Social Media Companies about Hack and Leak Operation Knew Hunter Biden Laptop Wasn't Russian Disinformation," House Committee on the Judiciary, July 20, 2023, https://judiciary.house.gov/media/press-releases/testimony-reveals-fbi-employees-who-warned-social-media-companies-about-hack.
28. Hans Mahncke (@HansMahncke), "Video from second presidential debate," Twitter, March 17, 2022, https://twitter.com/HansMahncke/status/1504463355725160452/video/1.
29. Public Statement on the Hunter Biden Emails, Politico, October 19, 2020, https://www.politico.com/f/?id=00000175-4393-d7aa-af77-579f9b330000.
30. Ben Schreckinger, "Justice Department's interest in Hunter Biden covered more than taxes," Politico, December 9, 2020, https://www.politico.com/news/2020/12/09/justice-department-interest-hunter-biden-taxes-444139.
31. United States v. Robert Hunter Biden, U.S. District Court for the District of Delaware, Indictment, July 12, 2023, https://storage.courtlistener.com/recap/gov.uscourts.cacd.907805/gov.uscourts.cacd.907805.1.0_1.pdf.

32. Biden Voter Messaging Survey Analysis, Media Research Center, November 2020, https://cdn.mrc.org/TPC-MRC+Biden+Voter+Messaging+Survey+Analysis+Nov+2020_final.pdf.
33. Matthias Williams and Natalia Zinets, "Biden assures Zelenskiy that NATO membership in Ukraine's hands, Kyiv says," Reuters, December 9, 2021, https://www.reuters.com/world/europe/ukrainian-president-zelenskiy-holding-talks-with-biden-adviser-says-2021-12-09/.
34. Email to Condoleezza Rice, Carnegie Endowment for International Peace, February 8, 2008, accessed August 5, 2024, https://archive.is/VfjTp.

Index

17 Intelligence Agencies 166, 169
ABC 11–12, 38, 54, 56, 58–59, 61–63, 156–157
Abedin, Huma 165
Abramovich, Roman 59–60
Abyshev, Sergei 72–75, 79
Access Hollywood tape 24, 120, 170
Afghanistan 41, 155, 188
Agalarov, Aras 80–81
Alfa Bank 20, 45, 65–66, 68, 73, 87–89, 129–145, 147, 157, 159, 161, 168, 184
Alptekin, Ekim 107
Ambush interview of Flynn 58, 62–63, 115, 176
America First 5, 179
Apelbaum, Yaacov xxx
Avakov, Arsen 124, 181
Aven, Peter 67, 130, 135, 142, 144–145

Baker, James (FBI counsel) 77, 134–139, 144, 160
Barr, William xiv, xxv, xxvi, 18, 91–92
Bartiromo, Maria 48, 52
Batty, Nate 138–139
Belton, Catherine 59–60, 159–161
Bensinger, Ken 177
Berkowitz, Jake 11, 14
Bernstein, Carl 174
Biden, Hunter 3, 22, 39, 43, 120, 182, 185–188
Biden, Joe viii, xi, xii, xiv, 2, 3, 10, 17, 24, 30, 43, 51, 120, 123–124, 167, 176–177, 179, 185–187, 189
Black, Charles 123

Black ledger 123
Blumenthal, Sidney 11
Brennan, John 22, 124, 137, 168–171, 173, 175–176, 188
Brin, Sergey ix
Brookings Institution xxii, xxvii, xxix, xxx, 28–29, 31–32, 134
Bucharest Declaration 2
Burisma 43, 177
Bush, George H.W. 4
Bush, George W. vii, 2, 6, 23, 58,
Buzzfeed vii, xvii, 22, 44, 67–68, 129, 177

Cambridge University 35, 41, 74, 122
Canberra, Australia 93
Caputo, Michael 107
Carson, Ben 48–49
Carter, Jimmy 116
CBS 91, 109–110, 156, 169
Central Intelligence Agency (CIA) xviii, xxv, 22, 24, 48, 94, 124, 136–137, 144, 154, 166–169, 187–189
Chalupa, Alexander 180–181
Chaly, Valeriy 124, 180–181
Chen, Shui-bian 4
China 3–5, 10, 43, 48, 54, 141, 182, 189
Ciaramella, Eric xiv
Clapper, James 167, 171–173, 175–176
Clinesmith, Kevin xxv
Clinton campaign xvii, xviii, xxii, xxxi, xxxii, xxxiii, 1, 5–6, 9–15, 17–18, 20, 25, 27, 34–35, 37, 47, 49, 51, 53, 59–60, 64, 74, 81, 84–88, 93, 109, 120–121,

129, 131–134, 136–137, 140, 143–144, 147–148, 150, 152, 154, 156–158, 163–164, 182, 189
Clinton Foundation xvii, 49
Clinton, Bill xvii, 1, 11, 23, 38, 58
Clinton, Chelsea 48–49, 59, 185
Clinton, Hillary viii, x, xv, xvii, xxxii, xxxiii, 1–2, 5–6, 10, 13, 21–24, 27, 35, 48, 60, 84, 88, 93, 99, 103–106, 110, 115–116, 120, 125, 133, 137, 142, 144, 154, 15, 167, 169, 175, 189
Clovis, Sam xxi, 73, 97, 101–102, 105, 121, 155
Cohen, Edward 158
Cohen, Michael 34, 160
Cold War ix, x, 3, 182
collusion x, xiv, xv, xix, xx, xxi, xxii, xxxiii, 1, 5, 13–15, 18–25, 31, 33, 35–39, 48, 53–54, 58–59, 81, 85, 98, 100, 106, 109–111, 137, 147, 149–150, 152–154, 159, 167, 170–171, 174–175, 177, 179, 181, 184–185, 188
Comey, James 21, 23, 38, 53, 58, 62, 66, 115, 122–123, 137, 154, 164–165, 168, 171–174, 176
Conway, Kellyanne 123, 181
Corn, David xxii, 58, 160
COVID-19 Intelligence Report 167
Crimea 2, 43, 151, 179, 180, 182
Crimeware 142, 144
criminalize diplomacy 124, 182, 186
Crossfire Hurricane xiv, 19, 23, 35, 38, 42, 48, 58, 80, 91–93, 95, 97, 99–101, 103, 105, 107–113, 115, 117, 122–123, 125–126, 132, 137, 168
Crowdstrike 131, 148–149
Crowly, Michael 151–152
Cruz, Ted 147–149

Dacey, Amy 131
Daily Beast 59
Danchenko, Igor ix, x, xv, xvii, xix, xxi, xxiii, xxv, xxvii, xxix, xxx, xxxi, xxxii, xxxiii, 11–12, 15–16, 18, 27–35, 51, 53–58, 62–67, 71–81, 83, 86, 92, 125–127, 134–135, 145, 172–173, 176

Dearborn, Rick 102
declassification 38, 121, 126
Democratic National Committee 2, 6, 12, 36, 56, 84–87, 93–96, 106, 108–110, 118, 131–132, 136, 147–150, 158, 164, 166, 180, 183–185
Denman, Diana 87, 149
Department of Justice (DOJ) xviii, xxiii, xxv, 30, 42, 75, 109–110, 112, 126, 160, 177, 183
Deripaska, Oleg 42, 133, 153
Dibble, Elizabeth 94, 115
Diveykin, Igor 154
Dolan, Charles 78
Domain Name System 129, 131, 139–141, 143
Dowd, John xx
Downer, Alexander xiv, xx, 13, 36, 48, 92–96, 99, 104–106, 108–113, 115–116, 118–120
Drudge, Matt 155
Dubelier, Eric 183
Durham Report xx, 31–32, 56, 91, 95, 111, 143
Durham, John xiv, xx, 17, 31–32, 51, 56, 86–88, 91–92, 95, 111, 136, 142–144, 172

election fortification 9
Elias, Marc 9–11, 87
Embassy of the United Kingdom in Moscow 14, 41
Embassy of the United States in Kiev 180
Embassy of the United States in London 94–95, 109
Embassy of Ukraine in Washington DC 181
European Council of Foreign Relations 103

Farkas, Richard xvi, 95–96
Fauci, Anthony 187
FBI Steele dossier matrix 160
Federal Bureau of Investigation (FBI) Chicago Field Office 106, 139
Federal Bureau of Investigation (FBI) congressional briefings xxv, 44, 81, 126

Index

Federal Bureau of Investigation (FBI) headquarters 20, 111, 137, 160
Federal Bureau of Investigation (FBI) leadership 16–17, 53, 91–92, 95, 108, 113, 115–116, 120, 138–140, 165, 171–172
Fédération Internationale de Football Association (FIFA) 21, 24, 44
Filkins, Dexter 130
Financial Times 59, 159, 161
Flynn, Michael xv, xix, xx, 23, 47, 58, 62, 74, 97, 100, 106–107, 110–111, 115, 122, 134, 157, 158, 161, 166, 176
Foer, Franklin 12–13, 140–141, 159
Fontaine, Barbara 67–68
Fool Nelson xiv, xix, xxv, xxvi, xxvii, 15, 32, 51, 72, 77, 96, 105, 131
Forbes 22, 48, 177
Ford, Gerald 122
Foreign Agents Registration Act (FARA) xvi, 47, 100
Foreign Intelligence Surveillance Act (FISA) xxiv, xxv, 19, 31, 26, 44, 58, 75, 80, 92, 119–120, 126, 150–151, 153–154, 156–157
Foreign Intelligence Surveillance Court (FISC) xxiv, xxv, 17, 53, 75, 117, 119–122, 126, 150, 153–154
Fox News 48–49, 52, 69, 93, 96, 99, 104, 108, 116, 119
Fridman, Mikhail 67, 135, 144–145
Fritsch, Peter xxii, 9, 61, 140, 145, 152–153, 159
FSB (Russian Federal Security Service) viii, xxii, xxiii, xxvi, 11, 41, 71, 73–74, 83–84, 169–170
Fusion GPS xvii, 9, 11–12, 15–16, 21, 71, 85–86, 131, 140, 144, 152–153, 157, 159, 161

Gaeta, Michael 19, 21, 35, 63, 91, 132
Garland, Merrick xxxii
Gates, Rick 102
geopolitical 2, 5, 148, 179, 184, 189
Georgia Tech 130
Gordon, J.D. 87
Govorun, Oleg 134–135

Graham, Lindsey xxvi, xxx, xxxii, 27, 32
Gregory, Paul 48–49, 177
Grenell, Richard 38, 160
Gubarev, Alexei 67
Gurganus, Julia 175–176

hacking of DNC 87, 109, 148, 158, 183–184
Halper, Stefan 35–36, 73–74, 116–122
Hamburger, Tom 15, 151, 158–159
Haspel, Gina 94–95, 115
Hayden, Michael 48, 188
Heathrow Airport 53, 71
Hellman, Scott 138–140, 143
Helsinki 24
Henry, Shawn 131, 148–149
Hicks, Hope 60, 160
High Court, London 60, 68, 161
Hill, Fiona xxix, xxx, 28
Horowitz Report ix, xxiii, xxv, xxvi, xxx, 93, 112–113, 160
Horowitz, Michael ix, x, xviii, xxiii, xxiv, xxv, xxvi, xxx, 19, 61, 74–75, 92–93, 112–113, 117, 118, 160, 173
Hosenball, Mark 12, 44, 140

India 3, 73, 131
Intelligence Community Assessment (ICA) xxi, 17–18, 22, 37–38, 148, 167–177
Ioffe, Julia 151
Isikoff, Michael xxii, 58, 133, 151–158, 181
Ivanov, Sergei 44, 151

January 24, 2017 61–62
January 5, 2017 173, 176
January 6, 2017 22, 174, 176
Jewish Americans viii, ix, 83–84, 170
Joffe, Rodney 20, 87, 130–132, 142–144, 147
Johnson, Joel 1, 9
July 24, 2016 13, 19, 85–86, 147, 149
July 26, 2016 13, 83, 94, 109
July 28, 2016 56, 85, 111, 136, 168
July 29, 2016 54, 56, 87–88, 111, 113, 132–134, 151

July 31, 2016 19, 56, 91, 111, 113
July 5, 2016 19, 21, 35, 54, 63, 83, 91, 164–165

Kellogg, Keith xxiii
Kendall-Taylor, Andrea 169
Kensington Wine Rooms 95
Kerry, John 6, 7
KGB (Committee for State Security of the Soviet Union) xxii, xxiii, xxvi, xxvii, 161
Khan, German 67, 135
Khrushchev, Nikita 2, 180
Kiev, Ukraine 3, 124, 180
Kislyak, Sergei 176
Kremlin xxiii, xxvi, xxxii, 1, 4, 6, 14, 18, 20–24, 33–34, 45–47, 64, 68, 71–72, 81, 83, 85, 96, 103, 106, 129, 133–135, 138, 143, 150, 153, 159, 167–168, 172–173, 175, 181, 189
Kudlow, Larry 187

La Repubblica 103
laptop, Hunter Biden 22, 39, 120, 185, 187–188
Laufman, David 30
Lewandowski, Corey xxiii, 102
Lewinsky, Monica 155
Lichtblau, Eric 139–140, 158
Litvinenko, Alexander 41
Lokhova, Svetlana 74, 122
London Centre of International Law Practice 96, 102, 106
Lorenzen, April 130
Lynch, Loretta 165

Maidan 43, 46, 180
Malaysia Airlines Flight MH17 45
Manafort, Paul xxvii, xxviii, 11, 27–28, 34, 39, 42, 47, 63, 85–86, 97, 100–102, 111–113, 121–125, 133–134, 151–155, 160, 180–181
Manchurian candidate 185
Mangiante, Simona xv, 157
Maremont, Mark 60–61

Martin, David 109–110
Mayer, Jane 158
Mayflower Hotel, Washington DC 97–98, 100
"Max" (Rodney Joffe) 130
McCabe, Andrew 38, 53, 61, 108, 111, 115, 126, 140, 172–174
McCarthy, Joseph ix, x
McIntrye, Stephen xiv, xv, xvi, xviii, xix, xxi, xxii, xxv, xxv, xxvi, xxx, xxxi, xxxii, 15, 32, 51, 54, 55, 77, 85, 105, 135, 188
McLaughlin, John 188
Meadows, Mark
Medium Blog 153
Meduza 79
Medvedev, Daniil 3
Medvedev, Dmitry 184
Meier, Barry 133, 152–153, 155
MI6 28, 41–42, 68, 88
Miami xviii, 45, 85, 109
Mifsud, Joseph 96–107, 117
military-industrial complex vii, x, 5,
Millian, Sergei xxx, xxxi, xxxii, 12–13, 51–69, 75, 77, 78–80, 86, 106, 122, 127, 150, 156–157, 159–160
Miss Universe competition 21
Mnuchin, Steve 183, 187
Monaco, Lisa 166
Mook, Robby 1, 13–14, 85–86, 93–94, 132, 134, 147–149
Morell, Michael 188
Mosk, Matthew 12–13, 54, 61–62, 156–158
MSNBC 110, 152
Mueller investigation xv, xvi, xx, xxi, xxii, 39, 88, 95–96, 98–100, 107, 183
Mueller Report xix, xx, xxi, xxii, 49, 81, 95, 99, 104
Mueller testimony 24–25, 183, 186
Mueller, Robert xiv, xx, 23, 38, 58, 81, 123, 183, 186
Musk, Elon 12, 77, 175
Myers, Steven Lee 139

Nakashima, Ellen 148–150, 158–159, 166

Index

Nalyvaichenko, Valentin 123–125
Napolitano, Andrew 48–49
National Security Letters 58
NBC 170
New Economic School, Moscow 155
New York Times 23, 94, 98, 123, 129, 133, 139, 140, 152, 153, 158, 166
New York, United States viii, 19, 52, 54–58, 63, 85, 165
Newsweek 155
Niemöller, Martin xi, xii
Nixon, Richard 2, 116
North Atlantic Treaty Organization (NATO) 2, 4–5, 147, 179, 181, 189
November 8, 2016 18, 103, 163–164
Nuland, Victoria 2–3, 24, 35, 42–43, 46, 91, 179, 180–181
Nunes, Devin xix, 35, 158

Obama, Barack vii, viii, x, xii, xviii, xxi; 2, 17, 23, 28, 37, 43, 93, 110, 122, 137, 148, 163–164, 167–168, 172–174, 176–177, 179, 182, 184
Obama, Michelle xviii
Ocasio-Cortez, Alexandria 88
October 3, 2016 80, 126, 154
October surprise 49, 120–121
Ohr, Bruce 42, 53, 160,
Ohr, Nellie 53, 63
Oxford University xvi, 11

Page, Carter xviii, xxii, xxiii, xxiv, xxv, 11, 14–15, 17, 19, 21, 35–36, 43–44, 58, 73, 75, 80, 85–86, 92, 111–112, 117, 119–120, 126, 150–154, 157, 159, 166, 168, 181
Page, Lisa 111–112, 125, 132, 140, 165
Painter, Richard 58
Palmieri, Jennifer 1, 6, 9, 131–134
Panetta, John 188
Papadopoulos, George xiv, xv, xvi, xix, xx, xxi, xxiii, 35–36, 39, 47–49, 58, 73–74, 92–111, 113, 115–122, 125, 153–155, 157, 168
"pee tape" xxxi, 21, 71, 75, 78–80

Perkins Coie xvii, 9–10, 14, 34–35, 87–88, 91, 132, 151, 154, 157
Peskov, Dmitry 34
Phares, Walid xxiii
Pientka, Joe 115
Podesta, John 1, 6, 47, 120
Politico 13, 109, 151
Polonskaya, Olga 96, 100
Pompeo, Mike 169
Poroshenko, Petro 43, 45–46, 123–124, 181
Porter, Kieran xxx
Powell, Sidney xx
Priest, Dana 158–159
Priestap, Bill 58, 81, 165
Prigozhin, Yevgeny 182–183
Project Charlemagne 47
Prokhorov, Mikhail 23
Protocols of the Elders of Zion ix, x, xi
Putin, Vladimir x, xv, xvii, xviii, xxvi, xxxi, xxxii, 4, 11–13, 16, 18, 22–24, 28, 30, 37–38, 42, 44–46, 49, 59, 65, 94–98, 103, 110, 133–135, 137–138, 143–145, 150–153, 158–160, 166–170, 174–175, 177, 180, 182, 187, 189
"Putin's niece" 96, 110
Pyatt, Geoffrey 2

Ratcliffe, John 13, 137
Reagan, Ronald 116, 120, 122
Reid, Harry 134
Republican National Convention 122, 147
RIA Novosti 54, 63–64
Rich, Seth 84
Ritz Carlton Hotel, Moscow 12, 71, 75, 78–80
Rogin, Josh 148–150
Rome, Italy 80, 99–100, 102–103, 126
Rosneft xviii, 15, 21, 43–44, 151
Ross, Brian 12, 54, 58, 157
Ross, Chuck 69, 73, 117
RT (Russia Today) 22, 158, 175
"Russia, if you're listening" 36, 109
Russian Embassy in Washington DC 16
Russian-American Chamber of Commerce xxxi, 52, 58, 62, 68, 86

sanctions xx, 23, 45, 47, 54, 67, 145, 151, 161, 170, 176, 182–183
Sanders, Bernie xi, 13, 84, 118, 164–165
Sanger, David 158
Schamel, Mark 29, 33, 65–66
Schiff, Adam 38, 170
Schmitz, Joe xxiii
Schrage, Steven 35
Schwartz, Rhonda 157
Sechin, Igor 15, 21, 43–44, 151, 153
Security Service of Ukraine (SBU) 123–124
Senate Committee on Homeland Security and Governmental Affairs 160
Senate Intelligence Committee xxi, 149, 172–173
Senate Judiciary Committee xxvi, 137, 171
September 19, 2016 20, 129, 135–136, 138
September 7, 2016 137, 154, 168
Sessions, Jeff xxi, xxiii
Shearer, Cody 11–12, 14, 78
Sidar, Cenk 32–33, 64
"signal to meet" 98
Simpson, Glenn xxii, 9, 35, 47, 53, 56, 58–59, 61, 63, 71, 132, 151–153, 156, 159
Slate Magazine 130, 140–143, 159, 161, 184
Smirnov, Alexander 177
Smith, Lee xix
Solomon, John 126
Soviet Union ix, 2–4, 52, 62, 84, 180
Sporre, Eric 139
St Petersburg 4, 22, 28, 74, 135
Steele dossier #112 65, 68, 87, 134–135
Steele dossier #132 44, 160
Steele dossier #137 44, 160
Steele dossier #139 44, 61, 159–160
Steele dossier #80 xvii, xviii, 21–22, 34, 57, 63, 66, 71, 73–75, 77–81, 83, 85, 88
Steele dossier #86 83–85, 170
Steele dossier #95 56, 64, 79–80, 85–89, 150
Steele dossier #97 22, 80
Steele, Christopher xvii, xix, xx, xxi, xxii, xxiii, xxiv, xxv, xxvii, xxx, xxxi, xxxii, 10–16, 19–23, 27–28, 30, 32–35, 41–47, 49, 51, 53–54, 56–69, 71–75, 78–81, 83–89, 91–92, 112, 125–127, 129, 132, 134–135, 145, 150, 154, 157–160, 170–171, 173, 176
Stein, Jill 23
Stephanopoulos, George 58, 156
Stone, Roger 39, 81, 110, 123
Strzok, Peter 16, 53, 62, 104, 106, 108–112, 115, 122, 125, 132, 137, 154, 165, 168, 171–172, 175–176
Sullivan, Jake 134, 144
Sussmann Text Message 136
Sussmann, Michael 10, 19–21, 66, 81, 87–89, 129–131, 134–139, 142, 144, 147–148, 157
Svoboda, Cyril 23
Swift Boat Veterans for Truth 6
Swiftboat email 1, 6, 9, 131
Swiftboat project 5–7, 9–11, 13, 15, 17–19, 23, 29, 32, 39, 48, 52, 57, 87, 131–133, 149, 151, 156, 163, 168, 182, 184

Tabard Inn 158
Talbott, Strobe 11
Tapper, Jake 104, 174, 177
Target Labs 33, 55
"Tea Leaves" (April Lorenzen) 130
Telegraph Newspaper 103
"The America We Deserve" 5
"The Apprentice" xvii
The New Yorker 42, 130, 158
Thompson, Erika 48, 94–95, 110
Time Magazine 9
Times of London, 101
Timofeev, Ivan 96–98, 100–101, 103, 106
Trubnikov, Vyacheslav 73–75
Trump administration 28, 38, 166, 168, 182
Trump campaign xvi, xix, xx, xxiii, 36, 38, 60, 74, 86–87, 91–93, 95–98, 101–103, 105, 107, 110–113, 115–116, 121, 130–132, 150, 152–155, 160, 169
Trump impeachment xiv, xxix, 3, 25, 38, 43, 182–83, 186–187

Index

Trump Organization 20, 34, 38, 52, 87, 130, 138, 142–143, 157
Trump Tower xxiii, 130, 132, 176
Trump, Barron 24
Trump, Donald x, xii, xiv, xv, xvii, xviii, xxi, xxii, xxviii, xxix, xxxi, xxxii, xxxiii, 1, 2, 4, 5–6, 9–24, 36, 39, 43, 52, 58–60, 67, 71, 80–81, 86, 92, 97, 103, 109, 111–112, 123–126, 131, 133–134, 137, 143, 151–152, 156, 158, 164–168, 170, 174–177, 179–187
Turk, Azra 36, 116
Twitter Files 77, 175
Tymoshenko, Yulia 46

Ukraine dossier 42–47
Ukrainian prosecutor xiv, 43, 186–187

Valdai Discussion Club 97, 99
Vietnam vii, xxi, 6
Vindman, Alexander 3, 186
Vixie, Paul 140–142
Vorontsov, Ivan 75, 77–80
Vox News 129

Waldman, Adam 42
Walkafyre xiv, xix, xxv, xxvi, xxvii, 15, 32, 51, 77, 118, 131
Wall Street Journal 9, 11, 60–62, 106
Warby, Mark 68
Washington DC 55, 87, 97, 100, 180–181

Washington DC establishment 5, 22, 182, 187
Washington Post 15, 47, 86, 87, 134, 148–151, 153, 158–159, 166, 170
Wasserman Schultz, Debbie 84
Webzilla 67
Weiner, Anthony 165
Weissmann, Andrew 81
Welker, Kristen 39
"well-developed conspiracy of co-operation" xxxi, 64, 85
Western alliance 4, 182
White House xiv, 58, 62, 115, 122, 126, 157–158, 166, 168, 176
Whitewater scandal 39
WikiLeaks xxxi, 1, 6, 13, 26, 74, 83–87, 89, 95, 108, 110, 150, 163, 185
Wimmer, Willi 23
Winer, Jonathan 11, 44–46
Wiseman, Jeffrey 118–119

Xi, Jinping 182

Yahoo News 133, 151, 153, 183
Yanukovych, Viktor xxviii, 27, 43, 112, 123, 133, 152, 180–181
Yatseniuk, Arsenyi 124, 181
Yota phone 131–132

Zelenskyy, Volodymyr 24, 43, 182, 186–187
Zlochevsky, Mykola 3